THE GOSPEL OF FREE ACCEPTANCE IN CHRIST

THE GOSPEL OF FREE ACCEPTANCE IN CHRIST

*An Assessment of the Reformation
and 'New Perspectives' on Paul*

CORNELIS P. VENEMA

THE BANNER OF TRUTH TRUST

THE BANNER OF TRUTH TRUST
3 Murrayfield Road, Edinburgh EH12 6EL, UK
P.O. Box 621, Carlisle, PA 17013, USA

*

© Cornelis P. Venema 2006

ISBN-10: 0 85151 939 3
ISBN-13: 978 0 85151 939 5

*

Typeset in 10.5 /14 pt Sabon at the
Banner of Truth Trust, Edinburgh
Printed in the U.S.A. by
Versa Press, Inc.,
Peoria, IL

CONTENTS

v

PREFACE

But now the righteousness of God has been manifested apart from the law, although the Law and the Prophets bear witness to it—the righteousness of God through faith in Jesus Christ for all who believe. For there is no distinction: for all have sinned and fall short of the glory of God, and are justified by his grace as a gift, through the redemption that is in Christ Jesus, whom God put forward as a propitiation by his blood, to be received by faith (*Rom.* 3:21–25).

When I was a graduate student at Princeton Theological Seminary in the 1970s, I elected to write a doctoral dissertation on John Calvin's understanding of the gospel. For Calvin the good news of salvation can be summed up in two words: 'acceptance' and 'renewal'. The grace of God in Christ brings a double benefit: the gift of free justification or a new status for sinners before God, and the gift of ongoing sanctification or the renewal of human life in obedience to God. On the one hand, the gospel declares that guilty sinners are freely accepted or justified on the basis of the work of Christ alone. On the other hand, the gospel promises that believers, who enjoy the grace of free acceptance with God, are being renewed after the image of Christ by the work of the Holy Spirit in them. The twofold plight of human beings as sinners before God is matched by a twofold solution: guilty sinners are set right with God and become heirs of eternal life; at the same time they are renewed in holiness and obedience to God's commandments.

Back in the 1970s, when engaged in this research, I could scarcely have imagined that some of the key features of Calvin's view of the gospel would become the focus of much contemporary theological debate. And yet in recent decades there has been a resurgence of ecumenical and theological interest in the subject of the good news of salvation, particularly the message of free justification before God on the basis of Christ's saving work. This resurgence has occurred in two areas. Within the sphere of ecumenical discussions of the gospel, a series of important dialogues have taken place between representatives of the Protestant churches and the Roman Catholic Church. The principal fruit of these dialogues was the remarkable *Joint Declaration on the Doctrine of Justification,* issued on 31 October 1999. In it the claim was made that a 'consensus' had been achieved on the substance of the gospel. By any measure, this was an extraordinary claim. Since the Reformation of the sixteenth century, Protestants and Roman Catholics have been deeply divided over the question of the nature of the gospel of justification. For the Protestant Reformers, as well as their spiritual descendants, the doctrine of justification is a watershed issue. Without true consensus regarding how believing sinners become right with God, there is no prospect of achieving unity in understanding the gospel of Jesus Christ.

In addition to these ecumenical discussions, which are ongoing and the subject of widely differing assessments, a second development has occurred, largely within the sphere of New Testament scholarship. A number of prominent Pauline scholars have argued for a very different reading of the apostle's doctrine of justification from that of most of the Western theological tradition, whether Protestant or Roman Catholic.

These writers claim that the debates regarding the gospel of justification in the sixteenth and subsequent centuries were skewed by a failure to read Paul's epistles *in their historical context.* When we interpret Paul in the historical setting of 'Second-Temple Judaism' (c. 200 BC – AD 200), we will discover that the question for Paul to which justification provides an answer is not the question of how sinners can 'find a gracious God' (Luther), but the question of whether Gentiles are also included as heirs of God's covenant promise to Israel. Justification is not so much a soteriological (doctrine of salvation) issue, which addresses the way sinners become right with God, as an ecclesiological (doctrine of the church) issue, which addresses the way Gentiles are included together with Jews in God's covenant family.

The following study was prompted by this renewed interest in the gospel of free justification. It is written from the conviction that the Protestant churches need to reacquaint themselves with their doctrinal heritage, especially their understanding of the gospel of free acceptance with God on the basis of Christ's redeeming work. Before abandoning the older perspective on Paul in favour of the new, evangelical believers need to understand what it is they are being asked to abandon. Furthermore, evangelical believers must take a careful look at the claims of authors who propose a newer and ostensibly better reading of the apostle Paul's understanding of the gospel. The newer perspective on Paul makes bold claims, some of which may be rather appealing in an age that favours the new over the old and has grown weary with the 'battle lines' of ancient debates. The newer perspective on Paul demands careful study and assessment. At stake is nothing less than the gospel itself, the church's proclamation of the good news of salvation in Christ. As the title of this book indicates, the purposes of the study are to summarize the older perspective of the Reformation (which understood justification to be the gospel's declaration that sinners are acceptable to God by the grace of Christ alone), to provide a general introduction to what is known as the 'new perspective' on Paul, and to assess critically the claims of the new perspective from a biblical and theological standpoint.

After an opening chapter, which offers a sketch of the main features of contemporary discussions on the doctrine of justification, the first part of the study summarizes the Reformation perspective on Paul's doctrine of justification. One of the unfortunate characteristics of contemporary discussions of the gospel is the relative neglect of the traditional Protestant understanding of justification. Though it may be true that there were differences of emphasis between the magisterial Reformers, especially Calvin and Luther, I argue in this opening part of the book that there is an identifiable 'Protestant' view of justification. In order to assess the claims of those who argue for a 'new' perspective on Paul's doctrine of justification, it is essential that we reacquaint ourselves with this 'older' perspective. In the opening part of the study, therefore, I provide an overview of the Reformation perspective in order to set the stage for the subsequent treatment of the newer perspective on Paul. Since the Reformation understanding of justification excludes human works from playing any role in the believer's justification before God, a separate chapter is also dedicated to this question and to the traditional dispute between Protestant and Roman Catholic interpretations of the second chapter of James.

The second part of the study summarizes the newer perspective on Paul's doctrine of justification. Though there are a number of authors who are associated with this new approach to the apostle's writings, the study primarily focuses upon three authors who have contributed several of its most important themes. The summary will offer a sketch of the principal features of new perspective authors. My purpose is not to trace all of the variations of viewpoint and distinctive arguments of the diverse authors associated with the effort to interpret Paul in a new way. For the purpose of this book, it is enough to identify the most important aspects of the newer approach.

The third and most important part of the study offers a critical assessment of the new perspective on Paul. A number of features of the new perspective are evaluated in terms of Paul's epistles. Since the new perspective claims that its reading of Paul is more attentive to the historical setting and the particular arguments of his epistles, this part of the study *appeals directly to Paul's writings* and challenges many of the claims of new perspective authors. On the basis of this critical assessment of the new perspective, the study concludes that the older perspective on Paul continues to warrant our loyalty. Though the historical studies associated with the new perspective may enrich our understanding of Paul's epistles in some respects, the new perspective ultimately offers a different gospel than that to which the Reformation bore witness – the gospel of free acceptance with God by grace alone.

Several additional characteristics of the following study deserve brief notice.

First, unlike many studies of the new perspective on Paul's doctrine of justification, this one does not restrict itself to the field of biblical studies, particularly the scholarly study of the apostle Paul.

There are a number of competent assessments of the new perspective, which have been written by authors whose specialty is the
academic study of the Pauline writings. Several of these studies have
offered trenchant criticisms of the new perspective. This book seeks
to fill a gap in the literature on the new perspective by treating its
claims within the broader framework of contemporary theological
discussion and interests.

Rather than leaving the discussion of the new perspective within
the relatively narrow confines of New Testament academic study, I
endeavour to interact in a responsible way with other significant
dimensions of the debate regarding the doctrine of justification.
Therefore, unlike many discussions of the new perspective, this book
includes a summary of the Protestant consensus on justification. It
also raises general questions regarding the method employed by some
new perspective authors in advancing their claims. Can we argue,
as new-perspective authors often do, that Paul's understanding of
justification requires our agreement with a certain kind of historical
scholarship on Second-Temple Judaism? Rather than staying within
the limits of New Testament Pauline scholarship, the book attends
to related, broader issues of Christian doctrine that are affected by
the newer perspective.

Second, the second and third parts of this book represent a revision of material that originally appeared in a lengthy series of articles
in *The Outlook*, a Reformed periodical in North America. I wish
to acknowledge with gratitude the permission granted me by the
Board of the Reformed Fellowship to revise these articles for publication. Though the introductory chapter and the first part of this
book are largely new, a section of the introduction, which summarizes recent ecumenical discussions of justification, is a revision
of a portion of a previously published chapter on the doctrine of
justification in contemporary discussion.[1] I also acknowledge grate-
fully the permission granted to me by Inter-Varsity Press (UK) to
include this section in this book. Even though parts two and three

---

[1] 'Justification by Faith: The Ecumenical, Biblical and Theological Dimensions of Current Debates', in *Always Reforming*, ed. A. T. B. McGowan
(Leicester: Inter-Varsity Press, 2006), pp. 289–327.

have been revised and expanded, my treatment of this subject retains the character of a study that is addressed to a general and not exclusively academic readership. Though the reader is referred throughout to the academic literature on the newer perspectives, I aim to speak to a broad readership that includes academics and non-academics. Since the newer perspectives on Paul have profound implications for the evangelical church's proclamation of the gospel in our time, it is only proper that evangelical believers and churches be introduced to a discussion that is often intimidating because of its highly academic character.

And third, the Scripture quotations throughout the book are taken from the English Standard Version (Crossway Bibles, 2001). Though this version is relatively new, it retains the literary qualities of its eminent predecessors (KJV, RV, ASV, RSV) and seeks to render the original languages in an 'essentially literal' manner.

There are several people who contributed to the preparation and publication of this volume whom I wish to acknowledge. I am grateful for the assistance of Jonathan Watson of the Banner of Truth Trust, who responded favourably when I first sent him a copy of my manuscript. I also wish to acknowledge and thank Glenda Mathes, a freelance writer and editor in Pella, Iowa, who willingly edited and improved an earlier draft of the book. I have also benefited from interaction with my faculty colleagues, J. Mark Beach, Alan Strange, and Mark Vander Hart, regarding the subject of justification and the new perspective on Paul. Since we are called to prepare our students for the ministry of the gospel of Jesus Christ, the emergence of the new perspective on Paul constitutes an inescapable challenge to study the Scriptures afresh and determine, as best as we are able, whether the Protestant church's historic understanding of the gospel remains true and compelling.

Ultimately, it is the gospel itself that is at stake in the debate regarding the Reformation and new perspectives on Paul. It is my hope that this study will contribute in some small way to a renewed appreciation for the gospel of God's free acceptance of his people in Christ, and an informed awareness of the threat to the evangelical church posed by the new perspectives on Paul. For this reason, I dedicate this book to my former and present students at

Mid-America Reformed Seminary. It is my prayer that they may joyfully and faithfully continue to herald the good news of God's gracious acceptance of believing sinners on the basis of the work of Christ alone.

CORNELIS P. VENEMA
Dyer, Indiana
Ascension Day
25 May 2006

JUSTIFICATION IN CONTEMPORARY DISCUSSION

While a graduate student at Princeton Theological Seminary in the late 1970s, I frequently joined in debate with students in the departments of theology and biblical studies regarding the merits of our respective fields of study. Our discussions often turned to the perception of a wide chasm between the interests of the academy and the pew. Those of us who were in the Department of Theology were especially critical of the discipline of biblical studies, seeing it as irrelevant to the life and ministry of the church. Did the church or the pulpit really need another lengthy article on some arcane feature of the biblical text? And, if the biblical texts were as hopelessly diverse and inconsistent in their teaching as the biblical students maintained, then what difference would it make what the text taught? After all, one text is as good as any other, and if they do not agree with each other, who is to say 'my text is better than yours'? To complicate matters further, there was the rather daunting problem of the historical distance between 'then' and 'now'. Even were we able to determine what these 'ancient texts' were saying, there was the additional problem of bridging the divide between what people in ancient times believed and what people believe today. So far as we would-be systematic theologians were concerned, it was rather unlikely that any help for the church's proclamation of the gospel would be forthcoming from the field of biblical studies.

Needless to say, the students of biblical studies were no more hopeful regarding the discipline of theology. Whatever the challenges facing students of the biblical texts, at least they were busy with actual texts. Better to confront the challenges of understanding the Bible than to ignore the texts altogether, as they accused the theology students of doing.

When I consider the development in recent decades of what is known as the 'new perspective on Paul', I am reminded of those graduate school debates. One of the more striking illustrations of the gap that continues to exist between contemporary biblical scholarship and the pulpit or pew is the emergence of this new view within biblical studies. In many Protestant churches, where adherence to the Reformation confessions is more than a matter of lip service, the teaching of justification by faith alone remains a matter of special emphasis. However, in the last several decades, Pauline scholars have engaged in a process of thoroughgoing deconstruction of this very doctrine. Indeed, so widespread and influential is this new reading of Paul, which claims that the Reformation got the gospel wrong, that it might be regarded as something of a consensus opinion among many contemporary biblical scholars. Articles and books, which address one or another feature of this new perspective, are being produced in such abundance that it has become virtually impossible for the non-expert to keep up with the subject.

Though there are some signs that the new perspective on Paul is making itself felt more widely in non-scholarly circles, so far it has largely been the subject of academic discussion. However, whatever the gap between academy and pulpit, lecture hall and pew, this new approach to the interpretation of Paul is so revolutionary and far-reaching in its implications that it seems likely it will, sooner or later, have a profound effect upon the life and ministry of the church. If the Reformation misunderstood the gospel, as the new perspective intimates, things cannot go on as before. Not only must this be reflected in a new understanding of the message of the gospel, but it also has rather obvious implications for the historic division between Protestantism and Roman Catholicism. It will also directly challenge churches whose confessions give summary expression to the gospel as it was understood at the time of the Reformation. Whatever the gap between academy and pew, ideas tend to have legs that will eventually carry them into the church. Seminary students who are taught by professors sympathetic to the new perspective will likely allow the seeds to germinate and produce fruit in their own ministries. Church members who are uninformed about the new perspective could easily be caught unawares. Furthermore, since the new perspective deals with issues as basic as the meaning of the gospel of Jesus Christ, Christian believers have the duty to assess its claims by the standard of the Word of God.

The need for a careful assessment of this new perspective on Paul hardly needs to be demonstrated. Not only is it likely to become an increasingly influential view within scholarly and more popular circles, but it is also addressed to a subject that is of special importance to the Christian church at an ecumenical and historical level. The importance of the new perspective is enhanced by the renewed interest in the doctrine of justification in recent ecumenical discussion, and by the prospect that it may offer a way forward in diminishing the historic divisions between Protestant and Roman Catholic views.

Though writers who are sympathetic to the new perspective often appeal to a biblical and textual basis for their position, the emergence of this new perspective on Paul cannot be isolated from the larger sphere of recent discussions about the doctrine of justification. At no time since the Reformation of the sixteenth century has justification taken centre stage as it has done in the biblical and theological discussions of the last ten years. Whether owing to a desire to overcome the historic polemics between Roman Catholic and Protestant, or to offer a fresh reading of the Pauline epistles, the appeal of a new, ecumenically more promising reading of the apostle Paul on the doctrine of justification can hardly be exaggerated. Before we consider and evaluate the new perspective on Paul, therefore, it will be useful to review the shape of this discussion and the place of the new perspective within it.

RECENT ECUMENICAL DISCUSSION[1]

Undoubtedly, a significant part of the appeal of the new perspective derives from the contemporary ecumenical interest in resolving the long-standing disagreement between Roman Catholic and Protestant understandings of the gospel. Though the new approach to Paul is largely a movement within the orbit of biblical theology, especially Pauline studies, it cannot be properly appreciated without a recognition that it has emerged within a framework of dissatisfaction with the divisions created by the sixteenth-century dispute about justification. Any approach to the teaching of Paul that promises to bridge these divisions will undoubtedly prove attractive to members of the Christian church who long for greater unity among its various branches. As is so often the case in theological studies, factors other than the interpretation of the Scriptures may have a significant formative influence in the development of new ideas. The contemporary desire to revisit the disputes of the sixteenth century and to find a new, unifying consensus is surely a significant factor in the emergence of this new perspective on Paul.

LUTHERANS AND CATHOLICS TOGETHER?

One of the most striking examples of recent ecumenical discussions regarding the doctrine of justification is the sustained dialogue in the last few decades between representatives of the Roman Catholic Church and the Lutheran churches. Since the Lutherans represent the first branch of Protestantism to object to the medieval Roman Catholic view of justification, these discussions are of particular significance. The principal reason for the separation between the Lutheran churches and the Roman Church was the disagreement regarding justification. For the Lutherans, justification is no less than the 'article of the standing or the falling of the church' (*articulus stantis et cadentis ecclesiae*).[2] Unless there is substantial agreement on this article, there can be no unity between the churches on the truth of the gospel. The remarkable feature of these recent discussions is not that they are taking place at a level unsurpassed since the early years of the sixteenth-century Reformation; rather, they have resulted in the issuing of joint statements, which ostensibly demonstrate that a united understanding of the gospel of free justification may now be a reality. If this proves to be the case, it will represent the most extraordinary advance in ecumenical unity within the western church since the sixteenth century.

During the course of the discussions between Roman Catholics and Lutherans, a series of documents has been produced, purporting to show that the old divisions of the past need no longer separate the two communions. The earliest indication of the course of these discussions was provided by the Helsinki Assembly of the Lutheran World Federation in 1963. Although this Assembly spoke only for the Lutheran churches, it did draw the conclusion that there was no longer any substantial difference between Rome and the Lutheran churches on the doctrine of justification. Subsequently, three major declarations by Lutheran and Catholic representatives were issued that claimed to show a growing consensus on the meaning of the gospel.[3]

The first of these declarations is included in the document *Justification by Faith,* which was the seventh in a series of joint statements by representatives of the Roman Catholic Church in the United States and the Lutheran World Ministries, a branch of the Lutheran World Federation.[4] This document included a 'Common Statement' that begins and ends with the affirmation that

> Our entire hope of justification and salvation rests on Christ Jesus and on the gospel whereby the good news of God's merciful action in Christ is made known; we do not place our ultimate trust in anything other than God's promise and saving work in Christ.[5]

While admitting that this affirmation did not resolve all of the remaining differences between Roman Catholic and Lutheran views—including the Lutheran insistence that 'God accepts sinners as righteous for Christ's sake on the basis of faith alone'[6]—the authors of the joint statement maintained that these differences were not 'church-dividing' in nature.[7] In the opinion of those who produced this statement, a consensus on the essential teaching of the gospel was achieved, which was sufficient to overcome the most significant historical differences between their respective traditions.

Shortly after the appearance of this first statement in 1983, a Joint Ecumenical Commission on the Examination of the Sixteenth-Century Condemnations, which was composed of a number of Roman Catholic and Lutheran theologians, produced a second statement, *The Condemnations of the Reformation Era*.[8] The impetus for the formation of this Commission was a visit by Pope John Paul II to Germany in 1980. This visit stimulated interest in the question whether justification was a doctrine that continued to divide Christians. As the name of this Joint Commission suggests, its task was to examine the condemnations of the Reformation period, particularly the Canons adopted at the Roman Catholic Council of Trent and the condemnations contained in the Lutheran confessional documents. The Commission concluded that the mutual condemnations of the Reformation era no longer apply to the teaching of the contemporary Roman Catholic and Lutheran communions. Despite the far-reaching character of this conclusion, responses from representatives of both communions were varied. Though some hailed the statement as an important breakthrough, others were more cautious and noted that the conclusion glossed over the reality of remaining differences on significant features of the doctrine of justification.[9]

Due in part to the divergence of opinion over this second statement, discussions between representatives of the Roman Catholic Church and the Lutheran World Federation continued. Their outcome was perhaps the most remarkable chapter in the yet unfinished dialogue between the two communions: the issuing of a *Joint Declaration on the Doctrine of Justification* in 1999.[10] This statement, which includes a supplementary 'Annex' that clarified some issues of continuing debate and an affirmation of the *sola fide* formula by Rome, was signed by official representatives of the Lutheran World Federation and the Roman Catholic Church on 31 October, a date chosen because of its association with the beginning of the Protestant Reformation. Two statements in this *Joint Declaration* capture its tenor and emphases. In a section entitled, 'The Common Understanding of Justification', the common teaching of the two communions is summarized:

> Together we confess: By grace alone, in faith in Christ's saving work and not because of any merit on our part, we are accepted by God and receive the Holy Spirit, who renews our hearts while equipping and calling us to good works.[11]

In a final section entitled, 'The Significance and Scope of the Consensus Reached', the two communions concluded that a fundamental consensus regarding the nature of the gospel now exists, despite some differences in expression:

> The understanding of the doctrine of justification set forth in this *Declaration* shows that a consensus in basic truths of the doctrine of justification exists between Lutherans and Catholics. In light of this consensus the remaining differences of language, theological elaboration, and emphasis in the understanding of justification described in [section 4] are acceptable. Therefore the Lutheran and the Catholic explications of justification are in their difference open to one another and do not destroy the consensus regarding the basic truths.[12]

Whether these and other declarations within the context of ecumenical discussions will prove to be a harbinger of greater unity between the Lutheran and Roman Catholic churches remains to be seen. That they represent a development of great historical significance cannot be denied. Inasmuch as the doctrine of justification was the great point of disagreement in the sixteenth century, declarations that purport to express a new-found consensus on this subject can hardly be exaggerated in terms of their ecumenical implications. At the very least, the doctrine of justification is seen as an issue of both theological and ecclesiastical importance.

Evangelicals and Catholics Together?

But it is not only in the broader context of ecumenical discussions between Lutherans and Roman Catholics that the doctrine of justification has achieved a position of prominence. Similar discussions have taken place between other branches of the Reformation and the Roman Catholic Church. Among the more important of these are those that have taken place in North America between a number of prominent evangelical theologians and representatives of the Roman Catholic Church. Though these discussions and the statements they have produced do not have the same level of official church standing as those between the Roman

Catholic and Lutheran communions, they are nonetheless a
significant part of the present renewed interest in the doctrine of
justification. Arising out of a desire to offer a unified witness in the
public square, Roman Catholics and evangelicals have been keen to
portray themselves as 'co-belligerents', combating the social and
moral decay of contemporary American society, who also share
many fundamental articles of the Christian faith. This shared faith
extends to some though not all aspects of the disputed doctrine of
justification.

Two documents, which were endorsed and signed by
representatives of both the Catholic and evangelical communities,
are of special importance. The first of these was produced in 1994
and bore the revealing title, 'Evangelicals and Catholics
Together'.[13] It included a summary statement regarding the doctrine of justification:

> We affirm together that we are justified by grace, through faith,
> because of Christ. Living faith is active in love that is nothing less
> than the love of Christ, for we together say with Paul: 'I have been
> crucified with Christ; it is no longer I who live, but Christ who lives
> in me; and the life I now live in the flesh I live by faith in the Son
> of God, who loved me and gave himself for me' (*Gal.* 2).[14]

Because the burden of this declaration was to demonstrate the
substantial similarities of viewpoint between evangelicals and
Catholics, the remainder of the document says nothing more about
differences between them on the subject of justification. The
doctrine of justification is treated as a point of consensus, rather
than a point of disagreement. However, the brevity of the statement
on justification allows for a considerable difference of opinion
among those who might find its wording agreeable. Evangelical
critics of the statement were able to point out that it says nothing
more than was said by the Roman Church at the Council of Trent.
The chief point of dispute – whether justification is by grace *alone*
through faith *alone* on account of the work of Christ *alone* – is
glossed over. It is not surprising, therefore, that the Evangelicals
and Catholics Together declaration received strong criticism from
theologians within the evangelical community.

Due to the perceived weaknesses of 'Evangelicals and Catholics Together', a number of its signatories joined with other evangelicals to prepare a sequel declaration. Published in 1997, it bore the title, 'The Gift of Salvation'.[15] Written in order to clarify some of the issues raised by the first statement—and to assuage concerns expressed within the evangelical community, it attempted to offer a more clearly evangelical statement on the doctrine of justification. Justification, it affirmed,

> is not earned by any good works or merits of our own; it is entirely God's gift, conferred through the Father's sheer graciousness, out of the love that he bears us in his Son, who suffered on our behalf and rose from the dead for our justification. Jesus was 'put to death for our trespasses and raised for our justification' (*Rom.* 4:25). In justification God, on the basis of Christ's righteousness alone, declares us to be no longer his rebellious enemies but his forgiven friends. And by virtue of his declaration it is so. We understand that what we here affirm is in agreement with what the Reformation traditions have meant by justification by faith alone.[16]

'The Gift of Salvation' is a clearer statement of the issues than the earlier 'Evangelicals and Catholics Together'. It affirms several traditional features of the Protestant view of justification; particularly that it is by grace alone, apart from works, and received through faith alone. However, despite the apparent consensus on key elements of the doctrine of justification, it also noted that there were areas of continued disagreement between Protestant and Catholic. These areas include

> the meaning of baptismal regeneration, the Eucharist, and sacramental grace; the historic uses of the language of justification as it relates to imputed and transformative righteousness; the normative status of justification in relation to all Christian doctrine; the assertion that while justification is by faith alone, the faith that receives salvation is never alone; diverse understandings of merit, reward, purgatory, and indulgences . . . [17]

This admission suggests that 'The Gift of Salvation', though offered to address criticisms of the earlier 'Evangelicals and Catholics Together' declaration, has not produced anything like a consensus within the evangelical community of North America. Not only are these declarations unofficial in character, and therefore without any ecclesiastical authority within the Catholic and evangelical communities, but they are also the subject of continued discussion and even considerable criticism within the evangelical community itself. Within this context, a third statement was drawn up from within the evangelical community, *The Gospel of Jesus Christ: An Evangelical Affirmation*.[18] As its title indicates, this document was intended to serve the evangelical community as a unifying testimony to the doctrine of justification in its Protestant understanding. Since the publication of this statement, discussion and controversy within the evangelical community in North America has ebbed.[19] Whether the doctrine of justification will be a further subject of discussion in the future between Catholic and evangelical representatives remains to be seen. As the Catholic and evangelical communities find themselves opposing common cultural and religious trends, it seems likely that further attempts will be made to resolve this crucial doctrinal point of contention.

THE ATTRACTION OF A NEW PERSPECTIVE FOR THE ECUMENICALLY MINDED

A common feature of the more recent ecumenical discussions regarding justification is a renewed interest in the witness of the Bible. It is often repeated that a new look at the Scripture texts will afford an opportunity to discover dimensions of the biblical gospel that will enrich the inherited understanding of the past.[20] The pathway forward invites, not a repetition of the opposing views of the past, but a new view that will serve to unite rather than divide the churches. Even though the new perspective is not a direct outcome of contemporary ecumenical discussions on justification, the fact that it parts company with the view of the Reformation and offers a fresh reading of the biblical text gives it a special attraction for those looking for a way through the thicket of long-standing disputes. Rather than simply revisiting the old disagreements of the

Reformation, the new perspective seeks to engage the biblical texts unencumbered by the inheritances of the past. This means that, whereas the old perspective led to the most significant division within the western Christian church, the new perspective offers an understanding of the gospel that may prove especially useful from an ecumenical point of view.

But it is not merely the new perspective's fresh reading of the biblical texts that makes it particularly attractive within the context of contemporary ecumenical discussions about justification. The very nature of the new perspective gives it a peculiar ecumenical significance. One of its special features is an emphasis upon justification as a unifying theme. Rather than leading to further rifts between various branches of the Christian church, justification is an inherently *ecumenical* teaching. From the point of view of the new perspective, it is ironic that past disputes about the doctrine of justification divided the church, when it is an essentially unifying theme in the Bible and especially in the theology of Paul.

THE REFORMATION PERSPECTIVE: JUSTIFICATION AS A CHURCH-DIVIDING TEACHING

From the vantage point of history, it is not difficult to illustrate how the doctrine of justification in its Reformation expression proved to be a church-dividing doctrine. When the sixteenth-century Reformers formulated the doctrine of justification, each of its principal themes was expressed polemically over against the teaching of the medieval Roman Catholic Church. For example, each of the 'solas' of the Reformation aimed to crystallize the difference between Protestant and Roman Catholic views. From the standpoint of the Reformers, believers are saved 'by grace alone' (*sola gratia*) and not by 'grace plus works' as the Roman Catholic Church taught. Justification, which was interpreted as an act of God whereby he accepts believers and reputes them to be righteous, was said to be based solely upon the work of Christ (*solo Christo*) and not upon any human work or merit. Furthermore, justification was a free gift of God's grace that was received by the instrument of faith alone (*sola fide*), apart from any works performed in obedience to the law. For the Reformers this doctrine of justification by grace alone on account of Christ alone through faith alone—to state it in the most precise form—was *the* article of the standing or the falling of the church. Failure to agree on the teaching of free justification, accordingly, could only bring about a parting of the ways between the true church of Jesus Christ and the false church. Thus, the Reformation view of the gospel, which sharply opposed the medieval Roman Catholic view, occasioned the most far-reaching division within the Christian church in her history. According to the Reformers, so serious was the corruption of the gospel in the Roman Catholic Church that they were compelled to regard it as no longer a true expression of the church of Jesus Christ on earth.

Though I do not intend at this point to offer a comprehensive consideration of the Reformers' view of justification, several of its features were bound to aggravate the division with Rome.

In the Reformation understanding of the gospel, justification was a benefit of Christ's saving work, the importance of which could not be overemphasized. Indeed, it was not only the Lutheran tradition that spoke of justification as the article of the standing or the falling church. Calvin, who had the highest regard for Luther's rediscovery of the gospel of free justification, insisted that this doctrine was 'the main hinge of the Christian religion'.[21] The implication of Calvin's use of this metaphor is that, if we should become unhinged at this point, then the whole of the Christian faith is in danger of collapsing. Since justification addresses the most basic religious question, namely, how offending sinners can find favour and acceptance with God, it lies at the heart of the saving message of the gospel. The answer it supplies calls our attention to the sheer graciousness of God, who justifies the ungodly on the basis of Christ's saving work alone. Any failure to appreciate the completely gratuitous nature of salvation, or to affirm categorically that sinners find acceptance with God through Christ in spite of their demerits, could only lead to a fundamental misconception of the gospel of God's saving grace in Christ, according to the Reformers.

They believed that such a misconception was the inevitable consequence of the medieval Roman Catholic doctrine of justification.

Because it emphasized obedience to the law as a partial, meritorious basis for the justification of believers, it profoundly compromised the gospel of grace. Though the Roman Catholic Church acknowledged the priority of God's grace in Christ for justification, the Reformers objected to its insistence, nonetheless, that the believer must co-operate with God's grace by obeying the commandments of God, and in so doing merit further or increased justification. According to such an understanding of the gospel, believers are saved, not by grace alone through the work of Christ alone received by faith alone, but by grace *plus works*.[22] The righteousness that makes believers acceptable to God is not exclusively the righteousness of Christ, but includes the good works of believers. Consequently, in his complaint against Rome, Luther especially emphasized the essential similarity between its teaching of salvation by meritorious good works and the Pharasaical or Judaizing teaching of salvation by obedience to the law. A similar emphasis is also present in Calvin's writings. Frequently, Luther and Calvin criticize the teaching of the medieval church by arguing that its understanding of justification was a repetition of an old error, which had earlier characterized the religion of the Pharisees and Judaism at the time when the New Testament was written. Just as the Pharisees trusted in their own righteousness before God as the basis for their claim upon his favour and mercy, so the Roman Catholic doctrine of justification by grace plus works encouraged a similar trust in one's own righteousness. The apostle Paul's arguments with the Judaizers in his letters to the Romans and Galatians, therefore, anticipated the Reformers' opposition to the Catholic doctrine of righteousness by works.[23]

Luther and Calvin also expressed their objection to Rome's teaching by insisting upon a sharp distinction between the law and the gospel, so far as the believer's acceptance with God is concerned. The law, at least in its first or 'theological use' (*usus theologicus*), is a mirror that teaches the believer to know his or her sinfulness before God. The law in this use can only condemn and expose the unrighteousness of sinners before God. In the first and second tables of the law, we are commanded to live a life of perfect love for God and our neighbour. However, there is no one who is righteous by this standard, who is able to keep the requirements of the law perfectly, and on that basis stand before God justified. Only Christ, who obeyed the law perfectly and suffered its penalty in the place of sinners, can obtain for them the righteousness that is acceptable to God. The contrast between the law and the gospel, therefore, is the contrast between the righteousness of the law and the righteousness of faith. Either we are saved (partly or wholly) by our obedience to the law or we are saved by Christ's obedience for us. Perhaps more than Luther, Calvin also spoke of a positive use for the law as a rule of gratitude in the Christian life.[24] Nevertheless, Calvin was as convinced as Luther that obedience to the law has no role to play in the believer's justification before God.

As a corollary to this contrast between the law and the gospel, Luther and Calvin rejected the Roman Catholic view of justification by faith and works. Though they acknowledged that faith works through love, they nevertheless insisted that believers receive the gift of God's grace and righteousness in Christ by the empty hand of faith alone. God grants and imputes to believers the perfect righteousness and obedience of Christ, which is received by faith only. Though the faith that receives God's grace in Christ is an active and fruitful faith, it does not justify on account of its fruit-bearing. What distinguishes faith as the appropriate instrument by which to receive God's grace is that it looks outside of itself to Christ alone as the only and perfect Saviour. Faith receives the righteousness of Christ freely imputed to believers by God.[25]

Each of these features of the Reformation doctrine of justification emphasized, so far as the Reformers were concerned, the insuperable difference between the gospel of free justification and the Roman Catholic teaching of salvation by grace and works. Each of them was formulated in a polemical setting that could only lead to a separation of the Protestant and Roman Catholic traditions. It is precisely the church-dividing implications of the old or Reformation perspective on Paul's view of justification that lends such importance to the recent ecumenical discussions, which we considered earlier in this chapter. Even though it is claimed that such discussions have achieved a growing consensus between Protestants and Catholics on the subject of justification, it is difficult to imagine that this consensus will prove substantive and enduring so long as the doctrine is considered within the parameters of the historic disagreements of the sixteenth century. The potential of a new perspective on Paul lies in part in its willingness to think outside of these parameters.

THE NEW PERSPECTIVE: JUSTIFICATION AS A CHURCH-UNITING DOCTRINE

Unlike the main features of the Reformers' understanding of justification, which were formulated in a polemical and church-dividing context, several features of the new perspective on Paul are especially attractive because of their church-uniting implications. There are, of course, considerable differences of emphasis and position among the writers who, broadly speaking, are identified with the new perspective. [26] However, it remains possible to identify several features of the new perspective on Paul that have a certain attraction to those engaged in ecumenical dialogue.

We have already noted one of these features: the desire to read the biblical texts without the burden of having to defend the positions of the past. Rather than simply restating the polemical positions of the sixteenth century, the new perspective claims to offer a new, and therefore unbiased, reading of the biblical and Pauline texts. Whereas so much of traditional Protestant scholarship on Paul has taken the Reformation as an uncontested starting point, authors of the new perspective claim to be motivated by a desire to read the biblical texts in their immediate, historical context.

When the biblical texts are read in their historical setting, the new perspective maintains that the Reformation's reading of the apostle Paul cannot be sustained. It argues that we need a comprehensive re-evaluation and re-assessment of the Reformation's interpretation of the patterns of religious belief among the Pharisees and the Jewish community contemporaneous with the writing of the New Testament. Contrary to the Reformation's claim that the Pharisees in particular, and Judaism in general, were representative of a 'works righteousness' religious practice, the new perspective maintains that Second-Temple Judaism emphasized

God's gracious election and initiative in embracing his people Israel. Judaism never taught that those who belonged to this covenant community did so by virtue of their own good works and acts of obedience to the law of God. Rather, Judaism was a religion of grace in which believers were brought into covenant relationship with God by the initiative of his electing love. To be sure, the members of the covenant community were obligated to obey the law of God in order to maintain their position within the community. But this obedience to the law was not the ground upon which Israel was embraced within God's favour. Therefore the Reformation's claim that Judaism was a legalistic religion, which anticipated the legalism of the Roman Catholic Church, is untenable according to the new perspective.

From an ecumenical point of view, one of the most attractive features of the new perspective is its explanation of Paul's polemic with Judaism. Whereas the Reformers regarded Judaism as a legalistic religion, the new perspective insists that the problem within Judaism was not the law as such, but Israel's claim to be the *exclusive* community of God's people. The boasting opposed by the apostle Paul in his epistles is not the claim to find favour with God on the basis of obedience to the law; rather, it is Jewish boasting in those 'works of the law' that *distinguish* them from Gentiles, and mark them off as the exclusive objects of God's favour and mercy. The problem tackled in the epistles was not the problem of a self-righteous boasting before God, which assumes that our standing with God is based upon meritorious good works; rather it was the exclusivistic claims of many Jews who maintained that they alone were numbered among the people of God by virtue of their keeping certain requirements of the law (circumcision, feast day observances, dietary laws) which distinguished or separated them from the Gentiles.

The new perspective argues that Paul's doctrine of justification, accordingly, was not the central theme of his gospel, nor was it addressed to the problem of legalism. The doctrine addressed the specific issue of *inclusion within the covenant community, particularly whether Gentiles are included.* Therefore, when Paul spoke of justification by grace through faith, apart from the works of the law, he was teaching that all become members of the covenant community through faith in Christ, not by submitting to the distinctly Jewish requirements of the law. The problem with Judaism, therefore, was not that it was a legalistic and self-righteous religion, but rather that it was unwilling to recognize the fulfilment of God's covenant promise to bring blessing to all the peoples of the earth, Jew and Gentile alike. It did not recognize the new reality of God's saving presence in Jesus Christ whereby Jew and Gentile are brought into the number of God's covenant people.

It is especially this feature of the new perspective on Paul that underscores its ecumenical implications. If Paul's formulation of the doctrine of justification was aimed at the narrow exclusivism of a party within Judaism that excluded the Gentiles from the company of God's people, it should serve a similar purpose today. Rather than leading to division within the Christian community, justification is, if it is anything, a church-uniting doctrine. Speaking of the social and practical application of Paul's doctrine of justification, James D. G. Dunn, for example, notes that

> We can now see more clearly what Paul was getting at when he created his classic antithesis: God justifies (accepts) people through faith and not by virtue of works of the law. He was not hitting at people who thought they could earn God's goodwill by their achievements, or merit God's final acquittal on the basis of all their good deeds. That theological insight is true and of lasting importance. But it is not quite what Paul was saying. ... To sum up, justification by faith as Paul formulated it cannot be reduced to the experience of individual salvation as though that was all there is to it. Justification by faith is Paul's fundamental objection to the idea that God has limited his saving goodness to a particular people.[27]

Similarly, N. T. Wright, in his popular introduction to the new perspective on Paul, *What Saint Paul Really Said,* calls attention to the ecumenical implications of this perspective for the contemporary church:

> Paul's doctrine of justification by faith impels the churches, in their current fragmented state, into the ecumenical task. It cannot

be right that the very doctrine which declares that all who believe in Jesus belong at the same table (*Gal.* 2) should be used as a way of saying that some, who define the doctrine of justification differently, belong at a different table. The doctrine of justification, in other words, is not merely a doctrine which Catholic and Protestant might just be able to agree on, as a result of hard ecumenical endeavour. It is itself the ecumenical doctrine, the doctrine that rebukes all our petty and often culture-bound church groupings, and which declares that all who believe in Jesus belong together in the one family.[28]

Such comments by significant proponents of the new perspective illustrate the considerable attraction this perspective holds within the context of contemporary discussions. In a period of church history marked by ecumenical endeavour, any new reading of the biblical text that serves the cause of church unity must have a special appeal. When this reading relates to the doctrine that has served most powerfully to divide the western church, its appeal can only be exponentially increased. It is a peculiar irony that the new perspective, upon the basis of a 'Protestant' appeal to a fresh reading of the Pauline texts, argues that the doctrine of justification serves the cause of church unity rather than disunity. If proven true, this would mean that the new perspective represents more than an argument against the old or Reformation view of justification. It also represents a movement to reopen discussion of a doctrine that in times past was injurious to the church's peace, in the name of healing the wounds and divisions of the past.

CONCLUSION

The new perspective on Paul requires our attention for a variety of reasons. It represents a significant, if not the most significant, development in Pauline studies that has occurred in recent decades. But it will likely prove to be far more than an intellectual current within the narrow guild of New Testament scholars. Ideas have legs, and those that address a subject as vital as that of the Christian gospel and its doctrine of justification will undoubtedly travel into the pulpits and pews of the church. Moreover, if what we have noted is true—the development and proposal regarding a new perspective on Paul occurring within the setting of heightened ecumenical interest in the subject of justification—then the new perspective becomes a subject of special importance. Whereas in the sixteenth century the doctrine of justification served to divide the western Christian church, the new perspective insists that, upon the basis of a fresh reading of Paul, it will prove to be the great ecumenical doctrine. The way forward ecumenically, according to exponents of this new perspective, is not to repeat the errors and divisions of the past regarding the doctrine of justification; rather, it is to rediscover what St Paul really said about justification, that God's purpose is to unite all peoples within his one covenant family.

NOTES

[1] Some of the material in this section is a revision and expansion of my chapter, 'Justification by Faith: The Ecumenical, Biblical and Theological Dimensions of Current Debates', in *Always Reforming*, ed. A. T. B. McGowan (Leicester: Inter-Varsity Press, 2006), pp. 289–327.

[2] Though this language is often attributed to Luther, it actually reflects the language of the *Smalcald Articles* (1537), an early Lutheran statement of faith that was later included among the Lutheran confessional documents with the *Formula of Concord* (1576). Article II.1 states, 'On this article [Christ alone is our salvation] rests all that we teach and practice against the pope' (quoted from Theodore G. Tappert, ed., *The Book of Concord: The Confessions of the Evangelical Lutheran Church* [Philadelphia: Fortress Press, 1959], p. 292). Luther, however, used similar language in his *Commentary on St Paul's Epistle to the Galatians* (ed. P. S. Watson; Grand Rapids: Baker Book House reprint, 1979 [1891]), p. 143: '[Justification is] the principal article of all Christian doctrine, which makes true Christians indeed.'

[3] For an extensive summary of these ecumenical discussions and documents, which includes a thorough bibliography of primary and secondary sources, see Anthony N. S. Lane, *Justification by Faith in Catholic-Protestant Dialogue: An Evangelical Assessment* (London: T. & T. Clark Ltd, 2002), pp. 87–126. Lane also treats high-level ecumenical discussions between Catholic and Anglican, and Catholic and Methodist, representatives. For our purposes, we will only summarize the discussions between Catholics and Lutherans, and Catholics and North American evangelicals. For a survey and critical evaluation of these Lutheran-Roman Catholic discussions which is written from a confessionally Lutheran standpoint, see Robert D. Preus, *Justification and*

Rome: An Evaluation of Recent Dialogues (Saint Louis: Concordia Publishing House, 1997).

⁴ H. George Anderson, T. Austin Murphy and Joseph A. Burgess, eds., *Justification by Faith. Lutherans and Catholics in Dialogue VII* (Minneapolis: Fortress Press, 1985). For a summary of the biblical discussions that form a background to this report, see John Reumann, *'Righteousness' in the New Testament* (Philadelphia: Fortress Press, 1982).

⁵ Anderson, Murphy and Burgess, eds., *Justification by Faith,* 'Common Statement', par. 4, 157.

⁶ 'Common Statement', par. 157.　　⁷ Ibid., par. 4.

⁸ K. Lehmann and W. Pannenberg, eds., *The Condemnations of the Reformation Era: Do They Still Divide?* (Minneapolis: Fortress Press, 1990). A chapter by W. Pannenberg, 'Can the Mutual Condemnations Between Rome and the Reformation Churches be Lifted?' (pp. 31–43), describes the process followed by the Joint Committee. The original document was printed in German: K Lehmann and W. Pannenberg, eds., *Lehrverurteilungen—kirchen-trennend? I: Rechtfertigung, Sakramente und Amt im Zeitalter der Reformation und Heute* (Freiburg: Vandenhoeck & Ruprecht, 1986). It should be noted that, though most of the participants in this project were Catholic and Lutheran, a few Reformed theologians also took part.

⁹ For a summary of the various responses to this document, see Lane, *Justification by Faith,* pp. 101 ff.

¹⁰ An English translation of this declaration was issued by the Lutheran World Federation and The Pontifical Council for Promoting Christian Unity (Grand Rapids: Eerdmans, 2000). The original declaration was published in German: *Gemeinsame Erklärung zur Rechtfertigungslehre* (Frankfurt am Main: Otto Lembeck, 1999).

¹¹ *Joint Declaration,* par. 15.

¹² *Joint Declaration,* par. 40. For an assessment of the significance of the *Joint Declaration* for the ecumenical movement, see the volume of essays, *Justification and the Future of the Ecumenical Movement: The Joint Declaration on the Doctrine of Justification,* ed. William G. Rusch (Collegeville, MN: Liturgical Press, 2003). For a critical appraisal of the *Joint Declaration* written from a confessionally Reformed standpoint, see W. Robert Godfrey, 'The Lutheran-Roman Catholic Joint Declaration', *The Banner of Truth,* Issue 432 (January 2000), pp. 17–20.

¹³ 'Evangelicals and Catholics Together: The Christian Mission in the Third Millennium', *First Things* 43 (May 1994), pp. 15-22. For other printings of this declaration, including discussion and responses by various authors, see Charles Colson and Richard John Neuhaus, eds., *Evangelicals and Catholics Together: Toward a Common Mission* (London: Hodder & Stoughton, 1996); T. P. Rausch, ed., *Catholics and Evangelicals: Do They Share a Common*

Future? (Downers Grove: Intervarsity Press, 2000); R. C. Sproul, *Faith Alone: The Evangelical Doctrine of Justification* (Grand Rapids: Baker, 1995); and Norman L. Geisler and R. E. MacKenzie, *Roman Catholics and Evangelicals: Agreements and Differences* (Grand Rapids: Baker, 1995).

¹⁴ Colson and Neuhaus, eds., *Evangelicals and Catholics Together,* p. xviii.

¹⁵ Like its predecessor, this document was printed in several publications: Timothy George, 'Evangelicals and Catholics Together: A New Initiative', *Christianity Today* (8 December 1997), pp. 34–8; 'The Gift of Salvation', *First Things* 79 (January 1998), pp. 20–3; and R. C. Sproul, *Getting the Gospel Right: The Tie that Binds Evangelicals Together* (Grand Rapids: Baker, 1999), 179–84. For critical assessments of this declaration, which are written from a classic Protestant perspective, see R. C. Sproul, *Getting the Gospel Right,* pp. 45–93; and Mark Seifrid, '"The Gift of Salvation": Its Failure to Address the Crux of Justification', *Journal of the Evangelical Theological Society* 42 (1999), pp. 679–88.

¹⁶ *Christianity Today* (8 December 1997), p. 36.   ¹⁷ *Ibid.,* p. 38.

¹⁸ For printings of this declaration together with responses and critical evaluation, see R. C. Sproul, *Getting the Gospel Right,* 95-195; *Christianity Today* (14 June 1999), pp. 51–6; J. N. Akers et al., eds., *This We Believe: The Good News of Jesus Christ for the World* (Grand Rapids: Zondervan, 2000); and P. R. Hinlicky et al., 'An Ecumenical Symposium on "A Call to Evangelical Unity"', *Pro Ecclesia* 9 (2000), pp. 133-49.

¹⁹ Though there has been a waning of interest in these earlier discussions between evangelicals and Catholics, a recent symposium at Wheaton College, which was devoted to current debates regarding justification and imputation, indicates that the subject of justification remains an important one for contemporary evangelicals. For a description of the conference and a printed version of the papers presented, see Mark Husbands and Daniel J. Treier, eds., *Justification: What's at Stake in the Current Debates?* (Downers Grove, IL: InterVarsity Press, 2004).

²⁰ Cf. e.g. John Reumann, *'Righteousness' in the New Testament,* Preface, xv: 'They [biblical studies] have also served to indicate not merely that, but more precisely how, the historical-critical approach [of contemporary exegetical science and biblical theology] can be useful in transcending old impasses and in presenting new insights.'

²¹ *Institutes* III.xi.1 (ed. John T. McNeill; Philadelphia: The Westminster Press, 1960). Calvin uses language similar to Luther's and the Lutheran tradition in a sermon on Luke 1:5–10: '[Justification is] the principle of the whole doctrine of salvation and the foundation of all religion' (as cited by Francois Wendel, *Calvin* [London: Collins reprint, 1963], p. 256). Though for Calvin justification was not the whole of the gospel—Calvin insisted that justified sinners were simultaneously sanctified by the grace of Christ's Spirit—it was no doubt the most pivotal feature of the good news of God's salvation in Christ.

[22] Cf. *The Canons and Decrees of the Council of Trent,* Sixth Session, Decree on Justification, Chap. 16 (quoted from Philip Schaff, *The Creeds of Christendom* [reprint; Grand Rapids: Baker, 1985 (1931)], 2:107), 'And, for this cause, life eternal is to be proposed to those working well *unto the end,* and hoping in God, both as a grace mercifully promised to the sons of God through Jesus Christ, and as a reward which is according to the promise of God himself, to be faithfully rendered to their good works and merits.' The doctrine of justification set forth at the Council of Trent represents the official dogma of the Roman Catholic Church. A careful reading of the Council's Sixth Session on the doctrine of justification will make clear that the Roman Catholic view does not teach justification by works, as is often alleged, but justification *by grace plus works.* Many Protestants have an inadequate appreciation for the fact that the Catholic view can readily speak of 'justification by grace through faith'. The initial grace of justification is entirely free and unmerited. Moreover, whatever 'increase' in justification occurs, it too is the fruit of the working of God's grace infused through the sacraments. The principal difference between Reformation and Catholic views, therefore, is that the former completely excludes the believer's works from playing any role whatever in his justification. This difference is expressed by means of the language not only of 'grace alone', but most especially of 'faith alone'.

[23] Calvin, for example, in his commentary on Philippians 3:8, spoke of the Roman Catholics of his time as 'present-day Pharisees' who uphold 'their own merits against Christ'. See *Calvin's New Testament Commentaries: Galatians, Ephesians, Philippians and Colossians,* ed. David W. Torrance and Thomas F. Torrance (Grand Rapids: Eerdmans, 1965), p. 274.

[24] Cf. Calvin, *Institutes* II.vii.12: 'The third and principal use, which pertains more closely to the proper use of the law, finds its place among believers in whose hearts the Spirit of God already lives and reigns.'

[25] The *Heidelberg Catechism,* an influential Reformed Catechism of the Reformation period, expresses clearly this understanding of justification by grace alone through faith alone in Q. & A. 61: 'Why do you say that you are righteous only by faith? Not that I am acceptable to God on account of the worthiness of my faith, but because only the satisfaction, righteousness, and holiness of Christ is my righteousness before God, and I can receive the same and make it my own in no other way than by faith only' (quoted from *Ecumenical and Reformed Creeds and Confessions* [Classroom edition; Orange City, IA: Mid-America Reformed Seminary, 1991]). Unless otherwise indicated, quotations from the Reformation confessions are taken from this source.

[26] For relatively brief surveys of the history and development of the new perspective, see Douglas Moo, 'Paul and the Law in the Last Ten Years', *Scottish Journal of Theology* 40 (1986), pp. 287–307; Frank Thielman, *Paul & the Law: A Contextual Approach.* (Downers Grove, IL: InterVarsity, 1994), pp. 9–47; Thomas R. Schreiner, *The Law and Its Fulfillment: A Pauline Theology of the Law* (Grand Rapids: Baker, 1993), pp. 13–31; Stephen Westerholm, *Israel's Law and the Church's Faith: Paul and His Recent Interpreters* (Grand

Rapids: Eerdmans, 1988); idem, *Perspectives Old and New on Paul: The 'Lutheran' Paul and His Critics* (Grand Rapids: Eerdmans, 2004), pp. 101–49, 178-200; Gerhard H. Visscher, 'New Views Regarding Legalism and Exclusivism in Judaism: Is there a need to reinterpret Paul?', *Koinonia* 18/2 (1999), pp. 15–42; and Guy Prentiss Waters, *Justification and the New Perspectives on Paul: A Review and Response* (Phillipsburg, NJ: Presbyterian & Reformed, 2004). It is almost impossible for a non-specialist to keep up with the literature on the new perspective. We will refer to additional sources in the second half of our study.

[27] James D. G. Dunn and Alan M. Suggate, *The Justice of God: A Fresh Look at the Old Doctrine of Justification by Faith* (Carlisle, UK: The Paternoster Press, 1993), pp. 27–8. Dunn goes on to spell out the radical implications for unity of this understanding of justification: '[T]oday we need to rediscover Paul's original teaching on the subject [of justification]. God accepts all who believe and trust in him: Gentile as well as Jew, black and white, Palestinian and Israelite, central American and US citizen, Roman Catholic and Protestant, Orthodox and Muslim' (pp. 28–9).

[28] *What Saint Paul Really Said: Was Paul of Tarsus the Real Founder of Chrsitianity?* (Grand Rapids: Eerdmans, 1997), p. 158.

PART ONE

THE REFORMATION
PERSPECTIVE ON PAUL

2

JUSTIFICATION BY FAITH ALONE

Though I have forgotten the name of the author and the periodical in which he was writing, I vividly remember reading a criticism of the Reformation understanding of justification. The author opined that, if the doctrine of justification was as important as the Reformers insisted it was, then it should be easy to understand. The good news of acceptance with God through faith in Jesus Christ, which lies at the heart of the Christian message, must be capable of a simple, uncomplicated presentation. However, this does not seem to be the case with justification. Discussions about justification often result in the issuing of complicated formulas and arcane terms that defy easy explanation. And so, the author concluded, the Reformation was undoubtedly wrong about justification, if for no other reason than its failure to provide a clear explanation of its meaning.

The author of this criticism was clearly not sympathetic to the Reformation doctrine of justification. Testimonies to the loss of a clear understanding of justification within contemporary Protestantism, however, can also be found among authors who are more sympathetic to the Reformation view. Michael Horton, who is associated with the Alliance of Confessing Evangelicals, tells of a personal experience that illustrates this loss in his book, *Putting Amazing Back into Grace.*[1] During an engagement at a Christian high school, Horton recounts how he had the opportunity to speak to some 160 students about the Reformation's view of the gospel. During the course of his presentations, he queried the students about the doctrine of justification and its meaning. Remarkably, *not one* of those 160 students, who were enrolled in this Christian high school, could give him even a simple definition of the doctrine. This anecdotal evidence suggests that, even among contemporary

evangelical Christians, the doctrine of justification is not appreciated or clearly understood.

Before taking up the subject of the new perspective on Paul,
therefore, we wish to begin with a consideration of the historic
Protestant understanding of the doctrine of justification. In new
perspective literature, references are often made to the old perspective on Paul, which presumably means the predominant view
of the Protestant Reformation. Seldom, however, do we find any
sustained treatment of the doctrine as it was advocated by the
Reformers. Assumptions are made regarding the nature of their
understanding, but these are frequently presented without citations
from the principal authors and confessions of the period. Therefore, a critical assessment of the new perspective, which presents
itself as a viable alternative to the old, requires an accurate understanding of the Reformation's doctrine of justification.

Admittedly, it is not possible in the brief span of two chapters
to give a complete account of the Reformation's doctrine.[2] Our
approach, therefore, will be to provide a brief sketch of some of the
Reformation's most dominant themes, appealing to the scriptural
and confessional statements that played an important role in the
development and articulation of historic Protestantism's view of
justification. In this chapter we shall begin by offering a summary
of the Reformation's teaching on this subject. In the next, we shall
address the oft-disputed subject of the relation between the apostle
Paul's doctrine of justification and the teaching of James. Since the
dispute between the Reformers and the Roman Catholic Church
turned in many ways upon the issue of justification by faith alone,
a consideration of the Reformation's handling of James, and the
relation between faith and works, is of vital importance to our
study.

THE NATURE OF FREE JUSTIFICATION

In order to summarize the Reformation view of justification, it is
important to keep in mind an accurate statement of the doctrine.
To say merely that believers are justified by grace through faith
does not adequately state the Protestant view. Classic Protestantism
maintains that sinners are justified before God *by grace alone* on

account of the work of *Christ alone*, and that this free justification becomes ours *by faith alone*. In setting forth the older Protestant perspective, we will consider successively each phrase in this traditional formulation of this doctrine. What did the Reformers understand by the term 'justification'? Why did they insist that this justification is 'by grace alone' on account of the work of 'Christ alone'? And what about their corollary insistence that this free justification becomes ours 'by faith alone'? These three questions will serve as an outline for the rest of this chapter.

A JUDICIAL DECLARATION OF ACCEPTANCE OR FAVOUR

One of the common ways of getting at the nature of the Protestant understanding of justification is to note that it views justification as a *forensic* or *judicial* declaration. Justification is a legal declaration by God, which pronounces the justified person to be righteous or acceptable in his sight. By contrast, the Roman Catholic view maintains that it includes a process of moral transformation equivalent to what, in evangelical terms, is known as the work of sanctification. The historic dispute between Protestant and Roman Catholic can be partially summarized, therefore, in the questions: Does justification *declare* someone to be righteous or acceptable to God, as the Reformers maintained? Or, does justification involve a process whereby someone is *made* righteous, as the Roman Catholic Church taught? [3]

When the difference between the Protestant and Roman Catholic views of justification is posed in these terms, it becomes apparent why some complain that the doctrine of justification devolves quickly into language and formulations that are obscure or unduly technical. Do we have to employ language like 'forensic' or 'judicial' in order to explain what is meant by justification? Though it is undoubtedly true that the language employed is sometimes technical—even the term 'justification' is derived from Latin and requires explanation—it is not that difficult to explain what is meant by asserting that justification is forensic in nature.

The word 'forensic' derives from a root that refers to the law court where decisions are made regarding the innocence or guilt of persons charged with a violation of the law. [4] This is the background to the contemporary use of the term 'forensics', which refers to the task of gathering evidence that will prove either the innocence or the guilt of someone charged with a crime. It is likewise used to denote a form of public speaking in which the speaker is required to argue for or against the truth of a certain proposition. If a school were to offer a course in forensics, it would likely be a course in public speech where the students would be asked to prove or disprove a thesis or claim. These various uses illustrate that the term has its home within the setting of a court of law. The principal concern of such a court is the declaration of a person's innocence or guilt.

When we consider this within a biblical and theological setting, it is not difficult to see its implications. To say that justification is a judicial or forensic act means that *it refers to God's pronouncement in his court that sinners are righteous, or innocent of any charge of guilt.* To be justified in a biblical setting is to be judged righteous and acceptable, so far as God is concerned. Just as forensics refers to a form of public speech in a court of law, forensic justification refers to God's declaration in the court of heaven regarding the innocence of his people.

Though there are many examples of this understanding of justification among the Reformers of the sixteenth century, we will cite only one from Calvin's *Institutes*.

> He is said to be justified in God's sight who is both reckoned righteous in God's judgment and has been accepted on account of his righteousness. . . . Now he is justified who is reckoned in the condition not of a sinner, but of a righteous man; and for that reason, he stands firm before God's judgment seat while all sinners fall. If an innocent accused person be summoned before the judgment seat of a fair judge, where he will be judged according to his innocence, he is said to be 'justified' before the judge. Thus, justified before God is the man who, freed from the company of sinners, has God to witness and affirm his right-eousness. . . . Therefore, we explain justification simply as the acceptance with which God receives us into his favour as righteous men. And we say that it consists in the remission of sins and the imputation of Christ's righteousness.[5]

As Calvin's statement indicates, the Reformers believed that the idea of justification was firmly rooted in the biblical teaching that God is the Judge of all persons. Though the terminology of justification is metaphorical, depicting sinners in legal terms as those who are called to appear before God as their Judge, for the Reformers it represented the real (or literal) situation of all persons in relation to God. As creatures originally created in God's image but now fallen into sin in Adam, all human beings are accountable to God and will be judged by him. God is the Judge of all the earth, and his judgments are always right. The issue of justification, so far as the Reformers were concerned, can hardly be exaggerated in terms of its importance. It is one matter to be summoned before a human court and adjudged innocent or guilty; but it is quite another matter to be summoned before God, and to be subject to his judgment.

This is why, for the Reformers, the question of justification is not one question among many but *the* religious question, the paramount question in life and death.[6] God's verdict respecting sinners depends upon such questions as: Are sinners acceptable to God or not? Are they in the right with him or in the wrong? In these respects, justification is principally a theological and soteriological doctrine. On the one hand, it assumes that God is the ultimate Judge before whom all sinners must give an account. And on the other hand, it assumes that the pivot on which the whole doctrine of salvation in Christ turns, is the issue of finding favour or acceptance with God in spite of human sin and unworthiness.

Scriptural and Confessional References

In the Reformers' reading of the Scriptures and especially the writings of the apostle Paul, this understanding of justification as a judicial pronouncement is commonly defended. Whether in Old Testament passages, which provide a background to New Testament usage, or in the epistles of Paul, justification – according to the Reformation's view – is God's act of vindicating and accepting his people as righteous in Christ.

The idea of justification as a judicial declaration did not originate with Paul, but is found already in the Old Testament.[7] In most of the Old Testament passages that use the term 'to justify', this is its sense. Two passages from the Old Testament will suffice by way of illustration. [8]

The first is found in Deuteronomy 25:1, a passage that provides instruction on the duties of a judge in Israel. In this passage judges are instructed, when a dispute is brought to their court, to 'justify' the innocent party and to 'condemn' the guilty. The word 'justify' in this passage clearly refers to the judgment that the judge is called upon to make in the court of his jurisdiction. He is obligated to declare in favour of the innocent person and to declare against the guilty. The judge's action does not make the person innocent or guilty; the judge simply pronounces the person to be innocent or guilty. Undoubtedly, in the act of pronouncing the court's verdict, the guilt or innocence, the righteousness or the lack thereof, of the one being judged is a paramount concern to the judge. So far as the meaning and the significance of the term 'to justify' is concerned, however, it *does not mean to make the justified one just*. It means *to declare him so*, to declare him to be in the right, to be without guilt.

The other example is Proverbs 17:15, where we read, 'He who justifies the wicked, and he who condemns the righteous are both alike an abomination to the LORD.' Here again the idea cannot be that the judge, when justifying the wicked or condemning the righteous, makes the wicked righteous or makes the righteous wicked. It is the verdict of the judge, the declaration pronounced in the court of law, that is at issue.

It is this Old Testament usage that predominates in the New Testament as well, especially in the epistles of Paul.[9] This is evident from the contrast Paul draws between 'to justify' and 'to condemn', from the court-room imagery and language that permeates his descriptions of justification, particularly in the opening chapters of Romans, and from his use of the terms to 'reckon' or 'impute' in connection with justification.

One of the most familiar passages in Paul's epistles is Romans 8:33-34, where the apostle says:

Who shall bring any charge against God's elect? It is God who justifies. Who is to condemn? Christ Jesus is the one who died—

more than that, who was raised—who is at the right hand of God, who indeed is interceding for us.

Romans 8, which opens with the great affirmation that 'there is now no condemnation for those who are in Christ Jesus' (verse 1), brings the opening chapters of the epistle to a kind of provisional conclusion. When Paul contrasts justification and condemnation in this passage, he is clearly picking up the theme of justification, which had preoccupied him in the previous chapters. The gospel of Jesus Christ, which is the power of God unto salvation (1:16), proclaims that God has acted in Christ to justify his people and thereby free them from all condemnation. The sharp antithesis between justification and condemnation in this passage confirms that the divine work of justification is akin to a declaration by God that believers are right with him, and not subject to the condemnation and death that sinners deserve. Earlier in Romans 5:16, which is set within the context of a sustained parallelism between the second Adam (Christ) and the first Adam, Paul draws a similar contrast between justification and condemnation: 'And the free gift is not like the result of that one man's sin. For the judgment following one trespass brought condemnation, but the free gift following many trespasses brought justification.' In both of these passages, the contrast drawn between justification and condemnation places the reader in the orbit of the courtroom of God where the verdict that ultimately matters is rendered.

Throughout Romans the use of the term justification is located within a legal framework. Though it may not be as clear in translation as in the original Greek, this is what we see in the remarkably powerful imagery of Romans 3:19–20:

> Now we know that whatever the law says, it speaks to those who are under the law, that every mouth may be closed and all the world may be accountable to God, because by the works of the law no flesh will be justified in his sight.[10]

Here the apostle dramatically portrays the plight of every sinner before the throne of God in the court of heaven. Like defendants in a human court whose guilt is evident beyond reasonable doubt, all are clearly guilty of having broken the law of God. They have, accordingly, nothing to say in their own defence. This is the sense of Paul's phrase, 'that every mouth may be closed'. To speak colloquially, sinners would be wasting their breath if they sought to excuse or exonerate themselves before God's judgment. The imagery and setting of this passage, which occurs at a crucial juncture in Paul's argument regarding justification is clearly legal. When he says that no flesh will be justified in God's sight, he means that no one will be found innocent or righteous on the basis of works performed in obedience to the law of God. Whether Jews or Gentiles, whether having the privilege of the law in written form or not, the same law serves to condemn as sinners all who have fallen short of its requirements.

In addition to passages in Paul's writings that contrast justification and condemnation, or that employ the imagery of the court-room when speaking of justification, there are also passages that speak of justification in terms of 'imputation' or 'reckoning'. In such passages, justification is closely linked with the believer's status before God. Like the person in court who has been declared innocent, the justified person is someone whom God reckons and declares to be innocent.

Just as we know a person's 'reputation' by listening to what the court of human opinion has to say about them, so we know a believer's 'reputation' by listening to what God reputes or declares him to be.[11] At several points in Romans 4, for example, the apostle uses the terminology of imputation to define what occurs when God justifies a believer. Citing Genesis 15:6, Paul appeals to the example of Abraham, the father of all believers, to prove that justification is a free gift in which God reckons believers to be righteous:

> For what does the Scripture say? 'Abraham believed God, and it was *counted* to him as righteousness.' Now to the one who works, his wages are not *counted* as a gift but as his due. And to the one who does not work but trusts him who justifies the ungodly, his faith is *counted* to him as righteousness (emphasis added).

By speaking of Abraham's faith as being reckoned for right-eousness, Paul aims to emphasize that justification is a free gift of God's grace, which is granted and imputed to believers (cf. verses 8, 10, 11). He is underscoring the nature of justification as something that concerns God's declaration regarding believers, namely, that they are in a righteous status before him. For the same reason, Paul also appeals to the example of David who, in spite of his actual sin and unworthiness, was a man against whom the Lord did not 'count' his sin (verse 8). In a similar way, Paul speaks of God not counting the sins of believers against them, when he reconciled the world to himself through the death of Christ (2 *Cor.* 5:19). The terminology of counting or reckoning in these texts illus-trates the legal nature of God's act of free justification. Rather than regarding believers as possessing the status of ungodly sinners, God in justification regards them as possessing the righteous status of Christ.

It is this biblical emphasis upon justification as a judicial declaration that is expressed in the confessions of the churches of the Reformation. These confessions define justification as a judicial act by which God, for the sake of Christ, accepts and declares his people to be righteous. The *Heidelberg Catechism,* a classic statement of the sixteenth-century Reformed churches, states that the primary benefit of faith in the Christian gospel is that believers are 'righteous in Christ before God' and therefore heirs of eternal life.[12] Its question and answer concerning justification explains how believers 'can stand before the tribunal of God' and be regarded as holy and innocent.[13] In the Westminster Assembly's *Larger Catechism,* which provides an authoritative account of the teaching of the English-speaking Reformed churches, justification is defined as 'an act of God's free grace unto sinners, in which he pardoneth all their sins, accepteth and accounteth their persons righteous in his sight'.[14] Likewise, in the symbols of historic Lutheranism, justification speaks of the believer's acceptance with God on the basis of the work of Christ. The *Augsburg Confession,* the first great summary of Lutheran teaching in the Reformation period, states in its fourth article that 'men can not be justified [obtain forgiveness of sins and righteousness] before God by their own powers, merits, or works; but are justified freely [of grace] for Christ's sake through faith, when they believe that they are received into favour, and the[ir] sins forgiven for Christ's sake.'[15] Likewise, in the *Formula of Consensus* – which was written to settle several divisive controversies within the Lutheran churches in the latter part of the sixteenth century – justification is defined as God's act in Christ whereby he forgives the sins of his people and counts them righteous and acceptable to him:

> [In justification] God remits to us our sins of mere grace, without any respect of our works, going before, present, or following, or of our worthiness or merit. For he bestows and imputes to us the righteousness of the obedience of Christ; for the sake of that righteousness we are received by God into favour and accounted righteous.[16]

THE GROUND OR BASIS FOR FREE JUSTIFICATION

Despite the difference of viewpoint between Protestant and Roman Catholic on the nature of justification, the principal point of difference between them relates to another issue, namely, the *basis* upon which believers are justified by God. Though the Reformers believed that the Roman Catholic view confused justification and sanctification by treating justification as though it involved a process of moral renewal, this was not their principal complaint against it. While it may surprise some contemporary Protestants, even the Council of Trent, in its reply to the Reformation's doctrine of justification, acknowledged that justification includes a judicial declaration by God. In the sixth session on justification, chapter 7, the Council of Trent defines justification in a way that includes God's act of declaring believers to be righteous: 'Not only are we *reputed* to be righteous, but we are *called* righteous, receiving justice within us.'[17] In this classic statement of Rome's position, justification includes what God reputes believers to be. Even though the Council of Trent adds that, in reputing believers to be righteous, God also makes them righteous, there is still a recognition that justification relates to the believer's standing and acceptance before God. According to the Reformation, the critical error of Roman Catholicism does not reside, therefore, in its failure to see that justification has to do with God's verdict regarding believers; rather it lies in a wrong conception of the verdict's *basis*.

According to Rome, God justifies believers in part on the basis of their own righteousness. Since justification includes a process of moral renewal whereby believers are made righteous, the righteousness that justifies is said to be an inherent or intrinsic righteousness (*iustitia inhaerens*).[18] When God justifies believers, he does not do so *solely* on the basis of the work and merits of Christ, which are granted and imputed to believers by grace; but *partly* on the basis of the work and merits of believers, which are the fruit of God's grace at work in them.[19] The basis for justification includes those meritorious works of believers that are the fruit of their co-operation with the grace of God, which is communicated through the sacraments (especially baptism, the mass, and penance). Furthermore, the justification of believers is maintained and increased when believers perform good works by the grace of God. Should believers fail to persist in co-operation with God's grace and in doing such good works, they risk the 'shipwreck' of their faith and the loss of their state of grace before God. Thus, justification includes not only the initial introduction of believers into a state of grace, but also their continual progress and growth through personal holiness in this state of grace ('further justification').[20] Viewed from the standpoint of the eschatological goal of salvation, the justification of believers is only secured at the end of this process, either after a period of purification in purgatory of the remaining effects of sin or immediately upon the death of the saints. The works of believers, which are acknowledged to be prompted by the grace of God in Christ, are the essential means or instrument by which believers enjoy and ultimately receive the fullness of salvation in communion with God.[21]

Grace Alone, Christ Alone

In response to Rome's teaching, the Reformers insisted that justification is wholly a free gift of God's grace. *Grace alone*—not grace plus the works of believers prompted by grace—is the exclusive source and basis for the justification and salvation of believers. So far as their acceptance with God is concerned, believers rest their confidence, not in anything that they might do in obedience to God, but in God's gracious favour demonstrated in the free provision of redemption through Jesus Christ. The sole basis for God's declaration of favour toward believers is his sheer grace in Christ.

No one familiar with the debates of the sixteenth century will have any difficulty acknowledging that the expressions, 'grace alone', and 'Christ alone', capture the spirit and form of the Protestant view of justification. However, due to the tendency within modern Protestantism to move in a pietistic direction, the significance of these expressions is not always fully appreciated. In the Reformation view of salvation, justification does not play the prominent role it does because of a *primarily subjective anxiety* about finding acceptance with God. When we consider the new perspective's view of Paul, we will see that proponents of the new perspective often regard the old view to be born principally out of Luther's (and since the time of Augustine even the Western church's) 'introspective conscience'.[22]

Because Luther and the Reformers were unable to find acceptance with God in the context of medieval Catholic teaching about justification, they came to insist upon the doctrine of justification by faith and not by works. This, however, fails to appreciate the God-centredness and Christ-centredness of the Reformation view.[23] From the perspective of the Reformation, the Roman Catholic view wrongly focused its attention upon the piety and works of believers. According to Rome, the fulcrum upon which a believer's standing with God turned was his or her own co-operation with the grace of God and progress in the way of holiness. To say that justification is a free gift of God's grace, which is granted to believers upon the basis of the work of Christ alone, is to refocus attention upon the *objective reality* of God's work for his people. For this reason, Luther argued that the doctrine of justification reflected a proper understanding of God as one who justifies the ungodly (*Rom.* 4:5). What undergirds the doctrine of justification is an emphasis upon God's grace and mercy in Christ. Consequently, the doctrine of free justification is an instance of

obedience to the first commandment, which requires that we let
God be the God who freely justifies believers in Christ.[24]

THE RIGHTEOUSNESS OF GOD IN CHRIST

Often the Reformation view of justification is associated with
Luther's discovery that the 'righteousness of God' is not a righteousness that demands obedience to the law as the basis for
justification, but a righteousness that is freely given to believers.
The righteousness revealed in the gospel of Jesus Christ, which is
the basis for the justification and acceptance of believers, is the gift
of a new status with God and not the demand for obedience to the
law. Whereas the medieval Roman Catholic view of justification
maintained that the righteousness, which is the basis for the
believer's justification, is an infused and inherent righteousness, the
Reformation view insisted that it is a righteousness that God
graciously grants and imputes to believers. Justification is by grace
alone because it is based upon a righteousness that does not look to
the believer's works of obedience to the law, but to the righteousness of Christ. To understand the Reformation view of the
basis of the believer's justification, some consideration has to be
given to the way the Reformers viewed the work of Christ and the
sharp contrast they posited between the law and the gospel.

According to the Reformers, the righteousness that justifies the
believer is an 'alien' righteousness (*iustitia aliena*), not a personal or
inherent righteousness. Though this terminology is often criticized,
the Reformers insisted upon it in order to emphasize that the
believer's justification rests upon the righteousness of another,
namely, Jesus Christ. The saving work of Christ reveals a righteousness from God that is perfect and sufficient to justify otherwise
ungodly and unacceptable sinners. By means of his suffering and
death, Christ bore the penalty and suffered the curse of the law on
behalf of his people who were guilty of its violation. Furthermore,
by means of his obedience, Christ met all the righteous demands of
the law on their behalf. Christ alone secures the justification of his
people. The righteousness of God, which is demonstrated in the
gospel, therefore refers to the work of Christ in which he satisfies
all the claims of the law of God on behalf of his people.[25]

Because the basis for the believer's justification is the right-eousness of Christ, it cannot be comprised of any works that the believer performs in obedience to the law of God. Consequently, a sharp distinction is drawn between the law and the gospel in the Reformation perspective. The law of God, when distinguished from the gospel, refers to the righteous requirements or obligations imposed by God upon his human creatures. Whether Jews, who received the law of God in written form through Moses, or Gentiles, who have the works of the law written upon their con-sciences, all human beings fail to live in perfect conformity to the law's demands (*Rom.* 2–3).

By the standard of the perfect law of God, all human beings stand condemned and are worthy of death as the wages of sin (*Rom.* 6:13). Though the law of God is good and holy, it can only require and demand from believers what they cannot do because of their sinfulness. The law, though it may promise life to those who perfectly do what it requires, can only actually condemn and frustrate those who seek to be justified by its means. No one can be justified by the works of the law, because no one actually does to perfection what the law in its entirety requires. Only the right-eousness of Christ, which includes both his perfect obedience to the law's demand and satisfaction of the law's penalty, can satisfy the requirements of God's law and thereby constitute the basis for the justification of believers. Contrary to the law's function to expose human sin and guilt, the gospel proclaims the good news that God freely grants to believers what could never otherwise be achieved: acceptance and favour with God on the basis of the righteousness of Christ.

An 'Imputed' Righteousness

To express the difference between their view of the basis for the justification of believers and that of the Roman Catholic Church, the Reformers spoke of 'imputation' or 'imputed righteousness' (*iustitia imputata*). This terminology was used to explain how the righteousness of Christ benefits believers. When God justifies believers in Christ, he does so, not by making them righteous, but by granting and imputing the righteousness of Christ to them.

Believers, who are joined to Christ by faith, are reputed to be righteous, not in themselves, but as those who are partakers of Christ's righteousness. In his great sermon on 'Two Kinds of Righteousness', Luther used the biblical analogy of the relationship between the bridegroom and the bride to describe how the righteousness of Christ is shared with his people:

> Therefore a man can with confidence boast in Christ and say: 'Mine are Christ's living, doing, and speaking, his suffering and dying, mine as much as if I had lived, done, spoken, suffered, and died as he did.' Just as a bridegroom possesses all that is his bride's and she all that is his—for the two have all things in common because they are one flesh [*Gen.* 2:24]—so Christ and the church are one spirit [*Eph.* 5:29–32].[26]

Calvin likewise maintains that believers are justified through union with Christ, which is the basis for God's counting them righteous:

> . . . 'to justify' means nothing else than to acquit of guilt him who was accused, as if his innocence were confirmed. Therefore, since God justifies us by the intercession of Christ, he absolves us not by the confirmation of our own innocence but by the imputation of righteousness, so that we who are not righteous in ourselves may be reckoned as such in Christ.[27]

Since this is not the believer's own righteousness, but the righteousness of Christ, the Reformers also spoke of the justified person as 'at once just and a sinner' (*simul iustus et peccator*). This expression was a deliberately provocative one, since it called attention to the sharp difference between the Roman Catholic view of justification that sinners are *made* righteous and the Reformation's view that sinners are *declared* righteous. It also drew a sharp line between the view that based the justification of believers *partly* on works and the view that based it *exclusively* upon the grace of God in Christ. By using this expression, the Reformers intended to emphasize that what distinguishes the grace of free justification is its focus on the *ungodly (iustificatio impii; Rom.* 4:5). Justification reveals the sheer grace of God who receives and welcomes sinners in spite of their utter unworthiness. Full acceptance and favour with God is not conditional upon the transformation of believers into righteous people. Full acceptance and favour with God are found in Christ whose righteousness is perfectly adequate for the need of believers. To say that a believer is 'at once just and a sinner', therefore, is to affirm that human sinfulness is not an insuperable obstacle to God's free grace. Grace triumphs even in the face of continued human sinfulness and unworthiness. The gospel of free justification provides the antidote to the law's condemnation by announcing that God's grace in Christ embraces those who merit his judgment and wrath.

SCRIPTURAL AND CONFESSIONAL REFERENCES

The Reformers were convinced that the good news of free justification upon the basis of the righteousness of Christ was not merely a theme in Paul's epistles; it is also one of the great themes of the Old and New Testament Scriptures.[28] However, in their defence of the Reformation view, they appealed particularly to Paul's presentation of free justification in his New Testament epistles, especially Romans and Galatians. Since our primary interest here is the Reformation's perspective on Paul, we will only consider the kinds of scriptural evidence to which the Reformers appealed in their writings. Though this represents somewhat too tidy an account of the Reformers' scriptural arguments, we will focus upon two such lines of evidence in particular. The first is an appeal to those passages that maintain justification to be a free gift of God's grace, granted to believers on the basis of the righteousness of Christ; the second is an appeal to those passages that show the futility of any attempt to be justified by the works of the law, since no one is able to do what the law requires.

ROMANS 3:23–26

With respect to the first line of evidence, the Reformers appealed to Romans 3:23–26, in which the sheer graciousness of justification is stressed:

> For all have sinned and fall short of the glory of God, and are justified by his grace as a gift, through the redemption that is in

Christ Jesus, whom God put forward as a propitiation by his blood, to be received by faith. This was to show God's righteousness, because in his divine forbearance he had passed over former sins. It was to show his righteousness at the present time, so that he might be just and the justifier of the one who has faith in Jesus.

The apostle Paul here restates a theme which he has argued throughout the first three chapters of Romans: all people, whether Jews or Gentiles, are sinners and are unworthy of being received into God's favour and of finding acceptance with him. Despite their unworthiness, however, God, by an act of his sheer grace, freely justifies those who have faith in Jesus Christ. Though sinners deserve the just consequence of their offences, namely, condemnation and death, God has revealed his righteousness by giving Christ as their redemption and propitiation. The righteousness of God is a righteousness that is given freely as a gift to all who believe the gospel. Thus, this passage stresses not only that justification is given by grace alone, but also that it is based upon the work of Christ alone. God demonstrated his righteousness in the cross of Christ, not by excusing sin or perpetually passing over the sins of those who disobey him, but by providing Christ as the one who would suffer the consequences of sin on behalf of all who are united to him by faith.[29]

ROMANS 4:25

In a similar passage, which forms a kind of sequel to what is presented in Romans 3:24-26, Paul declares that Christ 'was delivered up for our trespasses and raised for our justification.' According to the comprehensive perspective of this passage, the death and resurrection of Jesus Christ on behalf of his people constitute the sure basis for the justification of those who believe in him. In the Reformers' understanding of this passage, the work of Christ involved a great exchange. Though Christ had not himself sinned or offended, he was nonetheless given up to death 'on account of' the sins of his people. On the cross, Christ assumed the place of the guilty and suffered death on their behalf (cf. 2 Cor. 5:19); he substituted himself for his people by being put to death *on account of* their sins. This is the ground on which believers stand, says the apostle, with regard to their justification. Furthermore, the resurrection of Christ represents the justification and vindication of believers. Since Christ bore the consequences of sin on behalf of his people on the cross, his resurrection was God's declaration of both his and his people's righteousness. The great and complex event of Christ's death and resurrection constitutes the basis for the positive verdict of justification for all who are in union with him through faith. In the death of Christ, the trespasses of his people were punished; in the resurrection of Christ, the justification of his people was declared. The justification of believers occurs by virtue of their participation in the reality of Christ's death and resurrection on their behalf.

ROMANS 5:15–16

Another passage often invoked by the Reformers was Romans 5:15–16:

> But the free gift is not like the trespass. For if many died through one man's trespass, much more have the grace of God and the free gift by the grace of that one man Jesus Christ abounded for many. And the free gift is not like the result of that one man's sin. For the judgment following one trespass brought condemnation, but the free gift following many trespasses brought justification.

The chapter in which these verses are found describes the parallel or analogy between the first and the second Adams. Through the sin and disobedience of the first Adam, all in him have become sinners and are liable to condemnation and death. Through the obedience of the second Adam, however, all in him have been constituted righteous and are heirs of life eternal.[30] The righteousness that constitutes the basis for the justification of sinners is the righteousness of Christ. It also reveals the super-abounding grace of God, in that it is a free gift given to all united to Christ by faith. Negatively stated, the basis for the justification of believers is not their own righteousness; rather, it is Christ's righteousness, which is freely granted by God's grace to all who believe in him. Nothing that believers might bring before God commends them to his favour. By another's act – Christ's obedience – believers are constituted righteous and no longer liable to the condemnation that brings death.[31]

In such passages the apostle not only describes the righteousness of Christ as the basis for the justification of believers, but he also describes the futility of finding acceptance with God on the basis of any human obedience to the demands of the law. The Reformation interpretation of the Pauline teaching of justification, therefore, also emphasizes that the law of God exposes human sinfulness and the inability of sinners to obtain acceptance with God on the basis of their own righteousness. According to the Reformers, when the apostle describes the function of the law in relation to justification, he is opposing those whose boast rests upon their own claim to be righteous by the standard of the law. The fierceness of his opposition to the Judaizers in his epistle to the Galatians, for example, is aimed at those who claimed to be justified ultimately on the basis of their own works of righteousness.

When Paul argues in Romans 3 that there is no one who is righteous (verse 10), he does so to illustrate the inability of the law to provide a way of justification. Rather than finding acceptance with God on the basis of works performed in obedience to its requirements, the law silences the mouth of all human beings. Far from providing a way of justification before God, it functions to make known the sinfulness and the inability of all to fulfil its requirements (verse 20). Indeed, the law, which promises life to all who obey its demands, aggravates the problem of human sinfulness by causing sin to come alive and produce death in those who are unable to obey it (7:7–12). Though the law promises life to all who keep its commandments (10:8), those who seek to establish their own righteousness in this manner cut themselves off from the righteousness that comes by faith (9:30–10:13). Moreover, if anyone wishes to find blessing by means of obedience to the law, he is obligated to keep the whole law (*Gal.* 5:1). The law, which pronounces a curse upon all who do not continue in all things that are written in it, can only serve to place before sinners the fearful spectre of the curse and judgment of God (*Gal.* 3:13). Therefore, since the law can only expose and aggravate the problem of human sinfulness and guilt before God, it excludes all self-confident boasting on the part of those who might be tempted to find favour with God by doing the works of the law (*Rom.* 3:27; 4:4; *Phil.* 3: 1–11). In this way, the law serves the gospel by shutting off the way of acceptance with God by means of human works. All who become conscious of their sinfulness through the law are obliged to look elsewhere, namely, to the righteousness of Christ, as the only basis for their justification before God.

In the confessional statements of the Reformed churches the justification of believers is clearly based upon the righteousness of God in Christ, which is freely granted and imputed to believers by grace alone. This is the case in both the Lutheran and Reformed symbols. In the *Heidelberg Catechism,* the justification of believers is based exclusively upon the saving work of Christ in his satisfaction, righteousness and holiness:

> Q. 59. How are you righteous before God?
>
> A. Only by a true faith in Jesus Christ; that is, though my conscience accuse me that I have grievously sinned against all the commandments of God and kept none of them, and am still inclined to all evil, yet God, without any merit of mine, of mere grace, grants and imputes to me the perfect satisfaction, righteousness, and holiness of Christ, as if I had never had nor committed any sin, and myself had accomplished all the obedience which Christ has rendered for me; if only I accept such benefit with a believing heart.

This clearly affirms that the righteousness of God in Christ, which includes both his obedience to the law and satisfaction of its curse, is the only sufficient basis for the believer's right standing with God. *The Formula of Concord* confesses similarly that

> this very thing is our righteousness before God, namely, that God remits to us our sins of mere grace, without any respect of our works, going before, present, or following, or of our worthiness or merit. For he bestows and imputes to us the righteousness of the obedience of Christ; for the sake of that righteousness we are received by God into favour and accounted righteous.[32]

This statement is almost identical in language to the *Heidelberg Catechism*. The righteousness of Christ, which is granted and imputed to believers, is the basis for the favourable verdict God pronounces when he accepts believers in Christ.[33]

In addition to this clear testimony to justification's basis in the free grace and righteousness of Jesus Christ, the confessions of the Reformation also view the law of God in sharp contrast to the gospel, when it comes to the question of justification. This is as true for the Reformed confessions as it is for the Lutheran, though Lutheranism is perhaps better known for its insistence upon this contrast. The *Heidelberg Catechism*, for example, gives the summary of the law in answer to its third question: 'From where does the knowledge of human sin and misery derive?'[34] It also maintains that it is impossible for believers to obey the law as a means of self-justification. The law's demands only serve to remind believers that Christ alone, by his obedience and satisfaction, has obtained righteousness and eternal life for believers.[35] *The Formula of Concord* offers a classic definition of the distinction between the law and the gospel:

> . . . whatever is found in the Holy Scriptures which convicts of sins, that properly belongs to the preaching of the Law. The Gospel, on the other hand, we judge to be properly the doctrine which teaches what a man ought to believe who has not satisfied the law of God, and therefore is condemned by the same, to wit: that it behooves him to believe that Jesus Christ has expiated all his sins, and made satisfaction for them, and has obtained remission of sins, righteousness which avails before God, and eternal life without the intervention of any merit of the sinner.[36]

BY FAITH ALONE

So far our summary of the Reformation's perspective on justification has largely focused upon justification as a work of God in Christ. Far from being a subjective experience in the heart and life of believers, justification begins 'outside of us' (*extra nos*) in the gracious provision of Christ and his saving action on behalf of believers. It is not, primarily, a subjective experience in the human heart, but a judgment or verdict that God declares on behalf of his people, which is accomplished through the death and resurrection of Jesus Christ (*Rom.* 4:25). This needs to be emphasized, since the Reformation view is often represented in predominantly subjective or existential terms, as though it described an occurrence that begins and ends within the life-experience of believers. However, we still need to consider what the Reformers meant by their insistence that the grace of free justification is received 'by faith alone'. Paul's letter to the Romans begins by declaring that the righteousness of God has been revealed in the gospel 'from faith to faith, as it is written, "The righteous shall live by faith"' (1:17). For the Reformers, this summary of the gospel shows that justifying righteousness can only be properly received by way of a response of faith. Therefore, to complete our summary of the Reformation view of this doctrine, we need to consider how it understood faith as the instrument by which believers are freely justified.

Why 'Faith Alone'?

The Reformers' insistence that believers are justified by faith alone was an obvious corollary of their insistence that justification is a free gift of God's grace in Christ. If it is a free gift, which is based upon the righteousness of Christ graciously granted and imputed to believers, then it most emphatically is not by works. 'Grace alone', 'Christ alone', and 'faith alone', are corollary expressions; to say the one is to imply the others. If we are saved by grace alone, then works must be excluded as a necessary precondition for our being accepted into favour with God. If we are saved by the person and work of Christ alone, then nothing we do before God in obedience to the law could possibly complete or compensate for anything supposedly lacking in Christ. This is precisely what the term 'faith alone' asserts. It excludes from view every possible form of human work or achievement as the meritorious cause of God's favour towards sinners.

According to Rome, faith also plays an indispensable role in the reception of the grace of justification. The first step in the process of justification is a believing assent to and co-operation with the grace of God, which is communicated through the sacrament of baptism. For this reason, the Council of Trent acknowledges that faith alone is the 'foundation' or 'beginning' (*initium*) of the process of justification.[37] Faith alone, however, does not justify in the full sense. Such faith, which is only an assent to the gospel promise, must become a 'faith formed by love' (*fides caritate formata*) as it receives the further infusion of justifying grace by means of the Church's sacraments. Faith justifies only by virtue of its performance of good works, which are the fruit of the co-operation of the believer with the infused grace of God. Strictly speaking, the instrument of the believer's justification is the sacrament of baptism, not faith. However, through the grace that the sacrament communicates, believers are enabled to perform good works that merit further grace and justification. In the same manner in which the Reformation view insisted upon *faith alone* as the way by which the grace of free justification is received, the Roman Catholic view insisted upon *faith plus works* as the way by which justification is maintained and advanced.

One of the more vexing features of the disagreements between Protestant and Roman Catholic at the time of the Reformation was the problem of misunderstanding, and particularly so at this point of the dispute regarding the role of faith as the instrument of justification. When the Roman Catholic Church heard the Reformation claim that justification is by faith alone, they understood this to mean that an 'unformed' faith, that is, a faith that was a mere intellectual assent to the gospel, was an adequate way of receiving the gospel promise of justification and salvation. However, this was not the position of the Reformers, nor was it the reason for their insistence that the grace of free justification is received by faith alone. Luther, as much as Calvin, maintained that the faith which alone receives the grace of justification is not an 'alone' faith. The Reformers were not motivated by an antinomian rejection of the importance of good works as the necessary fruit of true faith.[38] In their understanding of salvation, believers who receive the free gift of justification are simultaneously renewed by the Spirit of Christ in the way of sanctification. Rather, their motivation in using the term 'faith alone' was to guard against any view that ascribed to works the power to justify. The distinct way in which they spoke of faith, however, was bound to raise questions in Roman Catholic minds about their motives. From the vantage point of the Roman Catholic understanding of faith, the Reformers' insistence on 'faith alone' seemed to imply that justification and salvation were granted to believers whether or not their faith was active and fruitful.[39]

THE CHARACTER OF FAITH

In their teaching on the role of faith as the exclusive instrument of justification, the Reformers argued that faith is peculiarly appropriate to the reception of free justification. This was not due merely to the fact that faith was a gift of God's grace in Christ (*Eph.* 2:6); all the various facets of the believer's response to the gospel are the fruit of God's gracious initiative in Christ and the gift-character of faith does not therefore distinguish it as the means of receiving the grace of justification. What distinguishes faith from other features of the believer's response to the gospel is its essentially self-effacing or self-denying quality. As the exclusive instrument for receiving the grace of free justification, faith boasts, not in itself or in any other human achievement, but in the grace of Christ alone. Faith answers to the free gift of justification in Christ, because it is principally the believer's humble acknowledgment that his only boast before God is the work of Christ alone.

To express the unique suitability of faith to receive the gift of free justification, the Reformers used various expressions. Calvin, for example, spoke of faith as an 'empty vessel' in order to stress its character as a receptacle that brings nothing to God but receives all things from him.[40] Luther used the striking analogy of a ring that clasps a jewel; faith has no value of itself, but clasps the jewel that is Christ and his righteousness.[41] Calvin also remarked that, in a manner of speaking, faith is a 'passive thing', because it is the cessation of all working and striving to obtain favour and acceptance with God in order to rest in a favour freely given in Christ.[42] What makes faith a suitable instrument for the reception of free justification is that it is marked by a readiness to humbly acknowledge that all honour in salvation belongs to God in Christ. As a receptive and passive acknowledgement of the sheer graciousness of free justification, faith is an act of trustful acceptance of what God freely grants in Christ. In the act of faith, the righteousness of God in Christ is acknowledged as the only basis for justification. When believers accept the free gift of justification by faith, they look away from themselves and focus their attention upon Christ, who is their righteousness. Faith, therefore, is the antithesis of all boasting in human achievement before God.

SCRIPTURAL AND CONFESSIONAL REFERENCES

The Reformers noted that this understanding of faith's character best accords with the doctrine of Paul's epistles. Paul speaks of the justification occurring 'through' faith and not 'on account of' faith.[43] Faith is not the basis for, but the means to obtain, the free gift of justification. Furthermore, he draws a sharp contrast between the righteousness that is by faith and that which is by the works of the law.

The Reformers noted that the apostle often emphasizes the instrumental role of faith in justification. In particular, he uses three related expressions to describe faith's role. In some passages, Paul uses the preposition 'through' with the genitive case to express the instrumental role of faith. Galatians 2:16 is an example of this kind of expression: '. . . we know that a person is not justified by works of the law but through faith in Jesus Christ.'[44] In other passages, the apostle uses the preposition 'out of' or 'by' with the genitive case to identify faith as the occasion, though not the cause or basis, for justification. Thus, in Romans 5:1 – a passage that played such an important role in Luther's discovery of the doctrine of free justification – Paul summarizes the argument of the early chapters of Romans by saying, 'Therefore having been justified by faith, we have peace with God through our Lord Jesus Christ, through whom also we have obtained our introduction by faith into this grace in which we stand.'[45] Paul also speaks of justification 'by faith' in passages that use 'faith' in the dative case; this expresses the idea of faith as the means or instrument by which the righteousness of God is received. For example, Romans 3:28 declares: 'For we hold that a man is justified by faith, apart from the works of the law.'[46] By means of these diverse expressions, the apostle consistently affirms the instrumental role of faith in justification.

Consistent with his use of these expressions is Paul's description of justifying righteousness as a righteousness that is of God. Since God grants and imputes this righteousness to believers, it can only be received by faith, and not by the works of the law. In Romans 1:17 Paul describes the righteousness of God as that which is 'revealed from faith to faith'. In Romans 3:22, he calls it the righteousness of God that is 'through faith in Jesus Christ for all who believe'.

Later in the epistle, Paul contrasts a righteousness that is 'based on works' with one that is 'by faith' (*Rom.* 9:32). Similarly, in Philippians 3:9, he speaks of being found in Christ, 'not having a righteousness that is my own that comes from the law, but that which comes through faith in Christ, the righteousness from God that depends on faith.' The primary theme of these verses is that believers are justified when, by the empty hand of faith, they receive what God freely grants in Christ.

Perhaps the most vigorous statement of the contrast between works and faith is found in the argument developed in Romans 4. Throughout this chapter Paul insists that justification is not granted to believers on the basis of their works. Unlike the labourer who receives a wage due for work performed, the believer is someone whose faith is 'counted for righteousness'.

Abraham stands as an example of this principle. Rather than obtaining righteousness by working, Abraham trusted in the God who justifies the ungodly (verse 5). Paul appeals to the examples of Abraham and David to illustrate the antithesis between faith and works; whereas faith receives what is freely given, works earn what is justly deserved. Thus, the apostle argues that the promise of justification or acceptance with God depends upon faith 'in order that [it] may rest on grace' (verse 16). There is a correspondence between the graciousness of justification and the receptivity of faith that makes it the only appropriate means by which to receive the promise of God.

The confessions of the Reformation articulate this insistence that faith is the only instrument by which believers receive the grace of free justification. Once again, we will only cite a few examples, the first of which is taken from the *Heidelberg Catechism:*

Q. 61. Why do you say that you are righteous only by faith?

A. Not that I am acceptable to God on account of the worthiness of my faith, but because only the satisfaction, righteousness, and holiness of Christ is my righteousness before God, and I can receive the same and make it my own in no other way than by faith only.

The *Heidelberg Catechism* is careful to note that faith is not itself a good work, an evangelical performance that is *in lieu of* other good works performed in obedience to the law of God. Faith is merely a means of receiving the righteousness of Christ and, as such, has no intrinsic value that contributes to the believer's justification. In the *Belgic Confession* – a popular confession of the European Reformed churches – the exclusive role of faith in receiving the grace of justification is similarly affirmed: '. . . they [good works] are of no account towards our justification, for it is by faith in Christ that we are justified, even before we do good works' (Article 24). Though this article deals primarily with the necessity of good works in the life of the believer who is indwelt by the Holy Spirit, it nonetheless excludes works altogether from any role in justification. Even 'before we do good works', we are justified on the basis of Christ's work alone, which is received by faith. In a similar way, *The Formula of Concord* confesses:

Faith alone is the means and instrument whereby we lay hold on Christ the Saviour, and so in Christ lay hold on that righteousness which is able to stand before the judgment of God; for that faith, for Christ's sake, is imputed to us for righteousness (*Rom.* 4:5).[47]

KEY FEATURES OF THE REFORMATION'S PERSPECTIVE

Having considered the Reformation's perspective on justification, we are in a position to delineate several features of it that are of special importance to the new perspective on Paul. When new-perspective authors contrast their understanding of Paul with the older perspective, they usually have several distinctive features of the latter in mind.

First, the Reformation perspective sees justification as a principal theme of the gospel. Since it answers the crucial question of how guilty sinners find acceptance with God, justification belongs to the heart of the Christian gospel and is a central motif in the writings of Paul. Though the gospel embraces more within its scope than this truth, justification is regarded as *the* article of 'the standing or the falling of the church', to use the language of historic Lutheranism, or the 'main hinge' of the Christian religion, to use the language of John Calvin. The doctrine of free justification, therefore, is not peripheral to the gospel, nor is it limited to Paul's writings; rather, it is integral to the great message of the whole Bible.

Second, the Reformation view maintains that justification is a primarily theological and soteriological theme. On the one hand, the doctrine reveals the character of God as a God of righteousness and grace, who justifies ungodly sinners on the basis of the work of Christ. In this respect, it is of great theological significance. On the other hand, it reveals the character of sinful human beings who can only be received and accepted by God on the basis of the righteousness of Christ alone. In this respect, justification is a thoroughly soteriological theme, explaining how otherwise guilty sinners can be received into God's favour. While it presupposes a number of other aspects of scriptural teaching, particularly Christ's obedience and death as a satisfaction for sin, it primarily addresses the question of the salvation of guilty sinners. Though the Reformers recognized that Paul developed his teaching on justification in opposition to the teaching of Judaizers, they did not consider justification to be an exclusively polemical doctrine that answers an ecclesiological question about how both Jews and Gentiles can be members of the one church of Christ.

Third, this Reformation perspective claims that the medieval Roman Catholic doctrine of justification compromised the gospel by emphasizing obedience to the law as a partial, meritorious basis for justification. According to the Reformers' reading of Paul, Rome's error was similar in form and substance to that of the

Pharisees and Judaizers in Paul's day. Just as the apostle opposed the erroneous view of those who claimed to find favour with God on the basis of their meritorious works, so the Reformers in their day claimed to be opposing a similar error. Luther especially emphasized the essential similarity between the Roman Catholic teaching of salvation by meritorious good works and the Pharasaical or Judaizing teaching of salvation by obedience to the law of God. But Calvin also charged Rome with the same error that had earlier characterized the religion of the Pharisees and Judaism in apostolic times.[48] Just as the Judaizers trusted in their own righteousness before God as the basis for their claim upon his favour and mercy, so the Roman Catholic doctrine of justification by grace plus works encouraged a similar trust in the righteousness of believers.[49] Paul's arguments with the Judaizers in his Roman and Galatian epistles anticipated the Reformer's opposition to the Roman Catholic doctrine of righteousness by works.

Fourth, the Reformers insisted that, when Paul speaks of 'works' or 'works of the law', he refers to any acts of obedience to the law that are regarded as the basis for acceptance with God. Part of Paul's argument against the Judaizers is that no one is able to do what the law requires, and this inability illustrates the contrast between the law and the gospel. Luther and Calvin understood the opposition between the law and the gospel to be one of two contrary methods of justification. The law, at least in its first or theological use, functions like a mirror that reveals one's own sinfulness before God. The law in this use can only condemn and expose the unrighteousness of sinners. In the first and second tables of the law, we are commanded to live a life of perfect love for God and neighbour. However, there is no one who is righteous by this standard, who is able to keep the requirements of the law perfectly. Only Christ, who obeyed the law perfectly and suffered its penalty in the place of sinners, can obtain for them a righteousness that is acceptable to God.

And *fifth*, the Reformation perspective viewed the righteousness of God, which is revealed in the gospel of Jesus Christ, as something that God freely grants and imputes to believers. For Luther and Calvin, the righteousness of God was not identified with the severe demand of the law, but with the gracious act by which God grants to believers a share in the righteousness of Christ. When God grants this to believers, they enter into a right standing with him. According to the Reformers, the righteousness of God refers to the work of Christ in which believers come to share. By means of his death and resurrection, Christ has obtained righteousness and life, favour and acceptance for everyone who believes in him. Salvation is a free gift, which is received by faith alone.

Notes

¹ *Putting Amazing Back into Grace: Who Does What in Salvation:?* (Grand Rapids: Baker, 1991, repr. 1994), pp. 167–8.

² For more complete summaries of the Reformation doctrine of justification, see John Calvin, *Institutes* III.xi; Herman Bavinck, *Our Reasonable Faith: A Survey of Christian Doctrine* (Grand Rapids: Baker Book House reprint, 1977 [1956]), pp. 439-68; James Buchanan, *The Doctrine of Justification* (Edinburgh: Banner of Truth reprint, 1991 [1867]); G. C. Berkouwer, *Faith and Justification* (Grand Rapids: Eerdmans, 1954); Robert Traill, *Justification Vindicated* (rev. ed.; Edinburgh: Banner of Truth, 2002 [1692]; John F. MacArthur, Jr., *et al.*, *Justification by Faith Alone* (Morgan, PA: Soli Deo Gloria, 1995); James R. White, *The God Who Justifies* (Minneapolis: Bethany House, 2001); R. C. Sproul, *Faith Alone*; Eberhard Jüngel, *Justification: The Heart of the Christian Faith* (New York: T. & T. Clark, 2001); Anthony N. S. Lane, *Justification by Faith*, pp. 17-44; John Owen, *The Works of John Owen*, vol. 5: *The Doctrine of Justification by Faith* (Edinburgh: Banner of Truth reprint, 1965 [1850–53]); Francis Turretin, *Institutes of Elenctic Theology* (Phillipsburg, NJ: Presbyterian & Reformed, 1994), 2:633–88; and Alister E. McGrath, *Iustitia Dei: A History of the Christian Doctrine of Justification* (2nd ed.; New York: Cambridge University Press, 1986, 1998), pp. 188–240.

³ Cf. the definition of justification in *The Canons and Decrees of the Council of Trent*, Sixth Session, Chapter 7: 'This disposition, or preparation, is followed by Justification itself, which is not remission of sins merely, but also the sanctification and renewal of the inward man, through the voluntary reception of the grace, and of the gifts, whereby man of unjust becomes just [*fit iustus*] . . . (Schaff, *The Creeds of Christendom*, 3:94).

⁴ The Latin root of the term is *forum*, the place of public discourse and adjudication of cases, which is the equivalent of our contemporary court of law.

⁵ *Institutes* III.xi.2.

⁶ Though I do not intend here to defend the Reformation's claim that the question of justification is *the* religious question, it is significant to note how the assumptions of the doctrine of justification are at variance with the assumptions of many moderns. There are those, for example, who say that the world in which we live today can no longer understand the doctrine of justification. The doctrine, because it belongs to the court of law, assuming that God is our Judge and that the law serves to expose our wrong-doing, militates against the common assumptions of modern people. We no longer think in legal categories. God is not thought to be in the business of judging sinners. The law is no longer preached or taught as having divine authority or serving to condemn us for our sins. Without disputing the need to communicate clearly the meaning of the biblical language in terms that modern people can understand, the church does not have the freedom to alter the gospel she proclaims. If that gospel includes elements that are legal in nature, it is incumbent upon theologians to explain this clearly in the contemporary context.

⁷ For a more complete statement of the Old Testament use of the term justification, see James Buchanan, *The Doctrine of Justification,* pp. 226–49; John Owen, *Works,* vol. 5:123–37; and James White, *The God Who Justifies,* pp. 76–88.

⁸ In addition to the passages cited, see *Exod.* 23:7; *1 Kings* 8:32; *Job* 32:2; *Isa.* 5:23.

⁹ It is sometimes argued that the Greek verb for 'to justify', *dikaioô,* has in common with the Latin verb, *iustificare* [a combination of *facere,* 'to make', and *iustus,* 'just'], the suggestion that justification refers to a moral process by which persons are made righteous. Leon Morris, *New Testament Theology* (Grand Rapids: Zondervan, 1986), p. 70, offers a helpful criticism of this suggestion: 'It is sometimes argued that the verb normally translated "to justify" (*dikaioô*) means "to make righteous" rather than "to declare righteous". But this agrees neither with the word's formation nor with its usage. Verbs ending in –*oô* and referring to moral qualities have a declarative sense; they do not mean "to make—." And the usage is never for the transformation of the accused; it always refers to a declaration of his innocence.' For a discussion of the way the translation of the Old Testament terms for justification into Greek and Latin has often misled readers to think of justification as a moral transformation, see McGrath, *Iustitia Dei,* pp. 4-16.

¹⁰ Cf. Douglas J. Moo, *The Epistle to the Romans* (Grand Rapids: Eerdmans, 1996), p. 205, who notes that Paul's terminology 'reflects the imagery of the courtroom. "Shutting the mouth" connotes the situation of the defendant who has no more to say in response to the charges brought against him or her. The Greek word translated "accountable" occurs nowhere else in the Scriptures, but it is used in extra-biblical Greek to mean "answerable to" or "liable to prosecution", "accountable". Paul pictures God both as the one offended and as the judge who weighs the evidence and pronounces the verdict.'

[11] It is interesting that the terms 'repute' and 'impute' have a common verbal root (in the Latin, *imputare*, 'to reckon' or 'to regard'). Since the language of 'imputation' seems foreign to modern English speakers, it is helpful to use the terms, 'repute' and 'reputation'. Few people should have difficulty recognizing what these terms mean.

[12] *Heidelberg Catechism*, Q. & A. 59: 'But what does it profit you now that you believe all this [the faith as summarized in the Apostle's Creed]? That I am righteous in Christ before God, and an heir of eternal life.' Cf. *Belgic Confession*, Articles 22–23.

[13] *Heidelberg Catechism*, Q. & A. 62: 'But why cannot our good works be the whole or part of our righteousness before God? A. Because the righteousness which can stand before the tribunal of God must be absolutely perfect and wholly conformable to the divine law....'

[14] *Westminster Larger Catechism*, Q. & A. 70.

[15] Schaff, *The Creeds of Christendom*, 3:10.

[16] Schaff, *The Creeds of Christendom*, 3:115–6. The widespread consensus as to the nature of justification among Protestants of the sixteenth century is evident from the statement on justification in *The Thirty-Nine Articles of the Church of England*, Art. 11 (Schaff, *The Creeds of Christendom*, 3:494), pp.'We are accounted righteous before God, only for the merit of our Lord and Saviour Jesus Christ by Faith, and not for our own works or deservings.'

[17] See Schaff, *The Creeds of Christendom*, 2:95.

[18] Cf. Schaff, *The Creeds of Christendom*, 2:95–6: 'For, although no one can be just, but he to whom the merits of the Passion of our Lord Jesus Christ are communicated, yet is this done in the said justification of the impious, when by the merit of that same most holy Passion, *the charity of God is poured forth*, by the Holy Spirit, *in the hearts* of those that are justified, and is inherent therein [*atque ipsis inhaeret*].'

[19] According to the classic statement of the doctrine at the Council of Trent, the righteousness on account of which we are justified, though it derives from the working of God's grace infused into us through the sacrament of baptism, is *our own righteousness*. Our being renewed in the way of Christian obedience and righteousness (to be sure, produced by God's grace in us) becomes a significant part of the ground for our justification by God. For this reason, those who obey the commandments of God and of the church, 'faith cooperating with good works, increase in that justice received through the grace of Christ and *are further justified*' (emphasis mine; *The Canons and Decrees of the Council of Trent*, Sixth Session, Chap. 10; Schaff, *The Creeds of Christendom*, 2:99). This has two serious and acknowledged consequences: first, Christ alone is no longer the believer's righteousness before God; and second, the believer cannot have any assurance of salvation (unless by special dispensation and revelation) since his own righteousness can scarcely provide any sure footing in the presence of God.

[20] *The Canons and Decrees of the Council of Trent*, Sixth Session, Chap. 10-16 (Schaff, *The Creeds of Christendom*, 2:99–110).

[21] See *The Canons and Decrees of the Council of Trent*, Sixth Session, Chap. 16 (Schaff, *The Creeds of Christendom*, 2:108): ' . . . We must believe that nothing further is wanting to the justified, to prevent their being accounted to have, by those very works which have been done in God, fully satisfied the divine law according to the state of this life, and to have truly merited eternal life.' Traditional Catholic theology distinguishes 'true merit' (*meritum de condigno*), which consists of those works performed by virtue of God's infused grace in the believer that justly deserve their reward, and 'half' or 'congruent merit' (*meritum de congruo*), which consists of those works performed by the believer's cooperation with the grace of God that receive a reward that is not strictly deserved. For a contemporary discussion of the subject of merit from a Roman Catholic perspective, s. v. 'Merit', *Sacramentum Mundi: An Encyclopedia of Theology*, ed. Karl Rahner (London: Search Press Limited, 1969), 4:11–14.

[22] Cf. Krister Stendahl, 'Paul and the Introspective Conscience of the West', in *Paul Among Jews and Gentiles and Other Essays* (London: SCM, 1977), pp. 78–96.

[23] Calvin, for example, claims that the foremost benefit of the doctrine of free justification is that the 'honour' of God is upheld, since this doctrine emphasizes his grace toward believers in Christ. See *Institutes*, III.xiii.1–2.

[24] For a discussion of the way Luther linked the affirmation of free justification with obedience to the first table of the law, see Paul Althaus, *The Theology of Martin Luther* (Philadelphia: Fortress Press, 1966), pp. 118–29.

[25] Cf. Louis Berkhof's definition of justification in his *Systematic Theology* (Edinburgh: Banner of Truth, reprint, 2003), p. 513: 'Justification is a judicial act of God, in which He declares, on the basis of the righteousness of Jesus Christ, that all the claims of the law are satisfied with respect to the sinner.' Traditional Reformed theology distinguished in this connection between the 'active' and 'passive' obedience of Christ. The purpose of this distinction was not to divide Christ's obedience into two chronological stages (the first being his earthly ministry, the second being his sacrificial death upon the cross) or even into two parts, but to distinguish two facets of the one obedience of Christ. Christ's active obedience refers to his life of conformity to the precepts of the law; Christ's passive obedience refers to his life of suffering under the penalty of the law, especially in his crucifixion (*Rom.* 5:12–21; *Phil.* 2:5ff; *Gal.* 4:4). For traditional presentations of this distinction and its significance for justification, see Louis Berkhof, *Systematic Theology*, pp. 379–82, 513ff.; Turretin, *Institutes of Elenctic Theology*, pp. 646-59; Buchanan, *The Doctrine of Justification*, pp. 314–38. I will return to this distinction between the active and passive obedience of Christ in Chapter 9.

[26] Quoted from John Dillenberger, ed., *Martin Luther: Selections from His Writings* (Garden City: NY: Anchor Books, 1961), pp. 86–7.

[27] *Institutes*, III.xi.3.

[28] For a discussion and illustration of the way Reformation theologians appealed to the teaching of the entire Scripture to support the doctrine of free justification, see Buchanan, *The Doctrine of Justification*, pp. 17–76; and Berkouwer, *Faith and Justification*, pp. 61–100.

[29] The Reformation perspective on justification is a corollary of its understanding of the atoning work of Christ. For a comprehensive treatment of the Reformation view of the saving work of Christ, see Robert Letham, *The Work of Christ* (Downers Grove, IL: InterVarsity, 1993); John R. W. Stott, *The Cross of Christ* (Downers Grove, IL: InterVarsity, 1986); Leon Morris, *The Apostolic Preaching of the Cross* (3rd ed.; Grand Rapids: Eerdmans reprint, 1965); and idem, *The Cross in the New Testament* (Grand Rapids: Eerdmans, 1965).

[30] I am not concerned here to address the question of the apparent universalism of verse 18, which speaks of 'justification of life to *all* men'. It should only be noted that, in the context, the apostle does make it clear that only those who through faith are joined to Christ benefit from his saving work.

[31] Though I am not devoting any special attention to the alternative view of the ground of justification in Roman Catholic teaching, it differs markedly from the Reformation's view at this point. According to the classic statement of the doctrine at the Council of Trent, the righteousness on account of which we are justified, though it derives from the working of God's grace infused into us through the sacrament of baptism, is the believer's *own righteousness*. See *The Decrees and Canons of the Council of Trent*, Sixth Session, Chapters 10–16 (Schaff, *The Creeds of Christendom*, 2:99–110).

[32] Schaff, *The Creeds of Christendom*, 3:115–6.

[33] *Westminster Confession of Faith*, Chap. 11.1, likewise affirms that Christ's righteousness, which consists of 'the obedience and satisfaction of Christ', is imputed to believers and is the sole basis for their justification before God.

[34] Q. & A. 3: 'Whence do you know your misery? Out of the law of God.'

[35] *Heidelberg Catechism*, Q. & A. 59–64.

[36] Schaff, *The Creeds of Christendom*, 3:127.

[37] Cf. *The Decrees and Canons of the Council of Trent*, Sixth Session, Chap. 8 (Schaff, *The Creeds of Christendom*, 2:97): 'Faith is the beginning of human salvation, the foundation, and the root of all Justification.'

[38] The Lutheran and Reformed confessions repeatedly affirm good works as the necessary fruit of true faith. See e.g.: *Heidelberg Catechism*, Q. & A. 64, 86–87, 91; *Belgic Confession*, Art. 24; *Westminster Confession of Faith*, Chap. 11.2; and *The Formula of Concord*, Art. 4.

[39] Calvin's rejoinder to this Catholic objection to the Reformation's view is well-known and often-quoted: 'It is therefore faith alone which justifies, and yet the faith which justifies is not alone; just as it is the heat alone of the sun which warms the earth, and yet in the sun it is not alone, because it is constantly conjoined with light' ('Canons and Decrees of the Council of Trent, with the Antidote', in *Selected Works of John Calvin: Tracts and Letters*, ed. Henry Beveridge [Grand Rapids: Baker Book House reprint, 1983 (1851)], 3:152).

[40] *Institutes*, III.xi.7.

[41] *Luther's Works*, ed. Jaroslav Pelikan and Helmut T. Lehmann, 55 vols. (American ed.; St. Louis: Concordia Publishing House, and Philadelphia: Fortress Press, 1955–1986), 26:89, 134 (hereafter, *LW*).

[42] *Institutes*, III.xiii.5.

[43] Orthodox Reformation theologians, therefore, speak of justification 'through faith but not on account of faith' (*per fidem sed non propter fidem*).

[44] εἰδότες δὲ ὅτι οὐ δικαιουται ἄνθρωπος ἐξ ἔργων νόμου ἐαν μη δια πίστεως Ἰησου Χριστου.

[45] Δικαιωθεντες οὖν ἐκ πιστεως εἰρηνην ἔχομεν προς τον Θεον δια του κυρίου ημων Ἰησου Χριστου. It is well known that Luther, when translating this verse, inserted the German word, *allein*, 'alone', in order to make this point clear. Cf. Charles Hodge, *A Commentary on Romans*, rev. ed. (Edinburgh: Banner of Truth, repr. 1997), p. 100, who cites instances of a similar insertion of 'alone' by Roman Catholic translators prior to the Reformation.

[46] λογιζόμεθα γαρ δικαιουσθαι πίστει ἄνθρωπον χωρὶς ἔργων νόμου.

[47] Schaff, *The Creeds of Christendom*, 3:116. Cf. the Westminster Larger Catechism, Q. & A. 73: 'How doth faith justify a sinner in the sight of God? Faith justifies a sinner in the sight of God, not because of those other graces which do always accompany it, or of good works that are the fruits of it, nor as if the grace of faith, or any act thereof, were imputed to him for his justification; but only as it is an instrument by which he receiveth and applieth Christ and his righteousness.'

[48] Calvin, for example, in his Commentary on Philippians 3:8, spoke of the Roman Catholics of his time as 'present-day Pharisees' who uphold 'their own merits against Christ.' See *Calvin's New Testament Commentaries*, 11:274.

[49] Cf. *The Canons and Decrees of the Council of Trent*, Sixth Session, Chap. 16 (Schaff, *The Creeds of Christendom*, 2:107), 'And, for this cause, life eternal is to be proposed to those working well *unto the end*, and hoping in God, both as a grace mercifully promised to the sons of God through Jesus Christ, and as a reward which is according to the promise of God himself, to be faithfully rendered to their good works and merits.'

3

CAN A 'LONELY' FAITH SAVE?

During the course of our consideration of the Reformation view of justification, we noted that misunderstanding was a troublesome problem of sixteenth-century doctrinal disputes. This was often aggravated by the fact that Protestant and Roman Catholic, in articulating their respective views, used the same terms in different ways.

Perhaps the most striking instance of misunderstanding between the two sides relates to their different uses of the term 'faith alone' in relation to justification. According to the Reformation view, believers are justified upon the basis of the righteousness of Christ, which God freely grants and imputes to them; therefore, this righteousness is received by the empty hand of faith alone. For the Reformers 'faith alone' *(sola fide)* was a watchword that preserved the distinction between justification and sanctification and emphasized the sheer graciousness of God's act in receiving sinners into his favour.

Though justified believers are also sanctified by the Spirit of Christ, the good works which are the fruit of faith play no role so far as justification is concerned. Faith alone justifies the believer, since faith is the believer's act of receiving what God graciously grants and imputes to them. If good works, even those that are the fruit of a living faith, are viewed as instrumental in justification, then the gospel of free justification is compromised and the confession of salvation by grace alone is imperilled.

Whenever good works are added to faith in relation to justification, Christ's work is no longer regarded as sufficient to save, but needs to be supplemented by human merit and achievement.

PAUL AND JAMES

The Protestant insistence upon faith alone was bound to provoke a negative reaction among Roman Catholic theologians. Since Rome's doctrine of justification views faith as a mere assent to the gospel promise, faith must be 'formed by love' in order for justification to be maintained and increased. To say that faith alone justifies equates to teaching that a mere intellectual acceptance of the gospel promise is sufficient to save. The Protestant teaching on justification implies, according to its Roman Catholic critics, that believers are justified by an *inactive* and *unfruitful* faith. One of Rome's principal objections to the Protestant view is expressed in the question raised at the beginning of Romans 6: 'What shall we say then? Are we to continue in sin that grace may abound?'

According to this objection, if justification occurs by grace alone, apart from any works done in obedience to the law of God, and if believers simply receive it as a free gift with the empty hand of faith, then such a doctrine will encourage believers to live careless and sinful lives. What motivation will remain to encourage a serious pursuit of holiness or obedience to the commandments of God?[1] According to Roman Catholic critics, the Protestant insistence that God justifies sinners by grace alone apart from works encourages carelessness with respect to the law and the gospel's call to holiness.

This objection has played an important role in the dispute regarding justification since the sixteenth century. A standard feature of Roman Catholic criticism of the Reformation view is that the doctrine of free justification dangerously undermines the need for good works in the Christian life. One form in which this criticism is expressed is the frequent complaint that the Reformation view represents a kind of 'legal fiction'. The Protestant doctrine of justification amounts to the claim that God treats sinners in justification *as if* they were righteous, when in fact they remain the sinners they were before.[2] According to this complaint, when sinners are saved, they are not really changed by God's grace and their lives undergo no real amendment. It is important to note, however, that what ultimately lies behind this objection is the implication that, when God declares men to be acceptable to himself, he *leaves them in their sins*: God's work of grace ends or terminates upon justification, and does not bring with it the grace of sanctification.[3]

This objection is most clearly crystallized in the traditional Roman Catholic complaint that the Reformers neglected the teaching of the apostle James. The scriptural basis for the Reformation's view was, according to this objection, too one-sidedly based upon an appeal to Paul's New Testament epistles. Consequently, when Rome condemned the doctrine of the Reformation at the Council of Trent, no portion of Scripture was more frequently cited than the epistle of James, especially the second chapter with its emphasis upon the role of works in justification. According to the Council of Trent, James 2:14–26 offers a convincing scriptural proof of the error of the Reformation's teaching regarding justification.[4] Contrary to the insistence that justification is by grace alone through faith alone, apart from works, the apostle James teaches that believers are also justified by their works. The believer's justification is based upon God's grace, to be sure; but this grace produces good works done in obedience to the law of God, which also form part of the grounds for the believer's justification.

From a historical point of view, this claim against the Reformers is rendered credible by Luther's rather critical and unsympathetic opinion of the epistle of James. By expressing a rather negative assessment of its teaching on justification, Luther gave credence to the traditional Roman Catholic complaint that the Protestant view of faith alone was one-sidedly Pauline and detrimental to an emphasis upon good works.

In his preface to the 1522 edition of the German New Testament, Luther remarked that the epistle of James is a 'right strawy' (*recht strohern*) epistle.[5] Though he had better things to say about James on other occasions, he nevertheless expressed his readiness to consign the epistle to the flames, rather than allow it to stand against the doctrine of justification by faith alone. From the Roman Catholic point of view, however, Luther's strong words expressed the general consensus of Protestantism and exposed the vulnerability of its emphasis upon justification by faith alone.

Due to the importance of this long-standing Catholic objection
to the Protestant view, our general sketch of the Reformation
perspective on justification requires that we look at the teaching of
James 2. Since it played a prominent role in the historic debates
between Protestant and Roman Catholic, a careful treatment of
James's teaching will clarify the meaning of the Protestant claim
that justification is by faith alone. Without a consideration of this
passage it is hardly possible to assess whether the traditional
Roman Catholic complaint against the Reformation doctrine of
justification is valid. Admittedly, our treatment of this passage will
take us a little out of the way from our primary focus upon the
Protestant perspective on Paul's teaching. Nonetheless, consideration of this passage, particularly in terms of the way it was
handled by the Reformers of the sixteenth century, will complete
our survey of the Reformation perspective on justification. Only
against the background of a full and accurate understanding of the
Reformation's perspective, will we be in a position to consider the
claims of the new perspective on Paul. Since some of these claims
include the role of works in the life of the believer, the Reformation
view of Paul and James, which is especially relevant to the issue of
faith's relation to works, is of clear value to our primary purpose –
the assessment of the new perspective and its criticisms of the
Reformation doctrine of justification.

Before we draw any conclusions about the implications of James
2:14–26 for the traditional dispute between Roman Catholic and
Protestant views, however, we need to have the passage itself in
clear focus. What is the line of James's argument in these verses?
What does he teach about the relation of faith and works, or
of faith and justification? Only when these issues have been
addressed, can we conclude with a comprehensive consideration of
the respective Roman Catholic and Reformation interpretations.
Since Calvin provides the most comprehensive and positive account
among the Reformers of the relation between Paul and James on
the doctrine of justification, we will regard his comments on this
passage to be of particular importance for evaluating the Reformation perspective.[6] When, subsequent to our reading of the passage,
we take up the historic difference between Roman Catholic and

Protestant views, we will be especially interested in the questions: Does the teaching of James 2 refute the Reformers' emphasis upon justification by faith alone? And, if it does not contradict the Reformers' view, how are we to understand its emphasis upon the role of works in the salvation and justification of genuine believers?

THE QUESTION: CAN A 'LONELY' FAITH SAVE?

JAMES 2:14-26

What good is it, my brothers, if someone says he has faith but does not have works? Can that faith save him? [15] If a brother or sister is poorly clothed and lacking in daily food, [16] and one of you says to them, 'Go in peace, be warmed and filled', without giving them the things needed for the body, what good is that? [17] So also faith by itself, if it does not have works, is dead. [18] But someone will say, 'You have faith and I have works.' Show me your faith apart from your works, and I will show you my faith by my works. [19] You believe that God is one; you do well. Even the demons believe—and shudder! [20] Do you want to be shown, you foolish person, that faith apart from works is useless? [21] Was not Abraham our father justified by works when he offered up his son Isaac on the altar? [22] You see that faith was active along with his works, and faith was completed by his works; [23] and the Scripture was fulfilled that says, 'Abraham believed God, and it was counted to him as righteousness' – and he was called a friend of God. [24] You see that a person is justified by works and not by faith alone. [25] And in the same way was not also Rahab the prostitute justified by works when she received the messengers and sent them out by another way? [26] For as the body apart from the spirit is dead, so also faith apart from works is dead.

Even a first reading of these verses will clearly show the reason why they have played such an important role in traditional Roman Catholic polemics against the Reformation. In the course of his argument James reaches a conclusion that seems startlingly at odds with the Reformation doctrine of justification. He writes:

Was not Abraham our father justified by works when he offered up his son Isaac on the altar? You see that faith was active along with his works, and faith was completed by his works. . . . You see that a person is justified by works and not by faith alone (2:21–23).

While the Reformers appealed to the writings of Paul to advance their claim that justification is by faith alone, James seems explicitly to reject the teaching of faith alone in his explanation of the believer's justification. According to him, Abraham's example confirms that a person is 'justified by works and not by faith alone'. This seems to be clearly opposed to the Reformers' reading of Paul on the subject of justification, and raises a serious question as to whether their view was too narrowly Pauline. If James's teaching is permitted to shape our understanding of the justification of believers, then the vigorous Reformation emphasis upon grace alone and faith alone stands in need of serious modification. Even a superficial reading of James 2 seems to support Luther's concern that it fits uncomfortably with that of Paul, to put it mildly, or explicitly contradicts it, to put it more bluntly.

Before drawing our own conclusions, we need to look carefully at the *context* for James's conclusion that Abraham was justified by his works. We also need to consider the *specific way* in which James speaks of justification. Only then can we determine how his statements relate to that of Paul. One of the best ways to interpret an argument is to discover the issue being addressed. This is particularly true when it comes to the interpretation of James 2:14–26.

What good is it, my brothers, if someone says he has faith but does not have works? Can that faith save him? (2:14).

James begins by explicitly raising a question for consideration. The question is consistent with the practical character of his epistle; it is full of instructions about how the Christian life ought to be practised. Though verses 14–26 form a clear unit, they are not an abrupt insertion into the epistle, but a continuation of James's exhortations to live in accordance with 'the royal law according to the Scripture' (1:8). The burden of the letter is that those who profess faith in Jesus Christ must live in a manner consistent with the gospel.

Within this context, James's question is quite straightforward and sets the stage for his subsequent argument. He asks whether there is any 'good' or 'benefit' when someone professes to believe but does not have 'works'. The reader is asked to imagine a person who makes a public declaration of faith in Jesus Christ, but whose faith is not accompanied by good deeds.

There are several linguistic features of this verse that help to clarify the force of James's question. First, he uses the present tense: 'What use is it, brothers, if a man *says* he has faith.' The focus is upon a professing believer, someone who is claiming to be a Christian. Second, James calls attention to the nature of this professed faith: 'Can *that* faith save him?' Literally, the text reads, 'Can *the* faith save him?'[7] The use of the definite article emphasizes that the faith of which this man boasts is a faith devoid of good works: it is a 'lonely' faith in the sense that it is unaccompanied by works. And third, James pointedly summarizes his question rhetorically, using a form that expects an emphatically negative answer. No one whose profession of faith is merely a matter of words should deceive himself by thinking that such a faith is able to save.

The precise form of James's question must be borne in mind in any consideration of this passage. James 2:14–26 is clearly framed by this question and its anticipated negative answer. In fact, so tightly governed by this question is this section that it would be possible to delete verses 15–25 and to place verse 26 immediately after verse 14.

> What good is it, my brothers, if someone says he has faith but does not have works? Can that faith save him? . . . For as the body apart from the spirit is dead, so also faith apart from works is dead.

The opening and closing verses form a kind of parenthesis around the intervening argument, which offers an extended illustration of James's principal point, namely, that a 'works-less' faith

– a mere professing-to-believe without any accompanying works – cannot save. The question here is similar in its implications to other familiar passages in Scripture. In Matthew 15:8, Jesus quotes the words of the prophet Isaiah: 'This people honours me with their lips, but their heart is far from me.' Isaiah describes people whose religion is of the lips and the teeth and the tongue alone. In a similar passage, Matthew 7:21, Jesus declares that 'Not everyone who says to me, "Lord, Lord", will enter the kingdom of heaven, but the one who does the will of my Father who is in heaven.' It is only the person who does the Father's will whom Jesus will acknowledge as one of his disciples. To those who do not do the Father's will, however, he will say, 'Depart from me, you workers of lawlessness"' (7:23). As in these comparable passages, James's focus is on a person who professes to believe, but whose life belies this profession.

> If a brother or sister is poorly clothed and lacking in daily food, and one of you says to them, 'Go in peace, be warmed and filled', without giving them the things needed for the body, what good is that? So also faith by itself, if it does not have works, is dead (2:15–17).

Having raised the passage's governing question, James offers a concrete example. The purpose of his illustration is to lend tangible force to the question in verse 14. This is evident from the repetition of the phrase, 'what good is that?' in verse 16. James once again anticipates that his readers will respond with an emphatic agreement that such 'deed-less' faith is of no good whatsoever.

The illustration is a simple one. A Christian brother or sister needs clothing and food. What good would it do, asks James, to wish such a person well, but to do nothing to help him or her? The expression here, 'Go in peace', is much like our English expression, 'Goodbye'; it literally means to wish someone well. Often, when conversations conclude with a 'goodbye', the expression is really little more than an empty phrase. The well-wisher who says 'goodbye' does not intend to do anything specific to address the recipient's need. The words are tossed out, but they do not express a heartfelt interest in the recipient's well-being. This is the kind of thing of which James is speaking here: a professing believer who wishes someone well, but has no real intention of acting upon his or her words. He wants to make a point similar to that made in 1 John 3:9–11, where the person who professes to love God but does not love his brother is exposed as a hypocrite.

Of what use, then, is a faith that has no accompanying good works, that is 'by itself', all alone, having no evidence that it is alive?

> But someone will say, 'You have faith and I have works.' Show me your faith apart from your works, and I will show you my faith by my works (2:18).

Verse 18 is one of the more difficult verses to interpret in this passage, since it is not clear which words belong to James's interlocutor and which words belong to James himself. A cursory review of the contemporary English translations will demonstrate how competent translators differ on the punctuation of this verse.[8]

Though the commentaries discuss this verse in quite technical and complicated terms, there are only three possible principal interpretations. The first takes the entire verse after the opening phrase to be the statement of an interlocutor or objector to James. This interpretation properly recognizes that the words James uses to introduce his interlocutor's statement, '*But* someone will say', clearly implies that an objection to James's argument is anticipated.[9] The problem with this view, however, is that the last part of the verse seems to be a statement that agrees with James's primary argument here, namely, that faith shows or demonstrates itself by works.

The second view punctuates the verse so that the objection of James's interlocutor is limited to the statement, 'You have faith but I have works.' However, the difficulty with this punctuation is that then the objector's statement does not appear to express a significant objection. Rather, it seems to amount to the assertion of a strange separation of faith and works, whereas James is arguing throughout the passage that they are inseparably linked.

Due to the problems posed by these two readings of verse 18, a third interpretation suggests that the text means:

But someone will say, 'Do you have faith?' And I *will say*, 'I have works. Show me *your faith* apart from your works, and I by my works will show you my faith.'[10]

Advocates of this third view argue that the phrase, 'You have faith', which introduces the objection of James's interlocutor, could be taken as a question, 'Do you have faith?'. They also note that the addition of the verbal idea, 'will say', after this question is permissible. However, what especially commends this particular reading of the verse is the way it fits in nicely with the context. Commenting on this point, James White argues that

> The result fits perfectly . . . with the context: the imaginary objector, responding to James's emphasis upon deeds, asks if James has faith at all. James, rejecting the abnormality already seen (faith that cannot prove its existence by actions), responds by saying that he possesses evidence, works, and that he can demonstrate the existence of his *real* faith by those very works. The objector cannot demonstrate the existence of faith without the corresponding actions.[11]

The latter part of this reading of verse 18 expresses James's point that there is an inseparable connection between faith and works. This then leads quite naturally to the emphasis of the next verse, which contrasts true faith that works with a false faith that does not work.

Despite the complexity of this verse and the various readings advocated by different interpreters, the main point, which is crucial to the right interpretation of the remainder of the passage, is not difficult to ascertain. Is there an inseparable link between (genuine) faith and works; or is it possible to separate them? James argues that true faith is a working, living faith; it is not lifeless or dead. Consequently, he speaks of a *synergy* between faith and works, when he describes saving faith as active 'along with' works (2:22).[12] He strongly opposes any separation between faith and works, which would tear asunder what properly belongs together. Faith and works are two sides of a single coin; if you have the one, you will necessarily have the other. As James White notes: 'The contrast in this passage is not between *faith* and *works* but between *dead faith* and *living faith*.'[13]

A further feature of verse 18 deserves comment. The insistence on the inseparability of faith and works occurs within a specific context, namely, how the claim to have faith is verified or confirmed. When someone makes a profession of faith, the issue of its genuineness comes into focus. The words 'show' or 'prove' at the end of verse 18 calls attention to this issue. What is at stake is the visible demonstration or proof of the claim to have genuine faith. By introducing this verbal idea, the inseparability of faith and works is not only emphasized but also placed within the specific context of *the genuineness of a person's profession of faith demonstrated to others*. To state the matter negatively, the setting is not whether such a profession is known to be true by God. Rather, assuming that God knows perfectly well whether a profession of faith is valid, James focuses his attention upon the question of *how others can be assured that the claim to have faith is true*.[14]

> You believe that God is one; you do well. Even the demons believe—and shudder! (2:19).

To illustrate the inseparability of true faith and works, James introduces the prospect of a species of faith that consists merely in giving one's assent to true propositions about God. The faith of someone who professes to believe, but who does no good works, is compared to the faith possessed by demons. Following closely the train of thought at the end of verse 18, James notes that a person may assent to the truth that 'God is one' and yet be devoid of good works. However, because this faith is literally a dead orthodoxy, such a believer is no better off than the demons. They also assent to the truth that God is one, but far from producing good works in them, their faith only causes them to tremble with fear. Such knowledge, which James is careful not to criticize,[15] is nevertheless not the expression of a true and living faith.

The preposition used in verse 19 reinforces this contrast. It speaks of the demons believing '*that* God is one'; they do not believe 'in' or 'upon' God. However in the New Testament true faith is spoken of as an act whereby a person believes 'in' or 'upon' or 'into' Jesus Christ or the promises of the gospel.

> Do you want to be shown, you foolish person, that faith apart from works is useless? (2:20).

James employs strong language in describing the person who would maintain that a dead and unfruitful faith is able to save.[16] The 'foolish person' is without soundness of mind; his thinking is vain and empty. Once again, as in verse 14, James here uses a rhetorical form that anticipates an emphatic negative response to his question.

One of the interesting features of verse 20 is the play on words used to underscore the apostle's main point that faith without works cannot save. The literal conclusion reached is 'the faith without works work-less is'. The word translated as 'useless' (ESV) is a combination of the negative prefix, *a-*, which means 'no' or 'non', and the noun for 'works'. Though it does not come through well in translation, this play on words expresses a kind of tautology: faith without works is workless, that is, it is barren, empty, unfruitful. And so we return to the question with which James began: Can the faith, which has no works, save anyone? What good is it, if a person claims to have faith, but has no works?

Before taking up the second half of this passage, we need to make two preliminary comments about the relation between the teaching of Paul and James.

First, the contrast governing James's discussion in this passage is one between a true faith, which is inseparably joined with works, and a false faith, which is barren and lifeless. Only the former can save, James argues, not the latter. Those whose faith is without works are self-deceived in their profession; their profession of faith is no better than the dead orthodoxy of demons. This contrast is quite distinct from that found in Paul between faith, which is the exclusive instrument of justification, and works, which play no role as the basis for justification.

Second, the issue James addresses seems quite distinct from that addressed by Paul, particularly with regard to his treatment of the doctrine of justification. James is concerned about how the genuineness of someone's profession of faith can be demonstrated. Or, to state the difference in other terms, James focuses upon the *justification of faith* in the presence of others, whereas Paul focuses upon the *justification of the ungodly* in the presence of God.

THE ANSWER: NO SALVATION WITHOUT A 'LIVELY' FAITH

Thus far in our treatment of James 2:14–26 we have focused primarily on whether a 'lonely' faith, barren of good works, can save. Having considered the question, we are now in a position to look at James's answer.

> Was not Abraham our father justified by works, when he offered up Isaac his son on the altar? You see that faith was active along with his works, and faith was completed by his works; and the Scripture was fulfilled that says, 'Abraham believed God, and it was counted to him as righteousness' — and he was called a friend of God (2:21–23).

James appeals to the example of Abraham in order to show that the faith which saves is always active in good works. Like Abraham, whose faith led him to willingly offer up his son Isaac on the altar in obedience to the Lord, so all believers must exercise an active faith 'along with' their works. There is a synergism, a mutual working-with the other, of faith and works in the life of the believer.

However, the remarkable feature of James's appeal to Abraham is his use of the expression, 'justified by works'. Though his words and argument have their own integrity and meaning – which has to be determined without undue concern for harmonizing with Paul – the apparent contrast with the statements of his fellow apostle can hardly be missed. Whereas Paul appeals to Abraham's example to prove that we are justified freely by grace alone through faith alone apart from works (*Rom.* 4), James appeals to Abraham as someone whose faith was lively and active in good works. Just as Paul cites Genesis 15:6 (which speaks of Abraham's faith being reckoned to him as righteousness), so also does James. But James's purpose in appealing to this Old Testament passage appears to be quite different from, even contradictory to, that of Paul. Paul does so in order to show that believers are justified apart from works done in obedience to the law. This is the point he labours to prove throughout Romans 4: Abraham was justified before he received the seal of the righteousness of faith in circumcision. Before Abraham had done anything in the way of obedience, his faith was reckoned to him for righteousness. But James refers to Abraham in order to make a different point, one that appears upon first reading to be contradictory to Paul's.

The crux of the difficulty here can be put in the form of a question: Does James 2:21–25 use 'justification' in the same sense as Romans 4? If the answer is yes, then the conclusion seems unavoidable: James is contradicting Paul. If so, then we seem to be confronted with a dilemma: either Paul is right, or James is right, but they cannot both be right.[17] You cannot say that believers are justified by faith apart from works of the law on the one hand, and then also say that believers are justified by works – at least not if the term justification is being used in the same sense in both instances. Any resolution of this issue must address the question whether James uses 'justification' in a sense different to Paul.

Those who insist that James is not contradicting Paul usually offer one of three possible interpretations of his claim that Abraham 'was justified by works'.

First, some appeal to the question governing this passage, 'Can that faith *save* him?', and argue that James is using 'justify' as a synonym for 'save'.[18] On this interpretation, James is using the term 'justify' to refer inclusively to all that belongs to salvation. However, the great difficulty raised by this interpretation is that we have no instance of a similar use of this term in the New Testament.

Second, some suggest that James uses the term, not to refer to the initial justification and acceptance of sinners, but to a *final justification* that occurs in the context of the final judgment.[19] The strength of this interpretation is that it takes the term 'justify' in a declarative sense; it refers to God's pronouncement regarding the righteousness of the believer in the context of the final judgment. This use is attested in Scripture (cf. *Matt.* 12:37) and correlates well with how Paul uses it. However, this interpretation gratuitously inserts into the passage the idea of a future or final justification. This seems at odds with James, who locates the justification of Abraham within the context of his offering of Isaac upon the altar (*Gen.* 22). He is not referring to a *future* justification, but to one occurring in the *present*.

Third, some interpreters maintain that James is using the term in a *demonstrative* sense, that is, to refer to the demonstration and proof of Abraham's righteousness.[20] Abraham was shown to be just by his deeds, which were the evidence of his living and fruitful faith. Unlike the first two interpretations, this third interpretation seems compelling. Not only does it do justice to the context of verse 21 within the argument of the passage, but it also appeals to a recognized scriptural use of the term 'to justify'. As we have already noted, James is opposing the idea that a dead and unfruitful faith may be saving. He is also concerned about how to test the genuineness of a public avowal of faith. In verse 18 he speaks of 'showing' a person's faith by works and again in verse 20 he speaks of 'showing' how faith without works is useless. The focus of attention, therefore, within the immediate context of verse 21, is the public demonstration of the genuine character of a person's claim to have faith. Thus, when James adduces the example of Abraham's faith working along with his deeds, he is providing an example of a deed that demonstrates Abraham to be a righteous person.[21] In this connection, it should be noted that James appeals to Abraham's readiness to sacrifice Isaac, an event that is recorded in Genesis 22 and not Genesis 15. In which ever way we take James's appeal to Genesis 15:6 in this verse, it is important to recognize that he is interested in the way Abraham's faith produced works, which demonstrated the patriarch's righteousness.

In addition to this important contextual consideration, it should also be noted that those who take James to be using the term 'justify' in this sense are not inventing a new use for the word. Rather, they are appealing to a use that is attested in the best lexicons and dictionaries of New Testament words.[22]

There are several New Testament passages that use the word in this way. For example, in Luke 7:35 Jesus speaks of how 'wisdom is *justified* by all her children.' Wisdom is known and demonstrated by its fruits. The familiar proverb, 'A gentle answer turns away wrath', illustrates the principle: a gentle and restrained response lowers the temperature of a dispute and is a demonstrable fruit of wisdom. Similarly Paul, quoting the Psalms in Romans 3:4, says, 'Let God be found true though every one were a liar, as it is written, "That you may be *justified* in your words."' The idea here is that God may be 'proved true' and reliable by the works that he performs. Or consider one other example, from 1 Timothy 3:16: 'Great indeed, we confess, is the mystery of godliness: He was manifested in the flesh, *justified* by the Spirit, seen by angels. . . .' The justification spoken of here is the vindication or demonstration of Christ's glory and person in his resurrection from the dead. These are all instances of a demonstrative or probative use of the verb 'to justify'. None of them allow the translation, 'to declare to be righteous before God'.

This demonstrative use best fits the context of James's statement that Abraham 'was justified by works'. Abraham, whom God reckoned to be righteous by faith, demonstrated and proved his righteousness by his willingness to sacrifice his son Isaac in obedience to God.[23]

This is also apparent from verse 22, which draws a general conclusion regarding the relation of faith and works. James notes that the synergy between faith and works does not allow them to be pulled apart. We cannot have the one without the other, James argues, because faith finds its 'completion' in its works. In the same way that a good tree bears good fruit and, in doing so reaches its *telos* or perfection, so faith is completed or perfected by its works.

Abraham's willingness to sacrifice Isaac 'fulfilled' what was declared already in Genesis 15:6: 'Abraham believed God, and it was counted to him as righteousness.' Since this text is cited by Paul in Romans 4:3 and Galatians 3:6 to prove that believers are justified before God by faith alone, James's appeal to it is regarded by some interpreters as clear evidence that his doctrine of justification differs from that of Paul.[24] For Paul justification is by faith alone; for James it is by faith together with its works. However, if James uses 'justify' in verse 21 to refer to the demonstration of Abraham's righteousness by his works, as we have argued, it is unnecessary to interpret his appeal to Genesis 15:6 in this way. James's appeal to Genesis 15:6 is the one occasion in which he specifically addresses the question of Abraham's righteousness *before God*, and in so doing he fully concurs with Paul's teaching: Abraham was justified before God by faith, not by works. When James speaks of Abraham's justification *before others*, he appeals to Genesis 22, because it records the way in which Abraham's faith was demonstrated or proved to be genuine. Consequently, James speaks of the event recorded in Genesis 22 as a 'fulfilment' of what was previously declared in Genesis 15. Fully consonant with the theme observed throughout this passage, Abraham's act of obedience served as a confirmation of the truth of God's earlier declaration regarding him in Genesis 15.[25]

> You see that a person is justified by works and not by faith alone. And in the same way was not also Rahab the prostitute justified by works when she received the messengers and sent them out by another way? For as the body apart from the spirit is dead, so also faith apart from works is dead (2:24–26).

James here brings his argument to a conclusion. Verse 24 boldly restates the principle already established from Abraham's example. Though made in generic terms, the point is the same as that made previously with respect to Abraham. He is using the term 'justify' in the same way as he used it in verse 21. Anyone whose faith produces works shows evidence of having a genuine faith. James also cites the example of Rahab as further confirmation. Rahab's readiness to protect the messengers who visited her in Jericho is an example of a true faith productive of good works. On the basis of her obedient faith, Rahab was justified, that is, confirmed or evidenced as a genuine believer.

James closes the passage by drawing a comparison to illustrate the intimate conjunction of faith and its works. In the same way that the body, if it were separated from the spirit, is dead, so faith, if it were separated from its works, is dead. Such a person whose faith is a 'lonely' faith, that is, a faith without works, cannot be saved.

Summary

We have discovered that one principal question is addressed throughout this passage: Can a deedless faith save anyone? The contrast governing this passage is one between a *living faith* on the one hand, and a *dead faith* on the other. A living faith is inseparably joined to its fruits; a dead faith is unaccompanied by any fruits. A living faith works in synergy with its deeds; a dead faith is devoid of any deeds.

Assuming this contrast between a living and a dead faith, James's major claim, from the opening verse of this passage to its close, is that a person is saved only by a faith that is accompanied by works. James makes this point negatively by insisting that a 'works-less' or deedless faith cannot save anyone. This point governs the shape of his argument and provides the context within which to consider the examples of Abraham and Rahab. Furthermore, it is especially significant that James focuses his attention upon the demonstration of a person's public profession of faith. He not only argues that a dead faith cannot save; he also argues that *we* can only know whether someone's claim to faith is genuine by the good works it produces.

The contrast drawn between a genuine and a false faith is placed within the context of the demonstration of true faith before others. Just as true faith is evident from the works it produces, so false faith is evident from its failure to produce any works. James's interest, therefore, is in the confirmation of true faith by its fruits. Just as a good tree demonstrates its goodness by the fruit it bears, so true faith is known by its works.

If we keep in mind these features of the passage, then the meaning of James's remarkable claim that Abraham was 'justified by works' becomes apparent. He does not use this term in the same sense that Paul does to describe how a believing sinner finds acceptance before God. Rather he uses it to describe how a professing believer is confirmed in his righteousness, that is, shown to be a just person whose faith is fruitful and active in good works. Therefore, the error James opposes is that of the person who makes an idle boast of faith.

A REFORMATION PERSPECTIVE ON
JAMES AND PAUL

We are now in a position to return to the issue of the Reformation perspective on James and Paul. As noted earlier, James played an important role in sixteenth-century discussions about the doctrine of justification, and continues to play a similar role today. According to the Roman Catholic Church, James 2 constitutes a clear refutation of the Protestant view that justification is by faith alone. Because James speaks of a 'justification by works', the inevitable question arises whether this historic claim of the Roman Catholic Church is valid. Does the teaching of James differ from the Reformation view that believers are justified by faith, and not by works?

We have already noted Luther's response to this objection. He was prepared, if necessary, to jettison the epistle of James in favour of the writings of Paul. For him, the doctrine of justification had to be preserved at all costs, even if this meant denying to James canonical status. Luther's negative opinion about James, however, does not tell the whole story so far as the Reformation view is concerned. Calvin, for example, in his *Institutes* addressed the question of the compatibility of the teaching of James and Paul, and maintained that, *when rightly understood,* they were fully compatible.

Calvin's treatment of the relation between the teaching of the two apostles is set within his extended exposition of the doctrine of justification in Book III of his *Institutes*. He proceeds on the presumption that James, as a minister of the gospel, does not differ from Paul in his basic teaching. Acknowledging that many Roman Catholic theologians viewed James's teaching as a contradiction of the Reformation doctrine of free justification, Calvin insists that James's 'statement must be so understood as not to disagree with Christ speaking through Paul's lips.'[26] Since the same Spirit speaks through James as through Paul, Calvin insists that their respective views must be in harmony.

Calvin then observes the particular concern addressed by James:

At that time there were many—and this tends to be a perpetual evil in the church—who openly disclosed their unbelief by neglecting and overlooking all the proper works of believers, yet did not cease to boast of the false name of faith.[27]

The occasion for the epistle was the empty boast of some professing believers whose lives were bereft of good works. Such a false or pretended faith is nothing but an 'empty image' of true faith. If we are to understand James, Calvin notes, then we must keep the epistle's purpose in mind: the author aims to expose the hypocrisy of those who claim to have faith, but are not genuine believers.

After making this initial observation, Calvin turns to the most important part of his case for the compatibility of James and Paul. Those who cite James against the Reformation's understanding of Paul are guilty of a '"double fallacy" [*duplicem paralogismus*]: one in the word "faith", the other in the word "justify".'[28] The key to resolve the difference between James and Paul lies in the recognition that the apostles are using these terms in quite distinct ways. Describing James's use of the word 'faith', Calvin notes that

> When the apostle labels 'faith' an empty opinion far removed from true faith, he is making a concession that in no way detracts from the argument. This he sets forth at the outset in these words: 'What does it profit, my brethren, if a man say he has faith but have not works?' He does not say 'if anyone have faith without works' but 'if he boast'. He states it even more clearly a little later where in derision he makes it worse than devils' knowledge, and finally, where he calls it 'dead'. . . . Obviously, if this faith contains nothing but a belief that there is a God, it is not strange if it does not justify![29]

In other words, James is not describing genuine Christian faith, which rests upon the assurance of God's mercy alone for justification; rather, he is talking about the dead or unfruitful faith that his opponents parade before others, as though it were the genuine thing itself. Though Calvin leaves the comparison implicit, he clearly means to emphasize that James's use of the phrase 'faith alone' (i.e. a dead, 'works-less' faith) is in no way comparable to Paul's use of the phrase 'faith apart from works'. The contrast in James is between a true and false faith; the contrast in Paul is between faith that rests upon God's mercy alone, and works that are regarded as the basis for the believer's acceptance with God.

The second, and perhaps more significant fallacy relates to the word 'justify'. Due to the care with which Calvin states this point, we will quote his discussion at some length:

> If you would make James agree with the rest of Scripture and with himself, you must understand the word 'justify' in another sense than Paul takes it. For we are said by Paul to be justified when the memory of our unrighteousness has been wiped out and we are accounted righteous. If James had taken that view, it would have been preposterous for him to quote Moses' statement: 'Abraham believed God' (*Gen.* 15:6; *James* 2:23), etc. For this is the context: Abraham attained righteousness by works because at God's command he did not hesitate to sacrifice his son (*James* 2:21). Thus is the Scripture fulfilled that says: 'He believed God, and it was reckoned to him as righteousness' (*James* 2:23). If it is absurd that an effect precedes its cause, either Moses testifies falsely in that place that faith was reckoned to Abraham as righteousness, or, from that obedience which he manifested by offering Isaac, he did not merit righteousness. . . . Therefore, either James wrongly inverted the order—unlawful even to imagine!—or he did not mean to call him justified, as if he deserved to be reckoned righteous. What then? Surely it is clear that he himself is speaking of the declaration, not the imputation, of righteousness. It is as if he said: 'Those who by true faith are righteous prove their righteousness by obedience and good works, not by a bare and imaginary mask of faith.' To sum up, he is not discussing in what manner we are justified but demanding of believers a righteousness fruitful in good works. And as Paul contends that we are justified apart from the help of works, so James does not allow those who lack good works to be reckoned righteous.[30]

In Calvin's interpretation of James 2, it is necessary to distinguish between the appeal to Genesis 15:6, which illustrates that Abraham was justified by God through faith alone, and the appeal to Genesis 22 which refers to Abraham's readiness to sacrifice Isaac upon the altar. Though Abraham was a justified person antecedent to his willingness to sacrifice Isaac, this willingness was a subsequent demonstration and confirmation of his righteousness. James, therefore, is using the word 'justify' to refer to the subsequent acting of Abraham's faith, which demonstrated and proved that he was a righteous person whose faith was genuine. The teaching of James and Paul are, accordingly, in full harmony. In this passage, James teaches two things, neither of which is contradicted in any way by the teaching of Paul: 'An empty show of faith does not justify, and a believer, not content with such an image, declares his righteousness by his good works.'[31]

Calvin, therefore, sees no reason to find James's view at odds with that of Paul. So long as we pay attention to the respective contexts of their writings, their teaching is fully compatible.

CONCLUSION

Though it has long been maintained by Roman Catholic representatives that the Reformation understanding of justification by faith alone is incompatible with the teaching of James, our consideration of this passage demonstrates otherwise.

In the Roman Catholic appeal to James, it is often assumed that the Reformers used the term 'faith alone' in the same way in which James uses it. When they spoke of justification by faith alone, they were understood as affirming that believers are accepted and saved by God, even though their faith was a dead or unfruitful faith.

From the perspective of the Roman Catholic Church, the Reformers' affirmation of justification by faith alone was contradictory to the teaching of James 2, which argues that a lonely or unfruitful faith cannot save anyone. However, in our treatment of James 2, as well as in our review of Calvin's handling of the relation between James and Paul, we have seen that there is a great difference in the way James and Paul use the word 'faith'. When James strongly repudiates the idea that 'faith alone' can save anyone, he is opposing what Calvin calls an 'empty image' of faith, not true faith. The great contrast that James draws is between such dead faith and true or living faith. This contrast is quite different from that which Paul draws between faith and works, so far as their role in the reception of free justification is concerned. The Reformation perspective on justification was not that a lonely faith, that is, a dead and unfruitful faith, was the instrument of justification.[32] Though faith alone receives the free gift of God's righteousness in Christ for justification, the faith that justifies is not an 'alone faith' but one that is always accompanied by fruitful works.[33] Consequently, one of the principal objections of the Roman Catholic Church to the Protestant view of justification completely misses the mark. Even Luther, who spoke rather incautiously regarding the teaching of James, emphasized, as much as Calvin and the other Reformers, that a true justifying faith is a lively and fruitful faith.[34] By speaking of 'faith alone' in respect to justification, however, they were unwilling to ascribe any value to the works of faith so far as the believer's acceptance with God is concerned.

Likewise, the Roman Catholic appeal to James 2 assumes that James uses the term 'justify' in the same way as Paul. On this assumption, it follows that James's insistence that a true believer is 'justified by works' confirms the Roman Catholic view. It is supposed that James teaches exactly what the Roman Catholic Church maintains, namely, that justification is maintained and increased by the merit of good works.

However, in our consideration of this passage, we argued that this is to misunderstand James's use of the term. Our reading of the passage is consistent with Calvin's claim that James and Paul use the word 'justify' differently, even as they use 'faith' differently. When Paul speaks of justification, he speaks of the act whereby believers are *accepted into God's* favour; justification is a gracious act of God whereby he pronounces the ungodly sinner to be acceptable to him in Christ. When James speaks of justification, he speaks of the way in which believers are *demonstrated* or *shown to be* righteous. Justification in Paul occurs *before God*; justification in James occurs *before others*. The Roman Catholic interpretation of James, therefore, fails to take into account the particular context within which James addresses the issue of justification.

The dispute between Roman Catholic and Protestant goes beyond the boundaries of their respective interpretations of James 2. In the broader theological framework of the Reformation view of salvation, free justification, which secures the believer's acceptance with God, is never separated from the Spirit's sanctification of believers in Christ. In order to preserve the sheer graciousness of the gift of free acceptance with God, the Reformers strongly insisted upon a distinction between justification and sanctification. However, they also maintained that all believers, who are united to Christ by faith, are simultaneously justified and sanctified.

As Calvin was fond of expressing it, Christ is not given to believers for righteousness without also being given to them for sanctification (*1 Cor.* 1:30). To separate justification and sanctification would be akin to separating Christ's deity and humanity. The benefits of Christ's saving work for his people include not only reconciliation with God through his cross, but also renewal in obedience to his commandments by the Holy Spirit. According to Calvin, you can no more separate justification from sanctification than you can separate Christ and his Spirit. Whenever Christ indwells the hearts of believers, he always subdues them to obedience by his Spirit. In the fullness of his office, Christ is not only a priest but also a king, who rules in the hearts of his people by his Spirit and Word.[35] The Roman Catholic Church's oft-repeated complaint, therefore, that the Reformation's view of justification undermines a life of good works, is without foundation.[36]

For the Reformers, 'faith alone', far from being detrimental to the Christian life of good works, is the only basis and source of Christian obedience. To place works before justification, as though they played a role in obtaining God's acceptance, alters the character of the Christian's life of obedience. Rather than good works being the fruits of thankfulness, which are born out of the grateful awareness of the believer's acceptance by God, they are regarded as a means to obtain favour with God. If works are performed to obtain God's favour, however, they are no longer performed in good faith. They become corrupted by a self-seeking desire to curry favour with God, or to wrest from God a reluctant acceptance and forgiveness. According to the Reformers, the Christian's freedom is a freedom to obey God, not a freedom to sin or continue in disobedience. However, the obedience of faith is not constrained by a fear of punishment or falling into disfavour with God. Rather, it is a joyful delight in God and his will, which springs from an awareness of God's undeserved favour in Christ.

When justification undergirds the believer's sanctification, Christian obedience is no longer coloured by an anxious uncertainty regarding God's grace. Calvin expresses this point in his comments on James and Paul, when he insists that we should not place good works, which are the inevitable *effect* of true faith, before faith, which is the only *cause* of good works. Unless believers are acceptable to God by faith in Christ, it is not possible for their works to be pleasing to him. At the same time, it is impossible for those who know the grace of free justification and who are united to Christ by faith, not to be renewed in good works.

Therefore, the Reformation view of justification does not teach that believers can be saved or justified by a 'lonely' faith, that is, a faith devoid of any good works. While carefully guarding the sheer graciousness of the believer's acceptance with God solely on the grounds of Christ's righteousness, the Reformation perspective insists that those who are justified by faith alone are also sanctified by faith. The believer's freedom in Christ is no occasion for disobedience; it inevitably leads to a life of free and heartfelt devotion to God and others.

NOTES

[1] This objection is stated or acknowledged in Roman Catholic and Protestant confessional documents. Cf. *The Canons and Decrees of the Council of Trent*, Sixth Session, Chapter 11, *et passim* (Schaff, *The Creeds of Christendom*, 3:100-2); and the *Heidelberg Catechsim*, Q. & A. 64: 'But does this doctrine [of free justification] make men careless and profane? By no means; for it is impossible that those who are implanted into Christ by a true faith should not bring forth fruits of thankfulness.'

[2] See *The Council of Trent*, Sixth Session, Chapter 11 (Schaff, *The Creeds of Christendom*, vol. 2:100), '. . . no one ought to make use of that rash saying, one prohibited by the fathers under an anathema, — that the observance of the commandments of God is impossible for one that is justified.' This is often expressed as well in the complaint that the formula, *simul iustus et peccator* (the justified is 'at once righteous and yet a sinner'), encourages a dangerous indifference to the necessity of good works in the Christian life. However, this formula was never intended to deny the necessity or reality of good works in the life of the believer. It was aimed at the idea that good works could be, in the whole or in part, the ground of the believer's justification. Because believers remain sinners still, however much their lives may be transformed by the working of the Spirit of Christ, they cannot be declared righteous upon the basis of who they are or what they have done.

[3] This objection is vividly described in a poem by W. H. Auden, entitled *Luther* (1940). He speaks of Luther's 'conscience cocked to listen for the thunder . . . The fuse of Judgment spluttered in his head . . . ' and concludes:

> All Works and all Societies are bad.
> The Just shall live by Faith, he cried in dread.
> And men and women of the world were glad,
> Who never trembled in their useful lives.

[4] See *The Council of Trent*, Sixth Session, Chapters 7 and 10 (Schaff, *The Creeds of Christendom*, 2:94–7, 99–100).

[5] LW, 35:362. For a summary and evaluation of Luther's diverse comments on James, see Timothy George, '"A Right Strawy Epistle": Reformation Perspectives on James', *Review & Expositor*, 83 (1986), 3, pp. 69–82. George concludes that Luther's emphasis upon justification was 'one-sided', but acknowledges that James received a 'more positive reception' in the Reformed tradition of Calvin and others.

[6] See Calvin, *Institutes*, III.xvii.11–12. For two recent treatments of James 2 that largely correspond to the view of Calvin, see Ronald Y. K. Fung, 'Justification in the Epistle of James', in *Right with God: Justification in the Bible and the World*, ed. D. A. Carson (Grand Rapids: Baker Book House, 1992), pp. 146–62; and James R. White, *The God Who Justifies*, pp. 329–54. Fung's article provides a fairly complete discussion of the debate about this passage in more recent literature.

[7] This is known as the anaphoric use of the definite article. Cf. Daniel B. Wallace, *Greek Grammar Beyond the Basics — Exegetical Syntax of the New Testament* (Grand Rapids: Zondervan, 1999), p. 219: 'The author introduces his topic: faith without works. He then follows it with a question, asking whether this kind of faith is able to save. The use of the article both points back to a certain kind of faith as defined by the author and is used to particularize an abstract noun.' Wallace ably refutes the unusual treatment of this passage by Zane C. Hodges (*The Gospel Under Siege* [Dallas: Redención

Viva, 1981], p. 23), who has to deny this sense of the definite article in verse 14 in order to make his case.

[8] For example, the NASB takes the whole verse as a statement of James' interlocutor; the ESV, the text I am using, the NIV, and the RSV restrict James' interlocutor to the phrase, 'You have faith and I have works.' For a thorough discussion of the various possible punctuations of this verse, see Fung, 'Justification in the Epistle of James', pp. 148–151.

[9] James uses the Greek conjunction, Ἀλλα ('but'), which indicates that a rebuttal is coming. See Fung, 'Justification in the Epistle of James', p. 149.

[10] For a defence of this punctuation, see White, *The God Who Justifies*, pp. 339-41; Heinz Neitzel, 'Eine alte *crux interpretum* im Jakobusbrief 2:18', *Zeitschrift für die neutestamentliche Wissenschaft* 73 (1982), pp. 289ff.; and Fung, 'Justification in the Epistle of James', pp. 149–50.

[11] *The God Who Justifies*, p. 340.

[12] The language of verse 22 employs a play on words. Literally, James says that 'faith works with works'.

[13] *The God Who Justifies*, p. 339. Cf. Peter H. Davids, *The Epistle of James* (Grand Rapids: Eerdmans, 1982), p. 125.

[14] See White, *The God Who Justifes*, p. 341; and Fung, 'Justification in the Epistle of James', pp. 150–1.

[15] It would be incorrect to conclude that James' view of true faith disparages the importance of knowledge of the truth. It is not the case that, so long as works are present, it matters not at all what someone believes. James does say that the person who believes God is one who 'does well'.

[16] See Davids, *The Epistle of James*, p. 126.

[17] One important aspect of the question of the relation of Paul and James concerns the priority of their writings. Is James responding to Paul's argument in Romans and Galatians? Or is Paul responding to James' argument in this passage? For a summary of the debate on this question see Fung, 'Justification in the Epistle of James', pp. 159–62. In my judgment, this question has no conclusive answer. Since James and Paul use the language of 'faith' and 'justify' differently, it is more likely that they are addressing quite different opponents. Cf. Alexander Ross, *The Epistles of James and John* (Grand Rapids: Eerdmans, 1967), p. 53, who suggests the analogy of two fighters who are not facing each other but standing back-to-back, fighting different opponents. John Owen, *The Works of John Owen*, 5:387, takes the same view: 'The design of the Apostle James is not at all to explain the meaning of Paul in his epistles, as is pretended, but only to vindicate the doctrine of the gospel from the abuse of such as use their liberty for a cloak of maliciousness and, turning the grace of God into lasciviousness, continue in sin under a pretence that grace had abounded unto that end.'

[18] See James H. Ropes, *A Critical and Exegetical Commentary on the Epistle of St. James* (Edinburgh: T. & T. Clark, 1916), p. 217.

[19] See Douglas J. Moo, *The Letter of James* (Grand Rapids: Eerdmans, 1985), pp. 109ff.; and Davids, *Commentary on James*, p. 132.

[20] See White, *The God Who Justifies*, pp. 346-7; Fung, 'Justification in the Epistle of James', pp. 153–4; Patrick J. Hartin, *James* (Collegeville, MN: Liturgical Press, 2003), pp. 153–4; R. V. G. Tasker, *The General Epistle of James* (Grand Rapids: Eerdmans, 1956), pp. 67–67; O. Palmer Robertson, 'Genesis 15:6: New Covenant Expositions of an Old Covenant Text', *Westminster Theological Journal* 42 (1980), pp. 286 ff.; and Luke Timothy Johnson, *The Letter of James* (Garden City, NY: Doubleday, 1995), p. 242.

[21] Cf. Johnson, *The Letter of James*, p. 242: 'Given the previous statement demanding the *demonstration* of faith, the translation here as "shown to be righteous" seems appropriate.'

[22] See Joseph Henry Thayer, ed., *A Greek-English Lexicon of the New Testament* (New York: American Book Co. ed., 1889), s.v. δικαιοω, p. 150: 'to show, exhibit, evince, one to be righteous'; Colin Brown, s.v. 'Righteousness, Justification', in *New International Dictionary of New Testament Theology*, gen. ed. Colin Brown, 3 vols. (Grand Rapids: Zondervan, 1975-1978), 3.370; and O. Michel, s.v. 'Faith', *New International Dictionary of New Testament Theology*, 1.605.

[23] Cf. Robertson, 'Genesis 15:6', p. 287: 'James intends to say that Abraham was "shown to be just" by his actions.'

[24] See Davids, *The Epistle of James*, pp. 129ff.; and Martin Dibelius, *James* (Philadelphia: Fortress, 1976), pp. 163–6, 168–74.

[25] See Fung, 'Justification in the Epistle of James', p. 155, who argues that, in his appeal to Genesis 15:6, James wholly concurs with Paul's view that the believer is justified by faith *before God*. However, when James speaks of the believer's justification *before others*, he appeals to his works as a demonstration or showing forth of his righteousness.

[26] *Institutes*, III.xvii.11. Elsewhere in his sermons and commentaries, Calvin presents the same view as he does in his *Institutes*. See my *The Twofold Nature of the Gospel in Calvin's Theology* (Ph.D. dissertation; Ann Arbor, MI: University Microfilms International, 1985), pp. 262–7.

[27] *Institutes*, III.xvii.11.   [28] Ibid. (((([29] Ibid.

[30] *Institutes*, III.xvii.12.   [31] Ibid.

[32] Cf. Francis, Turretin, *Institutes of Elenctic Theology*, 2:677: 'The question is not whether solitary faith (i.e., separated from the other virtues) justifies (which we grant could not easily be the case, since it is not even true and living faith); but whether it "alone" (*sola*) concurs to the act of justification (which

we assert); as the eye alone sees, but not when torn out of the body. Thus the particle "alone" (*sola*) does not determine the subject, but the predicate (i.e., "faith alone does not justify" [*sola fides non iustificat*], but "faith justifies alone" [*fides justificat sola*]). The coexistence of love with faith in him who is justified is not denied, but its co-efficiency or cooperation in justification is denied.'

[33] Cf. the following statement from the *Westminster Confession of Faith*, Chapter 11.2: 'Faith, thus receiving and resting on Christ and his righteousness, is the alone instrument of justification; yet is it not alone in the person justified, but is ever accompanied with all other saving graces, and is no dead faith, but worketh by love.' It is interesting that the proof texts that accompany this statement include *James* 2:14–26 and *Gal.* 5:6.

[34] Cf. Luther's comments in his *Preface to the Epistle of St. Paul to the Romans* (John Dillenberger, ed., *Martin Luther: Selections From His Writings*, p. 24): 'O, when it comes to faith, what a living, creative, active, powerful thing it is. It cannot do other than good at all times. It never wants to ask whether there is some good work to do. Rather, before the question is raised, it has done the deed, and keeps on doing it. A man not active in this way is a man without faith. He is groping about for faith and searching for good works, but knows neither what faith is nor what good works are. Nevertheless, he keeps on talking nonsense about faith and good works.'

[35] For a comprehensive study of Calvin's view of the relation between justification and sanctification, see my *The Twofold Nature of the Gospel in Calvin's Theology*, esp. pp. 112–282.

[36] It is unfortunate, therefore, that some contemporary evangelicals, who defend the Reformation's view of justification, link this view with what is called a 'non-lordship salvation' view. This view effectively says that a believer could be justified by faith alone, but not yet sanctified. This is not, however, the view of the Reformation. For a summary and critical assessment of this view, see Michael Horton, ed., *Christ the Lord: The Reformation and Lordship Salvation* (Grand Rapids: Baker, 1992); and Ernest C. Reisinger, *Lord & Christ: The Implications of Lordship for Faith and Life* (Phillipsburg, NJ: Presbyterian & Reformed, 1994). For a presentation of the non-lordship position, see Zane Hodges, *The Gospel Under Siege;* and idem, *Dead Faith: What Is It?* (Dallas, TX: Redención Viva, 1987).

PART TWO

A NEW PERSPECTIVE ON PAUL

4

A NEW PERSPECTIVE
ON PAUL : E. P. SANDERS
& JAMES D. G. DUNN

Ever since the sixteenth century, Protestant New Testament scholarship has been largely shaped by the Reformation perspective on the apostle Paul, which has been summarized in the first part of this book. Despite the influence of the eighteenth-century Enlightenment upon Protestant biblical scholarship, the Reformation perspective on Paul continued to hold sway until the latter part of the twentieth century. The dominance of the old perspective on Paul is attested, for example, in the work of two of the most influential Protestant theologians of the twentieth century, Karl Barth and Rudolf Bultmann. Though Barth and Bultmann differed from the Reformers and each other in significant respects, both claimed to be defenders of the old perspective on the apostle Paul's doctrine of justification.[1] In their neo-orthodox (or neo-Reformed) theology, some of the principal themes of the older Protestant emphasis upon justification by grace alone experienced something of a renaissance.

The dominance of the old perspective on Paul within Protestant biblical scholarship through a good portion of the twentieth century is all the more impressive in that one of the principal features of critical biblical scholarship is its claim to approach the biblical texts unfettered by traditional Christian theological dogma.[2]

The dominance of this older perspective does not mean, however, that the new perspective on Paul emerged suddenly or inexplicably. A historical review of the last one hundred years of biblical studies reveals a growing dissatisfaction with the traditional Protestant or 'Lutheran' understanding of Paul.[3] A confluence of factors has contributed to the desire for a new and fresh reading of Paul's writings. A truly comprehensive study of the new perspective on Paul would therefore require a careful examination both of the development of biblical and Pauline studies during this period and of the larger cultural context in which these studies were undertaken.

However, in keeping with the aim and focus of our study, we will restrict ourselves to a consideration of the principal authors who have played a formative role in the development of the new perspective. In doing so, we will be deliberately selective, ignoring some authors of considerable influence and presenting an overly tidy account of the emergence of this view.

Three authors are of particular significance: E. P. Sanders, J. D. G. Dunn and N. T. Wright. Though it is almost impossible to clear a way through the growing thicket of literature on this subject, a summary of their contributions will demonstrate the new perspective's main emphases.[4]

FORERUNNERS OF THE NEW PERSPECTIVE

Before considering Sanders' and Dunn's contributions, we need to explore briefly the historical background to Sanders' reassessment of Second-Temple Judaism. Although Sanders' work represents a significant point of departure for authors of the new perspective, it stands in a longer history of a revisionist treatment of Second-Temple Judaism and the writings of the apostle Paul. Within the orbit of New Testament studies in general and Pauline studies in particular, the debate regarding the accuracy of the Reformation's understanding of Paul spans a good part of the twentieth century. Though the new perspective only crystallized toward the end of the century, the contributions of several authors anticipated some of its features. In order to appreciate Sanders' contribution, we will begin with a brief treatment of several important forerunners of his view.

CLAUDE G. MONTEFIORE

The first figure of note in the pre-history of the new perspective is the Jewish theologian Claude G. Montefiore. In a highly influential study written early in the twentieth century (*Judaism and St Paul: Two Essays*) Montefiore argued that the religion of

Palestinian Judaism differed greatly from the picture of it that emerges from Paul's writings.[5] Although Paul portrays the Judaizers as proponents of a joyless, legalistic religion, rabbinic Judaism of the first century 'was a better, happier, and more noble religion than one might infer from the writings of the Apostle'.[6] Based upon his study of rabbinic Judaism, Montefiore claimed that it emphasized God's mercy and love as much as his holiness.

It taught that God gave the law to his peculiar people Israel, not that it might be a burden or means of salvation by works, but a means of life and blessing. Rather than encouraging pride and self-righteousness, rabbinic Judaism emphasized that the blessings of the covenant would only be inherited through God's grace and mercy. Furthermore, the religion of rabbinic Judaism made provision for God's gracious atonement for the sins of his people, and emphasized the mercy of God in their final vindication. As a result of his studies, Montefiore concluded that the only feature of Judaism that conflicted with this generally positive outlook was its particularism or tendency to exclude non-Jews from the reach of God's grace.

Though some aspects of Montefiore's interpretation of rabbinic Judaism are not embraced by proponents of the new perspective, his general portrait of Judaism has become a significant element within the new approach to Paul. Few New Testament students today agree with Montefiore's opinion that Paul was not a rabbinic Jew but a member of the diaspora, whose pre-conversion religion was of a distinctly more legalistic or graceless cast. However, many believe that Montefiore successfully refuted the traditional view of Judaism, demonstrating the importance of a proper understanding of it for a new interpretation of the New Testament. If Palestinian Judaism was a religion of grace, then the older view, which interpreted the apostle Paul's teaching on justification as an antidote to Jewish legalism, needs to be reassessed.

GEORGE FOOT MOORE

A second figure whose studies of Judaism have played an important role in the emergence of the new perspective on Paul, is George Foot Moore, an American rabbinical scholar. In a substantial and oft-quoted article in the *Harvard Theological Review,* Moore argued that the traditional Christian interpretation of Judaism was largely distorted by polemical interests.[7] Rather than providing an accurate and fair assessment of Judaism, most traditional views were improperly shaped by the desire to enhance some feature of Christian teaching on the one hand, and to refute Judaism on the other. As a result, Moore maintained, Judaism was largely misunderstood by the Christian theological tradition.

Moore's study of Judaism served two purposes, both of which are significant to the new perspective. One was to view Judaism on its own terms, and not in terms of the distinctive themes of Christian theology. According to Moore, Judaism needs to become the subject of genuine historical study rather than a foil for Christian polemics. The other purpose was to refute Protestant theology's distortion of Judaism. Rather than viewing Judaism through the lens of the New Testament letters of the apostle Paul, Moore insisted that Judaism deserved to be an independent subject of study. Such a study, he maintained, will shed as much light upon the New Testament as the New Testament sheds upon Judaism. Instead of taking the New Testament's account of Judaism as our standard, we must view Judaism from a historical perspective, seeking to discover its character without the bias or influence of Christian interests. Since the Reformation, much of the study of Paul's writings has served to support the Protestant, and especially Lutheran, polemic against Roman Catholicism's legalism. Roman Catholicism is regarded as little more than a later expression of the same legalistic religion that characterized Judaism at the time of the writing of the New Testament. Judaism is not viewed from the standpoint of its own witnesses. Rather, it serves as a kind of 'whipping boy' for the typical Protestant criticism of any religion that views obedience to the law as the means of finding favour with God.

Moore, like Montefiore before him, repudiated this whole approach.[8] In Moore's approach, historical studies of Judaism are granted precedence over the teaching of the New Testament. The primacy and authority of Scripture are subordinated to the findings of historical science.

ALBERT SCHWEITZER

Unlike Montefiore and Moore, the next figure of note, Albert Schweitzer, represents a trend in twentieth-century New Testament studies that disputes the centrality of the doctrine of justification in the Pauline understanding of the gospel. Though neither Montefiore nor Moore sought to reassess Paul's teaching within the framework of their portrait of Judaism, they did lay the groundwork for revisiting Paul's writings to see whether his teaching on justification was actually formulated in opposition to a legalistic distortion of the gospel. Schweitzer's work has quite a different focus. Rather than concentrating on Palestinian Judaism, Schweitzer focused his attention on the writings of the apostle Paul in order to directly challenge the Reformation's claim that justification was the centre of his religious thought. Schweitzer was among the first Pauline scholars of note to argue that justification is at best a subsidiary feature of Paul's gospel.

In *The Mysticism of Paul the Apostle,* Schweitzer maintained that the primary emphasis in the Pauline epistles is the believer's union with Christ.[9] With the coming of Christ, the law no longer remains in force as before. Though Paul argued for a kind of *status quo* position on the role of the law—it remains to be observed by Jews who become Christians, but it has no binding force on Gentiles—his real concern lies, not with observance or non-observance of the law's requirements, but with the believer's salvation through mystical union with the crucified and risen Christ.

Within this context the problem of justification is really only a minor and subordinate theme. According to Schweitzer, it was simply the apostle's solution to the problem of how Gentiles could be members of Christ without having to obey the requirements of the law. Justification plays no other role in Paul's understanding of the gospel.

Consequently, Schweitzer concluded that 'the doctrine of righteousness by faith is . . . a subsidiary crater [in Paul's thought], which has formed within the rim of the main crater—the mystical doctrine of redemption through the being-in-Christ'.[10]

KRISTER STENDAHL

The last figure for us to consider in this brief sketch of the background to E. P. Sanders' work is Krister Stendahl. Though a theologian in the Lutheran tradition, Stendahl has played a significant role in contesting the traditional Reformation claim that Paul's thought was dominated by the doctrine of justification. In a highly influential article, 'Paul and the Introspective Conscience of the West', Stendahl challenged the entire western tradition's reading of the apostle.[11] According to him, this tradition, beginning with Augustine but also including Luther, Calvin, and the preponderance of Protestant scholars to the present day, misread Paul as though he developed the doctrine of justification to solve the problem of his own troubled conscience. Stendahl argued that this represented a basic misreading of the Pauline epistles:

> Where Paul was concerned about the possibility for Gentiles to be included in the messianic community, his statements are now read as answers to the quest for assurance about man's salvation out of a common human predicament.[12]

The western tradition, and particularly its Protestant expression, read Paul's account of the doctrine of justification not as Paul intended, but as dictated by an introspective conscience. In Stendahl's view, however, Paul had a robust and confident conscience before God, and exhibited little or none of the anxiety about human liberation from the burden of sin that has characterized the western view of salvation. His doctrine of justification was not an attempt on his part to solve the problem of an uneasy conscience before God, but to account for how Gentiles are now included with Jews among the people of God.

E. P. SANDERS—PAUL AND PALESTINIAN JUDAISM

Though various forerunners contributed to the emergence of a new perspective on Paul,[13] the most influential and pivotal is undoubtedly E. P. Sanders. The two features in the work of his forerunners, which we have just considered, come together in Sanders' writing in a way that has given shape to the development of a new perspective on Paul. On the one hand, Sanders carries forward the programme of reassessing the traditional view of Judaism. On the other hand, he offers a revised view of Paul's understanding of justification, which corresponds more adequately to what is thought to be the historical context of the apostle's writings. Sanders stands, therefore, as a transitional figure in the development of a new perspective on Paul. The dissatisfaction with traditional Protestant treatments of first-century Judaism, which was earlier expressed by Montefiore, Moore, and others, comes into clear focus in Sanders. Once the older view of Judaism is repudiated, as he argues it must be, then it is no longer tenable to maintain the older Protestant view of Paul.

The 'Pattern' of Religion in Palestinian Judaism: 'Covenantal Nomism'

Sanders, who is Emeritus Arts and Sciences Professor of Religion at Duke University, North Carolina (where he taught from 1990–2005), published *Paul and Palestinian Judaism* in 1977, which is now generally regarded as the classic presentation of Second-Temple Judaism.[14] Despite its title, the primary focus of Sanders' highly influential study is the 'pattern of religion' that characterized Palestinian or Second-Temple Judaism. Following the lead of Montefiore and Moore, Sanders sought to describe Palestinian Judaism in its own terms. Unlike Montefiore and Moore, however, he writes as an ostensibly Christian theologian who is interested in the implications of his study of Palestinian Judaism for a proper interpretation of Paul's understanding of the gospel.[15]

Sanders endeavoured to compare the pattern of religion evident in Paul's writings with that found in Jewish literature belonging to the period between 200 BC and AD 200. By a 'pattern of religion', Sanders means the way a religion understands how a person 'gets in' and 'stays in' the community of God's people.[16] Traditional accounts of the differences between religions, particularly the differences between Judaism and Christianity, have focused upon the distinctive essence or core belief of these religions. In doing so, Judaism was often simplistically described as a 'legalistic' religion, which emphasizes obedience to the law as the basis for inclusion, while Christianity was described as a 'gracious' religion, which emphasizes God's free initiative in calling people into communion with himself. Similarly, descriptive accounts of different religions, which focus upon their distinctive 'motifs' or 'themes', often lead to a distorted picture, since they take one religion's ideas as normative and then apply them to the other. According to Sanders, the best way to get an accurate picture of Judaism and Christianity is to compare their respective accounts of the way people enter into and remain within the community of faith.

The first part of Sanders' study involves a comprehensive examination of Jewish literature during the two centuries before and after the coming of Christ. Sanders concludes that Judaism exhibits a pattern of religion best described as 'covenantal nomism', which he defines as follows:

> The 'pattern' or 'structure' of covenantal nomism is this: (1) God has chosen Israel and (2) given the law. The law implies both (3) God's promise to maintain the election and (4) the requirement to obey. (5) God rewards obedience and punishes transgression. (6) The law provides for means of atonement, and atonement results in (7) maintenance or re-establishment of the covenantal relationship. (8) All those who are maintained in the covenant by obedience, atonement and God's mercy belong to the group which will be saved. An important interpretation of the first and last points is that election and ultimately salvation are considered to be by God's mercy rather than human achievement.[17]

Contrary to the assumption that Palestinian Judaism was legalistic, Sanders appeals to literary evidence to support the view that it was a religion of grace. The theme of God's gracious election is consistently sounded, according to Sanders, within the literature of the period. God graciously elects Israel to be his people; he mercifully provides a means of atonement and opportunity for repentance in order to deal with their sins.

Therefore, Israel did not 'get in' the covenant by human achievement but by God's gracious initiative. Obedience to the law, however, is the required means of maintaining or 'staying in' the covenant. The people of Israel were obliged to obey the law in order to maintain the covenant relationship and secure their inheritance at the final judgment.

On the basis of his independent and unbiased investigation of Palestinian Judaism, Sanders endorsed the basic claim of Montefiore and Moore that traditional Christian theology has seriously misrepresented Judaism as a graceless religion. Palestinian Judaism's emphasis upon obedience to the law does not compromise the priority of God's gracious initiative in the covenant relationship, but highlights the importance of obedience as a means of staying in the covenant and vindication at the final judgment.

The Apostle Paul: From 'Solution' to 'Plight'

One obvious problem resulting from Sanders' conclusions about Palestinian Judaism is the apostle Paul's polemic against Judaism. If Judaism was not a legalistic religion, what are we to make of Paul's vigorous arguments against those who would find favour with God on the basis of works or human achievement? Is Paul combatting a kind of 'straw man' in his letters (especially in Romans and Galatians), when he objects to a righteousness that is by the works of the law? In his *Paul and Palestinian Judaism* and in a sequel, *Paul, the Law, and the Jewish People*,[18] Sanders suggests that Paul's understanding of the human plight was a kind of by-product of his view of salvation. Paul started with Christ as the 'solution' to the human predicament, and then worked backward to explain the 'plight' to which his saving work corresponds. Paul has been traditionally interpreted to teach that the problem of human sinfulness, which is made known and aggravated through the law's demand for perfect obedience, calls for a solution in Christ's person and work. However, Sanders maintains that we should also recognize that Paul's understanding of the problem of sin derives from his convictions about Christ. Paul, in effect, starts from the basic conviction that Christ is the only Saviour of Jews and Gentiles and on this basis develops a doctrine of the law and human sinfulness corresponding to it.

According to Sanders, Paul rejected the law as a means of salvation for two principal reasons: first, because salvation only comes through faith in the cross of Christ; and second, because obedience to the law as a means of salvation would exclude the Gentiles. *Paul, therefore, did not oppose the law because he found himself unable to keep its demands.* He was not a prototype of the sinner (cf. Luther) who, burdened by his inability to do what the law required, could only find comfort in Christ's righteousness. Passages like Philippians 3:6–9 do not offer a critique of the law as a means of salvation, but of the law as an alternative to faith in Christ. He argues that this passage actually expresses a considerable confidence regarding a righteousness that is according to law.

What Paul opposes, however, is clinging to a righteousness (however real) that is an alternative to faith in Christ. His opposition to the law expresses his prior conviction that faith in Christ is the only way to salvation and inclusion among the people of God. Any insistence upon the law as a means of salvation would undermine the exclusive claim of salvation through faith in Christ and prevent Gentiles from being included among the true people of God.

Thus, the great problem with Judaism *was not that it was legalistic.* Paul did not contest Palestinian Judaism's insistence upon zeal for the law. Nor did he object to Judaism on the basis of a conviction that no amount of effort to obey the law could ever make a person acceptable to God. His real (and only) objection to Judaism, according to Sanders, was that it denied the new reality of God's saving work through Christ. In words often quoted, Sanders concludes: 'In short, *this is what Paul finds wrong in Judaism: it is not Christianity.*'[19]

THE DOCTRINE OF JUSTIFICATION

Though Sanders does not give a great deal of attention to the doctrine of justification in his studies of Paul and Palestinian Judaism, it is evident that his conclusions have implications for how this doctrine is to be understood.

Sanders does not agree with the Reformation perspective that justification addresses the problem of how a sinner (whether Jew or Gentile) can find acceptance with God. Consistent with his view of how Paul moves from solution to plight, he believes Paul's doctrine addresses the issue of *who belongs to the covenant community*. Justification is more of an ecclesiological issue (Who are numbered among the people of God?) than an individual one (How can I, a sinner, find acceptance with a righteous God?). Paul's main objection to Judaism was not that it taught a doctrine of justification by works. After all, Judaism was a form of covenantal nomism that also emphasized God's gracious initiative in salvation, while requiring obedience to the law as a means of maintaining the covenant relationship. In these respects, Paul's pattern of religion does not differ significantly from Judaism. The problem with Judaism, as we have noted, is that it fails to recognize the new way of entrance into the number of God's covenant people, a way equally open to Jews and Gentiles who put their faith in Jesus Christ.

Sanders therefore focuses upon this issue of inclusion. Paul's doctrine developed in support of his conviction that all believers in Christ are members of the new covenant community. Judaism's problem was not that it confused grace and works, or taught that we become members of the covenant community by human achievement. God's righteousness was misunderstood, as though it referred to the way members of the covenant community maintain their status rather than to the way God places one within the covenant community. In a complicated but revealing statement of his position, Sanders declares:

> To be righteous in Jewish literature means to obey the Torah and to repent of transgression, but in Paul it means to be saved by Christ. Most succinctly, righteousness in Judaism is a term which implies the maintenance of status among the group of the elect; in Paul it is a transfer term. In Judaism, that is, commitment to the covenant puts one 'in', while obedience (righteousness) subsequently keeps one in. In Paul's usage, 'be made righteous' ('be justified') is a term indicating getting in, not staying in the body of the saved. Thus when Paul says one cannot be righteous by works of law, he means that one cannot, by works of law, 'transfer to the body of the saved'. When Judaism said that one is righteous who obeys the law, the meaning is that one thereby stays in the covenant. The debate about righteousness by faith or

by works of law thus turns out to result from different usage of the 'righteous' word group.[20]

This gives a fairly comprehensive statement of Sanders' view of justification. He interprets Paul's doctrine of justification to be his way of explaining how God embraces Gentiles and Jews as members of his new covenant community. Justification refers to one's status as a member of the community, and that status is obtained by Jews and Gentiles alike through faith in Christ. Since membership in the new covenant community is through faith in Christ, it cannot be based upon the law or obedience to it. If membership in the body of Christ is open to Gentiles as well as Jews, through faith in the crucified and risen Christ, then it may not be restricted to those to whom the law was previously given (the Jews) or to those who come 'under the law' as the Judaizers were insisting. The righteousness of God, furthermore, is God's active fulfilment of his covenant promise to embrace Gentiles together with Jews within the number of his people.

There are remarkable similarities between some of Sanders' conclusions and the traditional Protestant account of Paul's view of justification. He acknowledges that justification is by grace through faith in Christ. It is also a judicial act, which declares Jews and Gentiles alike to be in the status of belonging to the covenant people of God. As he puts it, it is an act of 'transfer' in which God reveals his righteousness, or covenant faithfulness, by fulfilling the promise of incorporating Gentiles as well as Jews into the covenant community.

However, it should also be noted that his understanding of Paul's doctrine has several features that substantially differ from the view of the Protestant Reformation. In his opinion, justification is *not central* to Paul's understanding of the gospel; what is central is faith in Christ as the only way of salvation for Jew and Gentile alike. Therefore, justification is a subordinate teaching in Paul's gospel. Now that faith in Christ is the one way of salvation for all people, obedience to the law may no longer be regarded as a requirement for membership in the covenant community. Paul does not base his argument for the doctrine of justification upon the

conviction that the law can only condemn and aggravate the problem of human sinfulness. It is not formed against the background
of legalism, or the teaching that obedience to the law is the way to
find favour with God. No such legalism was present in the
Palestinian Judaism of Paul's day, nor was it something from which
Paul claims to be delivered by his conversion to Christ. Paul's
doctrine of justification in the context of the new covenant is
derived from his basic conviction that the way of salvation is now
simply through faith in Christ.

PRELIMINARY SUMMARY

To summarize the main themes of Sanders' work which have
influenced later authors advocating a new perspective on Paul, it
may be helpful to list them as follows:

The traditional Protestant view of (Palestinian) Judaism seriously
distorts its true character. First-century Judaism did not teach that
a person is saved through works or human achievement; rather,
Judaism taught that God saved his people Israel on the basis of his
gracious election and mercy.

The traditional Protestant claim that the teaching of Roman
Catholicism was a new version of the old error of Pharisaism
(which teaches salvation through works) is therefore incorrect.

Palestinian Judaism exhibited a pattern of religion best described
as 'covenantal nomism'. One becomes a member of God's covenant
community *by grace*, and remains a member *by works* performed
in obedience to the law. 'Getting in' the covenant is by grace;
'staying in' (and being vindicated at the last judgment) is by
works.

Paul's argument with Judaism (and therefore the Judaizers) was
not aimed at its legalism. Nor was Paul's argument with Judaism
based upon the assumption that the law can only condemn Jews
and Gentiles alike as sinners. The starting point for Paul's quarrel
with Judaism was that it was not Christianity. Since salvation
comes to all (for Jews *and* Gentiles) who believe in the crucified
Christ, *the great problem of Judaism is its exclusivism, not its
legalism*. The problem with Judaism was not so much its insistence
upon the necessity of obedience to the law as its insistence that

Gentiles must become (through obedience to the law) Jews in order to be saved.

The apostle developed his doctrine of the human plight (of sin) from his doctrine of salvation through faith in Christ. Faith in Christ being the only basis for salvation, obedience to the (Jewish) law must not be imposed upon anyone as the basis for inclusion among God's people.

Paul's doctrine of justification is not the principal focus or emphasis in his writings. Justification by grace through faith in Christ was Paul's explanation of how God is fulfilling his promise to embrace Gentiles as well as Jews among his people. God's righteousness, which is the basis for the believer's justification, is his gracious act of including Gentiles among the number of his people. Justification is about who belongs to God's covenant people, not how a sinner can find favour with God through the perfect obedience and substitutionary sacrifice of Christ.

Justification, though it has to do with our standing before God or being numbered among his covenant people, does not require that God graciously grants and imputes the perfect righteousness of Christ to believers.

THE CONTRIBUTION OF JAMES D. G. DUNN

James D. G. Dunn, Emeritus Lightfoot Professor of Divinity at the University of Durham, England, has authored a number of substantial volumes on the apostle Paul.[21] While acknowledging his indebtedness to Sanders, Dunn has made his own significant contribution to this area of Pauline studies and has influenced another prominent new-perspective writer, N. T. Wright, whom we will consider in our next chapter.

AGREEMENT WITH SANDERS' VIEW OF JUDAISM

Dunn's starting point is his fundamental agreement with Sanders' assessment of Second-Temple Judaism. In a 1982 lecture, 'The New Perspective on Paul', Dunn acknowledges that Sanders' study, *Paul and Palestinian Judaism,* represents a 'new pattern' of understanding the apostle. Dunn credits Sanders with breaking the stranglehold of the older Reformation view that had dominated

Pauline studies for centuries. So far as he is concerned, any future assessment of Paul's teaching will have to reckon with Sanders' conclusions.

According to Dunn, the main conclusion to be drawn from Sanders' research is that the 'picture of Judaism drawn from Paul's writings is historically false'.[22] The idea that there is a basic antithesis between Judaism, which supposedly taught a doctrine of salvation by meritorious works of obedience to the law of God, and Paul, who taught a doctrine of salvation by faith apart from the works of the law, needs to be set aside once and for all. This simply does not fit with what the historical sources tell us about Second-Temple Judaism.

Dunn fully concurs with Sanders' argument that Judaism's pattern of religion was that of *covenantal nomism*: Israel, God's graciously elected people, were obliged to obey the requirements of the law (Torah), not as a way of obtaining favour with God but only as a way of preserving the covenant relationship first initiated by grace.

Because he largely agrees with this interpretation of Judaism, Dunn also shares Sanders' rejection of the Reformation's reading of Paul's doctrine of justification. The Reformers' reading of the apostle Paul was a fundamental misreading. Judaism at the time of Paul's writing did not teach that obedience to the law of God was a means of obtaining favour with God. Therefore, whatever the Judaizers' error was to which Paul responded in his epistles (especially Galatians and Romans), it was not the kind of legalism that characterized the medieval doctrine of justification. No such legalism was present in the Judaism of his day.

Dunn concurs, therefore, with Sanders' insistence that a new reading of Paul is required, one that acknowledges the basic correctness of Sanders' insights into the nature of Second-Temple Judaism. This means that whatever erroneous teaching about the law Paul opposes in his epistles, it cannot be the kind of legalism that the Reformation opposed. The doctrine of justification, which plays such an important role in the apostle's argument with some of his contemporaries, was not developed as an antidote to Judaistic legalism.[23] Therefore, according to Dunn, Paul's doctrine of justification must be reconsidered in the light of what we now know about Judaism.

SANDERS' FAILURE TO UNDERSTAND PAUL ON THE LAW

Despite Dunn's general agreement with Sanders' view of Judaism, he does find fault with the sharp distinction Sanders draws between Paul's understanding of the Christian faith and the religion of Judaism. Rather than interpreting the apostle's writings in relation to Judaism's 'covenantal nomism', Sanders represents him as making a clean break with his old religion. The system or pattern of religion that Paul articulated requires faith in the crucified and risen Christ as the means of gaining entrance into covenant with God. Contrary to the religion of Judaism, which continues to uphold the law of God and insists upon its abiding validity, Paul draws a radical contrast between faith in Christ and the law. According to the apostle's gospel, Judaism and the law must be abandoned in favour of the Christian religion. Consequently, despite Sanders' rehabilitation of Judaism as a religion of grace, he still treats Paul's new-found faith as though it required a wholesale abandonment of Judaism.

> He [Sanders] still speaks of Paul breaking with the law, he still has Paul making an arbitrary jump from one system to another and posing an antithesis between faith in Christ and his Jewish heritage in such sharp, black-and-white terms, that Paul's occasional defence of Jewish prerogative (as in *Rom.* 9:4–6) seems equally arbitrary and bewildering, his treatment of the law and of its place in God's purpose becomes inconsistent and illogical, and we are left with an abrupt discontinuity between the new movement centred in Jesus and the religion of Israel which makes little sense in particular of Paul's olive tree allegory in Romans 11.[24]

In spite of Sanders' groundbreaking insight into the nature of Judaism, he fails to provide a coherent or convincing explanation of Paul's relation to Judaism and its view of the law of God. Sanders leaves his readers with the impression that Paul rejected Judaism entirely, and embraced an understanding of the Christian faith that was largely disconnected from his Jewish past. In this respect, Dunn reckons that Sanders fails to do for the interpretation of Paul what he does so masterfully for the interpretation of Judaism: he fails to interpret Paul within the context of first-century Judaism. Particularly perplexing is his suggestion that the apostle repudiated the law of God altogether, as though it were wholly antithetical to the gospel of Christ. But if, within Judaism itself the law was never understood to be a means of meriting favour with God, why would Paul find it necessary to reject Judaism's view of it in order to emphasize God's grace in Christ? Was Paul rejecting the law as such, when he contrasts the works of the law with faith in Christ? These questions are left unresolved by Sanders and lead Dunn to take a closer look at Paul's teaching on the law in relation to justification. Sanders' assessment of Judaism raises, but fails to answer, the question: How does the new view of Judaism contribute to a new perspective on Paul? In Dunn's words,

> 'The new perspective on Paul', by forcing a reassessment of what Paul was reacting against [the Judaism of his day], has given fresh impetus to this line of inquiry. What was at issue between Paul and 'those of the circumcision'? Can we continue to speak in terms of Jewish boasting in self-achieved merit? What is it about 'works of the law' to which Paul objects this strenuously?[25]

Though Sanders has provided the basis for a new perspective on Paul, his own interpretation of the apostle's gospel fails to show how Paul's view of the law arises within the context of the Judaism of his day. If the problem with Judaism's understanding of the law was not legalism, then what was wrong with its teaching? To what error is Paul responding, when he speaks of a justification that is not according to 'works of the law' but according to faith?

The 'Works of the Law' as 'Boundary Markers'

If the apostle's writings are approached from the perspective of the new view of Judaism, Dunn argues, we will discover that Paul's objection was to *Jewish exclusivism,* not its *legalism.* The problem with the use of the law among the Judaizers whom Paul opposed was not their attempt to find favour with God on the basis of obedience to the law, but their use of the 'works of the law' to exclude Gentiles from membership of the covenant community. The Judaizers were emphasizing certain 'works of the law' which effectively served as 'boundary markers', distinguishing who did and who did not belong to God's covenant people. Paul's rebuke is directed against this *social* use of the law as a means of excluding Gentiles, and not against the use of the law as a means of self-justification.

According to Dunn, Paul's real objection to the Judaizers' appeal to 'works of the law' is clearly disclosed in passages like Galatians 2:15–16 and Galatians 3:10–14. A brief review of Dunn's handling of these passages will suffice to illustrate the shape of his argument.

GALATIANS 2:15–16

We are Jews by nature, and not sinners from among the Gentiles; nevertheless knowing that a man is not justified by the works of the law but through faith in Christ Jesus, even we have believed in Christ Jesus, that we may be justified by faith in Christ, and not by the works of the law; since by the works of the law shall no flesh be justified.

When read within the historical context of first-century Judaism, Dunn draws the following points from this passage:

1. Paul is using language that was typical of Jewish Christians ('we who are Jews by nature'), reflecting an understanding of what it means to belong to the covenant community, separated from Gentile sinners. These verses focus on the question of who belongs to God's covenant people and who does not.

2. Because Paul is speaking from within the context of a common Jewish understanding, his concepts of righteousness and what it is to be justified are likewise 'thoroughly Jewish'.[26] To be justified means, in this context, to be acknowledged by God as a member of his covenant people. God's righteousness in justifying his people is his covenant faithfulness expressed by way of his gracious and merciful 'verdict in favour of Israel on (*sic*) grounds of his covenant with Israel'.[27] Justification is not an exclusively initiatory act (as Sanders tends to argue) whereby God introduces

someone into the covenant community. Rather, as in the Judaism with which Paul was undoubtedly familiar, it is God's gracious 'acknowledgment that someone is in the covenant'. This understanding of justification—indeed the teaching of 'justification by faith' itself—was common to the Judaism of Paul's day and to the teaching of Paul. If we read the apostle Paul's language in this passage within the historical setting of Judaism, we will not conclude that he is introducing a new doctrine of justification, or that he is opposing a Jewish teaching that we can earn our acquittal with God on the basis of 'meritorious works'. Such a reading of Paul is incompatible with what we know about Judaism, which also emphasized the grace and covenant faithfulness of God in acknowledging those who are his people.

3. This leads Dunn to identify the crux of the issue in Galatians 2:15–16. When Paul attacks the idea of being justified by 'the works of the law', he is attacking an insistence upon observing those requirements of the law that served to distinguish the Jews from the Gentiles. The phrase 'works of the law' refers, not to all the observances required in the law of God, but to those 'particular observances' that 'functioned as identity markers . . . to identify their practitioners as Jewish in the eyes of the wider public.'[28] These observances—such as circumcision, food laws, and feast-days— 'were the peculiar rites which marked out the Jews as that peculiar people'. The 'works of the law', therefore, are those 'badges of covenant membership' that served to separate the true covenant people (the Jews), from those who were outside of the covenant (the Gentiles).

Upon the basis of these considerations, Dunn concludes that Galatians 2:15–16 does not present an attack upon Judaism or its 'covenantal nomism'. Paul was not opposing legalism. Rather, he was taking issue with the idea that the 'works of the law' – those observances that particularly distinguish Jews from Gentiles – are necessary badges of covenant membership. Paul teaches that faith in Christ is the chief badge of covenant membership. This does not mean, however, that Paul is disparaging the law or law-keeping in general. He only objects to the law being used 'as a Jewish prerogative and national monopoly'.[29] He has no objection to the law being understood in terms of its more basic command to love your neighbour as yourself (*Gal.* 5:14).

GALATIANS 3:10–14

Dunn also illustrates his interpretation of Paul's understanding of the law from Galatians 3:10–14. While admitting that any interpretation of Paul's writings must also consider his other epistles, especially Romans, Dunn believes that this passage confirms his own interpretation of Galatians 2:15-16 in particular and of the apostle's other writings as well.

The Reformation reading of this passage is well known. When Paul quotes Deuteronomy 27:26, he means to remind his readers that it is impossible to fulfil the law's demands and that all sinners lie under the curse of God for their failure to do so. Salvation does not come through our obedience to the law, but rather through the work of Christ who became a 'curse' for us. Christ, who alone kept the law perfectly, has become a curse by suffering the liability of the law on behalf of those who put their trust in him. The promise of salvation for Jew and Gentile alike comes by faith in Jesus Christ.

Dunn argues that such an interpretation represents a fundamental misreading of the passage. As in the earlier Galatian passage, Paul's concern is not chiefly about how a guilty sinner can find a gracious God or be saved, but about how God is pleased to acknowledge Gentiles as well as Jews as members of his covenant community. He develops his argument for this interpretation along lines similar to those used in his treatment of Galatians 2:15-16.

1. To understand Paul's point in this passage, we must recognize that he is 'deliberately denying what his fellow countrymen . . . would take for granted'.[30] The Jews understood 'being of the works of the law' to mean living in obedience to all that the law requires. Paul however argues that 'To be of the works of the law is *not* the same as fulfilling the law, is *less* than what the law requires and so falls under the law's curse.'[31] Paul's referencing the 'works of the law' is aimed at the Jewish claim that only those who fulfil the law's *ritual* requirements (circumcision, food laws, feast days) fall within the scope of God's covenant promise. Therefore the contrast in the passage is not between the law (which Paul continues to

affirm in its deeper meaning and demands, cf. *Rom.* 2:14–16, 26–29), and faith in Christ; it is between those who advocate obedience to the ritual requirements of the law (so far as they separate the Jews from the Gentiles) and those who advocate faith in Christ as the way whereby the promise of inclusion within the covenant is fulfilled. Accordingly, the curse of which Paul speaks in this passage is not some general curse upon all sinners who fail to do what the law demands. It is the particular curse that falls upon Israel when she exhibits a restrictive and nationalistic misunderstanding of the scope of God's grace.

2. The contrasts in verses 11–12 of this passage (e.g., between 'by the law' and 'by faith') are not to be interpreted absolutely. Paul is not disparaging the idea of 'doing the law' as such. He is not arguing that the law and faith are mutually exclusive; rather, the Judaizers have a misplaced set of priorities. Whereas many of his fellow-Jews emphasized faithfulness to the law's ritual requirements more than faith in Christ, Paul insists that faith in Christ is paramount. The call to faith in Christ surpasses Judaism, for it is only by faith in Christ that the promise of the covenant is *now* fulfilled for Jews and Gentiles alike. The relation between Judaism and Christianity is, in this respect, not so much an 'either/or' as it is a 'both/and', with the emphasis falling upon the 'eschatological life of faith' foreshadowed by Habakkuk 2:4.[32]

3. The words of verses 13–14, which speak of Christ having redeemed us 'from the curse of the law, having become a curse on our behalf', should not be interpreted in a general sense. Paul is not referring to a generalized curse or condemnation deserved by every sinner, and which Christ has vicariously suffered on behalf of his people. According to Dunn, 'The curse of the law here has to do primarily with that attitude which confines the covenant promise to Jews as Jews: it falls on those who live within the law in such a way as to exclude the Gentile as Gentile from the promise.'[33] The curse that Christ's death removes is the curse of a wrong understanding of the law, one that restricts the reach of God's grace to Jews alone.

Understood in this light, Galatians 3:10–14 confirms that Paul's polemic against the Judaizers was not a general polemic against legalism or the law as such. Paul was opposing Jewish exclusivism, the teaching that the covenant community was limited to those who obeyed the ritual demands of the law. Such 'works of the law' do not justify, that is, count as badges of covenant membership. The chief badge of covenant membership is faith in Christ.

REDEFINING THE DOCTRINE OF JUSTIFICATION

With this understanding of Paul's view of the 'works of the law', Dunn articulates a very specific understanding of the apostle's doctrine of justification. This can best be summarized in the following points:

1. Paul's doctrine of justification is not addressed to the problem of legalism. The Reformation view of justification proceeds from a false assumption, namely, that Paul's opponents were attempting to find acceptance with God on the basis of meritorious obedience to the law's requirements. According to the Reformers, justification answers the question, how a guilty sinner can find acceptance with God. However, the specific problem addressed in Paul's formulation of the doctrine is the exclusivism of those Jews who insisted upon obedience to the ritual requirements of the law as a prior condition for acceptance into God's favour and covenant membership.

2. Because Paul's doctrine has its roots in the traditional Jewish understanding of God's 'righteousness' as his covenant faithfulness, he uses the term, 'to be justified', to refer to God's gracious acknowledgment of his covenant people. Though Judaism also taught justification by faith, the Christian gospel fulfils and surpasses Judaism by teaching that God *now* graciously acknowledges *all who believe in Christ* as his covenant people. The gospel announces that God in his righteousness has declared that all who believe in Christ, whether Jews or Gentiles, are acceptable to him. Justification is by 'faith alone' in the sense that faith in the crucified and risen Christ is now the *chief badge* of covenant membership.

3. Justification, though it has to do with God's verdict or pronouncement regarding whom he acknowledges as his people, does not involve the kind of legal transaction that the Reformers taught. God does not justify believers by granting and imputing to them the righteousness of Christ. The righteousness of God is his

covenant faithfulness, not the righteousness of Christ. Dunn has no place in his understanding of the doctrine of justification for the idea of Christ's 'active' and 'passive' obedience. The death of Christ is not a vicarious or substitutionary atonement, which involved Christ's suffering the curse of the law against guilty sinners. Rather, it is a 'representative' death in which believers share or participate.[34]

4. Because justification is an act of God's covenant faithfulness, whereby he accepts those who are his people in Christ, it is not, strictly speaking, a 'once-for-all-act of God'. The relationship with God that justification declares requires a continual exercise of God's righteousness. Furthermore, the initial justification of believers is always with a view to God's final act of judgment and acquittal. Justification, consequently, has several stages in its progressive enactment. It begins with God's acceptance of the believer, and it ends with God's vindication of the believer who remains steadfast by the obedience of faith to the end.[35]

5. Though Dunn embraces the formulation of a justification 'by faith alone', he insists that the 'covenantal nomism' of Judaism is not rejected by Paul in favour of a gospel of justification. Faith in Christ, though the distinctively Christian badge of covenant membership, is not opposed to the basic requirements of the law of God (e.g., the love commandment, the 'law of Christ'). The apostle's understanding of the gospel does not deny but affirms the pattern of religion known as covenantal nomism. Believers are obligated to keep the law in order to confirm and maintain their covenant relationship with God. Without the obedience of faith, there can be no expectation of final vindication by God, since 'only the doers of the law will be justified' (*Rom.* 2:13).[36]

CONCLUSION

On the basis of a fresh new study of the historical sources, the new perspective claims that the older Protestant understanding of the apostle Paul stands in need of serious revision. The Reformers were convinced that Second-Temple Judaism was a legalistic religion, and that this constituted the background to the development of Paul's doctrine of free justification. However, the studies of

Montefiore, Moore, and especially Sanders, claim that Judaism was a religion of grace.

It was a form of 'covenantal nomism', which taught that one entered the covenant community of Israel by grace and was maintained in it by obedience to the law. If this revised portrait of Judaism is assumed as the background for Paul's articulation of the gospel in his writings, the proverbial rug is pulled out from underneath the feet of the Reformation's assumption that he was opposing Jewish legalism. The doctrine as found in Paul's epistles can no longer be regarded as his solution to the problem of finding acceptance with God on the basis of meritorious works, since no such problem obtained within the orbit of Second-Temple Judaism.

Once the older assumptions regarding Judaism and Paul's polemics with the Judaizers are debunked, the question arises: What was the problem to which Paul's doctrine of justification was an answer? Though writers of the new perspective offer various answers to this question, the predominant answer, which was anticipated to an extent by earlier writers like Schweitzer and Stendahl, is that Paul's doctrine of justification addresses the particular problem of Gentile inclusion among the covenant people of God.

As Dunn in particular argues, the problem Paul addresses is that concerning membership of the covenant community. The 'works of the law' to which Paul's opponents appealed as the basis for justification were not acts of obedience to the law of God in general. They were those that peculiarly identified or set the boundaries around the people of God, and that excluded the Gentiles from membership in the covenant.

Paul's doctrine of justification, accordingly, is not his general answer to the universal predicament of sinners before God, but a particular answer to the problem of Jewish exclusivism in the first century of the Christian era. Justification is a theme in Paul's understanding of the gospel of Christ to be sure; but it is not the kind of dominant theme that the older perspective on Paul imagined it to be.

Notes

[1] Cf. Rudolf Bultmann, *Theology of the New Testament,* vol. 1 (New York: Charles Scribner's Sons, 1951), pp. 270–329; and Karl Barth, *Church Dogmatics,* vol. 4/1: *The Doctrine of Reconciliation* (Edinburgh: T. & T. Clark, 1956), pp. 514–642.

[2] This disjunction between biblical theology, which aims merely to describe the teaching of the biblical texts, and dogmatic or church theology, is a significant feature of biblical studies in the modern era. Johann Philipp Gabler's inaugural address of 1787, 'Von der richtigen Unterscheidung der biblischen und der dogmatischen Theologie und der rechten Bestimmung ihrer beider Zeile [Concerning the Proper Distinction Between Biblical and Dogmatic Theology, and the Correct Aim of Their Distinct Parts]' (in *Biblische Theologie des Neuen Testaments in ihrer Anfangszeit* [Marburg: N. G. Elwert, 1972], pp. 272–84), is often regarded as a seminal statement of this disjunction.

[3] For a sketch of this history, see Westerholm, *Perspectives Old and New on Paul,* pp. 101–63; and Waters, *Justification and the New Perspectives on Paul,* pp. 1–89.

[4] As noted previously, James D. G. Dunn first coined this language in a 1982 address, 'The New Perspective on Paul.' In a recent address, 'New Perspectives on Paul', N. T. Wright argues for a multiplicity of new perspective views: '. . . there are probably almost as many "New Perspective" positions as there are writers espousing it.' This article is available at: http://www.ntwrightpage.com/ Wright_New_Perspectives.htm.

[5] London: Max Goschen, 1914.

[6] *Judaism and St Paul,* p. 87.

[7] 'Christian Writers on Judaism', *Harvard Theological Review* 14 (1921), pp. 197–254.

[8] The subject of Judaism, whether Second-Temple Judaism or the subsequent stages of its development within Mishnaic and Talmudic Judaism, is a complicated and controversial one. Though it goes beyond the boundaries of our study, it is interesting to note that the most prolific Jewish author and scholar of the history of Judaism today is Jacob Neusner. Neusner disagrees strongly with the portrait of Judaism presented by Moore and E. P. Sanders, the principal source of the new perspective's view of Second-Temple Judaism. According to Neusner, Moore and Sanders' treatment of Judaism is also ironically skewed by the concerns of Protestant Christian theology. See, for example, Jacob Neusner, *Rabbinic Judaism: Structure and System* (Minneapolis: Fortress Press, 1995), esp. pp. 7–27, 45ff. Remarkably, Neusner's positive portrait of Pharisaic Judaism seems to correspond rather closely to that of the long-standing tradition of Protestant scholarship. What is unique to Pharisaic Judaism is its view of the Torah ('the law') as a total way of life and redemption

in relationship with God. For Neusner's interpretation of Pharisaic Judaism, see his *The Rabbinic Traditions About the Pharisees Before 70*, 3 vols. (reprint; Atlanta: Scholars Press, 1999 [1971]).

[9] London: A. & C. Black, 1931.

[10] *The Mysticism of Paul the Apostle*, p. 225.

[11] In *Paul Among Jews and Gentiles and Other Essays*, pp. 78–96. Stendahl first gave this address to the Annual Meeting of the American Psychological Association in 1961.

[12] 'Paul and the Introspective Conscience', p. 86.

[13] One of these figures whose work is of special significance is W. D. Davies. Davies' study, *Paul and Rabbinic Judaism: Some Rabbinic Elements in Pauline Theology* (4th ed.; Philadelphia: Fortress Press, 1980), anticipates some features of Sanders' work, especially the claim that Paul was thoroughly shaped by his background within Rabbinic Judaism of the first century of the Christian era. Sanders acknowledges that Davies was, in this respect, a 'transitional figure' in New Testament studies. For Sanders' assessment of Davies' contribution, see his *Paul and Palestinian Judaism: A Comparison of Patterns of Religion* (London: SCM, 1977), pp. 7–12.

[14] *Paul and Palestinian Judaism: A Comparison of Patterns of Religion* (London: SCM, 1977).

[15] I use the term 'ostensibly', since Sanders does not hold an evangelical view of the inspiration and authority of the Scriptures.

[16] *Paul and Palestinian Judaism*, p. 17.

[17] Ibid., p. 422.

[18] Minneapolis: Fortress Press, 1983.

[19] Ibid., p. 552. Cf. Sanders' comment on p. 497: 'It is the Gentile question and the exclusivism of Paul's soteriology which dethrone the law, not a misunderstanding of it or a view predetermined by his background.'

[20] Ibid., p. 544.

[21] Among the more important sources for an understanding of Dunn's view are the following: James D. G. Dunn, 'The New Perspective on Paul', in *Jesus, Paul and the Law. Studies in Mark and Galatians* (Louisville: Westminster/John Knox Press, 1970), pp. 183-215; idem, 'Paul and "covenantal nomism"', in *The Partings of the Ways Between Christianity and Judaism and their Significance for the Character of Christianity* (Philadelphia: Trinity Press International, 1991), pp. 117-139; idem, 'Works of the Law and the Curse of the Law (Galatians 3.10-14)', *New Testament Studies* 31 (1985), pp. 523-42; idem, *The Theology of Paul the Apostle* (Grand Rapids: Eerdmans, 1998); and idem, *Word Biblical Commentary*, vol. 38a: *Romans 1-8*, and vol. 38b: *Romans 9-16* (Dallas: Word Books, 1988); idem, 'Yet Once More—"The Works of the Law": A Response', *Journal for the Study of the New Testament* 46 (1992),

pp. 99-117; and *idem*, ed., *Paul and the Mosaic Law* (Grand Rapids: Eerdmans, 1996).

[22] 'The New Perspective on Paul', p. 184.

[23] Cf. *The Theology of Paul*, p. 338. One of the important impulses that necessitates this new view of Judaism, according to Dunn, is the 'fundamental issue of Christianity's relation to Judaism, in particular the relation of Paul's gospel and theology to his ancestral religion' (p. 338). Dunn believes that it is no longer possible, in a post-Holocaust and post-Vatican II context, to embrace the older Protestant claim that Judaism and Catholicism are forms of legalism.

[24] 'The New Perspective on Paul', p. 188.

[25] The Theology of Paul, *p. 340.*

[26] 'The New Perspective on Paul', p. 190.

[27] Ibid. It should be observed that Dunn simply assumes at this point that the 'to be justified' means 'to be acknowledged as a member of the covenant community'. It is not, as the Reformation commonly understood it, an act whereby God receives a guilty sinner into fellowship with himself on the basis of the righteousness of Jesus Christ.

[28] 'The New Perspective on Paul', p. 192.

[29] Ibid., p. 200.

[30] 'Works of the Law and the Curse of the Law', p. 534.

[31] Ibid., p. 534.

[32] Ibid., p. 536.

[33] Ibid.

[34] *The Theology of Paul*, p. 386. Though this language is rather bland and unclear, it is Dunn's language. When we take up our evaluation of the new perspective on Paul, we will have to return to this way of viewing Christ's death, not as a substitutionary but as a representative death. One of the more disconcerting features of the new perspective is the absence of a significant treatment of Christ's atoning work in all of its dimensions. This is not surprising, however, since the doctrine of justification is only a reflex of a proper understanding of Christ's work. The gospel is always the gospel of Christ and the glory of his saving work. So soon as we diminish the problem of sin, we inevitably diminish the accomplishments of the Saviour.

[35] *The Theology of Paul*, p. 386.

[36] Ibid., p. 365; 'Works of the Law and the Curse of the Law', p. 535.

5

A NEW PERSPECTIVE ON PAUL: N. T. WRIGHT

Of all the authors who are to some extent identified with the new perspective on Paul, perhaps none is as prolific or widely known as Nicholas Thomas ('Tom') Wright. Though Wright prefers not to be identified with some monochrome development called 'the new perspective' (since he judges that there are significant differences among authors associated with this view), he clearly writes as one convinced that a return to the older Reformation view would be a turning back of the clock.[1]

However, unlike some of the prominent authors associated with the new perspective, Wright regards himself as an evangelical whose commitment to the great tenets of Christian orthodoxy is unswerving. While acknowledging he no longer sees things in black and white as once he did, Wright professes to be a deeply orthodox theologian who wants to present a fresh reading and defence of the gospel to the post-modern world.

Christianity Today featured Wright in an article by Tim Stafford, who described him as 'a big-hearted, friendly bear of a man, who loves to talk, loves to debate on television, loves to preach, and thoroughly enjoys being [as he then was] Dean of Lichfield Cathedral near Birmingham, England'.[2] Evidently Tom Wright represents a rare combination of scholarship and church-manship; not only is he a New Testament scholar and author, but he is also an Anglican divine who is deeply committed to the ministry of the gospel within the church.[3] In addition to his advocacy of a new reading of the apostle Paul, he is known for his contributions to the study of the New Testament, and to the contemporary 'third quest' for the historical Jesus.[4] One reason why many evangelicals hold him in high esteem is his defence of such truths as the physical resurrection of Christ, and the historical reliability of the main lines of the New Testament witness to Christ.

Due to his scholarly reputation and success in advocating positions that are relatively conservative by the standards of critical scholarship, therefore, Wright enjoys considerable favour among evangelicals. This is one reason why his views regarding Paul's gospel and the doctrine of justification have gained credence within the evangelical and Reformed community. His writings also illustrate how the new perspective on Paul is not merely a matter of academic interest, but one that has clear implications for the ministry and proclamation of the contemporary church.

WRIGHT AND THE 'NEW PERSPECTIVE'

Despite Wright's reluctance to identify himself with anything so monolithic as 'the new perspective on Paul', he is persuaded that the studies of Sanders and others require a fresh reading of the apostle. Sanders and Dunn in particular have irrevocably altered the landscape of biblical studies. Consequently, any simple return to the past, particularly to the debates and positions of the sixteenth-century Reformation, would be highly irresponsible. Despite his stated dislike for labels like 'the new perspective on Paul', or for a simple identification of his views with those of other writers sympathetic to this perspective, Wright ought to be regarded as a leading advocate of a new approach to Paul. So far as he is concerned, the new approach to Pauline studies is here to stay, and he clearly regards himself as one of its champions. He maintains that there are two critical reasons why it is necessary.

First, agreeing with Sanders, Dunn, and others, Wright believes that first-century Judaism was not legalistic in form. The idea that the Judaizers taught salvation on the basis of works-righteousness is largely a fiction, for the reasons we have already outlined in chapter 4. Whatever Paul's problems with Judaism were, they are not to be connected with legalism, since we know that Judaism advocated no such legalism in Paul's day.

Wright's endorsement of Sanders' new view of Judaism and its importance for understanding Paul's gospel is unmistakable. He says, 'the tradition of Pauline interpretation has manufactured a false Paul by manufacturing a false Judaism for him to oppose.'[5] Since it identifies Judaism as a form of legalism that anticipated the medieval Roman Catholic teaching of salvation by faith plus works, this interpretation of Paul fails to properly identify the true target of his polemical presentation of the doctrine of justification. Indeed, the Reformation's understanding of the gospel of free justification amounts to what Wright terms 'the retrojection of the Protestant Catholic debate into ancient history, with Judaism taking the role of Catholicism and Christianity the role of Lutheranism.'[6] Because the Reformation misunderstood the problem to which Paul was actually responding, it failed to grasp the real meaning of Paul's teaching on justification by faith.

Second, Wright also makes considerable use of Dunn's interpretation of Paul's dispute with the Judaizers and their understanding of the 'works of the law'. The problem with the Judaizers' appeal to the 'works of the law' was not its legalism, Wright insists, but its *perverted nationalism*. According to Wright,

> If we ask how it is that Israel has missed her vocation, Paul's answer is that she is guilty not of 'legalism' or 'works-righteousness' but of what I call 'national righteousness', the belief that fleshly Jewish descent guarantees membership of God's true covenant people. . . . Within this 'national righteousness', the law functions not as a legalist's ladder but as a charter of national privilege, so that, for the Jew, possession of the law is three parts of salvation: and circumcision functions not as a ritualist's outward show but as a badge of national privilege.[7]

The problem Paul confronted in his dispute with the Judaizers was a 'boasting' in national privilege, and an unwillingness to acknowledge that the covenant promise extends to Gentile as well as Jew.[8] The Reformation's claim, therefore, that Paul was opposing legalism when he articulated his doctrine of justification misses the mark rather widely. Paul was not opposing legalism, but nationalism. Consequently, the Reformation's reading of Paul transposes his understanding into a radically different key, when it treats the Judaizers as prototypes of a Roman Catholic doctrine of justification by (grace plus) works.

WRIGHT'S VIEW OF JUSTIFICATION BY FAITH

Wright's understanding of Paul's doctrine of justification by faith assumes these two pillars of the new perspective. Whatever the apostle Paul might mean by his insistence that justification is by faith and not by works of the law, it cannot be that sinners, whether Jews or Gentiles, are unable to obtain favour with God on the basis of their obedience to the law. Though this may well be true, no one in Paul's day would have thought otherwise. Paul's doctrine of justification must therefore be read in the historical context of the first century, and in the light of the Old Testament's teaching regarding the promise of the covenant. Wright believes that when Paul's gospel is read in this way, which requires that we set aside the mistaken approach of the Reformation, we will find that 'what Saint Paul really said' was rather different from what many have historically claimed.

THE 'GOSPEL' ACCORDING TO WRIGHT

Before taking up Wright's view of justification, it is important to note that he regards this doctrine as a subordinate theme in Paul's understanding of the gospel. To see the gospel merely as a 'system of how people get saved', is to seriously misrepresent its real meaning.[9] The gospel is not addressed to the guilty sinner's question, 'How can I find favour with God?' but rather answers the question, 'Who is Lord?' One of the unfortunate features of the Reformation and much evangelical thinking since, according to Wright, is the reduction of the gospel to 'a message about "how one gets saved", in an individual and ahistorical sense'.[10] In this kind of thinking, the focus of attention, so far as the gospel is concerned, is upon 'something that in older theology would be called an *ordo salutis,* an order of salvation'.[11] According to Wright, this kind of approach only distorts Paul's gospel and fails to do justice to the broader historical background and significance of Christ's saving work. Such an approach to the gospel focuses too narrowly on the issue of the individual's relationship with God, and not upon the reach of God's world-transforming power proclaimed in Jesus Christ. As a result of this inappropriate focus the older Reformation tradition was bound to exaggerate the importance of the doctrine of justification. Even were its understanding of justification correct, which it is not, it tends to focus upon what is only a subordinate theme in Paul's proclamation of the gospel in Wright's view.

If the gospel is not primarily about how people get saved, then what is its main focus? According to Wright it is essentially *the lordship of Jesus Christ*:

> Paul's new vocation involved him not so much in the enjoyment and propagation of a new religious experience, as in the announcement of what he saw as a public fact: that the crucified Jesus of Nazareth had been raised from the dead by Israel's God; that he had thereby been vindicated as Israel's Messiah; that, surprising though it might seem, he was therefore the Lord of the whole world.[12]

We will have occasion to return to the question of how Wright views the cross of Christ, especially in terms of its importance for justification. Here it only needs to be noted that the principal message of the gospel is 'Jesus is Lord and King'. Through the cross and resurrection of Jesus Christ, the one true God, who is the Creator of the world, has won a 'liberating victory . . . over all the enslaving powers that have usurped his authority'.[13]

Though Wright does not often clearly define what he means by the lordship of Jesus Christ, he does offer the following summary description:

> Paul discovered, at the heart of his missionary practice, that when he announced the lordship of Jesus Christ, the sovereignty of King Jesus, the very announcement was the means by which the living God reached out with love and changed the hearts and lives of men and women, forming them into a community of love across traditional barriers, liberating them from paganism which had held them captive, enabling them to become, for the first time, the truly human beings they were meant to be.[14]

The great theme of the gospel is this message of Jesus' lordship and its life- and world-transforming significance. Paul's gospel focuses upon the story of Israel's God, who created the cosmos and intends to redeem it through his people Israel, the new humanity, and claims that this story is being fulfilled in the person and work of Jesus, the Christ. Therefore to interpret Paul's message largely in terms of the question of individual salvation is to narrow the range of the apostle's vision. Justification is about who belongs to the family of God.

Such an understanding of the gospel's message has clear implications for Paul's doctrine of justification. Though an essential albeit subordinate theme in Paul's preaching, justification does not address the issue of how guilty sinners can find favour or standing with God. This would be to assume that Paul's gospel focuses upon the salvation of the individual rather than upon the lordship of Jesus Christ and the consequences of that lordship for the realization of God's covenant promises. However, when we view the gospel in terms of the lordship of Jesus Christ, the proper meaning and place of the doctrine of justification becomes apparent. 'Let us be quite clear', says Wright.

> 'The gospel' is the announcement of Jesus' lordship, which works with power to bring people into the family of Abraham, now redefined around Jesus Christ and characterized solely by faith in him. 'Justification' is the doctrine which insists that all those who have this faith belong as full members of this family, on this basis and no other.[15]

In order to appreciate the full meaning of this summary statement of the doctrine of justification, we need to consider briefly several distinct aspects of Wright's understanding. Chief among these are:

(1) his interpretation of the phrase 'the righteousness of God' as the basis for the justification of God's people;

(2) the precise meaning of the term 'to justify';

(3) the role of faith as the 'badge' of covenant membership or justification;

(4) the past, present, and future tenses of justification; and

(5) the relation between Christ's resurrection and the church's justification.

1. THE 'RIGHTEOUSNESS OF GOD'

Students of the Reformation are well aware that one of the key Pauline phrases for a proper understanding of justification is 'the righteousness of God' (*Rom.* 1:16–17; 3:21–26). Following Luther's 'discovery' that the righteousness of God is not so much the demand of God's law as the gift of his grace in Christ, the Reformers taught that we are justified by the free gift of God's righteousness in Christ, which is granted and imputed to believers. In this understanding, the righteousness of God is revealed through Christ who, by his obedience to the law and substitutionary endurance of its penalty, is the believer's righteousness before God. Justification is a judicial concept, and describes the way all of the requirements of the law have been met for the believer through the work of Christ. Those who receive the free gift of God's righteousness in Christ by faith stand acquitted and accepted before God.

Following the lead of Sanders, Dunn, and others, Wright insists that this Reformation view amounts to a profound misunderstanding of the phrase 'the righteousness of God'. He maintains that

> For a reader of the Septuagint, the Greek version of the Jewish scriptures, 'the righteousness of God' would have one obvious meaning: God's own faithfulness to his promises . . . God has made promises; Israel can trust those promises. God's righteousness is thus cognate with his trustworthiness on the one hand, and Israel's salvation on the other.[16]

Though the Reformation view rightly emphasized that the righteousness of God reflects a 'legal metaphor' taken from the law court, it apparently misapplied this terminology by misunderstanding the way the Hebrews understood the functioning of righteousness in the judgment of the court.[17] In the Hebrew court of law, there are three parties: the judge, the plaintiff, and the defendant. When the judge pronounces a verdict in the court in favour of the plaintiff or the defendant, we may say that he has been 'vindicated against the accuser; in other words, acquitted'.[18] This is the only meaning that the term 'righteous' has, when it is applied to the person in whose favour the judge acts: that person is, so far as the court's action is concerned, in the *status of being acquitted or righteous*. So far as the court's judgment is concerned, the person who is righteous has the status of being vindicated or being in favour with the court.

Even though Wright acknowledges, as the Reformers also insisted, that 'the righteousness of God' reflects a legal or forensic setting, he also argues that the vindication of someone in God's court *does not involve God's granting or imputing anything whatever to the person whom he vindicates.*

> If we use the language of the law court, it makes no sense whatever to say that the judge imputes, imparts, bequeaths, conveys or otherwise transfers his righteousness to either the plaintiff or the defendant. Righteousness is not an object, a substance or a gas which can be passed across the courtroom.[19]

When 'the righteousness of God' is revealed, Wright understands this to mean that God reveals his covenant faithfulness by keeping his promise to his people, vindicating them as 'righteous'. Since this righteousness is God's own faithfulness to his covenant promise, it is not something he can bestow upon or impart to his people.

2. WHAT IT IS 'TO BE JUSTIFIED'

It is claimed that just as the Reformers misunderstood 'the righteousness of God', so they also misunderstood Paul's use of the term 'justification'. In the popular mind, justification is taken to be the answer to the problem of sinners who try to find favour with God by doing good works. There is a sinful tendency in all of us to try to pull ourselves up by our own moral bootstraps, to seek to find favour with God on the basis of our achievements or efforts. Whether in the form of Pelagianism, which teaches that sinners are saved on the basis of the performance of good works in obedience to the law, or semi-Pelagianism, which teaches that sinners are saved on the basis of God's grace plus our good works—there is an inescapable tendency to base human salvation upon self-effort. The doctrine of justification is the only antidote to all such Pelagian or semi-Pelagian views of salvation, because it teaches that salvation is an unmerited gift of God's grace in Christ to sinners who receive the gospel promise by faith alone. In Wright's estimation, this popular opinion regarding justification, whatever its merits, 'does not do justice to the richness and precision of Paul's doctrine, and indeed distorts it at various points.'[20]

According to Wright, Paul's doctrine of justification did not serve to answer the 'timeless' problem of how sinners can find acceptance with God, but to explain how one can tell who belongs to 'the community of the true people of God'. When justification is interpreted in the light of its Old Testament and Jewish background, its covenantal nature will be recognized. The term does not describe how someone enters the community of God's people but rather *who belongs to that community*, both now and in the future. In Paul's Jewish context, Wright maintains that

> 'justification by works' has nothing to do with individual Jews attempting a kind of proto-Pelagian pulling themselves up by their moral bootstraps, and everything to do with the definition of the true Israel in advance of the final eschatological showdown. Justification in this setting, then, is not a matter of *how someone enters the community of the true people of God*, but of *how you tell who belongs to that community*, not least in the period of time before the eschatological event itself, when the matter will become public knowledge.[21]

Since justification has to do with God's recognition of who belongs to the covenant community, it is not so much a matter of 'soteriology as about ecclesiology; not so much about salvation as about the church'.[22]

It is argued that when Paul's teaching about justification is read within the context of Judaism's traditional understanding of the covenant, it identifies those who belong to the community of God's people. Within Judaism, justification does not refer to the way believers enter into a relationship with God but to the way believers are identified as belonging to his people.

'Justification' in the first century was not about how someone might establish a relationship with God. It was about God's eschatological definition, both future and present, of who was, in fact, a member of his people. In Sanders' terms, it was not so much about 'getting in', or indeed about 'staying in', as about 'how you could tell who was in'. In standard Christian theological language, it wasn't so much about soteriology as about ecclesiology; not so much about salvation as about the church.[23]

When the righteousness of God is revealed in the death and resurrection of Jesus Christ, God confirms his faithfulness to his covenant by securing the inclusion of all members of the covenant community. The community consists of all those who are baptized into Christ and marked by the 'badge' of covenant membership, which is faith. Justification refers, therefore, to the identification and inclusion of all believers, whether Jews or Gentiles, who are part of the covenant family of God.

3. Faith, the Badge of Covenant Membership

Since justification focuses upon God's declaration regarding *membership* in the covenant community, Wright interprets Paul's insistence that justification is by faith and not by works, in a manner that is quite similar to Dunn. The boasting of the Judaizers was not born of self-righteousness, but arose from a kind of misplaced nationalistic pride and exclusivism. The 'works of the law' were those requirements of the law that served to distinguish Jews from Gentiles and thereby exclude Gentiles from the covenant community.

However, now that Christ has come to realize the covenant promise of God to Abraham, faith in Christ is the *only badge* of membership in God's worldwide family, which is composed of Jews and Gentiles alike. Paul's insistence that justification is by faith expresses his conviction that with the coming of Christ God is 'now extending his salvation to all, irrespective of race' (p. 122).

Justification . . . is the doctrine which insists that all who share
faith in Christ belong at the same table, no matter what their
racial differences, as together they wait for the final creation.[24]

One of the surprising and provocative implications of this understanding of justification, according to Wright, is that it radically
undermines the usual polemics between Protestants and Catholics.
Whereas many Protestants have historically argued that justification is a church-dividing doctrine, according to Wright,
precisely the opposite is the case: Paul's doctrine of justification
demands an inclusive view of membership in the one family of
God.

Many Christians, both in the Reformation and in the counter-
Reformation traditions, have done themselves and the church a
great disservice by treating the doctrine of 'justification' as
central to their debates, and by supposing that it describes that
system by which people attain salvation. They have turned the
doctrine into its opposite. Justification declares that all who
believe in Jesus Christ belong at the same table, no matter what
their cultural or racial differences.[25]

Protestants who insist upon a certain formulation of the doctrine
of justification as a precondition to church fellowship, accordingly,
are guilty of turning the doctrine on its head. Rather than serving
its proper purpose of joining together all who believe in Christ as
members of one family (faith being the only badge of covenant
membership), it is transformed into the doctrine of justification 'by
believing in justification by faith'.[26]

4. JUSTIFICATION: PAST, PRESENT, AND FUTURE

One feature receiving special emphasis in Wright's understanding of justification is its nature as an eschatological
vindication of God's people. When God justifies or acknowledges
those who are members of his covenant community, he does so in
anticipation of their 'final justification' or vindication at the last
judgment. Justification occurs in three tenses or stages—past,
present, and future. The justification of God's covenant community

in the present is founded upon 'God's past accomplishment in Christ, and anticipates the future verdict.'[27]

In the *past* event of Christ's cross and resurrection, God has already accomplished in history what he will do at the end of time. Jesus, who died as the 'representative Messiah of Israel', was vindicated or justified by God in his resurrection from the dead. This event, Christ's resurrection, represents God's justification of Jesus as the Son of God, the Messiah, through whom the covenant promise to Abraham ('in your seed all the families of the earth will be blessed') is to be fulfilled. Because that promise comes through the crucified and risen Christ, it cannot come through the law (*Rom.* 8:3).

This past event of Christ's justification becomes a *present* reality through faith. All those who believe in Jesus as Messiah and Lord are justified, that is, acknowledged by God to be members of the one great family of faith composed of Jew and Gentile alike. Because the present reality of justification focuses upon membership in the covenant community—justification being, as we noted above, a matter of ecclesiology and not of soteriology—baptism into Christ is the event that effects this justification. 'The event in the present which corresponds to Jesus' death and resurrection in the past, and the resurrection of all believers in the future, is baptism into Christ.'[28]

Though justification has a past and present dimension, its principal focus lies in the future. At the final judgment or 'justification', God will declare in favour of his people, the covenant community promised to Abraham.

In this final justification, God's vindication of his people will even include a 'justification by works'. Commenting on Romans 2:13 ('It is not the hearers of the law who will be righteous before God, but the doers of the law who will be justified'), Wright insists that 'those who will be vindicated on the last day are those in whose hearts and lives God will have written his law, his Torah'.[29] Clearly justification does not exclude those 'works of the law' that are produced in the life of the obedient believer by the working of the Spirit.

5. JUSTIFICATION AND THE WORK OF CHRIST

One final feature of Wright's new view of justification, which remains rather undeveloped and unclear, is its basis in the work of Christ. As we noted above, he speaks of Christ's cross as a representative death and of his resurrection as a vindication by God. However, it remains rather unclear what Wright understands by Christ's atoning work and how it is related to the believer's justification.

One thing that does emerge clearly in Wright's limited treatment of this subject is his lack of sympathy for the historic view that Christ's cross involved his suffering the penalty and curse of the law on behalf of his people. In an extended treatment of Galatians 3:10–14, for example, Wright insists that its language 'is designed for a particular task within a particular argument, not for an abstract systematised statement'.[30] Galatians 3 is not about Christ suffering the curse of the law in the place of his people, all of whom have violated the law and are therefore liable to its curse. Paul is not talking about a general work of Christ that benefits sinful Jews and Gentiles alike. The traditional reading of this passage, which takes it to refer to Christ's substitutionary atonement, is, in Wright's view, mistaken.[31] If this passage is read in its first-century Jewish context and within the setting of God's covenant promise to Israel, it will become evident that Paul is talking about the curse of the exile, which Israel is experiencing as a people. Wright maintains that 'in the cross of Jesus, the Messiah, the curse of exile itself reached its height and was dealt with once and for all, so that the blessing of covenant renewal might flow out the side, as God always intended'.[32]

Wright's reading of Galatians 3 is rather characteristic of his general treatment of the subject of Christ's atoning work. Though it is clear that he has little sympathy for the older, Reformation understanding of Christ's saving work, what he is prepared to offer as an alternative remains rather obscure. Christ's death and resurrection are representative of Israel's exile and restoration. They are the means whereby the promise of the covenant is now extended to the whole worldwide family of God. However, because his understanding of Paul's gospel and the doctrine of justification has little, if anything, to do with the problem of human sinfulness and guilt, his understanding of the work of Christ likewise puts little emphasis upon the themes that have historically formed an essential part of the doctrine of Christ's atonement.[33]

A SUMMARY OF THE MAIN THEMES OF THE NEW PERSPECTIVE

During the course of this survey of the key proponents of a new perspective on Paul, we have acknowledged more than once that there are significant differences in viewpoint between them. No careful reading of the contributions of the three leading figures we have considered can fail to discern how they differ on several particular points. It is a little misleading, therefore, to speak of 'a new perspective' on Paul. As Wright has recently suggested, perhaps it would be more accurate to speak of 'new perspectives' on Paul.[34] Despite these differences, however, there are themes that clearly identify this perspective as a significant alternative to the older perspective of the Reformation.

Before we present our critical assessment of the new perspective, it will be useful to offer a summary of its main themes. This summary will also serve as an outline for the following chapters, each of which will offer a critical examination of these claims roughly in the order in which they are presented here.

(1) First, the new perspective is based upon a comprehensive re-evaluation and re-assessment of the patterns of religious belief among the Pharisees and the Jewish community contemporaneous with the writing of the New Testament. Contrary to the Reformation's claim that the Pharisees in particular, and Judaism in general, were representative of a 'works righteousness' religious practice, the new perspective maintains that Second-Temple or Palestinian Judaism emphasized God's gracious election and initiative in embracing his people, Israel. Judaism never taught that those who belonged to the covenant community were members of it by virtue of their own good works and acts of obedience to the law (Torah) of God. Rather, it was a religion of grace in which

believers were brought into covenant relationship with God by the initiative of his electing grace. To be sure, those who were members of the covenant community were obligated to obey the law of God in order to maintain their position within it. But this obedience to the law was not the ground upon which Israel was embraced within God's favour. Therefore, according to the new perspective, the Reformation's claim that Judaism was a legalistic religion, which anticipated the legalism of the Roman Catholic Church, is untenable.

The new perspective believes that the older reading of Paul paid insufficient attention to the historical background and context for his presentation of the Christian gospel. In order to understand the apostle's epistles, and for that matter the New Testament Scriptures, it is necessary to begin with a careful study and analysis of the Judaic background of Paul's gospel. When Paul was converted, he did not cease to be the man he was previously within Judaism. Instead he discovered in the gospel of Christ the fulfilment and realization of all that was true within Judaism. According to proponents of the new perspective, the error of the Reformation's reading of the apostle Paul stemmed from its failure to read his letters in their first-century context. This failure was due to the Reformation's pre-occupation with the teaching of medieval Roman Catholicism on the doctrine of justification. As a result the Reformers tended to view Judaism as a kind of proto-type of Roman Catholicism with its legalistic teaching about salvation.

(2) Second, the Reformation's insistence upon a sharp distinction between law and gospel in the believer's justification is likewise based upon a misreading of the gospel and of Paul's experience. Whereas the Reformers viewed the law as exposing human (whether Jewish or Gentile) sinfulness before God, the new perspective insists that the problem within Judaism was not the law as such, but Israel's claim to be the *exclusive* community of God's people. The boasting opposed by Paul in his epistles is not the claim to find favour with God on the basis of obedience to the law. Rather, it is the boasting in those 'works of the law' that *distinguish* Jews from Gentiles, and mark off the former as the exclusive

recipients of God's favour and mercy. According to the new perspective, the problem the apostle opposed was not one of a self-righteous boasting before God, which assumes that our standing with God is based upon meritorious good works. It was the exclusivistic claims of many Jews who maintained that they alone were numbered among the people of God by virtue of their keeping certain requirements of the law (circumcision, feast day observances, dietary laws), which distinguished or separated them from the Gentiles.

Contrary to the Reformation's claim that the gospel is the solution to the plight of human sinfulness (and therefore the gospel is really about how sinners can be saved), the new perspective maintains that Paul's gospel starts with the conviction that faith in Christ is the one way to inclusion among the covenant people of God. From that conviction Paul develops his particular view of the law, not as an instrument whereby our sinfulness is aggravated, but as an instrument whereby Israel sought to oppose the inclusion of Gentiles among the people of God. The problem with Judaism was not that the law was viewed as a means of self-justification before God, but that the law was misused as a means of excluding the Gentiles.

(3) Third, the new perspective argues that Paul's doctrine of justification, accordingly, was not the central theme of his gospel, nor was it addressed to the problem of legalism. Justification is a doctrine that addresses the specific problem of who is included within the covenant community, particularly whether Gentiles also are included. When Paul speaks, therefore, of justification by grace through faith, apart from the works of the law, he is teaching that all become members of the covenant community through faith in Christ, not by submitting to the requirements for inclusion among the Jews as a distinct people. This means that the problem with Judaism was not that it was legalistic and self-righteous; rather it was that Judaism was simply not Christianity. It did not recognize the new reality of God's saving presence in Jesus Christ whereby all are brought into the number of God's covenant people. 'Justification', therefore, is a covenant membership term; it identifies

those whom God acknowledges to be members of his covenant people. Furthermore, 'the righteousness of God', which is closely linked with the revelation of the justification of all who believe, refers to God's covenant faithfulness in action. The righteousness of God is not, as the Reformers commonly taught, something that is granted or imputed to believers who are united to Christ. Rather, the righteousness of God refers to what God has done in Jesus Christ to secure the inclusion of the Gentiles among his people in fulfilment of his covenant promises. 'The righteousness of God' and 'justification' must be understood in the context of the realization of God's covenant purposes in history through Jesus Christ.

(4) Some authors of the new perspective maintain that the Reformation's zeal to exclude good works altogether from playing any role in the believer's justification was inordinate. Just as Judaism taught that God's people are admitted into the covenant by grace, but kept in the covenant by a life of faithful covenant keeping, so the apostle Paul taught a kind of initial justification (or inclusion among the covenant people) by grace and a further or final justification by works. The new perspective maintains that the Reformation's understanding of justification failed to recognize that Paul developed the doctrine in relation to the specific problem of Judaizers who refused to include the Gentiles within the covenant people of God. It also failed to realize that, once a believer is included among the people of God, works done in obedience to the law play a legitimate role in 'maintaining' the covenant relationship. Indeed, when Paul says that 'only doers of the law will be justified' (*Rom.* 2:13), he is speaking of the final (or eschatological) justification in which the believer's works will play an important role. The answer, therefore, to the apparent problem of the Reformation's doctrine of justification—if we are saved by grace alone, then what becomes of the necessity of our good works?—is the recognition that justification has both an initial and a final reference. Believers enjoy their initial justification or inclusion among God's covenant people by grace alone, but their final justification is based in part upon their continuance in the way of obedience.

NOTES

[1] 'A *Reformation & Revival Journal* Interview with N. T. Wright: Part One', *Reformation & Revival Journal* 11/1 (Winter, 2002), pp. 117–39. The expression, 'turning back the clock', is Wright's (p. 128).

[2] *Christianity Today* (8 February 1999), p. 43. Since the writing of this article, Wright has become the Anglican Bishop of Durham.

[3] Wright's substantial volumes in New Testament studies and in the contemporary 'third quest' for the historical Jesus include: *The New Testament and the People of God* (Minneapolis: Fortress, 1992); *Christian Origins and the Question of God*, 3 vols. (Minneapolis: Fortress, 1992, 1996, 2003); *The Climax of the Covenant: Christ and the Law in Pauline Theology* (Minneapolis: Fortress, 1991); and *Who Was Jesus?* (Grand Rapids: Eerdmans, 1992). Among Wright's works that most directly represent his understanding of Paul and the doctrine of justification are the following: *What Saint Paul Really Said*; 'New Perspectives on Paul', www.ntwrightpage.com/Wright_New_Perspectives,htm; 'The Paul of History and the Apostle of Faith', *Tyndale Bulletin* 29 (1978), pp. 61-88; 'The Law in Romans 2', in *Paul and the Mosaic Law*, ed. James D. G. Dunn (Grand Rapids: Eerdmans, 1996), pp. 131-50; 'The Shape of Justification', www.thepaulpage.com/Shape.html; *The Letter to the Romans*, vol. 10 of *The New Interpreter's Bible* (Nashville, TN: Abingdon Press, 2002); and *Paul for Everyone: Romans Part 1, Chapters 1-8* (Louisville, KY: Westminster John Knox Press, 2004); and 'On Becoming the Righteousness of God: 2 Corinthians 5:21', in *Pauline Theology*, vol. 2, ed. David M. Hay (Minneapolis, MN: Augsburg Fortress, 1993), pp. 200-08. Wright has recently written a new book on Paul, *Paul in Fresh Perspective* (Minneapolis: Fortress, 2005). Unfortunately, the present study was completed before Wright's book was published, but this latest book does not seem to add anything significant to his previously published works.

[4] The 'third quest' for the historical Jesus is, as the language indicates, the third in a series of scholarly attempts to verify the historicity of the biblical Gospels' account of the life and ministry of Christ. For an account of the third quest, see Ben Witherington III, *The Jesus Quest: The Third Search for the Jew of Nazareth* (Downers Grove, IL: InterVarsity, 1997). For a summary and evaluation of the earlier quests, see Albert Schweitzer, *The Quest of the Historical Jesus: A Critical Study of Its Progess from Reimarus to Wrede* (New York: Macmillan, 1968 [1961]); Charles C. Anderson, *Critical Quests of Jesus* (Grand Rapids: Eerdmans, 1969); and Robert B. Strimple, *The Modern Search for the Real Jesus* (Phillipsburg, NJ: Presbyterian & Reformed, 1995).

[5] 'The Paul of History', p. 78.

[6] Ibid., p. 80.

[7] Ibid., p. 65. See *Romans*, pp. 139, 148–9.

[8] *What Saint Paul Really Said*, pp. 128–9. Cf. N. T. Wright, 'The Law in Romans 2', pp. 139–43.

[9] *What Saint Paul Really Said*, p. 45.

[10] Ibid., p. 60.

[11] Ibid., pp. 40–1. Cf. Wright, *Romans*, p. 403. Though it would take us too far from our focus in this study, Wright's basic theological convictions about the pre-eminence of narrative in the Scriptures militates against the formulation of anything like an *ordo salutis*, as it is understood in traditional Reformed theology. For a statement of Wright's theological method, see Wright, *The New Testament and the People of God*, pp. 31–80. For brief, critical assessments of the negative implications of Wright's emphasis upon the history of redemption (*historia salutis*) at the expense of the order of salvation (*ordo salutis*), see Waters, *Justification and the New Perspectives on Paul*, pp. 120–4; and my recent article, 'N. T. Wright on Romans 5:12–21 and Justification: A Case Study in Exegesis, Theological Method, and the "New Perspective on Paul"', *Mid-America Journal of Theology* 16 (2005), esp. pp. 52–4, 72–9.

[12] *What Saint Paul Really Said*, p. 40.

[13] Ibid., p. 47. See also Wright, *The Climax of the Covenant*, pp. 21–6; and Wright, *The New Testament and the People of God*, pp. 244–79.

[14] Ibid., p. 61.

[15] Ibid., p. 133. Cf. Wright, *Romans*, p. 481.

[16] Ibid., p. 96. For an extended treatment of Wright's understanding of 'the righteousness of God' in Romans, see his *Romans*, pp. 397–405.

[17] Wright does not believe, however, that the idea of righteousness and the 'legal metaphor' it reflects is the most important theme of the book of Romans or Paul's other epistles. In a very telling observation at the close of his discussion of justification in *What Saint Paul Really Said*, p. 110, he remarks that 'Romans is often regarded as an exposition of judicial, or law-court, theology. But that is a mistake. The law court forms a vital metaphor at a key stage of the argument. But at the heart of Romans we find a theology of love. . . . If we leave the notion of "righteousness" as a law-court metaphor only, as so many have done in the past, this gives the impression of a legal transaction, a cold piece of business, almost a trick of thought performed by a God who is logical and correct but hardly one we would want to worship.' This remark assumes the doubtful thesis that love and justice are not equally essential features of the gospel's revelation of God's character. To use a phrase from the *Heidelberg Catechism*, 'God is indeed merciful, but He is also just' (Q. & A. 11). Why should God's justice be diminished in order to make room for his love?

[18] *What Saint Paul Really Said*, p. 98. Cf. Wright, *Romans*, pp. 459-60.

[19] *What Saint Paul Really Said*, p. 98.

[20] Ibid., p. 113. Cf. p. 115: 'The discussions of justification in much of the history of the church, certainly since Augustine, got off on the wrong foot—at least in terms of understanding Paul—and they have stayed there ever since.'

[21] Ibid., p. 119 (emphasis Wright's). Cf. Wright, *Romans*, pp. 468, 497.

[22] *What Saint Paul Really Said*, p. 119.

[23] Ibid., p. 119. Cf. p. 120: 'Despite a long tradition to the contrary, the problem Paul addresses in Galatians is not the question of how precisely someone becomes a Christian, or attains to a relationship with God. . . . On anyone's reading, but especially within its first-century context, it has to do quite obviously with the question of how you can define the people of God: are they to be defined by the badges of Jewish race, or in some other way?' See also Wright, 'Curse and Covenant: Galatians 3:10-14', in *The Climax of the Covenant*, pp. 137–56.

[24] *What Saint Paul Really Said*, p. 122.

[25] Ibid., pp. 158-9.

[26] 'The Shape of Justification', www.thepaulpage.com/Shape.html. This article is Wright's response to Paul Barnett's critical evaluation of his understanding of justification. Barnett is an Anglican bishop from the diocese of Sydney in Australia. See 'Tom Wright and The New Perspective', www.anglicanmedia sydney.asn.au/ pwb/ntwright_perspective.htm.

[27] 'The Shape of Justification', p. 2.

[28] Ibid.

[29] *What Saint Paul Really Said*, pp. 126-7. Cf. Wright, *Romans*, p. 440: 'Justification, at the last, will be on the basis of performance, not possession.'

[30] *The Climax of the Covenant*, p. 138.

[31] Ibid., p. 150.

[32] Ibid., p. 141.

[33] For a discussion of the way Wright treats the work of Christ as 'representative' in Romans 5:12–21, see my 'N. T. Wright on Romans 5:12–21 and Justification', pp. 67–72.

[34] Cf. Wright, 'New Perspectives on Paul'.

PART THREE

A CRITICAL ASSESSMENT OF THE NEW PERSPECTIVE ON PAUL

6

SCRIPTURE, CONFESSION, AND HISTORICAL RECONSTRUCTION

Any evaluation of the new perspective on Paul faces a number of daunting challenges. Since a considerable part of the argument for a new approach to the apostle's teaching rests upon E. P. Sanders' historical reconstruction of the pattern of religion known as Second-Temple Judaism, some evaluation of this reconstruction is required. One of the oft-repeated claims of the new-perspective advocates is that the older view failed to read the Pauline epistles in their historical context, whether in terms of their Old Testament background or the Judaism prevalent at the time of writing. A particular historical understanding of Judaism, consequently, has become a major linchpin in the argument for a new view of Paul's teaching. This means that any evaluation of the new perspective that fails to reckon with the historical studies of Sanders and others is not likely to be regarded as adequate to the task.

Many authors who are sympathetic to the new perspective also insist that we need a new or fresh look at the Pauline epistles – one that is freed from the constraints of the older Reformation reading. To seek to defend the Reformation's understanding of the gospel is to risk the scorn of those committed to the long-overdue liberation of exegesis from dogmatic strictures. Defenders of the Reformation doctrine of justification are regarded as would-be 'guardians of orthodoxy', whose captivity to an older doctrinal system and paradigm makes their work outdated and out-of-step with modern scholarship.[1] If a revolution has occurred in Pauline studies, then those who are found on the pre-revolutionary side of this paradigm-shift risk being dismissed as the theological equivalent of 'flat earthers'. It is difficult to swim against the stream of what is now acknowledged to be the reigning paradigm in Pauline studies.[2]

In the view of many proponents of the new perspective, the older commentaries and treatments of the Pauline epistles are seriously handicapped by their assumptions regarding Judaism in the first century. A critical evaluation of the new perspective, therefore, calls not only for a consideration of the new understanding of Judaism associated with the work of Sanders, but also a re-reading of the Pauline epistles against the background of the new understanding of Judaism.

Though these challenges may seem daunting enough, there is the further complication of the fluid nature of the so-called new perspective. As we have previously noted, many who write in sympathy with the new perspective, object when this perspective is treated as though it were a monochrome rather than a polychrome movement with a variety of distinct viewpoints. Some authors specifically object to the language of 'the' or 'a' new perspective. Often it is noted that the new perspective embraces a cluster of viewpoints whose common thread is their divergence from the older Reformation view, not their positive agreement upon an alternative. Due to the tentativeness of many of the historical studies of first-century Judaism, it is frequently acknowledged that a great deal of further research is needed.

All of this contributes to a situation like that confronting a marksman in a shooting gallery. How is it possible to hit a target that is in constant motion and that, as soon as you get it in your sights, has bobbed up or down, or disappeared altogether?

As we embark upon our critical assessment of the new perspective in this and subsequent chapters, I am keenly aware of the limits of what we will be able to achieve. Admittedly, we will not be able to do justice to all the differences of viewpoint among advocates of a new perspective. Nor will we be able to deal adequately with the growing body of literature on various aspects of it.

What I propose to offer instead is an assessment that begins in this chapter by raising several key questions regarding the new perspective's reassessment of Second-Temple Judaism that are not adequately addressed by Sanders' study. Then in subsequent chapters, I will offer a defence of several key aspects of the

Reformation's understanding of Paul, which form the focus of the new perspective's criticism of the older view. However, my evaluation will remain, in the nature of the case, something of a preliminary assessment. A more complete and adequate evaluation would require a far more extended treatment of the issues only briefly considered in the pages that follow.[3]

SOME OBSERVATIONS ABOUT METHOD

Before we raise several questions regarding Sanders' approach to Second-Temple Judaism, we need to make some observations about theological method that are pertinent to our assessment of the new perspective.

One of the principal claims of the new perspective is that it offers a more exegetically-defensible treatment of Paul's writings in their historical context. N. T. Wright, for example, expresses some surprise at the strong criticisms that defenders of the Reformation view have brought against the new perspective. According to him, it is ironic that many critics of the new perspective fail to recognize that its advocates are seeking to honour the 'aim and method' of the Reformation itself:

> . . . the present controversy, from my own point of view, often appears to me in terms of a battle for the Reformers' *aims and methods*—going back to scripture over against all human tradition—against some of their theological positions (and, equally, those of their opponents, since I believe that often both sides were operating with mistaken understandings of Paul). I believe that Luther, Calvin, and many of the others would tell us to read scripture afresh, with all the tools available to us—which is after all what they did—and to treat their own doctrinal conclusions as important but not as important as scripture itself. That is what I have tried to do, and I believe I am honouring them thereby.[4]

The new perspective, Wright argues, ought to be regarded as a genuinely reformational project. Though the conclusions it draws regarding the doctrine of justification differ greatly from those of the Reformers, its aims and methods are thoroughly in accord with the Reformation principle of *sola Scriptura*. The final test of any perspective on Paul must be the writings of the apostle himself, not the conclusions of a prior age in the history of the church. Scripture is the ultimate arbiter in matters of Christian teaching, and it is the new perspective's professed concern to honour this principle in a consistent manner. If the Reformation view diverges from the actual teaching of the apostle Paul, then we must be prepared to abandon that view and embrace the fresh, exegetically more satisfactory, position espoused by authors of the new perspective.

Since so much of its case depends upon its appeal to Scripture against the older consensus of the Reformation, we need to consider briefly the subject of theological method before we proceed directly to our assessment of the new perspective's principal themes. Though this is a weighty subject in its own right, which demands more attention than we can give it here, there are two key principles that belong to a theological method that honours the Reformation. The first principle is that of *the priority of Scripture as the supreme authority in theology*. The second is that of *the subordinate, albeit real and unavoidable, authority of the ecclesiastical consensus* embodied in the creeds and confessions.

1. The Priority of Scripture

Wright is undoubtedly correct when he insists that any assessment of the new perspective's claims regarding Paul's understanding of the gospel must ultimately appeal to the epistles of the apostle. The debate regarding the correctness of the Reformation's understanding of the gospel may only be settled in a way that conforms to the Reformation's insistence that 'Scripture alone' is the supreme standard for theology. Just as the Reformers rested their case upon an appeal to the biblical writings, so contemporary interpreters of the apostle must make their case by appealing to an exegetically responsible handling of his acknowledged writings. The priority of Scripture in theological method holds true for the traditional Reformation understanding of Paul as much as that of the new perspective.

This acknowledgment has two consequences for an assessment of the new perspective. First, the priority of Scripture in theology lends credibility to the new perspective's claim that *we may not simply repeat the claims of the past* without regard to the findings of a new and fresh reading of the Pauline writings. If those defending the older perspective on Paul merely parrot the work of a prior age, but fail to directly engage the biblical writings themselves, their defence of the Reformation effectively belies the Reformation's own insistence upon the supreme authority of Scripture. Any defence of the Reformation's view that neglects to consider the biblical writings themselves is inconsistent and self-defeating.

The second consequence of the priority of Scripture, however, suggests a weakness in the method that often characterizes writers of the new perspective. Whatever the usefulness of Sanders' historical study of Second-Temple Judaism, we need to caution against the temptation to make the tentative results of such studies *the determining factor in our interpretation of biblical texts.* Since Paul's epistles were written on particular occasions and in special historical circumstances, historical studies play an important role in their interpretation. However, the conclusions of such studies must remain subordinate in authority to the arguments and specific claims of Paul's epistles themselves.

This observation ought not to lead to a defence of a kind of biblicism that ignores history. Rather, it ought to guard against a kind of historical scholarship that *inappropriately predetermines* the exegesis of biblical texts. For example, someone might argue on the basis of historical studies that the kind of Judaizing tendency the apostle Paul opposes in Galatians is not represented in the literature of Second-Temple Judaism. Consequently, the apostle Paul is guilty in Galatians of creating a 'straw man', a profile of a Judaizing tendency that simply did not exist in the first century, in order to make his case for a certain understanding of the gospel.

The point of this illustration is not to say that writers of the new perspective are necessarily guilty of such an approach. It is simply to warn against the real temptation of employing historical studies as a kind of matrix or grid for the reading of Paul's epistles, so that the actual teaching and arguments of the epistle are not the principal basis for determining Paul's view of things. *When determining*

Paul's view of the gospel, we must allow Paul's writings to have the first and last word. Nothing less than this is required, if we are to settle the question of what Paul understood by the gospel or the doctrine of justification.

One unavoidable issue arising in connection with this is the authenticity of all the canonical epistles which are ascribed to the apostle Paul. Readers of the New Testament are well aware that there are thirteen epistles explicitly assigned to Paul. However, most of the more prominent new-perspective authors follow the standard, critical consensus of New Testament scholarship that only recognizes seven of the canonical epistles to be genuinely Pauline.[5] In this consensus, Colossians, Ephesians, 2 Thessalonians, and the Pastoral Epistles, are regarded as deutero-Pauline and therefore not wholly reliable sources for determining the apostle's teaching. Though I do not concur with this critical view of the Pauline corpus, I will nonetheless restrict most of my appeal in what follows to passages in the generally acknowledged epistles. Since almost everyone acknowledges the authenticity of Romans, 1 and 2 Corinthians, Galatians, Philippians, 1 Thessalonians, and Philemon, references to these epistles will be treated as sufficient to determine Paul's teaching regarding the gospel and justification by faith. This will prevent us from becoming sidetracked by the important question of the authenticity of the canonical epistles of Paul.

2. The Authority of the Reformation Confessions

A somewhat more controversial subject is the place and role of the historic confessions of the Reformation in our understanding of the gospel. If the claims of the new perspective are granted, then it is not enough merely to take a fresh look at Paul's epistles. It also becomes necessary to view with suspicion the confessional statements, which summarize the gospel in general and the doctrine of justification in particular.

Key elements of these confessions — that justification is a central theme, if not *the* central theme, of Paul's understanding of the gospel; that justification answers the question of how ungodly sinners can find acceptance with God; that justification is by faith alone, now and in the future—must be rejected in the light of the new understandings of Judaism and the apostle Paul which are integral to the new perspective. N. T. Wright argues (as the title of his book – *What Saint Paul Really Said* – makes clear), that the Western tradition since Augustine has largely misunderstood the apostle Paul. Expressing an opinion that is common among writers of the new perspective, Wright insists that '. . . the discussions of justification in much of the history of the church, certainly since Augustine, got off on the wrong foot—and they have stayed there ever since'.[6] Even if you factor in the possibility that Wright is being deliberately provocative, his words, and the sentiment they express, can hardly lend encouragement to those who might view the Reformation confessions as a helpful summary of the teaching of the gospel.

At one level, of course, these sentiments respecting the correctness of the Reformation's reading of the gospel cannot be rejected out of hand. The confessions themselves acknowledge that they are subordinate to the teaching of Scripture and liable to correction if necessary. Even the most ardent subscriber to the Reformed confessions must be open to the possibility that they may contain error. This is really only another way of saying that Scripture is the supreme test of faith, and the confessions are true only by virtue of their agreement with Scripture.

However, at another level, these sentiments seem to betray a kind of pride, even recklessness, regarding the superiority of our present understanding of Scripture in contrast to the understanding of former generations. At the very least, they betray a kind of disrespect for the doctrinal consensus of the church, or an unwillingness to grant to the historic confessions a kind of presumption of 'innocent unless proven guilty'.

While the confessions of the Reformation are not beyond criticism, yet the modest point we wish to make is that the great burden of proof falls upon those who want to reject wholesale the heritage of the past. In the course of this study, we will show that this burden has not been met by advocates of the new perspective on Paul.

3. THE SUBORDINATE ROLE OF HISTORICAL RECONSTRUCTION

One final observation concerns the role and place of historical studies in the interpretation of the Pauline epistles. Such studies are an important component of any responsible approach to the interpretation of Scripture. For this reason, the study of the literature of Second-Temple Judaism provides an important context within which to read Paul's epistles. Knowledge of the historical setting is critical to the true interpretation of biblical texts. Thus, there can be no objection in principle to the study of the literature of Second-Temple Judaism to ascertain its implications for an accurate understanding of the apostle Paul.

However, though historical studies can significantly *illuminate* the meaning of biblical texts, great caution has to be exercised so as not to let the tentative conclusions of such studies 'trump' the apparent meaning of the text within its own canonical context. To argue, for example, that the apostle Paul 'could not be opposing any kind of legalism' because *we know from historical studies* that no such legalism existed at that time, is a dubious procedure. If the text seems to say something that does not fit in with our historical reconstruction, it may be that the conclusion drawn from our historical studies are incorrect or not directly relevant. When reading the Pauline epistles, great care must be exercised lest our reconstruction of their historical context becomes the governing key to their interpretation.

Perhaps a simple illustration of this point will help to make it clear. When Sanders summarizes his conclusions about Judaism in the time of Jesus and Paul, he offers the following remark:

> The possibility cannot be completely excluded that there were Jews accurately hit by the polemic of Matt. 23 [woes against the scribes and Pharisees], who attended only to trivia and neglected the weightier matters. Human nature being what it is, one supposes that there were some such. One must say, however, that the surviving literature [of Second-Temple Judaism] does not reveal them.[7]

The remarkable feature of this observation by Sanders is that it only grudgingly admits the remote possibility that the woes of

Matthew 23 may have hit a real and not an imaginary target. Whether Sanders' representation of Second-Temple Judaism is correct or not, it is striking that, upon the basis of the assured results of his study, he is reluctant to admit that the account of Matthew 23 might accurately represent at least one strand of first-century Judaism. It is not my purpose in citing this relatively small point in the larger context of Sanders' work to imply that this is characteristic of his work or the work of other proponents of the new perspective. But it does illustrate how easy it is to put the tentative hypotheses of historical studies above the scriptural texts.[8] This we may never do.

As we evaluate the new perspective we will need to keep these points in mind. When it comes to Paul's understanding of the gospel and the doctrine of justification, the principal source and standard must remain his own epistles. Neither the Reformation confessions nor the tentative conclusions of historical studies may stand alongside or parallel with the Scriptures in determining Paul's teaching.

Moreover, though the Reformation confessions are subordinate to the Scriptures, they must be granted considerable weight. Due to the tentativeness of the conclusions of historical studies—however useful and important they may be—they do not have the authority of Scripture or even of the church's confessional summaries of scriptural teaching.

QUESTIONS REGARDING SANDERS' VIEW OF SECOND-TEMPLE JUDAISM

It is appropriate that our critical assessment of the new perspective begins by raising several questions regarding its historical reassessment of Second-Temple Judaism. All of the primary writers who advocate a new approach to our understanding of the apostle's gospel, do so from the conviction that Sanders' study of Judaism requires a 'revolution' in Pauline studies. N. T. Wright well expresses this consensus, when he asserts that Sanders

> dominates the landscape [of Pauline studies], and, until a major
> refutation of his central thesis is produced, honesty compels one

to do business with him. I do not myself believe such a refutation can or will be offered; serious modifications are required, but I regard the basic point as established.[9]

Since the work of Sanders plays such a fundamental role in the development of the new perspective, a critical evaluation of it may not bypass Sanders' claims regarding the nature of Judaism at the time of the writing of the New Testament.

In our earlier summary of Sanders' work, we noted that he rejects the older view, which treated Paul's understanding of the gospel as a response to legalism, as a fundamental misreading of Second-Temple Judaism. The Reformation wrongly assumed that Paul formulated his gospel in opposition to a legalistic distortion that was characteristic of Judaism.

However, Sanders argues, the literature of Second-Temple Judaism pervasively witnesses not to a religion of legalistic works-righteousness but to a view of the law undergirded by God's covenant grace. Rather than exhibiting a pattern of religion marked by human initiative and finding favour with God on the basis of works of obedience to the law, this literature reveals a view in which God's gracious election precedes any required response on the part of his people. Second-Temple Judaism was not a form of 'Pelagianism' that regarded the covenant relationship as a kind of moralistic human achievement. Whatever obligations of obedience to the law were required of the covenant people, they were required as a response to the initiatives of God's grace. For this reason, Sanders describes this pattern of religion, which was pervasive to Second-Temple Judaism, as 'covenantal nomism'.[10] Covenantal nomism understands that we 'get in' the covenant relationship by grace, and we 'stay in' or 'maintain' the covenant relationship by works.

I would like to raise four key questions regarding Sanders' work. These will put us in a better position to see whether his arguments have the significance that many of the new-perspective authors claim for them. After this preliminary evaluation of Sanders' treatment of Second-Temple Judaism, we will take up the claims of the new perspective regarding Paul's understanding of the gospel.

1. How Strong Is the Case for 'Covenantal Nomism'?

No one who takes the trouble to read Sanders' studies on the subject of Second-Temple Judaism with care can doubt that he has canvassed a wide diversity of sources. In his *Paul and Palestinian Judaism* (1977), Sanders painstakingly sorts through the available literary evidence for an understanding of Judaism in the period between 200 BC and AD 200. Though Sanders' work has been reviewed in a great number of articles and monographs, it remains in a class by itself as among the most significant and comprehensive evaluations of the pattern of religious thought in the Judaism contemporaneous with the New Testament era.

The only studies that are comparable in their reach and length are two recent volumes of essays on Second-Temple Judaism edited by D. A. Carson, *Justification and Variegated Nomism*.[11] Though the various contributors to these studies raise a number of important questions regarding Sanders' findings, the assumption throughout is that Sanders' work has become a benchmark for our approach to Judaism in relation to the teaching of the apostle Paul. At the very least, these volumes suggest that future roads to Second-Temple Judaism will have to go through Sanders.

More important than the sheer breadth of Sanders' studies of Second-Temple Judaism, however, is the strength of his case. Though there are a number of cautions regarding Sanders' work that need to be issued, there can be little doubt that the case he makes for Judaism's teaching of 'covenantal nomism' is strong.

In the literature of Second-Temple Judaism, there is little evidence of a pattern of religion that views God's covenant with his people Israel as based upon something other than God's gracious initiative. God's election of Israel to be his people is the commonly attested view of how one 'gets in' the covenant community. Though there is an equally strong emphasis upon the need for obedience to the requirements of the law to 'maintain' the covenant relationship, it is also generally acknowledged that God has provided a means of atonement for sin or transgression when this obedience falls short. Thus, the covenant people of God are not obliged to merit or obtain favour with God by their obedience. Not only is the covenant relationship founded upon God's gracious initiative ('getting in'), but it is also sustained ('staying in') by God's merciful acceptance of people whose obedience falls short of perfection. Despite the differences among various segments of Judaism, the basic structure of what Sanders calls 'covenantal nomism' seems quite pervasive: the covenant relationship is established and administered by God's gracious and merciful initiative, while it is maintained by obedience to the law as an expression of resolve on the part of the covenant people.

Though Sanders' case for the pervasive presence of 'covenantal nomism' in the literature of Second-Temple Judaism is quite strong, this does not mean that it is without significant weaknesses. Some of these are due to problems of method or the failure to give adequate consideration to some key sources. The most significant weakness, however, has to do with the *nature* of what Sanders calls 'covenantal nomism'. Before elaborating further on this issue, I will simply mention a few 'flies in the ointment' in Sanders' study of Judaism.

First, *a significant shortcoming of Sanders' work is that he focuses primarily upon what he calls the 'pattern of religion' in Second-Temple Judaism.* For Sanders, a pattern of religion is exhibited primarily in terms of the way a person 'gets in' the religious community and then 'stays in'. Covenantal nomism is, accordingly, Sanders' term for the pattern of religion within Judaism that regards 'getting in' as a consequence of God's gracious initiative and 'staying in' as a consequence of the person's resolute commitment to God and obedience to his law. Though this approach serves usefully as a way of bringing some order into an immensely complex subject, namely, the religious views and practices of Second-Temple Judaism, it is rather reductionistic. As Sanders admits, his idea of a pattern of religion is not so much interested in the religious themes and teachings of the various strands of Judaism; it is more interested in the way it exhibits a certain pattern of understanding of how one becomes and remains a member of the religious community. What he terms 'covenantal nomism' becomes, therefore, a very general viewpoint that is able to accommodate quite a variety of ideas and practices. To the extent that it accommodates such diversity, it becomes a rather flexible and imprecise pattern. Most importantly, as we shall see, the broad range of positions that are compatible with covenantal nomism includes some that are more 'legalistic' than others.[12]

Secondly, in his development of this idea of a pattern of religion within Judaism, Sanders gives little attention to the way Second-Temple Judaism views the *future* (eschatological) vindication of the covenant community. By downplaying the future aspect of God's dealings with the covenant community, Sanders is able to emphasize the divine initiative in graciously electing the covenant community. However, if the final vindication of those who belong to the community is given greater emphasis, the covenant member's works of obedience to the law can be understood in a way that overshadows the grace that initiates the covenant. We will have occasion to return to this issue in the following section. But to neglect the role obedience to the law plays in the future justification/vindication of God's people represents an imbalance in Sanders' description of Judaism's pattern of religion.[13]

Thirdly, despite the extraordinary reach of Sanders' scholarship, the findings of a number of contributors to *Justification and Variegated Nomism* suggest that some of the significant literature of Second-Temple Judaism does not fit Sanders' idea of covenantal nomism.[14] Some of this literature places little emphasis upon God's gracious initiative of election.[15] Sometimes the primary emphasis falls upon the future vindication of those who distinguish themselves by their obedience to the law; in other instances it falls upon the obedience of the covenant members as that which 'merits' God's continued favour and final acceptance of them.[16]

Fourthly, though it hardly seems fair to fault Sanders for failing to consider all the sources in his remarkably extensive study of Second-Temple Judaism, there are some noteworthy omissions in his research. One reason behind the publication of *Justification and Variegated Nomism* was the need to give attention to these sources. For example, among the more important omissions from Sanders' original study are the works of Josephus, a first century Jewish historian, and *2 Enoch* – a third century BC apocalyptic (prophetic revelation) source.[17]

Because of these weaknesses in Sanders' approach to the study of Second-Temple Judaism, it is an exaggeration to say that his work represents a settled and consensus view. Second-Temple Judaism remains a lively field of inquiry among Jewish and Christian scholars, and so the claim that Sanders' conclusions are sufficiently established to require a new reading or re-evaluation of the writings of the apostle Paul is unwarranted.

2. Does 'Covenantal Nomism' Beg the Question?

Even though Sanders has mustered a considerable body of evidence to establish that the pattern of religion in Second-Temple Judaism was 'covenantal nomism', there is an intriguing 'begging of the question' that characterizes his claims and those of many advocates of the new perspective. Could what Sanders calls 'covenantal nomism' take a form that corresponds to what historians of Christian doctrine call 'semi-Pelagianism'?

Sanders and other new-perspective authors are fond of arguing that Second-Temple Judaism exhibits no substantial traces of Pelagianism, the idea that God's people find favour with him on the basis of their own moral efforts. In this respect, as we have acknowledged, Sanders has made a compelling case. Whatever the diversity of teaching and practice within the various branches and sects of Second-Temple Judaism, few if any practised a religion that was the equivalent of a kind of 'pulling oneself up to God by one's moral bootstraps'.[18]

The glaring weakness of Sanders' case, however, is that he does not seriously consider whether 'covenantal nomism' could accommodate a form of religious teaching that regards salvation and acceptance with God as being based upon grace *plus* good works. Covenantal nomism is a sufficiently elastic pattern for the religion of Second-Temple Judaism that it could express a kind of a semi-Pelagian view of the relation between God and his people. That Second-Temple Judaism was not full-blown Pelagianism is not surprising.[19] In the course of history, Pelagianism is a 'rare bird' in the aviary of Jewish and Christian theology. Few have argued that salvation does not require the initiative and working of God's grace but is simply based upon human moral achievement. Where

Pelagianism has appeared, therefore, it has commonly been condemned by the major branches of the Christian church. Semi-Pelagian views, however, are quite often found in the history of Christian theology. Though these views may speak of God's gracious initiative in salvation, they also insist that human salvation does not end with this good beginning. According to semi-Pelagianism, those who find favour and acceptance with God are those who freely cooperate with his grace and complement it by a life of good works that merits further grace and final salvation.

Accordingly, when the Reformers of the sixteenth century opposed the doctrine of justification in the medieval Roman Catholic Church, they did not oppose (let alone claim to oppose) it because it was Pelagian, as writers of the new perspective intimate. The Reformers, including Luther and Calvin, objected to the teaching that sinners are justified by God *partly* on the basis of his grace in Christ and *partly* on the basis of their willing cooperation with this grace, which includes good works that increase the believer's justification and merit further grace.

The Roman Catholic Church, whose teaching was criticized as a re-statement of the kind of works-righteousness that the early church (including Paul) opposed, was not criticized for its Pelagianism. What prompted the Reformation was the conviction that the Roman Catholic Church taught that God's grace in Christ was not a sufficient basis for the believer's acceptance into and continuance in favour with God. The parallel, therefore, drawn by the Reformers between the teachings of the Roman Catholic Church and the Judaizing heresy was that both wanted to make human works subsequent to the initiative of God's grace a partial basis for present and future justification.[20]

It is not enough to demonstrate the absence of a Pelagian view of salvation by works; what is required is the further demonstration that a form of semi-Pelagianism did not mark Second-Temple Judaism. The Reformation understanding of Paul's opposition to the Judaizers does not stand or fall with the claim that Second-Temple Judaism was rife with Pelagianism. Paul's polemics against those who emphasized the need for 'works of the law' in justification need only have been addressed to a species of Christian heresy that was the product of a particular strand of teaching within Second-Temple Judaism. The Reformation understanding of Paul's teaching only requires the presence of a semi-Pelagian emphasis within some branches of Judaism and which was also present among the apostle's opponents.

The irony here is that Sanders' description of covenantal nomism closely resembles a textbook description of semi-Pelagian teaching and therefore lends unwitting support to the Reformation argument. Covenantal nomism fits rather comfortably with the idea that the present and future justification of the righteous depends upon works of obedience to the law that follow upon and are added to God's gracious initiative.[21] Since this is the case, Sanders' covenantal nomism bears remarkable formal similarities to the semi-Pelagianism that marked the medieval Roman Catholic doctrine of justification.[22] The Reformation claim that Paul was opposing a doctrine of justification by (grace plus) works is more accurate than authors of the new perspective are willing to acknowledge. At the very least, Sanders' understanding of Second-Temple Judaism does not demonstrate the need for a new understanding of the teaching of the apostle Paul which authors of the new perspective propose.

3. What Role Is Played by the Fear of Anti-Semitism and Other Social Concerns?

Proponents of the new perspective on Paul often criticize the Reformers of the sixteenth century for reading the debates of their own age (between Protestant and Roman Catholic) back into the debates between the apostle Paul and his opponents in the New Testament period. According to this criticism, the Reformers' reading of the apostle was historically inaccurate because it permitted the interests of their own day to shape their understanding of the context within which Paul laboured. Rather than permitting historical studies to determine the character of Second-Temple Judaism, the Reformation read its conflict with Rome into the polemics of the first century of the Christian era. What we need, therefore, is the kind of study of Judaism represented by the work of Sanders, namely, one that is based more upon historical scholarship than the theological polemics or prejudices of the sixteenth century.

The intriguing feature of this criticism of the Reformation is that it invites the question whether something similar may not be true of the writings of new-perspective authors. No student of the Reformation would deny the powerful role that the Reformers' conflict with Rome played in their reading of Paul's writings. On this score, authors of the new perspective are no doubt correct. However, if the Reformers were influenced by the circumstances of their own time, the question may also be raised whether something similar may not also be true of new-perspective authors. Are there, perhaps, cultural and historical factors that might help to explain why they are so anxious to take another look at Second-Temple Judaism? Are there features of the older view of Judaism that have become particularly objectionable within the contemporary context of historical and biblical studies?

To this question the answer is undoubtedly 'Yes'. One of the more subtle features of the new perspective is the role played by a fear of anti-Semitism. Frequently, new-perspective authors decry the pervasive presence of an implicit anti-Semitism in the traditional polemics of the Reformation. If, as the Reformers are said to have taught, Judaism is infected with a pattern of religion that is legalistic and moralistic, this can easily reinforce stereotypical and critical attitudes toward Jews. The presence of remarks in Luther's writings that exhibit a crude and harsh criticism of Judaism, when coupled with the sad history and reality of Christian anti-Semitism, constitutes a sorry chapter in the history of the church and its theology.

Writers advocating a new perspective on Paul often note the implications of this older view of Judaism for relations between Christian and Jewish communities. Because of the intensity of the attacks upon the alleged legalism and moralism of the Jewish tradition, particularly in its Rabbinic expressions, Christian theology has often been blamed for contributing to a negative attitude toward the Jewish community. It is not that the Reformers and those in the Reformation tradition were anti-Semites.[23] However, by articulating a stereotypical and largely negative portrait of the role of the law in Judaism, the older tradition, especially in its Lutheran expression, contributed to the shaping of a largely negative and critical picture of Judaism. Though often cited by defenders of the new perspective,[24] this concern about 'Christian' anti-Semitism is most pronounced in the writing of James D. G. Dunn, a significant proponent of the new view.[25]

As we noted in our introductory chapter, the concern of new-perspective authors to combat negative and stereotypical views of Judaism is also coupled with a desire to formulate the doctrine of justification in a way that overcomes the divisive polemics of the Reformation period. Whereas the Reformation treated the doctrine of justification in opposition to Roman Catholicism, the new perspective, which maintains that justification answers the ethnic exclusivism of Paul's opponents, treats it as a *socially inclusive* doctrine.

N. T. Wright, for example, insists that, because it emphasizes that Gentiles and Jews are included in the covenant family of God, justification is the great *ecumenical* doctrine of the Christian faith.[26] Thus, the cultural and social concerns of the present day (to promote racial and social harmony) are served by a fresh understanding of justification as an inclusive doctrine. The doctrine of justification, far from serving to divide groups along racial and theological fault lines, encourages the practice of racial, social, and even theological reconciliation. The new perspective's revision of the Reformation's understanding of justification, accordingly, fits well the contemporary cultural milieu with its emphasis upon ecumenicity and harmony in the midst of acknowledged differences.[27]

There are several problems, however, with this contemporary concern to avoid presenting Judaism in a negative light and to offer a doctrine of justification more congenial to the modern spirit.

First, though the concern to resist anti-Semitism and unduly negative portraits of Judaism is no doubt legitimate, students of Second-Temple Judaism must carefully avoid the temptation to allow it to skew their findings. If it is alleged that the older portrait of Judaism was inappropriately shaped by the Reformers' disagreement with medieval Catholicism on the doctrine of justification, then the newer portrait must not be shaped by an inordinate fear of discovering something that might be objectionable to contemporary Christian theologians. To argue that the older view of Judaism was unduly influenced by the theological debates of the sixteenth century is to wield a double-edged sword.

Second, one of the ironies of the new perspective's study of Second-Temple Judaism is that it shares the Reformation conviction that 'legalism' is highly objectionable. Even though definitions of legalism vary, Sanders' analysis of Second-Temple Judaism assumes that legalism is any view that bases Israel's relationship with God upon the moral achievements of the covenant people. By such a standard, he concludes that Second-Temple Judaism was not legalistic. However, as our earlier comments on semi-Pelagianism suggest, legalism can take more subtle forms.

One of these forms appears to be present in some of the literature of Second-Temple Judaism. In such legalism, obedience to the law complements God's grace and constitutes an important part of the basis for God's continuing favour and final vindication of his people. Now, from the standpoint of historic Protestantism this modified form of legalism is objectionable. What is often not appreciated, however, is that this kind of legalism might be a perfectly acceptable viewpoint so far as some branches of Second-Temple Judaism are concerned, just as it is acceptable to some branches of the historic Christian church.

This observation reminds us that in our historical studies we have to be careful to allow distinct patterns of religious expression to have their own integrity. Why should we assume that a *Christian* concern about legalism in any of its forms must be shared by Second-Temple Judaism? There is a real danger at this point of introducing a kind of Christian imperialism into historical scholarship. The studies of the new-perspective authors are, in this respect, just as slanted in their concern about Judaism being labelled 'legalistic' as were those of the Reformers in their opposition to medieval Catholicism. Though the results of the newer and older studies may be markedly different, they proceed from remarkably similar, and decidedly theological, assumptions about the propriety of viewing a person's acceptance with God as though it were based upon their moral achievements.

Thirdly, in the writings of many new-perspective authors, especially those of Dunn and Wright, some expressions of Second-Temple Judaism are regularly characterized as a form of racial exclusivism. The appeal to the works of the law among the Judaizers whom Paul opposed was born out of a resistance to the reception of non-Jews or Gentiles as full members of the covenant community. According to Dunn, for example, the great problem Paul faced in his opposition to the Judaizers was their unwillingness to admit non-Jews into the covenant community, unless they submitted to those boundary markers which distinguished Jews from non-Jews.

The intriguing feature of this position is that it ascribes to first-century Judaism a kind of *racism* that is by some standards no more attractive than the *legalism* ascribed to Judaism by the older perspective.

One of the frequent objections to the older view of Judaism is that it perpetuated a stereotypical and negative picture. The problem with the new perspective's portrait of Judaism in the first century is that it could easily perpetuate a different yet equally stereotypical and negative picture of Judaism. Though it is difficult to rank sins, charging Paul's opponents with a form of Jewish racism does not appear to be much of an improvement upon charging them with legalism.[28]

These problems illustrate the point that the new perspective, no less than the Reformation view of justification, represents far more than a scholarly rediscovery of the real nature of Second-Temple Judaism or the gospel according to Paul. It is also a perspective which is born out of a desire to understand the gospel in a manner that is more congenial to the ecumenical emphasis and social agenda of contemporary mainstream Christian theology. Though the writers of the new perspective maintain that their position is the product of careful historical scholarship and biblical exegesis, the role played by these broader cultural and social factors should not be ignored or denied.

4. WHAT ABOUT THE DISTINCTION BETWEEN OLD TESTAMENT AND SECOND-TEMPLE JUDAISM?

A final question facing the new perspective relates to the distinction between Old Testament and Second-Temple Judaism. Does the new perspective adequately take into account the difference between the teaching of the Old Testament and the kind of religious practice that characterized Judaism in the first century AD?

One claim made by new-perspective authors is that the Reformation reading of Paul fails to recognize the important continuities between his understanding of the gospel and Judaism. According to the new perspective, Paul did not repudiate Judaism when he became an apostle of Christ. Rather, his teaching and understanding of the gospel are in significant continuity with his Jewish background. By drawing a sharp contrast between the 'law' and the 'gospel', the Reformation, and especially Luther, failed to appreciate the extent to which Paul viewed the gospel of Christ as the 'end' or 'fulfilment' of the law.[29]

The Reformation interpreted Paul's doctrine of justification by faith apart from works as though it were a 'new' teaching that was unknown to Judaism. However, the new perspective argues that Paul's teaching was in more substantial continuity with Judaism than the Reformation perspective allows. By drawing a sharp contrast between law and gospel, the Reformation failed to recognize the important similarities between Judaism and Paul's understanding of the gospel. Whereas Paul viewed the gospel of Christ as a fulfilment of the law and Judaism, the Reformation understanding of justification encourages a reading of Scripture that does not do justice to the Old Testament background of Paul's writings.

Though this is a complicated subject which we will take up again in our consideration of Paul's teaching on justification, one of the weaknesses of the new perspective at this point is its occasional failure to bear in mind that there are at least two distinct ways in which we may speak of Judaism. When the apostle Paul's relationship to Judaism is considered, it is important to remember that his opposition to a particular form of Judaism in the first century AD is not tantamount to an opposition to Judaism as such. Nor does it require the conclusion that Paul taught a conflict between the gospel of Christ and the teaching of the Old Testament (Judaism).[30] The Reformation view that Paul opposed a form of Jewish-Christian legalism does not mean that his teaching was somehow at odds with the teaching of the Old Testament. In the Reformation understanding, the apostle was combating a *distortion* of the Old Testament's teaching, when he confronted those who insisted upon obedience to certain requirements of the law as a basis for acceptance with God. In other words, Paul's opposition to the Judaizers was an opposition to a contemporary distortion of the teaching of the Old Testament, not to Judaism as such.

If this distinction between Old Testament and Second-Temple Judaism is borne in mind, the new perspective's claim that the Reformation failed to consider fully the continuity between Paul's gospel and the teaching of Judaism is placed in a different light. So far as the Reformation view of justification is concerned, the problem was not with Judaism itself, nor with the Old Testament; rather, Paul's problem with the Judaizers was that they had perverted the grace of God into a means of self-justification. Or, to put the matter in the language of Paul's epistle to the Galatians, the Judaizers had failed to reckon with the truth that the promise of the gospel predated the giving of the (Mosaic) law by some 430 years (*Gal.* 3:17–18).

CONCLUSION

By raising these four questions regarding the new perspective's understanding of Second-Temple Judaism, we have only set the stage for a more substantive evaluation. We must now turn to a direct treatment of Paul's writings and ask, Do these writings favour the older Reformation perspective or the new perspective on Paul? As we have argued, the most important measure of the new perspective is the teaching of the apostle himself in his New Testament epistles. Consequently, the remainder of our evaluation of the new perspective will be occupied with a direct treatment of Paul's writings and understanding of the doctrine of justification.

The questions we have raised, however, lead us to believe that the new perspective has overrated the significance of Sanders' view of Second-Temple Judaism. They also raise serious doubts over the bold claims of new-perspective writers. We do not need a revolution in our understanding of Paul's doctrine of justification for, as we have briefly shown, there is nothing in the new perspective's interpretation of Second-Temple Judaism that in itself is sufficient to warrant such a revolution.

NOTES

[1] Cf. N. T. Wright, *What Saint Paul Really Said*, pp. 19-20; and Wright, 'New Perspectives on Paul'.

[2] Cf. D. A. Carson, 'Summaries and Conclusions', in *Justification and Variegated Nomism*, vol. 1: *The Complexities of Second Temple Judaism*, ed. D. A. Carson (Grand Rapids: Baker, 2001), p. 505: 'At least in the Anglo-Saxon world, it is not going beyond the evidence to say that the new perspective is the reigning paradigm.'

[3] There are already several excellent studies that are more or less critical of the new perspective and that offer a defence of the essential correctness of the Reformation's understanding of Paul. In addition to some we have already cited and others that we will cite, see, for example, Seyoon Kim, *Paul and the New Perspective: Second Thoughts on the Origin of Paul's Gospel* (Grand Rapids: Eerdmans, 2001); Simon J. Gathercole, *Where is Boasting? Early Jewish Soteriology and Paul's Response in Romans 1-5* (Grand Rapids: Eerdmans, 2002); Colin G. Kruse, *Paul, the Law, and Justification* (Peabody, MS: Hendrickson, 1996); Thomas R. Schreiner, *The Law and Its Fulfillment*; Frank Thielman, *Paul and the Law*; Mark A. Seifrid, *Christ, Our Righteousness: Paul's Theology of Justification* (Downers Grove, IL: InterVarsity, 2000); and Stephen Westerholm, *Israel's Law and the Church's Faith*.

[4] 'New Perspectives on Paul'.

[5] E. P. Sanders, *Paul and Palestinian Judaism*, p. 431, expresses the consensus: 'I take the sources for studying Paul to be the seven letters whose authenticity is unquestioned: Romans, 1 and 2 Corinthians, Galatians, Philippians, 1 Thessalonians and Philemon.'

[6] *What Saint Paul Really Said*, p. 115.

[7] *Paul and Palestinian Judaism*, p. 426. One significant weakness in Sanders' approach is evident from this comment. The literature of Second-Temple Judaism is no doubt a principal source for ascertaining its religious practice and teaching. However, what is represented in the literature may differ from what was the case in practice. The proverbial 'man in the pew' often subscribes to a pattern of religion rather different from that formally expressed in the

literature of his tradition. For our purpose this means that, even were the literature of Second-Temple Judaism devoid of any 'legalism' or legalistic teaching, legalism may well still characterize the actual practice of segments of the Jewish community. To state the point differently, Paul could have responded to a form of legalism within Judaism which is not well represented in the literature that is extant.

[8] It is interesting that this comment of Sanders relates to the subject of the profile of the Pharisees in the New Testament. Though there is virtually no significant literary evidence that would help to identify Pharisaism in the first century (Josephus is the best source, though he writes as a defender of a party within Pharisaism), there is rather ample New Testament literary evidence regarding them. It is difficult to suppress the impression that the New Testament evidence, because it paints a rather unflattering picture of the Pharisees, constitutes something of an obstacle to Sanders' claims regarding the nature of Second-Temple Judaism. As we noted earlier (Chapter 4, note 8), Neusner, a leading Jewish scholar of Judaism, argues for a view of the Pharisees that seems closer to the traditional position. For an excellent discussion of the subject of historical reconstruction in New Testament studies, see Moisés Silva, 'The Place of Historical Reconstruction in New Testament Criticism' (in *Hermeneutics, Authority, and Canon*, D. A. Carson and John D. Woodbridge, eds. [Grand Rapids: Zondervan, 1986], pp. 109–33). Silva offers a helpful discussion of the Pharisees and rightly notes that their 'relaxation' of the requirements of God's law could encourage a kind of legalism in which one's standing with God is partly based upon moral achievement.

[9] *What Saint Paul Really Said*, p. 20.

[10] Sanders, as we have noted previously, uses this terminology to emphasize that we become members of the covenant by grace, but maintain our membership by obedience to the law. His term 'nomism' (from the Greek word, *nomos*, meaning law) means to emphasize the role of works of obedience to the law in maintaining the covenant relationship.

[11] Vol. 1: *The Complexities of Second Temple Judaism*; and vol. 2: *The Paradoxes of Paul* (Grand Rapids: Baker, 2004). The first of these volumes examines E. P. Sanders' thesis regarding Second-Temple Judaism. The second treats the writings of Paul in order to assess the claims of the new perspective. I should note also that the work of Neusner, which I cited earlier (Chapter 4, note 8), represents a significant alternative interpretation of Pharisaic Judaism as one strand among the Judaisms of this period.

[12] Cf. Peter Enns, 'Expansions of Scripture', in *Justification and Variegated Nomism*, 1:73–98. Enns makes a similar point at the conclusion of his study. He notes that Sanders tends to identify salvation with Israel's election, and then downplays the role of works in obtaining salvation for those who belong to the covenant community. According to Enns (p. 98), 'It might be less confusing [than Sanders' categories of 'getting in' and 'staying in'] to say that *election* is by grace but *salvation* is by obedience.'

[13] Cf. Simon J. Gathercole, *Where is Boasting?*, pp. 1–34. Gathercole, who critically evaluates the claims of the new perspective in terms of Paul's opposition to Jewish 'boasting' in Romans 1–5, rightly notes that Sanders fails to deal with the eschatological dimension of Judaism. When God's final verdict regarding his people is made to rest upon their obedience to the law, a kind of 'legalism' is affirmed. Though it may not be the 'legalism' that says we 'get in' the covenant by works, it is nonetheless one that says we are 'finally vindicated' by our obedience to the law. As we shall argue in what follows, one of the principal problems with Sanders' argument is that he works with a simplistic view of 'legalism', namely, the Pelagian idea of salvation by moral achievement apart from the initiatives of God's grace.

[14] Cf. Daniel Falk, 'Psalms and Prayers', in *Justification and Variegated Nomism*, 1:7–56.

[15] Cf. Philip R. Davies, 'Didactic Stories', in *Justification and Variegated Nomism*, 1:99–134; Richard Bauckham, 'Apocalypses', in *Justification and Variegated Nomism*, 1:135–88.

[16] Cf. Markus Bockmuehl, '1QS and Salvation at Qumram', in *Justification and Variegated Nomism*, 1:381-441.

[17] Cf. Paul Spilsbury, 'Josephus', in *Justification and Variegated Nomism*, 1:241–60. The omission of Josephus from Sanders' 1977 study is particularly striking, since Josephus, who writes as a member of a party of the Pharisees, is perhaps the single most comprehensive literary source for an understanding of Pharisaism in the first century of the Christian era. In Josephus' account of the relation of the religious community to God, little emphasis is placed upon God's gracious initiative. According to Josephus, the Jews were at a distinct advantage among the nations because God had given them the law of Moses and through obedience to the law they were able to live in the hope of the resurrection. *2 Enoch,* a work that Sanders does not consider, presents an even more unqualified form of legalism: those who keep the law merit their eternal reward and favour with God.

[18] N. T. Wright, *What Saint Paul Really Said,* p. 119. Cf. Wright, *Romans,* pp. 459–61.

[19] I am aware that I am using these terms, 'Pelagianism' and 'semi-Pelagianism', in an anachronistic and somewhat inexact fashion. For my purposes, however, it is enough to recognize that there is a considerable difference between a view that ascribes human salvation to moral achievement (Pelagianism) and a view that ascribes human salvation to God's grace *plus* good works that complete or complement the working of God's grace (semi-Pelagianism).

[20] Cf. Moisés Silva, 'The Law and Christianity: Dunn's New Synthesis', *Westminster Theological Journal* 53 (1991), p. 348: 'Sanders (along with biblical scholars more generally) has an inadequate understanding of historical Christian theology, and his view of the reformational concern with legalism does not get to the heart of the question.' I fully concur with Silva's observation and am happy to note that he speaks as a biblical and not a systematic theologian.

[21] Seyoon Kim, *Paul and the New Perspective*, p. 65.

[22] Cf. D. A. Carson, 'Summaries and Conclusions', in *Justification and Variegated Nomism*, p. 1:544: 'Nevertheless, covenantal nomism as a category is not really an alternative to merit theology, and therefore is no response to it. . . . By putting over against merit theology not grace but covenant theology, Sanders has managed to have a structure that preserves grace in the "getting in" while preserving works (and frequently some form or other of merit theology) in the "staying in".'

[23] Cf. E. P. Sanders, *Paul and Palestinian Judaism*, p. xiii. Sanders is quite explicit that he does not wish to accuse the older interpreters of Judaism of anti-Semitism.

[24] Cf. N. T. Wright, *What Saint Paul Really Said*, p. 19; Frank Thielman, *Paul and the Law*, pp. 45–7.

[25] James D. G. Dunn, *The Theology of Paul the Apostle*, p. 338: 'If post-Vatican II theology could no longer simply restate the old debate between Protestant and Catholic in the traditional terms, post-Holocaust theology could no longer stomach the denigration of historic Judaism which had been the dark-side-of-the-moon corollary to the Christian doctrine of justification.'

[26] *What Saint Paul Really Said*, p. 158: 'Paul's doctrine of justification by faith impels the churches, in their current fragmented state, into the ecumenical task. It cannot be right that the very doctrine which declares that all who believe in Jesus belong at the same table (Galatians 2) should be used as a way of saying that some, who define the doctrine of justification differently, belong at a different table. . . . The doctrine of justification is in fact the great *ecumenical* doctrine.'

[27] For a treatment of the *social* implications of the new perspective's understanding of justification, see James D. G. Dunn and Alan M. Suggate, *The Justice of God*. Dunn summarizes these implications in a striking way (p. 29): 'God accepts all who believe and trust in him: Gentile as well as Jew, black and white, Palestinian and Israelite, central American and US citizen, Roman Catholic and Protestant, Orthodox and Muslim.'

[28] Cf. Seyoon Kim, *Paul and the New Perspective*, p. 61, n. 212: 'In this post-Holocaust age, any attempt to exonerate even the ancient Jews of what modern people deem negative may be laudable. But in order to exonerate them of a 'works-righteousness' religion, the New Perspectivists as a whole and Dunn especially tend to present them emphatically as what in our modern language can only be termed as "racists" and "(religious) imperialists" . . .'

[29] Cf. Dunn, *The Theology of Paul the Apostle*, pp. 368–71.

[30] A key to understanding Paul's contrast between the 'law' and the 'gospel', as we shall see in our next chapter, lies in the recognition that he sometimes uses the language of 'law' to refer to the Old Testament Scriptures or the Mosaic administration of the covenant as a whole, and sometimes to refer more narrowly to the commandments and obligations of the law.

7

WHAT DOES PAUL MEAN BY 'WORKS OF THE LAW'?

So far our evaluation of the new perspective on Paul has addressed several general matters of method and the understanding of Second-Temple Judaism associated with the work of E. P. Sanders. However, the most important test facing the new perspective is whether it faithfully and accurately interprets the writings of the apostle Paul. Does the new perspective offer a more compelling interpretation of the Pauline epistles, especially with regard to the apostle's doctrine of justification, than the interpretation historically associated with the Protestant Reformation? Since the new perspective advertises itself as a more faithful reading of Paul than that of the Reformers, it is critical that we test its claims against the text of the apostle's epistles.

One of the key features of the new perspective is the way it interprets Paul's use of the terms the 'law' and the 'works of the law'. In the older Reformation view, Paul's doctrine of justification by faith alone stood in stark contrast to any doctrine of justification by works performed in obedience to the law. An important aspect of the Reformation's interpretation was the claim that justification is by faith alone apart from the works of the law. Since no sinner, whether Jew or Gentile, is able to keep the law of God perfectly, there is no possibility of finding acceptance or favour with God by works. In the Reformation view of Paul's writings, the doctrine of justification was treated as, among other things, the apostle's answer to a kind of Jewish-Christian legalism, which taught that we are justified by works performed in obedience to the law. This doctrine answers the question of how an unrighteous sinner can find favour with God. As we have seen in our survey of the new perspective, this older Reformation view, especially in its handling of Paul's understanding of the law, has been roundly rejected. According to Sanders, the apostle developed his doctrine of justification from the prior vantage point of his conviction that salvation comes by faith in Christ. The problem with Judaism was not its legalism—after all, no such legalism was present in Second-Temple Judaism. Rather, the problem with Judaism was that it was not Christianity. Paul's analysis of the human 'plight' (no justification by works of the law) was the fruit of his prior conviction that the 'solution' (justification by faith) to the human predicament can only be found in Christ.

In Sanders' reading of Paul's writings, therefore, the doctrine of justification does not address the predicament of human sinfulness and inability to keep the law. Paul's diagnosis that no one is justified by the works of the law is a by-product of his basic conviction that faith in Christ is the only way of incorporation into the new covenant community.

Moreover, according to two of the principal authors of the new perspective, James Dunn and N. T. Wright, Paul's teaching about the works of the law is addressed primarily to a *social* problem, namely, the inclusion of Gentile believers together with Jews as members of the covenant people of God. When Paul speaks of the works of the law, he is not referring to any general obligations of obedience which are required by the law; rather, he is speaking particularly about 'boundary markers' that separated Jews from Gentiles (for example, circumcision, dietary requirements, and Sabbath or feast day provisions).

The real problem that was the occasion for the development of Paul's doctrine of justification was the failure of some Jewish-Christian opponents to embrace Gentiles as well as Jews among the covenant people of God. The promise of inclusion within the covenant family of God, according to those who insisted upon adherence to the boundary-marker requirements of the law, was restricted to Jews or those who became identified as Jews by their adherence to such requirements. According to Paul, however, justification by faith means that Gentiles are also included in the covenant community, though they are not under any obligation to identify with the Jewish covenant community by undergoing circumcision or fulfilling these requirements of the law. Therefore, according to this understanding of Paul's writings, the works of the law do not refer to general obligations of obedience to the law as a basis for justification or acceptance with God.

In order to evaluate these claims of the new perspective, we need to address three distinct, though related, questions:

1. First, what does Paul mean by the 'works of the law' or 'works', when he insists that no one is justified by them? Do the works of the law refer exclusively to what Dunn and Wright call the 'boundary markers' of the law?

2. Second, does the apostle oppose the teaching of justification by works on the basis of his conviction that no one is able to do what the law requires? Or, is the real and primary occasion for Paul's argument against justification by the works of the law, his conviction that, since the coming of Christ, the only way of inclusion among the people of God is through faith in Christ (arguing, as Sanders puts it, from 'solution' to 'plight')?

3. And third, is it correct to claim, as the Reformation did, that Paul opposed the Judaizers for teaching that justification rests upon human obedience to the requirements of the law? Does the apostle Paul oppose a legalistic distortion of the doctrine of justification, which taught that acceptance with God depends in some measure upon works of obedience to the law?

A PRELIMINARY OBSERVATION: THE VARIOUS USES OF THE TERM 'LAW'

Before directly taking up these questions, it will be helpful to begin with a preliminary observation regarding the apostle Paul's use of the term 'law' in his writings. One of the great difficulties in comprehending Paul's understanding of the law is the diversity of ways in which he uses the term. Sometimes he speaks in a highly favourable way about the law, whereas on other occasions he speaks rather negatively about it. Any failure to pay close attention to the way the term 'law' is used in a particular passage can lead to serious misunderstanding. Or, to the put the matter differently, if it is assumed that Paul is using 'law' in a uniform way throughout his writings, the likelihood of misunderstanding is very great. The context in each instance must always be carefully considered before determining what Paul means by his various references to the law.

For our present purpose it is enough to note the following distinct ways in which Paul uses this term in his epistles.[1]

1. The most important use of the term refers to the administration of the *law of Moses* (*Rom.* 2:17–27; 5:13–14; 7; 10:4–5; *Gal.* 3:10–12,17–24; 5:3–4). In Romans 5:13, for example, speaking of the disobedience of Adam and its consequence, the apostle notes that 'until the law sin was in the world'. The 'law' in this passage refers to the law as it was given through Moses.

2. Even though the most important use of the term refers broadly to the law of Moses, it is significant to note that he also speaks of the law of Moses in both a *broader* and *narrower* sense. In the broader sense, it refers to what might be called the Mosaic administration of the covenant, which in its comprehensive teaching is fully compatible with the gospel of 'righteousness by faith' (e.g. *Rom.* 3:21; cf. *Rom.* 8:4). However, in a narrower sense, the law of Moses often refers specifically to the obligations and demands of the law (e.g. *1 Cor.* 9:8; 15:56; *Rom.* 2:12–13, 23-27; 3:20–21, 28; 4:15; 5:20; 7:5, 7–9; 8:4; 13:8–10; *Gal.* 2:16, 19; 3:10; 5:3, 14). When speaking of the law in this narrower sense, the apostle emphasizes that it belongs to a particular era of the history of redemption, *after* the giving of the promise to Abraham some 430 years earlier (*Gal.* 3:17) and *prior* to the coming of Christ in the fullness of time (*Gal.* 3:24; 4:1–7; *Rom.* 6:14–15). Moreover, in the more specific sense of the commandments of the law of Moses, Paul emphasizes the contrast or antithesis between 'the righteousness of faith' and 'the righteousness of (obedience to) the law' (*Rom.* 4).

3. Sometimes the apostle uses 'law' to refer to something like a 'principle', 'order', or 'rule' (*Rom.* 3:27; 7:21, 23, 25; 8:2). In these passages, 'law' refers to a rule that governs human life and conduct. For example, in Romans 7:21 Paul says that 'I find it to be a law that when I want to do right, evil lies close at hand.' Here 'law' simply refers to a principle that governs the lives of those who want

to do what pleases God: they find that the temptation to do otherwise lies close at hand.

4. Consistent with the usage of 'law' as referring to the Mosaic law, Paul also often uses the term to refer to the Old Testament Scripture as a whole or more particularly to the Pentateuch, the first five books of the Bible written by Moses (*1 Cor.* 9:8–9; 14:21, 34; *Rom.* 3:19, 21; *Gal.* 4:21–31).

5. In Romans 2:14–15, 26–27, Paul declares that the Gentiles, to whom 'the [Mosaic] law' was not given, have the 'work of the law written on their hearts' (verse 15). Though this passage does not explicitly assert the common theological distinction between the 'moral' and the 'ceremonial' law, it does suggest that the moral requirements of the Mosaic law are in some sense known by those to whom the law was not given, as it was to Israel. Even the Gentiles, who do not have the written law of Moses, know what the law requires.

6. The apostle also contrasts the 'law of Christ' (*Gal.* 6:2; cf. *1 Cor.* 9:21) to the law of Moses, since it does not require circumcision. This law of Christ is the distinctive norm of conduct for those who are united to Christ by faith and who walk in step with the Holy Spirit. For those who are united with Christ and indwelt by his Spirit, there is a sense in which there is no longer a need for the detailed written ordinances of the law. The believer's life in the Spirit of Christ expresses itself in a freedom and maturity of obedience that no longer wholly depends upon the specifying of the law's precepts and prohibitions.

1. WHAT IS MEANT BY THE 'WORKS OF THE LAW'?

Within the richness and complexity of Paul's use of the term 'law', the most pressing question raised by the new perspective is the meaning of Paul's expression 'the works of law' and of the more general but related expression 'works'. Particularly in his treatment of the doctrine of justification, the apostle uses these expressions to draw a contrast between justification by faith and justification by the works of the law. The new perspective maintains that this expression is primarily used by Paul to refer to 'boundary-marker' requirements in the Mosaic law, such as circumcision, dietary requirements, and other ceremonial distinctives. Accordingly, we should not take these expressions as references to general (moral) requirements of obedience to the law of God, which neither Jews or Gentiles are able to meet in order to find favour with God. Rather, the 'works of the law' are those 'badges' that distinguish Jews from Gentiles and prevent those who do not submit to them from being numbered among the covenant people of God and the heirs of the promise to Abraham.

Therefore, the Reformation understanding of the expression, which interprets 'works of the law' as a reference to human deeds performed in obedience to the commandments of God, fails to correctly grasp the context of Paul's dispute – a context of Jewish exclusivism rather than Jewish legalism.

However, this pivotal claim of the new perspective—that the 'works of the law' are simply 'badges' of covenant membership that served to exclude Gentiles from the covenant community—*cannot be sustained by a careful reading of the Pauline epistles*. Though we will not attempt to consider all the evidence from Paul's writings, it is not difficult to show that the works of the law refer to more than the boundary-marker requirements of the law. This can be demonstrated from Paul's use of this terminology in Galatians and Romans, the two epistles that give most direct and sustained attention to the doctrine of justification.

A. The 'Works of the Law' in Galatians

The use of this phrase in Galatians is especially significant, since the historical context of this epistle seems most agreeable to the new-perspective claim that the works of the law are boundary-marker requirements. It is quite clear, for example, that those whom Paul opposes in this epistle were stipulating that circumcision was a necessary pre-condition for inclusion among God's covenant people. For this reason, the Judaizers were denying the inclusion of the Gentiles among the people of God in spite of the fulfilment of God's covenant promise to Abraham. In Galatians 2, where the problem Paul confronts is described, it is evident that the 'circumcision party' demanded the circumcision of Gentile believers so that they might 'live like Jews' (cf. verses 3, 7–9, 12–14). However, even though this demand was the occasion for Paul's letter to the Galatians, an examination of how he uses the expression 'works of the law' indicates that the problem went deeper than a mere appeal to the boundary-marker requirements of the law.

I. Galatians 2:15–17

We ourselves are Jews by birth and not Gentile sinners; yet we know that a person is not justified by *works of the law* but through faith in Jesus Christ, so we also have believed in Jesus Christ, in order to be justified by faith in Christ and not by *works of the law*, because by *works of the law* no one will be justified [emphasis added].

The immediate occasion for Paul's assertion, that no one is justified by works of the law, was the circumcision party's claim that the Gentiles must 'live like Jews' in order to be received into the fellowship of God's people. This passage seems, therefore, to lend support to the new perspective's position.

There can be little doubt that Paul was opposing Jewish-Christians who appealed to the works of the law and who were unprepared to acknowledge that the promise to Abraham extended also to Gentiles. However, his use of this expression elsewhere in Galatians indicates that much more is involved than merely the boundary-marker requirements of the law. This becomes evident when we consider such passages as Galatians 3:10–14; 5:2–4; and 6:13. In them the apostle argues that his opponents' insistence upon obedience to the works of the law as a means of justification imperils the gospel of Christ. If justification is by such works, then the one who is justified is under obligation to find life and blessing by means of obedience to the *whole* of the law. But Paul reminds the Galatians that this is the way of the curse and death.

II. Galatians 3:11–14

For all who rely on works of the law are under a curse; for it is written, 'Cursed be everyone who does not abide by all things written in the Book of the Law, and do them.' Now it is evident that no one is justified before God by the law, for 'The righteous shall live by faith.' But the law is not of faith, rather 'The one who does them shall live by them.' Christ redeemed us from the curse of the law by becoming a curse for us—for it is written, 'Cursed is everyone who is hanged on a tree'—so that in Christ Jesus the blessing of Abraham might come to the Gentiles, so that we might receive the promised Spirit through faith.

What is striking about these familiar verses is the way the apostle Paul *enlarges* the principle of his opponents. Those who would be justified by such works as circumcision and the other 'boundary-marker' requirements, are reminded that the law pronounces a curse upon everyone who fails to keep 'all things' that are written in the 'Book of the Law'. Therefore, if anyone seeks to be justified by the works of the law, and thereby escape the curse of God, he will have to abide by *everything* the law requires. The least failure to do so will inevitably bring about the curse of Deuteronomy 27:26. Though the particular works of the law which his opponents emphasized were undoubtedly what Dunn and others call 'boundary markers', Paul insists upon the general principle that God's judgment rests upon everyone who fails to obey the whole law.

Furthermore, it is instructive that the requirements of the law, within the context of Deuteronomy 27, include more than circumcision, dietary laws, and feast day (Sabbath) provisions. Also included are prohibitions against idolatry, dishonourable behaviour toward one's father or mother, incest, and murder (*Deut.* 27:15, 16, 20, 24). It is not enough, therefore, to keep the former requirements in order to be justified; one must also live in conformity to all that the law enjoins. For this reason, the apostle also appeals to the principle of the law enunciated in Leviticus 18:5: 'The one who does them [the things required in the law] shall live by them.' If life and the blessing of favour with God are to be based upon doing what the law prescribes, then the way of life can only be found in the perfect performance of everything demanded by the law.[2]

The implication of Paul's argument is clear: since no one abides by all things written in the book of the law, all are under its curse and unable to find life on the basis of obedience to it. That no one is justified by the 'works of the law' expresses a truth that goes far beyond the occasion of the Judaizers' unwillingness to embrace Gentile believers who were uncircumcised and disobedient to the law's so called boundary markers.[3]

III. GALATIANS 5:2–4

Look: I, Paul, say to you that if you accept circumcision, Christ will be of no advantage to you. I testify again to every man who accepts circumcision that he is obligated to keep the whole law. You are severed from Christ, you who would be justified by the law; you have fallen from grace.

In this passage the apostle clearly states that his opponents were insisting upon circumcision as an identifying marker and entrance requirement for inclusion among the people of God. This is again a reminder of the particular occasion for the apostle's polemics in Galatians. However, according to Paul, the Judaizers' insistence that Gentile believers submit to circumcision in order to be admitted into the covenant people of God is tantamount to requiring submission to 'the whole law'. The law and its obligations cannot be treated piece-meal, as though it were possible to be justified by obedience to certain of its requirements (e.g. boundary markers).[4]

If his opponents want to base their justification with God upon such things as circumcision, they must also assume the full burden of the law in order to be justified. The implication here, though unstated, is clear enough: because his opponents have not met and cannot meet this burden, they have embraced an obligation that is beyond their reach.

Moreover, to seek justification in the way of obedience to (certain) requirements of the law is inimical to the grace of Christ. Either a person is justified freely through faith in Christ or through obedience to the law: there is no middle way.

IV. Galatians 6:13

For even those who are circumcised do not themselves keep the law, but they desire to have you circumcised that they may boast in your flesh.

In this verse the apostle admittedly uses an *ad hominem* (concerning the person) argument. He charges his opponents, in effect, with a kind of hypocrisy. When the Judaizers insist that others be circumcised in order to be justified, they do so in order that they may 'boast' in the 'flesh' of others, even though they themselves are guilty of not having kept the law. When the apostle Paul speaks here of the failure of his opponents to 'keep the law', he cannot be referring to their failure to fulfil the boundary-marker requirements of the law for they were undoubtedly circumcised. What he is referring to rather is their failure to recognize the consequence of their boast in the flesh, namely, that such boasting requires a great deal more conformity to the whole law than they are able to perform. Thus, Paul's opponents stand condemned by their own boast.

In each of these three passages, then, Paul is contending with a larger issue than merely whether circumcision, for example, is a necessary precondition for inclusion among the people of God. Though new-perspective authors are quite correct in their emphasis upon the particular historical occasion for Paul's argument in Galatians, they do a great injustice to the way Paul answers his opponents.

B. 'Works' and 'Works of the Law' in Romans

The epistle to the Romans also uses the terms 'works' and 'works of the law' in a way that *clearly goes beyond* the limitations of certain boundary-marker requirements of the Mosaic law. Even though it is plausible that the term 'works of the law' initially has a more limited application in the argument of Galatians, in Romans it serves to show how *no human acts of obedience can justify anyone before God*. No works of any kind, whether performed by Jews or Gentiles, whether in conformity to the written law of God (through Moses) or that which is written upon human consciences, can be a basis for a sinner's justification. Whatever limited value the new perspective's understanding of the works of the law may have for a reading of Galatians, it is completely unsatisfactory with respect to the argument the apostle musters in his epistle to the Romans.

THE USE OF THE TERM 'WORKS' IN ROMANS

One feature that distinguishes Romans from Galatians is Paul's use of the term 'works' as a general reference to human deeds or acts. Though clearly linked to the expression, 'the works of the law', as we shall see below, it implies the broader and more general idea of *any human performance or deed*. Therefore, when it is used in connection with the doctrine of justification, therefore, 'works' refers to any act of obedience to the will of God that might play a role in procuring salvation or justifying any sinner before God (cf. *Rom.* 9:32).[5]

I. ROMANS 2:6

The first instance of this general use of 'works' occurs in Romans 2:6: 'He [God] will render to each one according to his works.' The context for Paul's declaration here is the certainty of God's righteous judgment. All will be judged, and this judgment will be in terms of the works or deeds performed by all, whether Jew or Gentile. In his development of this theme throughout chapter 2, the apostle makes it evident that his use of 'works' is inclusive. He speaks, for example, of those 'who do evil' (verse 9) and of those 'who do good' (verse 10). He also distinguishes between those who do evil 'under' the law and those who do evil 'without' the law (verse 12). To God, who shows no partiality, it makes no difference whether one is a Jew or a Gentile.

What matters is whether any human being can perform deeds or acts that are good and therefore pleasing to God. The burden of Paul's argument in the latter part of this chapter is that even Jews who are tempted to 'rely on the law and boast in God' are at no advantage in relation to the Gentiles. Even those who would teach the law to others stand condemned by its prohibitions against lying, idolatry, adultery, and the like.[6]

II. ROMANS 4

Paul's use of the same term in chapter 4 also confirms this general reference to human deeds or acts. Though we will consider in the following section how this chapter uses the more specific expression, 'works of the law', Paul begins by noting that Abraham was not justified by 'works'. To ascribe Abraham's justification to his works would contradict the truth of his justification by faith (verses 2–3). In order to underscore this opposition between faith and works in Abraham's justification, the apostle uses the analogy of a person who works for wages. Anyone who works for wages does not receive them 'as a gift but as his due' (verse 4). Thus, if Abraham were justified by works and not faith, he would be counted righteous on the basis of *deeds that have their just reward or wage*. However, Abraham's justification was by faith (alone). The contrast drawn by Paul in Romans 4 is between someone who works and earns a wage, and someone who believes and receives a gracious free gift (cf. *Rom.* 4:16). 'Works', in this contrast, refer to human actions that merit their due.

To further illustrate this contrast, Paul appeals to the example of David. Even though David undoubtedly kept what Dunn and others term the 'boundary markers' of the law, he was counted righteous 'apart from works' (verse 6). Despite David's 'lawless deeds' and 'sins' (verse 7), God accepted him by not counting his sins against him. Though Paul goes on to note that God's acceptance and forgiveness of David did not depend upon his circumcision (10–12), the point made by his general reference to David's works is to exclude *all works* (including, most notably, circumcision) as a basis for his forgiveness with God.

III. ROMANS 9

One particularly important instance of the use of the term 'works' is found in Romans 9, which addresses the question of the effectiveness of God's Word and promise in the salvation of his elect people. Speaking of God's election of Jacob rather than Esau, though both were sons of the same parents, Paul notes that the 'calling' of Jacob was on the basis of 'God's purpose of election' and not of 'works' (verse 11). The reference to 'works' in this passage is explained earlier, where the apostle declares that neither Esau nor Jacob 'had done anything either good or bad'. Here, then, the term refers to *any human deed or act in the most general sense possible*. Nothing done or accomplished by either of these two boys is the basis for the election of the one and the non-election of the other.[7]

THE USE OF THE EXPRESSION 'WORKS OF THE LAW' IN ROMANS

In addition to these instances where Paul uses the general expression 'works', the apostle also speaks more specifically in chapter 3 about the 'works of the law' (verses 20, 28). Within the context of his argument (*Rom.* 2–4), this expression is closely associated with the more general term 'works'. Though it may refer more particularly to obedience to the Mosaic law's commandments, especially with regard to circumcision, the thread of the argument through these chapters indicates that it is a fairly general expression. The 'works of the law' include any human deeds, whether performed by Jews or Gentiles, which are conformed to what might be termed the *moral claims* of the law.[8]

I. ROMANS 3:20

The first instance of the use of this expression is found in Romans 3:20: 'For by works of the law no human being will be justified in his sight, since through the law comes knowledge of sin.' The context of this statement is Paul's extended indictment of Gentiles and (especially!) Jews for their failure to keep the requirements of the law. Particularly instructive is his argument that the Jews have failed to abide by the requirements of the law in respect to the prohibitions of theft, adultery, and temple desecration (*Rom.* 2:17–29). The law's function to expose the reality of sin, therefore, includes *all failures to keep the obligations of the law*. It is not that the law exposes the Jews for their failures in respect to the 'boundary markers' of the law. Nor is the primary fault, according to Paul, the improper imposition of these requirements, including circumcision, upon the Gentiles. Rather Paul, or more precisely the law, finds fault with both Jews and Gentiles because they do not do what it requires of them.

II. ROMANS 3:28

The only other instance in Romans where this expression is found is in chapter 3: 'For we hold that one is justified by faith apart from works of the law' (verse 28). Upon first reading in its context, this text might appear to favour the idea that the 'works of the law' refer specifically to 'boundary-marker' requirements such as circumcision. For immediately after this verse the apostle underscores that God is the God of Gentiles and Jews alike, and not of Jews alone. Whether someone is circumcised or uncircumcised, does not matter, since justification is by faith and not by 'works of the law'.

However, it is not possible to restrict Paul's use of the 'works of the law' in this text to circumcision as a boundary-marker requirement of the law. Nor is it possible on that basis to restrict the reach of Paul's point about justification by faith 'apart from works' to the issue of who belongs to the people of God, as is taught by the new perspective. In the context of the argument in Romans 3 and 4, it is clear that Paul is maintaining that *all sinners, whether Jews or Gentiles, fail to keep the requirements of the law in all of its stipulations.* In Romans 3 the apostle sums up his indictment against all sinners by saying 'None is righteous, no, not one.' This is the prior context for the statement of Romans 3:28. Moreover, in Romans 4, as we previously noted, the apostle speaks quite broadly of the principle of 'works' in opposition to 'faith': whereas faith receives freely what God's grace grants, works obtain the reward on the basis of merit or wages due.

The problem with appealing to 'works of the law' as a means of justification is that it begs the question whether anyone can satisfy such a demand.

Though we still need to address the second and third questions raised in our introduction to this chapter, it is evident from a study of the relevant Scriptures that the new perspective's insistence that the 'works of the law' refer particularly to the boundary markers of the law *cannot be sustained*. The apostle's opposition to the teaching of justification by 'works of the law' does not simply refute a Jewish-Christian refusal to include Gentiles among God's people.

Though this may well be an important part of the occasion for Paul's treatment of justification in his writings, he clearly wishes to oppose any doctrine of justification by works in the most radical and general manner possible. No 'works of the law' of any kind whatsoever can possibly justify someone in the presence of God. Any appeal to justification by 'works of the law' utterly fails in the face of the truth that 'all have sinned and fall short of the glory of God' (*Rom.* 3:23).

2. DOES THE LAW EXPOSE HUMAN INABILITY?

Having treated the first of our three questions in the preceding, we shall now take up the second and third. Does Paul argue in his epistles that the law exposes human inability before God? Does he also oppose a form of teaching that expressed a kind of legalistic insistence upon justification by works of obedience to the law's stipulations?

As noted earlier, these questions go to the heart of the new perspective's claims that the Reformation reading of the apostle was inaccurate and therefore seriously mistaken; that the claim that Paul taught that no one is able to do what the law requires and thereby find acceptance with God misses the real point of the apostle's gospel. He focused not so much upon the question of how sinners can find acceptance with God as upon the question of how the promise to Abraham now includes Gentiles as well as Jews. The problem posed by his opponents was not their claim to self-justification before God, but their exclusion of Gentiles who believed in Christ from receiving the inheritance promised to Abraham.

Writers of the new perspective are well aware of Paul's polemics against any righteousness before God that comes by way of the law. In Galatians 2:16 the apostle insists that righteousness comes through faith in Jesus Christ, and not by the works of the law. Indeed, if righteousness were to come through the law, Christ would have died for no purpose (*Gal.* 2:21). Or, to cite the familiar words of Romans 3:21: 'But now the righteousness of God has been manifested apart from the law.' However we interpret this contrast between law-righteousness and faith-righteousness, Paul's clear insistence upon it is undeniable.

According to the new perspective, however, the Reformation's explanation of this contrast between law and faith misses the mark. According to the Reformation view, the law principally functions as a 'teacher of sin'. This is its so-called 'first use' (*usus paedagogicus*).[9] Accordingly, one of the law's most important functions is to make known, even to aggravate, the problem of human sinfulness and inability before God. By itself the law serves only to expose and diagnose the problem of human sinfulness. No one is able to perform what the law requires and therefore the law serves the purpose of condemning before God all, whether Jews or Gentiles, who fail in this regard. In this way, the law leads the condemned sinner to Christ who, because he perfectly kept the law and suffered its curse, is the believing sinner's righteousness before God.

New-perspective advocates offer a very different interpretation of the 'problem with the law'. Sanders maintains that Paul's primary objection to the law is based upon his Christology. Because Paul teaches that faith in Christ is the way of salvation, he rejects the law. According to Sanders, Paul argues from 'solution' (faith in Christ) to 'plight' (not by the law). Therefore, the apostle is not arguing against the law because he believes it to be inherently defective or unable to provide a means of salvation; rather, the law and Judaism are simply not Christianity.[10]

In a modification of this approach, Dunn and Wright argue that Paul's problem with the law was due, not to the inability of Jews or Greeks to do what it requires, but to its 'exclusivism'.[11] The Judaizers who insisted upon obedience to the law did so in order to exclude non-Jews from membership in the covenant community. Paul primarily opposed the law in its 'social' function, namely, as an instrument of Jewish exclusivism, rather than in its 'theological' function, namely, because it only served to expose human sinfulness before God. Whether one takes the approach of Sanders or Dunn/Wright to the problem of the law, neither approach leaves much room for an emphasis upon the law's condemning or accusing function. Viewed from the perspective of the progress of redemptive history, the law is simply deficient and is now superseded by the coming of Christ.

We will consider several relevant passages in Paul's writings that support the Reformation understanding of the law's function in exposing human inability. These passages illustrate a significant feature of the apostle's theology of the law, namely, that *it excludes any form of justification on the basis of obedience to its requirements.*

I. GALATIANS 3:10

In this passage, which we considered earlier with respect to Paul's use of the expression 'works of the law', the apostle writes, 'For all who rely on works of the law are under a curse; for it is written, "Cursed be everyone who does not abide by all things written in the Book of the Law, and do them."'

To appreciate the point Paul makes in this verse, it is critical to observe that it falls within the context of his preceding claim that no one can be justified by 'works of the law' (cf. *Gal.* 2:16; 3:5). Though no explanation was given previously as to why this is the case, Galatians 3:10 clearly intimates that *it is due to the inability and failure of every human being to abide by all things written in the book of the law.* The opening conjunction, 'for', indicates that Paul is now offering an explanation of the failure of the law as a means of justification.

The problem lies in the impossibility of anyone perfectly keeping its requirements. To escape God's curse, it is necessary to do all that the law demands; but since no one obeys the law perfectly, no one can hope to escape the law's curse by attempting to perform its stipulations. The conclusion, therefore, is that all who seek to obtain salvation by means of the law fall under the curse of God.

As we argued previously, when considering this text in connection with Paul's use of the expression the 'works of the law', the problem addressed goes beyond the failure of his opponents to observe the 'boundary-marker' requirements of the law. This is apparent from the citation of Deuteronomy 27:26. In the context of this Old Testament passage (*Deut.* 27-30), the people of Israel were threatened with the divine curse for any failure to observe the law of God. Those who hope to obtain the blessing of God, in terms of their obedience to the law's requirements, may only hope to do so by perfectly obeying the law. *Any failure, even with respect to the least demand of the law, forfeits the blessing of God and brings the certain prospect of judgment.* Therefore, if anyone seeks to find favour with God on the basis of the works of the law, he will undoubtedly be sorely disappointed.[12]

II. Galatians 5:3

Since we also treated this verse in our previous consideration of Paul's use of the terms 'works' and 'works of the law', we will restrict our comments here to the question of human inability. The apostle here solemnly warns his opponents that their insistence upon the obligation of circumcision carries with it the further obligation to do all that the law requires. 'I testify again to every man who accepts circumcision that he is obligated to keep the whole law.'

When the apostle uses the word, 'again' here, he means to refer to something he had previously written. It is quite likely that this is a reference to Galatians 3:10, and that the point being made is quite similar. Those who accept circumcision and require it of others in order to acknowledge their inclusion among the covenant people of God must recognize that they assume thereby *an oblig-ation to the whole law.*

Since his opponents link their justification before God with circumcision (cf. *Gal.* 5:4), they must be warned that they have embarked upon a course that obligates them to perfectly perform everything in the law.

Nothing less than obedience to the law in its entirety will serve to justify them. The most obvious interpretation of Paul's argument at this point is that he believed no one was capable of such obed-ience to the whole law. The problem confronting his opponents is not simply that they have chosen a way of justification other than that of faith in Christ; *it is also that they have chosen a way of justification that is beyond the realms of human possibility.* Those who seek to be justified by the law will only find frustration and defeat owing to their utter inability to keep entirely the law's obligations.

III. ROMANS 3:9–26

One of the more significant and extended passages on the subject of the law's exposure of human inability is Romans 3:9–26. This passage, which follows a lengthy treatment of the way God's wrath is being revealed against all the ungodliness and wickedness of men (*Rom.* 1:18–2:29), presents a powerful indictment of all sinners, Jews and Gentiles alike, before the judgment of God. After an opening section that outlines the privileges and advantages that belong to the Jews (verses 1–8), the apostle Paul appeals to a variety of Old Testament texts (verses 9–18) in order to prove that 'all, both Jews and Gentiles, are under the power of sin' (verse 9). Whatever advantages the Jews may possess, including the rite of circumcision and the reception of the oracles of God, these are of no value so far as their standing before God is concerned. 'There is none righteous, no, not one', says the apostle (verse 10). 'All have turned aside; together they have become worthless; no one does good, not even one' (verse 12). Unrelentingly, he adduces a variety of scriptural passages to prove the point that all have sinned and fall short of the glory of God.

What is especially important to our purpose, however, is the way Paul sums up the role of the law in his indictment of human sinfulness:

> Now we know that whatever the law says it speaks to those who are under the law, so that every mouth may be stopped, and the whole world may be held accountable to God. For by the works of the law no human being will be justified in his sight, since through the law comes knowledge of sin (verses 19–20).

The imagery of this passage is compelling and dramatic. The law is represented as functioning much like a prosecutor in a court of law, though the court here in question is the court of heaven. So compelling is the prosecutor's case, that every mouth is stopped or silenced. No word can be offered in defence that would answer the law's accusations. Thus, the apostle concludes that no human being can find justification before God by the works of the law. The law serves only to make sin known. It cannot and does not serve to

justify anyone before the judgment of God. Since the law is powerless to serve as a means of justification, the apostle concludes that
the only way to find forgiveness and favour with God is through
faith in Jesus Christ (verses 21–26). Only on the basis of Christ's
atoning work by his blood-shedding death can sinners be justified
by God's grace as a gift.

The Law Aggravates the Problem of Sin

In Romans 3:9–26 and the other passages we have considered, it
is evident that the apostle regarded the law, at least in one of its
uses, as an instrument that exposes human inability and sinfulness.
Consistent with such an emphasis are other passages in Paul's
writings that speak of the law's function *of making known* and
aggravating the problem of human sin and guilt before God. In
Romans 3:20, he speaks of the way the knowledge of sin comes
'through the law'. Rather than serving as a means of justification,
the law serves as a means of disclosing the inescapable guilt of all
human beings who fall short of its requirements. Remarkably, in
some of these passages the apostle can even speak of the law, not
only in its disclosure of human sin, but also in its *stimulation* of
further sinfulness. In Romans 5:20, for example, we read that 'the
law came in to *increase* the trespass, but where sin increased, grace
abounded all the more.'

Similarly, in the well-known and much-disputed passage in
Romans 7, Paul, while affirming that the law is 'holy and righteous
and good' (verse 12), notes that it is powerless to effect what it
demands. Due to human depravity and sin, the law's demands only
'make sin known' (verse 7) and serve to 'arouse our sinful passions'
(verse 5). When the law declares, 'you shall not covet', it makes sin
come alive and thus brings death (verses 9–10).[13] Because the law
by itself can only aggravate and expose the reality of human sin and
guilt, the apostle describes the ministry of the law (of Moses) in
2 Corinthians 3 as a 'ministry of condemnation' and 'of death'
(verses 7, 9). Unlike the ministry of the Spirit of Christ, which gives
life from the dead, the ministry of the 'letter' can only kill (verse 6).

One of the more significant ways in which the apostle sets forth
the law's function of exposing and aggravating the problem of

human sinfulness is his use of the expressions, 'under the law' and 'under sin'. These are used synonymously in Romans 6:14: 'For sin will have no dominion over you, since you are not under law but under grace.' By using these expressions as synonyms, Paul suggests that to be 'under the law' is tantamount to being under the tyranny of sin. To be 'under grace' is tantamount to being freed from the power and dominion of sin.

In Galatians, the apostle also uses language that intimates a close connection between the law and the problem of human sin. For example, he speaks of those who are 'under a curse' due to their failure to abide by all that is written in the book of the law (3:10). He speaks of those who are 'imprisoned under sin' by the Scripture, 'so that the promise by faith in Jesus Christ might be given to those who believe' (3:22). When speaking of 'Scripture' in this text, Paul is probably referring to the Torah, the inscripturated administration of the Mosaic covenant. All who are 'under the law' (3:23; 4:4-5; 5:18), remain 'under a pedagogue' (3:25), 'under guardians and managers' (4:2), and 'under the elements of the world' (4:3). In all of these expressions, the apostle underscores the sharp contrast between being under the law, which can only bring the curse and death due to its violators, and being 'in Christ', which brings blessing and life to all who through faith are joined to him.

In the older Reformation understanding of these expressions, the law's role as a 'pedagogue' was primarily viewed in negative and personal terms.[14] By means of this kind of language, Paul was understood to emphasize the way in which the law of Moses condemned all who failed to abide by its provisions. However, among writers of the new perspective, it is often argued that this represents a failure to read Paul's argument in terms of its *salvation-historical* framework.

According to this view, when Paul speaks of the law as a 'pedagogue' or a 'guardian', he means only to stress its role at an earlier point in the course of redemptive history, namely, during the period of Israel's adolescence or immaturity. In this period, the role of the law was primarily positive, ensuring Israel's life and preserving her against sin until the coming of Christ. The law functions, therefore, in a positive manner to prepare Israel for the coming of Christ. But now that Christ has come, the law has been superseded and surpassed. To remain 'under the law', therefore, would be to deny the significance of Christ's coming and the way in which he surpasses the law. This understanding of Paul's language regarding the law, particularly the expression of being 'under the law', offers a substantial alternative to the Reformation claim that the law's pedagogical function was to expose the power and guilt of human sinfulness.

Though it is undoubtedly true that Paul's descriptions of the law and what it means to be 'under the law' are shaped by his conviction regarding the progress of redemptive history, any attempt to treat the law in unduly *benign* terms fails to do justice to Paul's language. The problem with the law is not simply that it is surpassed or even displaced by the new covenant in Christ; rather the law held its subjects 'captives', and 'imprisoned' them 'until the coming faith would be revealed' (*Gal.* 3:23; cf. 3:22). No doubt, in doing so the law served to lead its subjects by the hand to Christ, in whom righteousness is revealed and the promise of the covenant realized. In this respect, the law and the promise in Christ are companions, and the law as guardian serves the blessed purpose of preparing its subjects for the coming of Christ. Nevertheless, the particular way in which the law does this is *by aggravating and revealing the problem of human transgressions*.

In this connection, it is important to note that Paul's language about the law as 'pedagogue' and 'guardian' occurs in the context of Galatians 3:19, 'Why then the law? It was added because of transgressions, until the offspring should come to whom the promise had been made.' When Paul uses the language, 'because of transgressions', to explain the purpose for which the law was given, it does not seem likely that he is speaking positively about the law. Though some suggest that this language expresses the idea of a 'restraint' upon sin, this is not consistent with the language Paul uses regarding the law in the immediate context of Galatians 3:19ff. or, for that matter, in the argument of the whole epistle. In the verses that follow he maintains that the law captivates all under the power of sin (verses 21–22). In the context of his argument in this epistle, the apostle insists that justification occurs not by the works of the law but by faith in Jesus Christ. This insistence would be buttressed by an argument that the law *exacerbates* the problem of sin; however, it would be weakened by the claim that the law actually served the benign purpose of *diminishing* sin. Such a claim could hardly reinforce Paul's opposition to his Jewish-Christian opponents who taught that obedience to the law serves as an instrument for justification. Furthermore, a similar expression is used by Paul in Romans 5:20: 'Now the law came in to increase the transgression.' Galatians 3:19 probably says more than Romans 5:20, namely, that the law not only exposes but also provides the occasion for increased transgressions.

3. DID PAUL OPPOSE 'LEGALISM' OR BOASTING IN HUMAN STRENGTH?

The last question to be addressed regarding Paul's view of the law is whether he articulated his doctrine of justification over against a legalistic teaching of salvation upon the basis of works performed in obedience to the law. Though the new perspective argues that this was not a significant problem in Paul's day, there is evidence in Paul's writings that his opponents were putting their confidence before God in their own works of obedience to the law. There is also evidence that the 'boasting' of some of Paul's Jewish-Christian opponents was not simply a boasting in national privilege and distinction, but also a boasting in obedience to the requirements of God's law.[15] Once again our procedure in addressing this question will be to consider briefly several key passages.

I. ROMANS 3:27–4:8

At the outset of this section of Paul's argument in the opening chapters of Romans, the apostle refers to a kind of 'boasting' that is wholly excluded by the 'law of faith' (verse 27). The reason for the exclusion is then set forth: 'For we hold that one is justified by faith apart from works of the law' (verses 27–28). The implication of Paul's explanation is that some of his opponents were boasting of their works performed in obedience to the law. Such boasting militates against the truth of the gospel which Paul had summarized previously in Romans 3:21–26. If we are justified by God's grace 'as a gift, through the redemption that is in Christ Jesus', then it would be contrary to God's grace in Christ to appeal to any of our own law-works in respect to our justification. The boasting, then, to which Paul refers in these verses refers to a legalistic emphasis upon works of the law as a means of justification.

Immediately after these verses, however, Paul raises the question, 'Is God the God of Jews only? Is he not the God of Gentiles also? Yes, of Gentiles also' (verse 29). This question, which Paul poses in conjunction with his exclusion of boasting, leads some writers of the new perspective to argue that the problem Paul identifies in this passage is not legalism but Jewish exclusivism. E. P. Sanders, for example, notes that there is no evidence to suggest that Paul opposes legalism in this passage. According to Sanders, in this passage Paul simply observes that no one is justified by works and therefore there is no ground for boasting. There is no evidence to suggest that Abraham or any other member of the Jewish covenant community was boasting of their righteousness before God.[16]

Dunn, as might be expected, takes a slightly different approach: the problem Paul opposes is 'privileged status as *attested* and *maintained* by the law.'[17] Paul does not condemn a boast that focuses primarily in the performance of works of the law, which are regarded as the basis for finding acceptance or favour with God; rather, he tackles and condemns a boasting that is born out of a kind of Jewish exclusivism, which regards God's covenant favour and grace as a peculiar privilege reserved for those who are Jews and not Gentiles.

Though there may be an element of truth in Dunn's interpretation, neither his nor Sanders' approach adequately explain Paul's argument in this passage. When Paul sweepingly rejects all works of the law as the basis for our justification, it is hardly likely that he is addressing a merely imaginary or hypothetical opposition. He is not shadow boxing when in strong language he speaks of how boasting is 'shut out' by the law of faith (3:27). The question, 'What becomes of our boasting?', is not merely rhetorical. Furthermore, when he suggests that Abraham, whose faith was reckoned to him for righteousness, has nothing to 'boast about before God' (4:2), he makes a broad and inclusive point regarding *all human boasting about works before God.* For this to be true, it is not necessary to assume that Abraham was himself guilty of such boasting; it only needs to be the case that, if works were the basis for our justification, then we would have an occasion for boasting. However, as the apostle vigorously argues in Romans 4:4–8, the principle operative in justification is that of grace and not of works. When God justifies the ungodly, he counts as righteous *those who have not worked and therefore have no basis in themselves for a claim upon God's grace.* The kind of boasting that most properly fits within this context, therefore, is not a boasting in racial privileges or Jewish distinctives, but in any performance or work that might be regarded as the ground for our justification. In other words, *the argument of Romans 3:27–4:8 constitutes a frontal attack upon any form of legalism.* Why would the apostle present an argument that over-reaches its target? It is more accurate to deduce that his arrow is aimed at a very real target.

It should also be observed that there is something rather unlikely in Dunn's explanation. As he himself acknowledges, the boast of some in their 'privileged status' included their claim to have received the law and to maintain themselves by it before God. It is hard to see how this differs in any significant way from the Reformation claim that Paul was opposing legalism when he articulated his doctrine of justification. After all, boasting in the privilege of covenant status, *which is confirmed and maintained by means of the law,* is hardly distinguishable from a boasting in works before God. To share this boast, one would have to become a Jew, and to become a Jew, one would have to attest and maintain this status by works.[18]

II. ROMANS 9:30–10:8

Romans 9:30–10:8 is an especially important passage for the question of whether Paul opposed a form of legalism in his articulation of the doctrine of justification. The critical question answered by Paul in this passage is why many of his Jewish kinsmen stumbled at the gospel of Jesus Christ. In the opening sections of Romans 9, the apostle argues that the unbelief of the Jews does not represent a failure of God's Word. Throughout the course of redemptive history, God's 'purpose of election' distinguished those who were 'children of the promise' from those who were not (9:8, 11). Far from representing a failure of God's Word, the unbelief of many of Paul's fellow-Jews was the occasion for the realization of God's purpose to bring salvation to the Gentiles. In this way, God's promise through Hosea was being fulfilled: 'Those who were not my people I will call "my people", and her who was not beloved I will call "beloved"' (9:25).

After providing this initial answer to the question regarding Israel's unbelief, Paul goes on to develop more specifically the occasion for Israel's resistance to the gospel (9:30–10:8). Why, he asks, did Israel 'who pursued a law that would lead to right-eousness . . . not succeed in reaching that law' (verse 31)? The answer is that Israel 'did not pursue it by faith, but as if it were based on works' (verse 32). By pursuing righteousness on the basis of works, Israel 'stumbled over the stumbling stone' and thereby fulfilled the prophecy of Isaiah 28:16. The fault Paul finds with this pursuit is not simply that Israel sought righteousness on the basis of works. Seeking to be obedient to the law of God is not Israel's offence. The fault, according to the contrast Paul draws in these verses at the close of chapter 9, is that this pursuit was not 'by faith'.

The likeliest explanation, therefore, of Paul's words at the close of Romans 9 is that he is exposing the bad-faith attempt on the part of many within Israel to obtain a righteousness that is based upon works performed in obedience to the law rather than upon faith in Jesus Christ. It is noteworthy that the 'works' in question, as was true of Paul's use of this term in Romans 4, *refer to any human act or achievement that might be regarded as meriting or earning a wage*. In other words, Paul opposes in these verses *more* than a Jewish nationalism that insisted upon obedience to the boundary-marker requirements of the law. There is nothing in the immediate context to suggest that he is only referring to such things as circumcision or dietary requirements.

As if the point were not clear enough at the end of Romans 9, the apostle goes on at the outset of chapter 10 to reiterate his explan-ation of the principal reason Israel stumbled through unbelief.

For, being ignorant of the righteousness that comes from God, and seeking to establish their own, they did not submit to God's righteousness. For Christ is the end of the law for righteousness to everyone who believes (10:3–4).

The apostle here explicitly characterizes the unbelief of Israel as symptomatic of a kind of *self-righteousness*. Rather than submitting to the righteousness of God, which is granted to all who believe in Christ, Israel sought to establish her own righteousness. The language Paul uses in these verses is similar, as we shall see below, to the language of Philippians 3:9. It clearly expresses a negative judgment upon Israel's attempt to obtain righteousness by some other means than through faith in Christ. Furthermore, it cannot be maintained that the only problem Paul diagnoses is that Israel had failed to make the transition to the new circumstance in redemptive history. Though there is a considerable debate regarding Paul's use of the language of Christ as the 'end' of the law, the primary reason that Paul identifies for Israel's failure to believe in Christ was her pursuit of a righteousness of her own. Undoubtedly, Israel's unbelief represented, as proponents of the new perspective argue,[19] a pride in her covenant privilege over against the Gentiles and a failure to see that the law finds its fulfilment or goal in Christ. But if the question is pressed regarding the reason for this unbelief, pride, and failure, then it cannot be denied that the apostle ascribes it to *Israel's boast in her own righteous observance of the law*.

An important part of Paul's argument in this passage is his citation of Leviticus 18:5 in Romans 10:5: 'For Moses writes about the righteousness that is based on the law, that the person who does the commandments shall live by them.' Since Paul also cites this passage in Galatians 3:12 in a negative way to argue that life and blessing cannot come by way of obedience to the commandments of God, it is most likely that he cites it here for the same purpose. Though obedience to the commandments brings life and blessing in fellowship with God, such obedience lies beyond the reach of anyone, including the zealous Israelite who seeks thereby to establish his own righteousness before God. Thus, Paul appeals to Leviticus

18:5 in the context of his argument in this passage to prove the futility of any attempt to pursue righteousness by the law instead of by faith. The citation of Leviticus 18:5 confirms that Paul is opposing a use of the law as a means of justification by works.

Paul's use of Leviticus 18:5 in this passage raises an interesting question regarding the meaning of this text in its original Old Testament setting. According to that setting, Leviticus 18:5 seems to be used to positively commend obedience to God's commandments as the way of blessing within the covenant community. When Paul cites this text, however, he seems to concede the way it was used by his opponents as a commendation of securing righteousness before God through obedience to the commandments. Paul's appeal to this text seems to approve the 'legalistic' interpretation of it by unbelieving Israel.

Perhaps the best answer to this question is one suggested by Moisés Silva.[20] According to Silva, it is likely that Paul's use of Leviticus 18:5 in this passage is 'coloured' by the interpretation of his opponents. Since his opponents were probably using this text to support their pursuit of justification by obedience to the commandments of God,

Paul cites it, *in the limited setting of the issue of justification,* to prove that the law cannot serve as the *source* of our righteousness before God. Silva maintains that, in other contexts, Paul could speak of the law in the most positive of terms. In Romans 10:5, however, he turns the tables on his opponents' use of this text by arguing that the law cannot be 'life-generating', though it might in other contexts be life-preserving.

Because Paul focuses exclusively upon the law in respect to justification, he can argue that the law cannot play the role his opponents ascribe to it. The law, when viewed narrowly (by itself, as consisting merely of God's commandments), only reminds us that the way to obtain life and favour with God is through faith in Christ rather than through obedience to its commands. The law *by itself* enunciates a principle—'do this and live'—that compels the conclusion that justification cannot come by the law but only by faith in Christ.[21]

III. PHILIPPIANS 3:2-11

The last passage we will consider in this connection is Philippians 3:2–11. It is of particular interest since authors of the new perspective have significantly reinterpreted it.

E. P. Sanders, for instance, argues that it should not be read in overly personal terms. The apostle is basically arguing that, since salvation now comes through faith in Christ, there is no room left for the law as the way of righteousness. According to Sanders, Paul is not arguing here against those who boast of their 'own' righteousness before God. For example, when the apostle says that his life under the law was a 'gain' (verse 7), he speaks positively of the law and its usefulness prior to the coming of Christ.[22] For his part, Dunn treats this passage in the same context as many others in Paul's writings; the righteousness that Paul rejects is a Jewish covenantal exclusiveness, which prevents Gentiles from participating in the blessings of the covenant. Therefore, Paul is not opposing a kind a legalism in this passage, but a Jewish claim to covenant privilege and blessing that excludes the Gentiles.[23]

One of the more remarkable features of the handling of Philippians 3:2–11 by writers of the new perspective is the way Paul's representation of his life under Judaism is interpreted. When he declares that he was 'as to righteousness, under the law blameless', he positively affirms his own accomplishments by the standard of the law of God. Paul did not articulate his doctrine of justification on the basis of any conviction that he was an incompetent sinner, who was incapable of doing what the law requires and thereby commend himself to God. On the contrary, he expresses a considerable confidence in his own righteousness when measured by the standard of the law. The problem with the law, therefore, is not that no one can do what it requires and thereby be justified.

Here, as in so many other places in Paul's polemics regarding justification, the apostle either wants to maintain that the law has been supplanted by the coming of Christ or serves as a barrier to the inclusion of the Gentiles. The problem with those who boasted of their own righteousness was not that they were failing to abide by the requirements of the law. Indeed, Paul regards himself as a paramount example of someone whose righteousness by the standard of the law was 'blameless' and exemplary. We have to look for the problem elsewhere.

There are, however, several serious difficulties with this interpretation of Philippians 3:2–11. In the first place, it is difficult to defend the idea that Paul actually means to assert his own 'blamelessness' by the standard of the law. To be sure, when compared to the boast of his opponents, Paul does not hesitate to compare himself favourably with them. As much as anyone, he has the right to place his confidence in the flesh. 'If anyone else thinks he has reason for confidence in the flesh', he asserts, 'I have more: circumcised on the eighth day, of the people of Israel, of the tribe of Benjamin, a Hebrew of Hebrews; as to the law, a Pharisee; as to zeal, a persecutor of the church.' By the standard of blamelessness used by those whom he opposes, Paul compares rather favourably. But can we really take this to mean that Paul believed that his own righteousness was sufficient to commend him to God's favour? If we are to take his self-testimony in other passages seriously, the answer to this question must be a resolute 'No'.[24]

Furthermore, the credentials the apostle cites to prove his 'blamelessness' by the standard of the law are inconsistent with Sanders' and Dunn's interpretation of this passage. If the problem were primarily the failure of his opponents to see that salvation is *now* only through Christ or the insistence that the Jews have privileges from which the Gentiles are excluded, why does Paul speak of his achievements in such broad terms? The law-righteousness that Paul describes here *exceeds or goes beyond* what Dunn and others refer to as the 'boundary-marker' requirements of the law. This righteousness includes a broad range of acts of obedience born of a zeal to serve and obey God. By describing his righteousness in such broad terms, Paul refutes the boast of those who were undoubtedly making similar claims for their own legalistic accomplishments.

Moreover, if Sanders is correct that the problem with Paul's opponents was that they were not up-to-date so far as the new circumstance in redemptive history was concerned, it is odd that the apostle does not simply assert the same. Why does he not simply state that the problem with those who do not receive Christ by faith is that they are living in the past?

The argument of this passage, however, proceeds rather differently. Paul not only assumes that his opponents are guilty of a misplaced confidence in their own flesh; they are also, on that account, unwilling to receive the righteousness that is from God by faith. The language used throughout this passage is strongly personal and even existential. He speaks of those whose confidence is in their own flesh and righteousness (verse 4). He also speaks quite emphatically in the first person, not only when he compares his own righteousness with theirs but also when he speaks of the righteousness that is from God. In the strongest possible terms, he states:

> I count everything loss for the sake of Christ. Indeed, I count everything as loss because of the surpassing worth of knowing Christ Jesus my Lord. For his sake I have suffered the loss of all things and count them as rubbish, in order that I may gain Christ and be found in him, not having a righteousness of my own that comes from the law, but that which comes through faith in Christ, the righteousness from God that depends on faith (verses 7–9).

For these reasons, we are convinced that Paul opposes a kind of boasting in the flesh that is characteristic of all legalism. Rather than relying by faith upon the righteousness that is from God, those who place their confidence in the flesh look to their own achievements as the basis for their commendation before God. Just as in the case of the boasting mentioned in Romans 3:27–28 and Romans 4:1–5, this boasting or confidence reflects an unwillingness to acknowledge God alone as the source of our justification in Christ. Such confidence is sinful in that it fails to give the praise and honour to God, to whom it properly belongs.[25]

CONCLUSION

A significant part of the new perspective's criticism of the Reformation perspective on Paul relates to its view of his understanding of the law of God. In our examination of the new perspective's claims regarding Paul's theology of the law, however, we have not found them to be warranted by a reading of Paul's writings. Based on our study of these Scriptures, each of the questions we raised regarding the new perspective's handling of Paul's treatment of the law, leads us to the conclusion that the Reformation's understanding of Paul's arguments ought to be preserved while that of the new perspective ought to be rejected.

The new perspective interprets Paul's terminology regarding 'the works of the law' or 'works' as being primarily restricted to the boundary-marker requirements of the law, which distinguish Jews from Gentiles. However, we have seen from his own writings that Paul uses this terminology in a much broader sense. No doubt the occasion for Paul's rejection of justification by the works of the law included the exclusivism of Judaizers who insisted upon obedience to the law's boundary markers before Gentiles could be acknowledged as members of the covenant community. Nevertheless, Paul's argument goes well beyond the issue of the inclusion of Gentiles through obedience to these boundary-marker requirements. According to the apostle, no one, whether Jew or Gentile, can be justified by the works of the law, because no one is able to do what the law requires. The works of the law, which are excluded as a basis for justification, include any acts of obedience to all the requirements of the law. These include circumcision and other boundary-marker stipulations; but Paul understood them to include all the other stipulations contained in the law.

The reason Paul adduces for arguing that no one can be justified by obedience to the law is not simply that faith in Christ is now the only badge of inclusion within the covenant family of God. The tendency of the new perspective is to explain Paul's opposition to the works of the law exclusively on the basis of the transition that occurred in the history of redemption with the coming of Christ: now that Christ has come, it is no longer necessary to submit to the law's boundary-marker requirements in order to be numbered among the people of God. However, this explanation of Paul's opposition to justification by works of the law is totally inadequate. One of the important elements in Paul's explanation of the futility of being justified by the works of the law is the inability of any sinner, whether Jew or Gentile, to do what the law requires. Therefore, anyone who hopes to find life and blessing from God on the basis of his own observance of the law will experience only futility, frustration, and finally damnation. Since no one can do what the law requires, justification on the basis of the law is impossible.

Paul also clearly opposes a form of legalism in his rejection of the works of the law as a means of justification for sinners. The 'boasting' of Paul's opponents is not merely a pride in their identity as Jews and members of the covenant community. Their boasting also included the idea that, as recipients of the law of God, they were able to commend themselves to God's favour and acceptance on the basis of their own obedience to its requirements. In the final analysis, the new perspective's suggestion that the problem Paul opposed was a form of Jewish exclusivism, not Jewish legalism, is not sustainable.

The Reformation perspective, which identified the boasting of Paul's opponents as a boasting in their own achievements under the law, more accurately explains the occasion for Paul's writing against them. Indeed, the new perspective's assumption, that Jewish exclusivism represents an alternative form of boasting to that of Jewish legalism, is untenable. For this boast was intimately related to the idea that, as recipients of the law, their obedience to the law's requirements would grant them a privileged status before God.

NOTES

[1] For more detailed summaries of Paul's uses of the language of 'law', see Thomas R. Schreiner, *The Law and Its Fulfillment*, pp. 33–40; Douglas J. Moo, '"Law", "Works of the Law", and Legalism in Paul', *Westminster Theological Journal* 45 (1983), pp. 73–100; Stephen Westerholm, 'Torah, *nomos*, and Law: A Question of "Meaning"', *Studies in Religion* 15 (1986), pp. 327–36; and Colin G. Kruse, *Paul, The Law, and Justification*, pp. 287–90. For a survey of the discussion of Paul's view of the law among New Testament scholars, including writers of the new perspective, see Veronica Koperski, *What Are They Saying About Paul and the Law?* (Mahwah, NJ: Paulist Press, 2001); Heikki Räisänen, *The Torah and Christ: Essays In German and English on the Problem of the Law in Early Christianity* (Helsinki: Finnish Exegetical Society, 1986),

pp. 3–24; Heikki Räisänen, *Paul and the Law* (Philadelphia: Fortress, 1986); and A. Andrew Das, *Paul, the Law, and the Covenant* (Peabody, MS: Hendrickson, 2001). Räisänen's studies argue that Paul's diverse uses of the law include several inconsistencies or anomalies that are incapable of harmonization. Das' study concludes that, whereas the new perspective properly calls attention to Paul's 'ethnic' use of the law as an instrument for distinguishing Jews from Gentiles, it fails to deal adequately with Paul's teaching that the law requires a perfect obedience that uncovers human sinfulness.

[2] In our earlier summary of the positions of James D. G. Dunn and N. T. Wright, we noted the way they treat this passage. See James D. G. Dunn, 'Works of the Law and the Curse of the Law', pp. 215–41; and N. T. Wright, *The Climax of the Covenant*, pp. 137–56. Though Wright's handling of this passage allows for a more general disobedience on the part of Israel to the law of God, which was the occasion for the curse of Israel's exile that Christ assumed as her representative, he believes the passage does not speak of each individual's disobedience to the law. Both tend to restrict Paul's argument with those who appeal to the 'works of the law' to an objection to Jewish exclusivism.

[3] See Das, *Paul, the Law, and the Covenant*, pp. 145–70, for an extended treatment of these verses that leads to the same conclusion. Cf. James M. Hamilton, 'N. T. Wright and Saul's Moral Bootstraps', pp. 152–5.

[4] Cf. James 2:10: 'For whoever keeps the whole law but fails in one point has become accountable for all of it.'

[5] For a more extended defence of this claim than that provided in what follows, see Douglas J. Moo, '"Law", "Works of the Law", and Legalism in Paul', pp. 90–9; and Charles E. B. Cranfield, '"The Works of the Law" in the Epistle to the Romans', *Journal for the Study of the New Testament* 43 (1991), pp. 89–101.

[6] N. T. Wright, 'The Law in Romans 2', pp. 131–50, argues that the criticism of the law-breaking of the Jews in this passage is addressed to their unwillingness to include Gentiles in the covenant community, not their moral failures or defects. Consistent with the general tendency of the new perspective, Wright takes the case Paul makes in this passage to be framed by a historical-redemptive question of the inclusion of Gentiles among God's people as heirs of the promise to Abraham. Thus, Paul's case regarding the law and the works of the law is aimed at the question of covenant status, not how individuals who are sinners can find favour with God. Though he does speak of the general problem of human sin in his commentary on Romans, Wright still contends that the principal issue is the inclusion of Gentiles within the worldwide family of God. Cf. Wright, *Romans*, esp. pp. 464–86.

[7] For instances of a similar, general use of the language of 'works' in Paul's epistles, see 2 Cor. 11:5; Col. 1:21; Gal. 5:19. For instances of this usage in passages that are not universally acknowledged as authentically Pauline, see Eph. 2:9-10; 5:11; 1 Tim. 2:10; 5:10, 25; 6:18; 2 Tim. 1:9; 4:14; Titus 1:16; 2:7, 14; 3:5, 8, 14. Even if we were to grant the view that these latter texts are

not Pauline, which I do not, they minimally suggest that an author influenced by Paul took him to exclude all boasting in any works whatever in the matter of salvation (*Eph.* 2:9).

[8] It should be noted that close parallels to this language of the 'works of the law' can be found in the literature of Second-Temple Judaism. In these parallels, 'works of the law' and 'works of righteousness' refer to acts of obedience to the whole law, whether in its so-called ceremonial or moral requirements. For a brief treatment of these parallels and sources that consider them, see Schreiner, *The Law and Its Fulfillment,* pp. 52–54. These parallels are of particular significance, since the new perspective properly insists upon a reading of Paul's writings *in the context* of Second-Temple Judaism.

[9] Writers in the Reformed tradition usually distinguish this use of the law from two other uses: the 'political or civil use' *(usus politicus sive civilis),* which refers to the law's function in restraining sin within the civil order, and the 'didactic or normative use' *(usus didacticus sive normativus),* which refers to the law's function in ordering the believer's life of gratitude.

[10] E. P. Sanders, *Paul and Palestinian Judaism,* pp. 442–7, 474–511.

[11] Dunn, 'Works of the Law and the Curse of the Law', pp. 215–41; Wright, 'The Law in Romans 2', pp. 131–50.

[12] I deliberately use the singular here to reject an interpretation of this passage that regards the curse in exclusively 'corporate' terms. Cf. Wright, *The Climax of the Covenant,* pp. 137–56, who argues that Paul would have excluded himself from this predicament (after all, Paul says in Philippians 3:6 that he was 'blameless' with respect to the law!). Though this argument is highly unlikely when you consider Paul's self-testimony in other passages (*Rom.* 7; *1 Cor.* 15:8–9; cf. *1 Tim.* 1:15), it fails to do justice to the singular forms Paul uses in Galatians 3:10–13 ('everyone', 'no one', 'the one').

[13] Cf. Thomas Schreiner, *The Law and Its Fulfillment,* p. 73: 'Paul takes a step further . . . in his theology of the law. Most Jews of his day believed that a greater understanding of the contents of the law would curb the sinful impulse and prevent sin from dominating a person's life. Paul turns this theology on its head by saying that the law does not restrain sin but *stimulates* and *provokes* it.' Also cf. Westerhom, *Perspectives Old and New on Paul,* pp. 422–9.

[14] Hence the language of the 'pedagogical' or 'first use' of the law, as a means of exposing human disobedience and guilt. See note 9 above.

[15] The presence of legalism in the teaching of Paul's opponents does not require that they relied exclusively upon their own works to find favour with God. It only requires that they insisted upon works performed in obedience to God as a (partial) means of self-justification. Paul's opponents were no doubt familiar with the themes of God's grace and election of Israel. As we have earlier argued, they were not full-fledged 'Pelagians' (to speak anachronistically). The question is, however: Did they insist upon works performed in obedience to the law as an indispensable ground for the believer's justification

before God? And did they believe that they were capable of performing what the law required? Legalism includes both elements: the insistence upon obedience to the law as a means of justification, and the corollary conviction that such obedience is possible for sinners.

[16] E. P. Sanders, *Paul, The Law, and the Jewish People*, pp. 33–5.

[17] Dunn, 'Yet Once More — "The Works of the Law"', p. 113.

[18] Cf. Simon J. Gathercole, *Where is Boasting?* Based upon his study of the motif of 'boasting' in Second-Temple Judaism and the argument of Romans 1–5, Gathercole concludes that the boast was not only made in relation to others (Gentiles) but also *in relation to God* before whom the faithful Jew expected to be vindicated/justified for his adherence to the law.

[19] James D. G. Dunn, *Romans 9-16*, pp. 581–95.

[20] 'Is the Law Against the Promises? The Significance of Galatians 3:21 for Covenant Continuity', in William S. Barker and W. R. Godfrey, eds., *Theonomy: A Reformed Critique* (Grand Rapids: Zondervan, 1990), pp. 163–7.

[21] Silva, 'Is the Law Against the Promises?', p. 165: 'On the basis of Paul's positive statements about the law, I wish to argue that the apostle did indeed regard the law as leading to life — but not as life generating! — and that therefore he would have affirmed the truth expressed in Leviticus 18:5. On the other hand, he vigorously denied that the law could be the *source* of righteousness and life; indeed, he denied not merely that the law could be such but also the view that God had given it (ἐδόθη, 3:21) with such a purpose (otherwise, it would be opposed to the promise).'

[22] Sanders, *Paul, The Law, and the Jewish People*, pp. 44–5.

[23] Dunn, *Romans 9-16*, p. 588.

[24] See the references cited earlier in note 7.

[25] Cf. *1 Cor.* 1:29, 31; 4:7; *2 Cor.* 5:12; *Gal.* 6:4, 13.

8

'THE RIGHTEOUSNESS OF GOD' AND JUSTIFICATION

Now that we have considered the new perspective's understanding of Paul's use of the terms 'works' and 'works of the law', we are in a position to take up the important question of his understanding of the terms 'the righteousness of God' and the 'justification' of believers. Corresponding to its claims regarding Paul's use of 'works' or 'works of the law', the new perspective argues that Paul uses 'the righteousness of God' and 'justification' in ways very different from those suggested by the Reformers.

In order to appreciate the new perspective's understanding of God's righteousness and the justification of believers, we need to recall briefly the Reformation's understanding of these phrases. 'The righteousness of God' was understood primarily to be a gift from God, which was granted and imputed to believers in Christ.

When the Reformers pointed to Paul's doctrine of justification by faith, they claimed to have discovered something that was missing from the traditional teaching of the medieval Roman Catholic Church. The latter understood the righteousness of God primarily in terms of the *demand* upon sinners to obey the law in order to be justified. If sinners are to be justified and received into God's favour, they must keep the law and thereby satisfy the obligations of God's righteousness. Salvation, in this medieval view, required that believers co-operate with God's grace and, by obeying the law, maintain their favour with God. For Luther and the Reformers, however, the chief point of emphasis was upon the righteousness of God as the *gift* of a righteous status, which is freely granted and imputed to believers on account of Christ's saving work. The righteousness of God is freely given to believers for the sake of Christ's work, and this righteousness restores believers to favour with God. Rather than stressing the believer's own righteousness,

which comes from obedience to the righteous requirements of the
law, the Reformers taught that the righteousness whereby sinners
are justified is not their own, but an 'alien' or 'imputed' righteousness, which is from God and received through faith alone.[1]

Medieval and Reformation theology, it should be noted,
commonly assumed that the righteousness of God ordinarily refers
to God's moral character: God is righteous and requires righteousness on the part of his image-bearers. His creatures' failure to live
in accordance with the moral demands of his law is culpable
demerit that requires punishment. The righteousness of God, therefore, refers both to God's moral character, which demands righteous conduct from his creatures, and to his moral government,
which metes out punishment upon those whose conduct is unrighteous. In traditional theological terminology, the righteousness of
God was understood to be an essential attribute of God, which
is expressed administratively in God's moral government of all
things, and distributively in his just reward and punishment of
saints and sinners respectively.

Within this context the key question was: How can God, who
must act in accordance with his own righteousness, accept or justify
sinners who have disobeyed his law and deserve condemnation and
death? What made this question so compelling in the Reformation
period was the common assumption of Protestant and Roman
Catholic alike that God could not justify sinners at the expense of
his own righteousness. The righteousness of God had to be satisfied
in order for sinners to find favour with God.

Though Romanist and Reformation theology had this assumption in common, the great divergence between their respective
understandings of justification came into focus upon the question
of whether the righteousness that justifies the believer is *wholly
God's gift* in Christ or consists *partly in the believer's good works.*
In the Reformation view, the perfect obedience and sacrifice of
Christ upon the cross fully satisfied the righteousness of God.
Believers, who receive by faith alone the free gift of God's righteousness in Christ, are justified. The righteousness that justifies
believers is, accordingly, an alien or external righteousness. In the
Roman Catholic view, by contrast, the righteousness of God

requires that forgiven sinners maintain and increase their justification by good works which merit further grace. The righteousness of God is not merely given and imputed to believers, but is also required of believers in order for them to be justified. In the language of the sixteenth-century debates, the Reformers insisted that believers are justified by an 'alien' or 'imputed' righteousness, whereas the Roman Catholic Church insisted that believers are justified in part by an 'inherent' righteousness.

For our purpose, the principal point is that the Reformation understanding of justification maintained that 'the righteousness of God' is something freely given to believers in Christ, and not something that continues to demand obedience as a basis for justification.

Furthermore, as is evident from this debate regarding the righteousness of God, the Reformers understood the term 'justification' to refer to a judicial act of God, whereby guilty sinners were declared or pronounced righteous or innocent. Upon the basis of the righteousness of God in Christ, freely granted and imputed to believers, God declares sinners forgiven and acceptable to him. Because Christ satisfied the obligations and demands of God's righteousness for his people, God can simultaneously be just and the One who justifies the guilty (*Rom.* 3:26). 'Justification', therefore, does not refer to an ongoing process of moral renewal in righteousness (sanctification), but to a definitive, judicial (forensic) act that anticipates the final judgment.

When God justifies the ungodly, he declares their innocence before his tribunal. Justification, according to the Reformers, was of paramount importance because it addresses the great religious question of where sinners, whether Jews or Gentiles, stand with God. Are they acceptable to him? Or are they under a condemnation that brings death? According to the Reformers, the gospel, especially as it is expressed in the writings of the apostle Paul, announces the good news that believers, on account of the work of Christ in his life, death, and resurrection, are constituted righteous and the heirs of eternal life. Though not the whole of the gospel, this gracious act of free justification was understood to be at its heart.

THE NEW PERSPECTIVE'S VIEW OF
THIS TERMINOLOGY

In the writings of new-perspective authors, quite a different account is often given of Paul's understanding of 'the righteousness of God' and the believer's 'justification'. It is argued that these terms must be approached from the standpoint of their usage in the Old Testament and in Judaism. Unlike the rather abstract and general way in which the Reformation spoke of 'the righteousness of God' and 'justification', the new perspective aims to place this language within the context of the history of redemption, and particularly within the setting of the realization of God's covenant promise to Abraham. Though there are a variety of viewpoints, I will cite N. T. Wright's explanation of this terminology as some-what representative of the consensus among advocates of the new perspective.[2]

Wright claims that readers of the Septuagint, the Greek trans-lation of the Old Testament, would have readily understood the term 'the righteousness of God'. In the Septuagint, it refers commonly to 'God's own faithfulness to his promises, to the covenant'.[3]

God's 'righteousness', especially in Isaiah 40–55, is that aspect of God's character on account of which he saves Israel, despite Israel's perversity and lostness. God has made promises; Israel can trust those promises. God's righteousness is thus cognate with his trust-worthiness on the one hand, and Israel's salvation on the other. And at the heart of that picture in Isaiah there stands, of course, the strange figure of the suffering servant through whom God's right-eous purpose is finally accomplished.[4]

According to Wright, therefore, the righteousness of God does not refer to God's moral character, on account of which he pun-ishes the unrighteous and rewards the righteous. This common medieval idea of God's 'distributive justice' is little more than a 'Latin irrelevance'.[5] Rather, the righteousness of God is *his coven-antal faithfulness in action*. When God acts to fulfil his promises to Israel, he demonstrates or reveals his faithfulness and reliability as one who will accomplish his saving purposes on his people's behalf.

This covenant faithfulness refers both to a 'moral quality' in God (God is righteous, that is, faithful) and to an 'active power which goes out, in expression of that faithfulness, to do what the covenant always promised'.[6]

Though the righteousness of God is primarily to be identified with God's covenantal faithfulness in action, Wright also argues that this terminology, in its Old Testament and Jewish context, makes use of a legal or forensic (court-room) metaphor. The righteousness of God is a phrase that is derived from the Jewish idea of the law court in which three parties are present: the judge, the plaintiff and the defendant. Each of these parties has a distinct role to play in the court's proceedings: the judge is called upon to decide the issue and to do so in a proper manner, that is, justly and impartially; the plaintiff is obliged to prosecute the case and bring an accusation against the defendant; and the defendant is required to answer the accusation and seek acquittal.

In the functioning of this law court, what matters finally is not the moral uprightness or virtue of the plaintiff or the defendant, but the *verdict of the judge*. When the judge decides 'for' or 'against' either the plaintiff or the defendant, we may say that one of them has the *status of being righteous* so far as the court's judgment is concerned. The term 'righteous', when used within the framework of the court's pronouncements, means that the court has decided in the plaintiff or the defendant's favour. The 'righteous' person, therefore, is not the person who is morally upright, but the person in whose favour the court has decided. So far as the judgment of the court goes, 'the righteous' are those whom the court vindicates or acquits, 'the unrighteous' are those whom the court finds against or condemns. In these respects, 'the righteousness of God' and 'justification' are thoroughly legal or forensic in nature.

Even though Wright affirms the forensic nature of this terminology in a way that is a little reminiscent of the Reformation view of justification, he maintains that the idea of the imputing or imparting of God's righteousness to believers makes no sense in this context.

> If we use the language of the law court, it makes no sense whatever
> to say that the judge imputes, imparts, bequeaths, conveys or

otherwise transfers his righteousness to either the plaintiff or the defendant. Righteousness is not an object, a substance or a gas which can be passed across the courtroom.[7]

Rather than being something that God imputes to others, the righteousness of God refers to God's faithfulness in acting on behalf of his covenant people, vindicating or acquitting them so that they are in a state of favour with him. When God acts in the person of Jesus Christ, he acts to realize his covenant purposes for Israel. The death and resurrection of Jesus Christ, which reveal God's righteousness or covenant faithfulness, are the means whereby God deals with sin and vindicates his people through Christ their 'representative'.[8] God's promise that, in the future (eschatological) day of salvation and judgment, his people will be vindicated, has been accomplished through the representative death and resurrection of Christ. Thus, in the death and resurrection of Christ, God has acted to secure the promise of covenant favour and blessing for all, whether Jews or Gentiles, who believe in Christ. The righteousness of God, thus understood, cannot be imparted to believers, since it is identified with God's covenant faithfulness in action.

Thus, according to the new perspective, it is only within this context that a proper understanding of 'justification' can be reached. This doctrine is not principally about how guilty sinners, who are incapable of finding favour with God by their works of obedience to the law, can be made acceptable to God, but about *who belongs to the number of God's covenant people.* The primary location of Paul's doctrine of justification, Wright insists, is not soteriology (how sinners are saved) but ecclesiology (who belongs to the covenant family). When Paul's treatment of justification is read within the context of Judaism's historic understanding of the covenant, we discover that 'Justification in this setting . . . is not a matter of *how someone enters the community of the true people of God,* but of *how you tell who belongs to that community.*'[9] In a comprehensive statement of his view, Wright maintains that justification terminology functions as a description of those who belong to the covenant people:

'Justification' in the first century was not about how someone might establish a relationship with God. It was about God's eschatological definition, both future and present, of who was, in fact, a member of his people. In Sanders' terms, it was not so much about 'getting in', or indeed about 'staying in', as about 'how you could tell who was in'. In standard Christian theological language, it wasn't so much about soteriology as about ecclesiology; not so much about salvation as about the church.[10]

When God reveals his righteousness in the death and resurrection of Jesus Christ, he demonstrates his covenant faithfulness by securing the inclusion of all members of the covenant community; they are those who are baptized into Christ and are marked by the 'badge' of covenant membership, which is faith. Justification, therefore, refers to the inclusion within the covenant community of all those, whether Jews or Gentiles, who believe in Jesus Christ.

This approach to the terminology of justification explains the significance of Paul's insistence that justification is by 'faith' and not by 'works of the law'. As we have noted previously, Wright and other new-perspective authors regard the phrase 'works of the law' as a reference to 'boundary-marker' requirements in the (Mosaic) law, which served to exclude Gentiles from the promise of inclusion within the covenant family of God. Justification is 'by faith', and not by obedience to the 'works of the law', because it announces that God, in his covenant faithfulness, now intends to include Gentiles as well as Jews in the number of his covenant people. Commenting on Romans 3:21–31, Wright offers an explanation that is consistent with what we have already seen from our consideration of Paul's use of the 'works of the law':

> The passage is all about the covenant, membership in which is now thrown open to Jew and Gentile alike; *therefore* it is all about God's dealing with sin in the cross and resurrection of Jesus, because that was what the covenant was intended to do in the first place . . . 'Where then is boasting?' asks Paul in 3:27. 'It is excluded!' This 'boasting' which is excluded is not the boasting of the successful moralist [as in the Reformation view]; it is the

racial boast of the Jew, as in 2:17–24. If this is not so, 3:29 ('Or is God the God of Jews only? Is he not of Gentiles also?') is a *non sequitur*. Paul has not thought in this passage of warding off a proto-Pelagianism, of which in any case contemporaries were not guilty. He is here, as in Galatians and Philippians, declaring that there is no road into covenant membership on the ground of Jewish racial privilege.[11]

Faith alone is the 'badge' of covenant membership, because it excludes any boasting in covenant privilege on the part of the Jews. Through faith in Jesus Christ, Jews and Gentiles alike enjoy the privilege of 'present justification', that is, inclusion among the covenant people of God. This present justification 'declares . . . what future justification will affirm publicly (according to 2:14–16 and 8:9–11) on the basis of the entire life'.[12]

'THE RIGHTEOUSNESS OF GOD' IN ROMANS

To assess the validity of the new perspective's understanding of the terminology of 'the righteousness of God' and 'justification' is not an easy task. A full assessment would require a series of studies of the use of these terms in the Old Testament, in Second-Temple Judaism, and in all of the writings of the apostle Paul.[13] However, the most important factor in such an assessment is the Pauline epistles themselves: do Paul's letters, especially Romans and Galatians, support the claims of the new perspective regarding these terms?

We will begin by looking at the way 'righteousness of God' is used, particularly in Romans.[14] Then we will consider the related issue of the use of the term 'justification' in Paul's writings.

Romans is particularly important for an understanding of Paul's use of 'the righteousness of God'. Though similar expressions are used in his other epistles, this is the only one to use the expression on several occasions (*Rom.* 1:17; 3:5, 21, 22, 25, 26; 10:3; eight times in all). Though it is used on one other occasion in Paul's epistles (2 *Cor.* 5:21), its prominence in the book of Romans is clearly evident. Indeed, the expression is used in two places (*Rom.* 1:17; 3:21–26) that comprehensively set forth the primary theme of the whole epistle. For this reason, the use of the expression in Romans is decisive for arriving at an accurate interpretation of Paul's use of the term.

I. Romans 1:17

The first occurrence of the term is found in Romans 1:16–17, a passage generally viewed as a thematic statement of the epistle's message. Here the apostle affirms his unashamed commitment to the gospel, in which the righteousness of God is revealed.

> For I am not ashamed of the gospel, for it is the power of God for salvation to everyone who believes, to the Jew first and also the Greek. For in it the righteousness of God is revealed from faith to faith, as it is written, 'The righteous shall live by faith.'

Though these verses make clear that Paul regarded 'the righteousness of God' as a central theme of his preaching, the passage itself does not explain what he means precisely by this phrase. It is therefore necessary to turn elsewhere for light on this subject.

Writers of the new perspective, including N. T. Wright, turn to the Old Testament for help.[15] A number of Old Testament references speak of the righteousness of God in connection with God's actions in saving his people. In these passages, the term occurs within the context of actions performed in accordance with covenant obligations and commitments. Hence, when God's righteousness is described, it is often expressed in terms of his fidelity to his people and reliability in securing the promises made to them. The righteousness of God is, in this respect, relational or covenantal terminology. One example is found in Psalm 31:1: 'In you, O Lord, I take refuge; let me never be put to shame; in your righteousness deliver me!' Another is Exodus 15:13: 'You have led in your steadfast love [Septuagint reads 'righteousness'] the people whom you have redeemed; you have guided them by your strength to your holy abode.' In such passages, where God's righteousness seems to be equivalent to his covenant faithfulness, a variety of terms are used to express the way God is faithful to his people in securing their salvation.[16] If this is the specific background to Paul's language in Romans 1:17, we could paraphrase his words to read something like, 'The gospel reveals the faithfulness of the covenant Lord in keeping his promises made to his people.'

In addition to this possible Old Testament background to Paul's use of 'the righteousness of God' in Romans 1:17, there is another, closely related Old Testament usage that may have been an influence on Paul's thinking.[17] Often, Old Testament references to God's righteousness are used as equivalents for his saving action on behalf of his people.

When God intervenes on behalf of his people in order to save them, his righteousness is revealed. Psalm 51:14 is an example of this use: 'Deliver me from blood-guiltiness, O God, O God of my salvation, and my tongue will sing aloud of your righteousness.' Perhaps an even clearer example is Isaiah 46:13: 'I will bring near my righteousness; it is not far off, and my salvation will not delay.' In this prophetic declaration, the coming-near of the Lord's righteousness is parallel to the swift coming of salvation for his people. Examples of this identification of the righteousness of God with his saving activity on behalf of his people abound in the Old Testament (e.g. *Psa.* 22:31; 35:28; 40:10; 69:27; 71:15, 16, 19, 24; 88:12; 98:2; 119:123; *Mic.* 6:5; 7:9; *Isa.* 51:5, 6, 8).

Since the covenant faithfulness of the Lord is especially revealed in his saving acts on behalf of his people, it is not difficult to combine this second use of the term with the first. In both instances, the righteousness of God is a term that functions within the context of God's covenant relationship with his people. When the righteousness of God is revealed, God is revealed as One who faithfully and reliably acts to secure his people's well-being.[18]

If either one or the other, or some combination of both these uses of the term lies behind Paul's statement in Romans 1:17, it may seem that this passage confirms the view of the proponents of the new perspective.

The righteousness of God is not, then, connected with something God gives to believers that enables them to enjoy a status of favour with him in spite of their sinfulness. Rather, it is God's demonstration of his covenant-keeping character, and of his accomplishments that secure the redemption of his people.

Before drawing this conclusion too hastily, however, we need to consider two further lines of evidence; one from the Old Testament, the other from the epistle to the Romans.

First, in the Old Testament use of the term righteousness, there is also to be found a strongly forensic or legal emphasis that includes the idea of God granting to his people a righteous status and, at the same time, condemning their enemies or adversaries. This use fits well with the Reformation view that the righteousness of God in Romans 1:17 is a right standing or status that God freely grants to his people. And second, keeping in mind the close connection between the righteousness of God and faith in this passage ('the righteousness of God is revealed *from faith to faith*'), an important clue to the meaning of this terminology may be found in other passages in Romans in which righteousness and faith are clearly connected.

Examining the Old Testament passages in which the righteousness of God occurs reveals a thoroughly judicial setting. When God acts righteously, he does more than act in accordance with a general kind of covenant faithfulness or saving intention. He rules and orders the affairs of his creation and of his human image-bearers particularly, in a way that is right and in accordance with his own righteous character. Thus, it is in righteousness that God punishes the wicked and secures the salvation of the righteous. In Psalm 98, for example, the revelation of God's righteousness to the nations involves not only God's acts of faithfulness in bringing his people salvation, but also his righteous judgments upon his enemies. The salvation that the righteousness of God brings includes the coming of the Lord in order to judge the nations. God's righteousness is, therefore, an expression of his kingly and judicial dominion over the creation and all its creatures. Because God is righteous in this sense, he rules and administers the circumstances of his creatures in a way that is just. For this reason, the language of 'ruling and judging' are often intimately linked with God's righteousness (e.g. *Psa.* 72:1-3; *2 Sam.* 8:15; *1 Kings* 10:9; *Jer.* 22:3; *Prov.* 31:8-9).[19]

The righteousness of God involves more than a simple restoration of a proper relationship between God and his people. In his righteousness, God maintains order and justice; he simultaneously vindicates his people, and brings retribution upon their enemies (*Psa.* 143:1-3; *Jer.* 22:3). Summarizing this use of the terminology of God's righteousness, Mark Seifrid observes that

> The concept of 'God's righteousness' in the Hebrew Scriptures cannot be reduced to the meaning 'salvation' or the like, since it always functions within the context of a legal dispute or contention. When God works salvation for his people, he establishes justice for them (and for himself) over against their enemies and his. Saving righteousness and wrath parallel one another, since they are different aspects of the same event. Correspondingly, along with the references to a 'saving righteousness' of God, there are a number of passages in which punitive or retributive conceptions are associated with the 'righteousness of God'.[20]

The significance of this pervasively forensic or judicial use of the term 'God's righteousness' should be apparent. The righteousness of God cannot simply be identified with something like God's faithfulness to his promises, or his saving acts to secure the redemption of his people. This term indicates that God's faithfulness and saving action are demonstrated in his judgments, which include the *vindication of the righteous and the punishment of the wicked*. Integral to God's righteousness are his actions as the righteous and just Ruler and Judge of the nations. Thus, the administration of God's justice occurs in a legal framework, which includes, as an essential component, the element of a legal contention or dispute. When God's covenant word and law are violated, God's righteousness is expressed in retributive justice (e.g. *Isa.* 5:16; 10:22). God's righteousness secures the salvation of his people, but also brings judgment upon the wicked (*Psa.* 7:17; 9:4, 8; 50:4-6; 97:2). Thus, Psalm 119 can speak on five occasions of 'the judgments of your [God's] righteousness' (verses 7, 62, 106, 160, 164), each of which refers to God's condemnation of the wicked.

Within this judicial or forensic framework, the righteousness of God is intimately linked to God's acts of judgment, which include, respectively, the acquittal of his people and the condemnation of the wicked.[21]

Another important clue to the meaning of 'the righteousness of God' in Romans 1:17 is the phrase 'from faith to faith'. This phrase is further explained by Paul's appeal to Habakkuk 2:4: 'The righteous shall live by faith.' This link between righteousness and faith is a characteristic theme of the Roman epistle. It occurs in other important passages (3:21–22; 10:3; cf. 10:6), and in each instance faith is the appropriate response to God's righteousness. Through the response of faith, believers come to benefit from the saving power of the gospel of Jesus Christ, which reveals the righteousness of God. Consistent with the more general use of the term 'righteousness' in Romans, these passages indicate that righteousness is something that God grants or communicates to believers, and which involves the restoration of believers to favour with him. In Romans 5:17, for example, the 'righteousness' that acquits believers of condemnation and death is God's 'gift' to them (cf. *Phil.* 3:9). Similarly, in Romans 10:3–6, Paul draws a close parallel between 'the righteousness of God' and the 'righteousness based on faith'. Though we will have occasion in what follows to deal more directly with the issue of the imputation of Christ's righteousness to believers, these passages illustrate that the righteousness of God is not simply God's own character as One who is faithful to his promises. The righteousness of God is also something that can be granted or given to those who respond appropriately to its revelation, that is, to those who receive this righteousness by faith.

If we put these lines of evidence together, the outcome strikingly resembles the Reformation view of God's righteousness. Though the righteousness of God can undoubtedly refer to his faithfulness to his covenant promise in saving his people, the special character of God's righteousness is expressed in his acts of judgment, which secure the acquittal of his people and the condemnation of the wicked. Against the background of the Old Testament idea of God's righteousness, Paul is affirming that the gospel of Jesus Christ reveals God's judicial action in securing the righteous status of his people before him. What is remarkable about the gospel of God's righteousness in Christ is that God has, in the person and work of his Son, entered into judgment on behalf of *the ungodly*. By virtue of Christ's work, God has obtained righteousness for all who believe in him. All who receive the free gift of right standing with God on the basis of the work of Christ are the beneficiaries of God's righteousness; they are freed from condemnation and granted right standing with God the Judge.[22] God's righteousness reveals his covenant faithfulness to secure his people's salvation, to be sure; but it especially reveals God's powerful intervention in his own court to grant a righteous status to believers on the basis of the work of Christ.

II. ROMANS 3:21–26

Like Romans 1:17, this passage plays a pivotal role in outlining the epistle's major theme. In this summary statement of his major argument, Paul returns to the theme of the righteousness of God and directly affirms that it is received 'through faith in Jesus Christ' (verse 22).

> But now the righteousness of God has been manifested apart from the law, although the Law and the Prophets bear witness to it—the righteousness of God through faith in Jesus for all who believe. For there is no distinction: for all have sinned and fall short of the glory of God, and are justified by his grace as a gift, through the redemption that is in Christ Jesus, whom God put forward as a propitiation by his blood, to be received by faith. This was to show God's righteousness at the present time, so that he might be just and the justifier of the one who has faith in Jesus.

In order to interpret Paul's meaning, it is critical to understand how he uses 'the righteousness of God' within the context of his argument in Romans 1:18–3:20. In it we are presented with a sustained and withering indictment of all human beings, Jews and Gentiles alike, who as sinners lie under the wrath and judgment of God. Beginning with the well-known words of Romans 1:18 ('For the wrath of God is revealed from heaven against all ungodliness and unrighteous of men'), the apostle carefully sets out the grounds for this indictment and his conclusion in Romans 3:10 that 'none is righteous; no, not one.' In the case both of Gentiles who sinned 'without the law' and of Jews who sinned 'under the law' (2:12) there is no escape from the just judgment of God, before whom every mouth is stopped and the whole world is accountable (3:19). Whatever advantages the Jews may have enjoyed, including the privilege of receiving the law and the oracles of God (3:2), the conclusion of Paul's argument is reached in the words of 3:22–23: 'For there is no distinction: for all have sinned and fall short of the glory of God.' The background, then, for Paul's return to the theme of the revelation of 'the righteousness of God' at this juncture in his epistle is *thoroughly judicial*: the whole human race, when summoned before the One who will judge the world (cf. 3:6), stands condemned before God. The possibility of being justified before God on the basis of 'works of the law' is utterly excluded.

When interpreted within this context, Paul's use of the term 'the righteousness of God' clearly refers to something more than God's faithfulness to his covenant promise or his saving acts on behalf of his people. No doubt the themes of God's faithfulness and saving action are included; but what especially characterizes 'the right-eousness of God' is his *justifying* action, that is, his restoration of believers to the status of acquitted and forgiven sinners. This explains why the apostle, after having spoken of the revelation of the righteousness of God, goes on to speak of how sinners 'are justified by his grace as a gift, through the redemption that is in Christ Jesus, whom God put forward as a propitiation by his blood, to be received by faith. This was to show God's right-eousness . . . ' (3:24–25). The gospel reveals God's saving power in the work of Christ through whom believers are justified, that is, receive a right standing with God.

What is remarkable about Romans 3 is the way the apostle describes the work of Christ, which reveals God's righteousness. When God graciously justifies guilty sinners, he does so because of Christ's work for them. Paul describes it by the use of two rich biblical terms, 'redemption' and 'propitiation'. Though it is difficult to explain these terms briefly, it is important to note how they relate to the nature of God's righteousness as revealed in the gospel. 'Redemption' refers to Christ's work by which he purchases with his blood his people's release from the bondage of sin. Typically, redemption in the Scriptures emphasizes the related ideas of the 'payment of a price' and the 'securing of release' from captivity. In the context of Paul's argument in Romans 1–3, it is not difficult to see that the redemption Christ effected includes a payment for the wages of sin and the obtaining of freedom from sin's consequences (cf. *Rom.* 6:13). Though there is a great deal of dispute regarding the meaning of the term 'propitiation', the context again is decisive. The apostle has been describing at some length the reality of the revelation of God's wrath against guilty sinners. He also speaks of the way God in his patience formerly (under the circumstances that obtained prior to Christ's coming) had 'passed over' sins (3:25).

This contextual evidence confirms that the work of Christ in 'propitiation by his blood' was nothing other than his substitutionary endurance of the wrath of God against his people on account of their sin.[23] In this way (that is, in the way of Christ's redemptive and propitiatory work), the gospel is a revelation of God's righteousness in justifying his people.

A further feature of this passage is the clear way in which it speaks of the bestowal of the gift of justification to believers. God's righteousness is not simply revealed in the gospel of Jesus Christ. The righteousness of God is not exclusively the objective work of Christ for believers. God's righteousness, according to the terms used in this passage, is also a *gift* that is subjectively received through faith.

When speaking of God's righteousness it is not enough to speak of the work of Christ in redemption and propitiation. We must also speak of the way the benefit of this work, namely, a new status of righteousness before God, becomes the possession of believers. More clearly than in Romans 1:17, Romans 3 speaks of a righteousness that justifies because it is granted to believers by God's grace as a gift.

The somewhat tautological expression, 'by his grace as a gift', underscores two features of God's justifying work: firstly, it is an act of sheer grace and, therefore, antithetical to works of any kind whatever; and secondly, it involves a transaction whereby God gives a righteous status to believers who are united to Christ through faith. Paul's insistence here that justification is received by faith clearly demonstrates that the righteousness of God is something that is granted to believers. Though this was already evident in Romans 1:17 in the phrase 'from faith to faith', it becomes particularly clear in Romans 3.

III. ROMANS 10:3

'For, being ignorant of the righteousness that comes from God [literally, of God], and seeking to establish their own, they did not submit to God's righteousness.' This text, though it does not elaborate upon the way the righteousness of God is exhibited in the gospel, is quite similar in emphasis to Romans 3:21–26. The righteousness of God is not only his saving activity in justifying his people, but also his granting of the benefit of that activity to those who believe. A sharp contrast or antithesis governs this passage (as is also found in earlier passages in the same epistle), between the righteousness that is from God and received through faith, and the righteousness that is inherent and obtained by works. Between these alternatives, there is no middle ground. As the apostle Paul puts it in the following verse: 'For Christ is the end of the law for righteousness to everyone who believes' (verse 4).

In the immediate context of this verse, Paul speaks about his fellow Jews who 'have a zeal for God, but not according to knowledge' (verse 2). This language parallels his observations at the end of Romans 9, that they 'pursued a law that would lead to righteousness', a pursuit that was not 'by faith' but 'by works' (31–32; cf. *Phil.* 3:9). When the language of these verses is coupled with that of Romans 10:3 and 10:5 ('For Moses writes about the righteousness that is based on the law, that the person who does the commandments shall live by them'), the following conclusion is unavoidable: Paul is opposing a misguided endeavour to obtain righteousness by means of obedience to the law of God rather than by faith. Either righteousness is received by faith or it is obtained by works.

In this context, 'the righteousness of God', which is revealed in God's gracious work in Jesus Christ, refers especially to the new status of acceptance with God that comes to those who believe. In a manner that fully conforms to Paul's usage elsewhere in Romans, 'the righteousness of God' refers both to God's gracious provision in Jesus Christ and to the *gift of a new status* (justification) to those

who receive that gift in the way of faith, not works. However, as
we have previously noted, the way of 'works' in these verses is not
limited to the so-called 'boundary-marker' requirements of the law
– circumcision, dietary laws, and the like. Paul's objection to those
whose zeal for the law is misguided is not limited to their Jewish
exclusivism; it also and most emphatically includes their attempts
to establish a righteousness of their own that is based upon their
obedience to the law as such.[24]

SUMMARY

In the epistle to the Romans, 'the righteousness of God' is used
in such a way as to include several themes. It refers in a general way
to the covenant faithfulness of God in action, which secures the
promise of salvation for his people. But it also refers more specifically to a special kind of saving action, namely, God's work as a
righteous Judge who secures the acquittal of his people from condemnation before him. The righteousness of God, in this respect,
includes both his saving work through Jesus Christ and the imparting of the benefit of that work to those who receive it through faith.

God's righteousness is objectively revealed in Christ's death and
resurrection for guilty sinners (cf. *Rom.* 4:15); but it is also
subjectively granted to those who acknowledge the benefit of
Christ's saving work with a believing heart. 'The righteousness of
God', therefore, clearly speaks of the justifying work of God in
Christ and the reception of the benefit of that work through faith.
In these respects, the Reformation understanding of this termin-
ology closely reflects the apostle's usage.

THE MEANING OF JUSTIFICATION

Paul's use of 'the righteousness of God' forms an obvious basis for
an understanding of how he uses the related term 'justification' in
his epistles, because the justification of the ungodly is the great
benefit and result of the revelation of God's righteousness. Whereas
'the righteousness of God' refers primarily to God's gracious action
in Christ, which constitutes the basis for his granting a righteous
status to believers, 'justification' refers to the subjective benefit of
this saving action. Those to whom God grants righteousness as a

gift (which can only be received through faith, cf. *Rom.* 4:16) are freely justified.

Though writers of the new perspective insist that 'justification' is a 'covenant membership' term, identifying those whom God acknowledges as his covenant people, such a view is inadequate and ought to be rejected on several counts. Like the claim that the righteousness of God refers to God's covenant faithfulness in action, this interpretation of justification is far too general and imprecise to explain its specific meaning in Paul's writings. If we say that 'the righteousness of God' is his faithfulness to his covenant promise, we still need to ask, how does that faithfulness come to expression? And what exactly does the term 'righteousness' tell us about the way God's faithfulness is demonstrated? As we have argued, this terminology particularly emphasizes the judicial context for God's action in securing the acquittal/vindication of his covenant people, and bringing judgment/condemnation upon his enemies. It assumes that God is Judge and King, that he maintains justice and order in his dealings with his creatures, and that he acts justly in acquitting the righteous and condemning the wicked. The same holds true for the related term 'justification'. No doubt justification finds its meaning within the context of God's establishing a relationship with those whom he acknowledges as his covenant people; but this does not yet tell us what precisely 'justification' means, and why this word is especially appropriate as a description of what God does when he brings sinners into his covenant family. Obviously, 'justification' functions within the context of the covenant, as does most scriptural terminology so far as it deals with the relationship of God and his people. The question is, however, what does *this particular* term tell us about the nature of this relationship.

Perhaps the most serious problem with a simple identification of 'justification' with the new-perspective idea of 'belonging to the covenant people' is that it fails to do justice to the biblical context. If we consider only the context for Paul's treatment of justification in Romans 1–5, we discover that it answers the problem of human sin and guilt before the judgment of God. The apostle's treatment of this problem in these chapters contradicts Wright's genial suggestion that first-century Jews were not particularly troubled by the prospect of the final judgment and the wrath of God, or whether they would 'get to heaven' in the future.[25] Though there is an ecclesiological dimension to the terminology of justification (Who belongs to the covenant family? Are Gentiles as well as Jews included?), *the principal issue* is quite emphatically of a *soteriological* and *theological* nature. Paul's argument in Romans 1–5 raises far deeper questions than merely that which asks, Who belongs to the covenant people of God? The question raised is: How can guilty sinners, who have culpably broken the law of God and are subject to condemnation, be received into favour with a righteous God whose wrath is being poured out upon all the ungodliness and unrighteousness of men? Such is the importance of this context for our understanding of 'justification' that we must now briefly review the argument of these chapters in Romans.

The epistle's theme is stated at the outset: immediately after Romans 1:16–17, which announces that 'the righteousness of God is revealed from faith to faith', the apostle declares that 'the wrath of God is revealed against all ungodliness and unrighteousness of men' (verse 18). The good news that God justifies the ungodly occurs, accordingly, against the dark background of God's just displeasure with all guilty violators of his law. For this reason, the problem resolved by the revelation of God's righteousness is not whether God is faithful to his covenant, *but whether he is in the right when he justifies those who by virtue of their sin and guilt are worthy only of condemnation and death*. It is not God's faithfulness to his promise that is in question; rather, the question is whether human beings, who are on trial before God on account of their sins and offences, can find favour or acceptance with God. Having announced God's righteous wrath in Romans 1:18, the apostle then turns in Romans 2 to the reality of this impending judgment. A 'day of wrath' is coming when God 'will render to each one according to his works' (2:5–6). This day will reveal God's judgment by Christ Jesus upon the deeds of all, including the 'secret things of men' (verse 16). The setting for the demonstration of 'the righteousness of God' and the 'justification' of believers, therefore, is clearly one of trial and judgment before God.

Within this solemn setting the apostle proceeds after the manner of a prosecutor in a courtroom to detail the universal sway of sin and guilt among Jews and Gentiles alike. At the beginning of chapter 2, he hints that his Jewish readers might be tempted to affirm his indictment of Gentile sinners and offenders, while excluding themselves. However, he forcefully argues that *all* have sinned, whether they are Gentiles 'without the law' or Jews 'under the law' (2:12). Those who might be tempted to boast before God because of their privileged position, including their possession of the covenant mark of circumcision, are reminded that 'circumcision indeed is of value if you obey the law, but if you break the law, your circumcision becomes uncircumcision' (2:25).[26] In order to prove that Jews as much as Gentiles are at no advantage before God, Paul cites evidence of an *ad hominem* nature to illustrate how they also have disobeyed the law of God. Despite their boast, they are as guilty as the Gentiles of the sins of hypocrisy, stealing, adultery, and temple desecration (verses 21–22). And so he draws the inescapable conclusion: 'You who boast in the law dishonour God by breaking the law' (verse 23).

The whole point of this section of the epistle is to establish, within the context of the announcement of God's wrath against all the ungodliness and unrighteousness of men, that 'none is righteous; no, not one' (3:10). The law of God, far from being able to serve as an instrument of self-justification before God, pronounces its verdict upon Jew and Gentile alike. In the heavenly court before God, Jews and Gentiles share the common predicament of having nothing exculpatory to say in their own defence. When confronted with the demand and accusation of the law of God, every mouth is stopped and the whole world is held accountable to God.

The significance of all this for Paul's understanding of justification cannot be overstated. In this setting, justification cannot merely mean something like 'covenant membership'. After all, the Jews who were circumcised were members of the covenant people of God. Nor can justification be reduced to Paul's answer to the question: Are Gentiles also members of the covenant family? To reduce the meaning of justification to the inclusion or non-inclusion of Gentiles within the covenant family is to miss the real point. That point, as the Reformers rightly understood, was about the gracious provision in Christ for the justification of all believing sinners. Since no one can possibly be included within the covenant family of God on the basis of the works of the law, God has demonstrated his righteousness in providing a Saviour whose obedience and propitiatory death provide the basis for being received into his favour. In the setting of the argument of Romans, therefore, the term 'justification' refers to God's act of granting believers a status of favour and righteousness on account of the work of Christ. Justification is all about the forgiveness of sins and the granting of a new status of righteousness in Christ to otherwise guilty, condemned sinners. It is not simply about, 'Who is a member of the covenant', but goes to the deeper issue of, 'Who has a right to stand before God, despite his sin and unworthiness.' Justification is about God as the One who justifies the ungodly, and it is about nothing if not the *salvation* of guilty sinners. Only within the framework of these deeper theological and soteriological issues does the obvious ecclesiological issue regarding the inclusion of Gentiles have a place.

To illustrate the meaning of justification, it may be useful at this point to cite another passage: 'Who shall bring any charge against God's elect? It is God who justifies. Who is to condemn?' (*Rom.* 8:33–34). This dramatic affirmation confirms that justification refers to a judicial act of God, which pronounces otherwise guilty sinners righteous on the basis of the work of Christ. It is impossible to paraphrase these verses by inserting the term 'covenant membership' in the place of justification. For this passage includes anyone who might bring a charge against God's people. No matter what the charge, God has assumed the burden of answering it for his elect in Christ. By virtue of Christ's death and resurrection for sinners, God himself has entered into judgment on behalf of his people. In Christ he has answered the charge by assuming the place of the guilty and suffering his own displeasure against sin. What is the consequence? There is no possibility of a charge being brought against those whom he has justified, whose acquittal and righteousness he has established. 'There is therefore now no condemnation for those who are in Christ Jesus' (*Rom.* 8:1).[27]

The last observation to be made about the use of 'justification' in Paul's writings relates to the role and character of 'faith'. Consistent with their view of justification as covenant membership, Dunn and Wright speak of faith as 'the badge' of covenant membership. Faith in Jesus Christ is the mark that distinguishes Jews and Gentiles alike as members of the covenant family of God. Though this idea of faith as a kind of badge of covenant membership fits well with the notion that justification is all about covenant membership, it suggests something quite different from that which we find in Paul's writings. If anything may be said to be a badge of covenant membership, perhaps it would be something like the mark of circumcision or baptism (cf. *Rom.* 2:26; 4:11). Abraham, for example, received the rite of circumcision after his faith was 'reckoned' to him for righteousness. The reason Wright wants to speak of faith as a badge of membership is obvious. It keeps the idea of justification within the realm of ecclesiology and the identity of the family of God. If as we have argued, however, justification refers to the gracious act whereby God pronounces the innocence or righteousness of believers, faith more properly must be understood as the instrument whereby we receive the gracious gift of justification. The next chapter will consider this more fully by specifically addressing the way the believer's justification is based upon the imputation of the righteousness of Christ. The role of faith in justification cannot be adequately explained if justification is reduced to 'covenant membership'.

CONCLUSION

The use of 'the righteousness of God' and 'justification' in Paul's writings is well reflected in the writings and teachings of the sixteenth-century Reformers.

While the righteousness of God undoubtedly has a reference to God's action in fulfilling the promises of his covenant, the *objective revelation* of God's righteousness in Christ is also closely linked to the *subjective reception* of that righteousness by faith. Through faith believers receive the free gift of God's righteousness in Christ, and are placed in a new status of favour and acceptance with God. The Reformers' emphasis upon the gift-character of God's righteousness accurately reflected this feature of Paul's teaching. God's righteousness is revealed in the gospel of Christ, who endured the just punishment of sin on behalf of his people and secured their favourable standing with God. Consistent with the Old Testament usage of God's righteousness, Paul emphasizes the way it reveals God's judgment against the wicked and his vindic- ation of the righteous. What particularly distinguishes Paul's teach- ing, moreover, is that God has in righteousness acted to save the ungodly, to secure the salvation of otherwise undeserving and guilty sinners. Consequently, those who seek to establish their own righteousness before God on the basis of the works of the law demonstrate an unwillingness to receive what God freely grants in Christ. Furthermore, those who boast of their own righteousness fail to acknowledge the futility of any attempt to find favour with God by means of the law.

When Paul speaks about the justification of the ungodly, which occurs when the free gift of God's righteousness in Christ is received by faith, he speaks in a way that finds a faithful echo in the Reformation witness to the gospel. Here, too, the new perspective is in serious error, *not so much in what it affirms as in what it denies*. Though justification in Paul is related in a way to covenant membership and inclusion, its peculiar focus is upon the question of how guilty sinners, whether Jews or Gentiles, can be properly introduced and established in a right relationship with God.

The justification of the ungodly speaks to the ecclesiological question of the inclusion of Gentiles within the covenant com- munity; but it also speaks in a deeper and more significant manner to the salvation of all sinners on the basis of the work of Christ. Soteriology and ecclesiology are correlated in Paul's teaching in a way that the new perspective tends to diminish. In the apostle's doctrine of justification, the question of the inclusion of Gentiles is an important one; but the most important question has to do with how God can, consistent with his own righteousness, receive any sinner into favour with himself. It is this question that justification principally addresses and answers.

Notes

[1] Expressed grammatically, this means that the Reformers took the genitive in the expression, 'the righteousness *of* God', as a genitive of origin, that is, the righteousness that is *from* God.

[2] For a critical assessment of the way the term 'the righteousness of God' has been interpreted by authors of the new perspective, see Mark A. Seifrid, 'Righteousness Language in the Hebrew Scriptures and Early Judaism', in *Justification and Variegated Nomism*, 1:415–42. Contrary to the claim that this language refers primarily to God's saving action as an expression of his covenantal faithfulness, Seifrid demonstrates that it especially refers to God's retributive righteousness in punishing the disobedient and vindicating the righteous.

[3] Wright, *What Saint Paul Really Said*, p. 96. Cf. Wright, *Romans*, pp. 97–405.

[4] Wright, *What Saint Paul Really Said*, p. 96.

[5] This language is Wright's (*What Saint Paul Really Said*, p. 103).

[6] Wright, *What Saint Paul Really Said*, p. 103. For this reason, Wright regards the traditional grammatical debate whether the genitive in 'righteousness *of* God' is 'possessive' or 'subjective' to be beside the point. The righteousness of God is both God's being righteous (possessive) and God's acts of righteousness (subjective). God's covenant faithfulness expresses itself in deeds performed to fulfil his covenant promises.

[7] Wright, *What Saint Paul Really Said*, p. 99. Cf. Wright, *Romans*, pp. 398–400. One of the most striking omissions in Wright's discussion of the law-court imagery is his neglect to note the distinctively *Christian* use of this imagery in Paul's writings. Wright does not adequately represent the way Christ enters the court on behalf of his people (as their advocate, substitute, and representative), having obeyed the law and suffered its curse in their place. As we shall argue in Chapter 9, the imputation of Christ's righteousness to believers is only a way of expressing the believer's participation in Christ and his saving work. Wright's caricature of imputation does not fairly represent the Reformation view.

[8] Wright, *Romans*, pp. 470–7; Wright, *What Saint Paul Really Said*, pp. 106–7.

[9] Wright, *What Saint Paul Really Said*, p. 119 (emphasis Wright's). Cf. Wright, *Romans*, pp. 481–2.

[10] Wright, *What Saint Paul Really Said*, p. 120. Wright offers a similar comment on Paul's argument in Galatians: 'Despite a long tradition to the contrary, the problem Paul addresses in Galatians is not the question of how precisely someone becomes a Christian, or attains to a relationship with God . . . On anyone's reading, but especially within its first-century context, it has to do quite obviously with the question of how you define the people of God: are they to be defined by the badges of Jewish race, or in some other way?' (*What Saint Paul Really Said*, p. 122).

[11] Wright, *What Saint Paul Really Said,* pp. 128–9. Cf. Wright, *Romans,* p. 479.

[12] Wright, *What Saint Paul Really Said,* p. 129. As we noted in our introductory presentation of the new perspective, justification occurs in three 'steps' or 'phases', which correspond to the past event of Christ's resurrection, the present event of incorporation into Christ through faith, and the future event of the final judgment. In this statement of Wright's, an important question is raised regarding the role of the final judgment in the justification of believers: is the final phase of justification based, at least in part, on works or, as Wright puts it, the 'whole life' of the believer. We will address this subject in Chapter 10.

[13] For a good, brief summary of the debate regarding this terminology, see Douglas J. Moo, *The Epistle to the Romans,* pp. 63–90.

[14] In one important respect, my consideration of this terminology at this point is incomplete. In Chapter 9, I will consider directly the question of the legitimacy of the doctrine of an 'imputation' of the righteousness of Christ to believers. If Paul teaches such a doctrine, as I shall argue he does, then that has direct bearing on the question of the meaning of 'the righteousness of God'.

[15] Cf. e.g. Wright, *Romans,* pp. 393–405; Sam K. Williams, 'The "Righteousness of God" in Romans', *Journal of Biblical Literature* 99 (1980), pp. 241–90; James D. G. Dunn, *The Theology of Paul the Apostle,* pp. 340–6; and Manfred T. Barauch, 'Perspectives on "God's righteousness" in recent German Discussion', in *Paul and Palestinian Judaism* by E. P. Sanders, pp. 523–42.

[16] Cf. Isa. 63:7 (parallel with 'loving-kindness'); Isa. 38:19 ('covenant favour'); *Psa.* 36:6 ('truthfulness'); *Psa.* 88:12 ('mercy'); and *Psa.* 145:7 ('goodness'). See Moo, *The Epistle to the Romans,* p. 82, for a more extensive list of texts and discussion of this use of the term 'God's righteousness' in the Septuagint translation of the Old Testament.

[17] Cf. James D. G. Dunn, *Romans 1-8,* pp. 36–49.

[18] It should be noted that, contrary to the suggestion among new perspective authors that this feature of the meaning of 'the righteousness of God' was largely absent among the Reformers, Calvin was well aware of this usage. Cf. John Calvin, *Commentary on the Book of Psalms,* vol. 2 (reprint; Grand Rapids: Baker, 1979 [1843]), p. 96: (on Psa. 71:16) '*The Righteousness of God,* as we have just now observed, does not here denote that free gift by which he reconciles men to himself, or by which he regenerates them to newness of life; but his faithfulness in keeping his promises, by which he means to show that he is righteous, upright, and true toward his servants.' For a discussion of Calvin's recognition of this use of 'the righteousness of God', see my *The Twofold Nature of the Gospel in Calvin's Theology,* pp. 292–7.

[19] See Mark A. Seifrid, *Christ, Our Righteousness,* p. 40.

[20] *Christ, Our Righteousness,* p. 43. Old Testament texts that speak of God's righteousness in retribution against the wicked include: *Neh.* 9:33; *Deut.* 32:4-

5; 2 *Chron.* 12:6; *Psa.* 7:10, 12; 11:5-7; 50:6; *Isa.* 1:27; 5:16; 10:22; *Lam.* 1:18; *Dan.* 9:7, 14, 16. Thus, Wright's comment that this meaning is a 'Latin irrelevance' is at best overstated, but likely incorrect.

[21] This emphasis provides an Old Testament background to Paul's description in Romans 1:18ff. of how the wrath of God is being revealed against all the 'ungodliness and unrighteousness of men'.

[22] Cf. Wright, *What Saint Paul Really Said*, p. 110: 'Romans is often regarded as an exposition of judicial, or law-court, theology. But that is a mistake. The law court forms a vital metaphor at a key stage of the argument. But at the heart of Romans we find a theology of love.' If our analysis is correct, then Wright's statement is seriously misleading at two points. Judicial theology is not merely metaphorical; it expresses the reality of God's own nature as one who is righteous and who acts accordingly. Furthermore, Wright's subordination of God's righteousness to his love inappropriately plays God's attributes off against each other. It would be more proper to say that, just as God *is* loving, so he *is* righteous.

[23] For fine expositions of this understanding of Christ's cross as a propitiation for sin, see Leon Morris, *The Apostolic Preaching of the Cross*, pp. 144–78; and D. A. Carson, 'Atonement in Romans 3:21–26', in *The Glory of the Atonement: Biblical, Theological & Practical Perspectives*, ed. Charles E. Hill and Frank A. James III (Downers Grove, IL: Intervarsity, 2004), pp. 119–39.

[24] Cf. Moo, *The Epistle to the Romans*, p. 636: 'The Jews failed to "submit" to God's righteousness not only because they did not recognize God's righteousness when it arrived but also because they were too narrowly focused on seeking a righteousness in connection with their obedience to the law.'

[25] Wright, *What Saint Paul Really Said*, p. 118.

[26] In verse 13, Paul speaks similarly: 'For it is not the hearers of the law who are righteous before God, but the doers of the law who will be justified.' The Reformation's reading of this text usually takes it as a kind of 'hypothesis contrary to fact'. Since no one is, strictly speaking, a 'doer of the law', no one is justified by the law. However, among writers of the new perspective, this text is interpreted differently. In their view, Paul is positively affirming that in the final judgment only those who do what the law requires will be justified/vindicated. Cf. Wright, *What Saint Paul Really Said*, p. 126; and Wright, *Romans*, p. 440. I will consider this text more directly in Chapter 10, which addresses the subject of justification and the final judgment.

[27] One way to test the new perspective's claims regarding the meaning of the terms 'the righteousness of God' and 'justification', is to try to paraphrase Paul's language by substituting terms like 'covenant faithfulness' or 'covenant membership'. Though the substitution might seem plausible in a few instances, it generally makes little sense. See Charles E. Hill, 'N. T. Wright on Justification', *IIIM Magazine Online* 3/22 (May 28 to June 3, 2001), pp. 1–8.

9

JUSTIFICATION AND THE IMPUTATION OF CHRIST'S RIGHTEOUSNESS

Though not always adequately acknowledged, the chief difference between the classic Protestant and Roman Catholic views of justification relates to the *ground* of the believer's justification. The long-standing conflict between Reformation and Roman Catholic teaching was never primarily about the nature of the justifying verdict.[1] Does God justify sinners partly on the basis of his grace in Christ and partly on the basis of their own works performed in co-operation with his grace? Or does God justify sinners wholly on the basis of the righteousness of Christ, which is freely granted and imputed to believers?

The nub of the issue, therefore, can be stated in terms of these questions: Does the believer's justification depend entirely upon an imputed righteousness? Or does it partly depend upon an infused righteousness – the believer's own works of obedience, stemming from the prior working of God's grace by his Spirit?

No matter how one evaluates the older disputes between Protestant and Roman Catholic theologians on the doctrine of justification, it is apparent that the issue of imputation was the bone of contention. Whether one speaks of faith as the *exclusive instrument* of justification (*sola fide*) or of Christ's mediatorial work as the *exclusive basis* for justification (*solo Christo*), the essential point remains the same: God's righteousness in Christ is the gracious and only ground upon which the sinner can stand justified before God.[2] The righteousness by which sinners are justified is not their own but an alien or external righteousness. Only on account of Christ's obedience to the requirements of the law and his substitutionary endurance of its liability (his so-called 'active' and 'passive' obedience) can the sinner find favour with God. Justification through faith on account of the work of Christ requires a gracious transaction, a granting and imputing of the righteousness of Christ to believers so that this righteousness becomes as much theirs as his. Only by being united to Christ by faith can anyone find acceptance with God. The implication of this union for the believer's justification is expressed by the term 'imputation', according to the traditional Protestant teaching.

Considering the importance of the doctrine of imputation to this historic dispute, it is noteworthy that among authors of the new perspective on Paul this doctrine is generally neglected or openly repudiated.[3] In a passage cited earlier, N. T. Wright, dismisses the idea of imputation as incompatible with the functioning of justification within Judaism:

> If we use the language of the law court, it makes no sense what-ever to say that the judge imputes, imparts, bequeaths, conveys or otherwise transfers his righteousness to either the plaintiff or the defendant. Righteousness is not an object, a substance or a gas which can be passed across the courtroom.[4]

According to Wright and others, since Paul's understanding of justification was informed by the typical understanding of the way the law court functions in Judaism, Paul does not employ the idea of imputation as an essential part of God's justifying the believer. Though Wright affirms the forensic nature of justification—that is, it relates to a person's status in the judgment of the court—he rejects the idea that righteousness is granted and imputed to the justified person.

Due to the pivotal importance of the doctrine of imputation to the historic Reformation view of justification, its dismissal by writers of the new perspective requires our attention.[5] Moreover, just as we previously considered the new perspective's claims regarding 'the righteousness of God' and 'justification', we also need to consider whether its dismissal of the idea of imputation is biblically warranted. Does the doctrine of imputation enjoy the kind of scriptural warrant claimed for it by the historic symbols of the Reformation?[6]

We will begin by examining briefly several key passages that teach the doctrine of imputation, after which we will identify and comment on several theological corollaries integrally related to the biblical doctrine of imputation.

AN EXAMINATION OF SEVERAL KEY BIBLICAL PASSAGES

A number of key biblical passages have played a critical role in the classic Protestant understanding of justification on the basis of the imputed righteousness of Christ. Though they deserve more extensive treatment than we are able to give them, we will simply identify them and provide a short account of their bearing upon this issue.

I. ROMANS 4:2–6 (GENESIS 15:6)

For if Abraham was justified by works, he has something to boast about, but not before God. For what does the Scripture say? 'Abraham believed God, and it was counted to him for righteousness' (ἐλογίσθη αὐτω εἰς δικαιοσύνην). Now to the one who works, his wages are not counted as a gift but as his due. And to the one who does not work but trusts him who justifies the ungodly, his faith is counted as righteousness, just as David also speaks of the blessing of the one to whom God counts righteousness apart from works.

In this passage, Paul directly links justification with imputation. In order to illustrate that Abraham's (and, therefore, the believer's) justification was not 'by works', the apostle appeals to Genesis 15:6 where Abraham's faith is said to be 'counted (λογίζεται) to him for righteousness'.[7] Since God's justification of Abraham involved his act of 'crediting' or 'accounting' Abraham's faith for righteousness, he justified Abraham 'apart from works'.

Though this passage places the idea of imputation in the centre of Paul's understanding of justification, it also presents an immediate problem. When Paul quotes Genesis 15:6, 'it [that is, faith] was counted to him for righteousness', he seems to treat faith as though it were Abraham's righteousness before God. On this reading of the text, Paul could be teaching that Abraham's right-eousness *consisted of his faith*. If that were the sense of the text, then the conclusion seems unavoidable that Paul understood justification to be based, not upon Abraham's works (of obedience) but upon his faith, which stands in lieu of his works. This reading would mean that the righteousness, which was the ground for Abraham's justification, was not external to him, but his own act of believing God. Even though imputation is central to Paul's understanding of justification, the righteousness imputed, so far as this text is concerned, is not the righteousness of Christ, as in the historic Protestant view. Rather, it is a kind of subjective right-eousness, a righteousness that is equivalent to Abraham's act of believing God. In such an understanding, we might say that Abraham was justified not only 'by' but 'on account of' his faith.[8]

However, there are several reasons for rejecting this inter-pretation of Paul's terminology and his citation of Genesis 15:6.[9]

First, it should be noted that the expression Paul uses, 'counted *for* righteousness', contains a preposition (εἰς) that is best translated 'with a view to' or 'in order to'. If we were to render the expression in literal, albeit clumsy English, it would say that Abraham's faith 'was counted *with a view to* righteousness'. This is different from saying that Abraham's faith 'was counted *in the stead of* right-eousness', suggesting that his faith was his righteousness before God. In Romans 10:10, Paul uses the same preposition in a way that clarifies its meaning, when he says that 'with the heart one believes *unto* (εἰς) righteousness'. Here faith is that which moves toward and lays hold of Christ himself as our righteousness.

As J. I. Packer puts it, commenting on Romans 4:2,

> When Paul paraphrases this verse [*Gen.* 15:6] as teaching that Abraham's faith was reckoned for righteousness (*Rom.* 4:5, 9, 22), all he intends us to understand is that faith—decisive, whole-hearted reliance on God's gracious promise (verses 18ff.)—was *the occasion and means of* righteousness being imputed to him. There is no suggestion here that faith is the ground of justi-fication (emphasis added).[10]

Second, in the context of Paul's appeal to Genesis 15:6, he utilizes the connection between wages and debts to illustrate how imputation occurs, not in the manner of wages earned but as a free gift.

> Now to the one who works, his wages are not counted as a gift but as his due. And to the one who does not work but trusts him who justifies the ungodly, his faith is counted as righteousness (verses. 4–5).

This illustration draws a sharp contrast between wages, which are accounted to a wage-earner, and the gracious gift, which is accounted to a non-wage-earner (one who does not work). When God accounts or reckons Abraham's faith for righteousness, it is equivalent to his granting Abraham a free, unearned gift. This understanding of God's act of imputation in the justifying of the believer does not fit in with the idea that the righteousness imputed to Abraham consists of his (subjective) faith. Though faith may be the occasion and instrument for the reception of this righteousness, it cannot be the righteousness that is actually the ground of Abraham's justification. If that were the case, the point Paul is making—that the imputation of Abraham's faith for righteousness is like the free gift which is accounted to someone who has not worked for it—would be undermined.[11]

And third, there are several indications from the broader context of Paul's argument in Romans 3–4 that the righteousness of faith is not a subjective righteousness, but an objective, *external* right-eousness that is granted and imputed to believers. In Romans 4:16, for example, the apostle sets forth the great reason why justification is 'by faith' and not 'according to works':

> That is why it depends on faith, in order that the promise may rest on grace and be guaranteed to all his [Abraham's] offspring—not only the adherent of the law but also to the one who shares the faith of Abraham.

Faith is instrumental to receiving the gift of justification precisely because it looks outside of itself to God's gracious promise in Christ. The apostle also insists that, because justification is an act toward the *ungodly,* it must occur *apart from works* (*Rom.* 4:5). It requires a positive imputation of righteousness to the believing sinner. Immediately after his appeal to Genesis 15:6, therefore, he cites David as an Old Testament example of the way God 'counts righteousness apart from works'. Though David was a sinner, the Lord did not count his sins against him (verse 8, quoting Psalm 32), but accounted him righteous. The expression Paul uses to speak of David's justification, 'counted him righteous', is equivalent to his earlier words, 'to justify the ungodly'. It is also equivalent to the terminology of Romans 3:28: 'For we hold that one is justified by faith apart from works of the law.' The point of all these expressions is to exclude any thought of an inherent righteousness as the basis for God's free justification.[12] Justification involves a free and positive granting or imputing of righteousness to the believer, which is received by faith.

Admittedly, in these passages Paul does not explicitly identify this imputed righteousness as the righteousness *of Christ.* However, as we shall see, this is the obvious implication of the apostle's teaching. How could it be otherwise, when the faith by which sinners receive God's gift of righteousness trusts 'in him who raised from the dead Jesus our Lord, who was delivered up for our trespasses and raised for our justification' (*Rom.* 4:24–25)? The object of faith is the crucified and risen Christ, who is the believer's righteousness from God (cf. *1 Cor.* 1:30).

II. ROMANS 5:12–19

Although Romans 4 does not explicitly identify the righteousness that is the basis for the believer's justification, several key passages in Paul's epistles clearly identify it as Christ's righteousness. They affirm that God freely grants and imputes the righteousness of Christ to believers. The first of these passages is Romans 5:12–21, especially verses 16–21.

> And the free gift is not like the result of that one man's sin. For the judgment following one trespass brought condemnation, but the free gift following many transgressions brought justification. If, because of one man's trespass, death reigned through that one

man, much more will those who receive the abundance of grace
and the free gift of righteousness reign in life through the one
man Jesus Christ. Therefore, as one trespass led to condemnation
for all men, so one act of righteousness leads to justification and
life for all men. For as by the one man's disobedience the many
were made sinners, so by the one man's obedience the many will
be made righteous (δίκαιοι καταστaθήσονται οἱ πολλοί). Now the law
came in to increase the trespass, but where sin increased, grace
abounded all the more, so that, as sin reigned in death, grace also
might reign through righteousness leading to eternal life through
Jesus Christ our Lord.

This passage, which closes Paul's summary treatment of the
doctrine of justification in Romans 3–5, crucially compares and
contrasts the first Adam and the second Adam (Christ). Just as all
who are 'in Adam' are subject to condemnation on account of his
one trespass, so all who are 'in Christ' receive justification and life
on account of his one act of righteousness. Though these verses
bristle with difficult questions of interpretation, we will focus only
on those things that have a direct bearing on the subject of
imputation and justification.[13]

We begin by noting the manner in which Paul connects the one
trespass of the first man Adam with the fact that 'all sinned' (verse
12) and are under the reign of death. Though some attempt to
explain the phrase 'all sinned' by taking it to refer to the actual sins
of all men, this does not fit well with the nature of Paul's argument.
The burden of the apostle's argument is that there is an *immediate
link* between *the one trespass of the one man Adam* and the reign
of death *and the judgment that brings condemnation upon the
many*. For this reason Paul emphasizes that death reigned from
Adam to Moses, 'even over those whose sinning was not like the
transgression of Adam, who was a type of the one who was to
come' (verse 14). Even though the trespass was Adam's, and his
alone, death, the consequence of this trespass, reigned over all.
Accordingly, the apostle insists that the 'one trespass led to
condemnation for all men' and that 'the many were made sinners'
(verses 18–19). Because of the union of all with Adam in his one

trespass, God imputes or reckons to all men the guilt of this trespass and its judicial consequence of death. This is the sense in which we may say that 'all sinned' in Adam, and all bear, as a consequence, the judicial liability of condemnation and death.

In a similar way, the apostle links the one man's obedience (literally, 'the act of righteousness of one') with the making righteous of the many. Just as death reigned through the disobedience of the first Adam, so 'the free gift of righteousness reign[s] in life through the one man Jesus Christ.' So far as the doctrine of imputation is concerned, the critical phrase in these verses is 'the free gift of righteousness'. The many who are made righteous, who receive justification and life through Christ's work, are not made righteous on account of their own deed or deeds. Rather, God's grace 'super-abounds' toward the many who are, through union with Christ, partakers of his righteousness.

The critical point in Paul's argument regarding the doctrine of imputation is his insistence upon the direct (or immediate) participation of all who are united with Christ in his one act of obedience. Just as Adam's sin (and not the sins of all men) constitutes all as sinners under the judicial sentence of condemnation and death, so Christ's obedience (and not the obedience of the many) constitutes the many as righteous and under the judicial sentence of justification and life. The dominant theme in the apostle's argument is the judicial implication of our union with the first and second Adams: God counts or reckons as guilty all who are in Adam; he counts or reckons as innocent all who are in the second Adam, Christ.

A further question arising in connection with this passage relates to the meaning of Paul's words, 'the one act of obedience/righteousness'. Do these refer, to use the technical theological terminology, to Christ's passive obedience alone (that is, his cross), or does it refer to Christ's active and passive obedience, 'one act' signifying the whole of his life of obedience? John Murray provides a helpful answer to this question:

> If the question be asked how the righteousness of Christ could be defined as 'one righteous act', the answer is that the righteousness

of Christ is regarded in its compact unity in parallelism with the one trespass, and there is good reason for speaking of it as the one righteous act because, as the one trespass is the trespass of the one, so that one righteousness is the righteousness of the one and the unity of the person and his accomplishment must always be assumed.[14]

Christ's obedience upon the cross epitomizes his whole life of obedience. The cross does not exhaust Christ's obedience but reveals it in its most striking form (cf. *Phil.* 2:8: 'becoming obedient to the point of death, even death on a cross'). Indeed, were it not for the entirety of Christ's obedience from the beginning to the end of his ministry, it would not be possible to speak of his having died 'the righteous for the unrighteous, that he might bring us to God' (*1 Pet.* 3:18). Even though the reference to the 'one act of righteousness' in Romans 5 describes Christ's death upon the cross, it is not possible to separate this act of obedience from his entire life 'under the law' (cf. *Gal.* 4:4).

III. PHILIPPIANS 3:8–9

Indeed, I count everything as loss because of the surpassing worth of knowing Christ Jesus my Lord. For his sake I have suffered the loss of all things and count them as rubbish, in order that I may gain Christ and be found in him, not having a righteousness of my own that comes from the law (μη ἔχων ἐμην δικαιοσύνην την ἐκ νόμου ἀλλα την δια πίστεως Χριστου), but that which comes through faith in Christ, the righteousness from God that depends on faith (την ἐκ Θεου δικαιοσύνην ἐπι τῇ πίστει).

This remarkable testimony was written by Paul in the context of his fierce and unyielding opposition to certain persons who were placing their confidence before God in the flesh (verse 3). Though the apostle does not explicitly identify his opponents, it appears that they were those who were boasting of their own religious pedigree and credentials, particularly circumcision, on the basis of which they sought to commend themselves to God. In his initial reply the apostle engages in an extended *ad hominem* argument. If his opponents would place their confidence before God in such things, then he has even more reason for so doing: 'circumcised on the eighth day, of the people of Israel, of the tribe of Benjamin, a Hebrew of Hebrews; as to the law, a Pharisee; as to zeal, a persecutor of the church; as to righteousness, under the law blameless.'

However, unlike his opponents, Paul's confidence was not resting on 'a righteousness of my own that comes from the law'. His boast, rather, is in 'the righteousness from God that depends on faith'. This righteousness comes 'through faith' to those who are 'found in Christ'. Though Paul does not explicitly speak of God imputing or reckoning the righteousness of Christ in these verses, the idea is certainly present. Those who are *united with Christ through faith* receive, *on that account*, a righteousness from God. This righteousness, Paul insists in the most emphatic of terms, *is not his own righteousness* but a *righteousness that comes from outside himself*. God freely bestows an *alien* righteousness to Paul and to all who are in union with Christ.

IV. 2 CORINTHIANS 5:19–21

In Christ God was reconciling the world to himself, not counting their trespasses against them, and entrusting to us the message of reconciliation. Therefore, we are ambassadors for Christ, God making his appeal through us. We implore you on behalf of Christ, be reconciled to God. For our sake he made him to be sin who knew no sin, so that in him we might become the righteousness of God.

Perhaps no passage in Scripture more clearly teaches the doctrine of imputation than this one. The reconciling work of God in Christ took place when Christ, who 'knew no sin', was 'made to be sin'. In an inscrutable manner, God regarded the sinless Christ as though he were sin. On the other hand, God did 'not count [our] trespasses against [us]'; he did not treat or regard us in a manner consistent with our condition and circumstances as sinners. By these means—not counting our sins against us, making and treating Christ as though he were sin—we 'become the righteousness of God in him'. Here then, as in those passages we have previously considered, Paul does not expressly speak of the granting and imputing of Christ's righteousness to believers. However, no other interpretation can legitimately claim to do justice to these verses. It is only by virtue of our union and participation in Christ that we benefit from his saving and reconciling work. Charles Hodge's comments on this passage well express this truth:

> Our sins were imputed to Christ, and his righteousness is imputed to us. He bore our sins; we are clothed in his right-eousness. . . . Christ bearing our sins did not make him morally a sinner . . . nor does Christ's righteousness become subjectively ours, it is not the moral quality of our souls. . . . Our sins were the judicial ground of the sufferings of Christ, so that they were a satisfaction of justice; and his righteousness is the judicial ground of our acceptance with God, so that our pardon is an act of justice. . . . It is not mere pardon, but justification alone, that gives us peace with God.[15]

According to this reading of 2 Corinthians 5:19, the justification of believers on account of the work of Christ involves a great transaction: the sins of believers are imputed to Christ and the righteousness of Christ is imputed to them.

THEOLOGICAL COROLLARIES

The biblical basis for the doctrine of imputation includes more passages than those we have briefly considered. However, these sufficiently illustrate Paul's teaching that the justification of sinners occurs by means of the reception of the righteousness of Christ, granted and imputed to them by God and received through faith. No basis other than Christ's righteousness—comprising the entirety of his mediatorial work, not only his death for sin but also his perfect life of obedience—can make a sinner acceptable to God.

The importance of the doctrine of imputation can also be confirmed by its intimate connection with other biblical and theological themes. Consequently, we conclude our treatment of imputation by noting its relationship to several theological corollaries. Criticisms of the idea of the imputation of Christ's righteousness to believers often fail to recognize these corollaries and the broader theological framework within which the Reformation view ought to be understood.

I. Sola Fide, Solo Christo

According to the Reformers, justification is 'by faith alone' (*sola fide*), not because the faith that alone justifies is an alone faith (that is, without works), but because it is *the exclusive instrument or means to receive the free gift of righteousness*, which is the basis for our acceptance with God. If the doctrine of imputation emphasizes that the ground of justification lies outside of us in a righteousness that God grants and imputes to us, then *faith alone* answers to the act by which God justifies sinners. A gift can only be received; it cannot be earned. Faith, therefore, as a receiving instrument is just the response that answers to the granting and imputing of the righteousness which justification requires. Similarly, to say that our justification is 'on account of Christ alone' (*solo Christo*) is equivalent to saying that it is on account of the righteousness of Christ, which becomes ours through imputation. The doctrine of imputation serves as an indispensable safeguard against the teaching that sinners can find acceptance with God on the basis of any righteousness other than that of Christ alone.

II. Substitution, Union, and Imputation

Just as imputation affirms what is expressed by the use of the terms 'faith alone' and 'Christ alone', it also affirms what belongs to the biblical themes of Christ's substitutionary atonement and the believer's union with Christ. If Christ's life, death and resurrection occurred by God's design *for* or *in the place of* his people, then it follows that all that he accomplished *counts as theirs,* so far as God is concerned. How could Christ's work on their behalf and for their benefit not be reckoned to their account, if indeed it is *just as though they had performed it.*[16] Furthermore, when believers become united to Christ through faith, they participate in all the benefits of his saving work. Faith is the 'empty hand' by which believers receive all that Christ has accomplished for them. To say that God grants and imputes the righteousness of Christ to believers is, accordingly, to acknowledge what is required by the doctrines of Christ's substitutionary atonement and the believer's union with Christ through faith. Luther, in his well-known sermon, 'Two Kinds of Righteousness', illustrates this point by appealing to the analogy of the bride's intimate union with the bridegroom:

> Therefore a man can with confidence boast in Christ and say: 'Mine are Christ's living, doing, and speaking, his suffering and dying, mine as much as if I had lived, done, spoken, suffered, and died as he did.' Just as the bridegroom possesses all that is his bride's and she all that is his—for the two have all things in common because they are one flesh [*Gen.* 2:24]—so Christ and the church are one spirit [*Eph.* 5:29–32].[17]

The correlation between the various themes of Christ's substitutionary work, union with Christ, and the imputation of Christ's righteousness to believers, sheds light on recent claims that Paul has no doctrine of imputation but only of incorporation into Christ. Don Garlington, for example, has argued that the modality for the believer's becoming the righteousness of God is union with Christ, not the imputation of Christ's righteousness to believers.[18]

The element of truth in this claim is certainly that the believer's justification by faith only occurs by virtue of his or her incorporation or participation in Christ. Nothing that God does for believers in Christ can benefit them, unless they are joined to him by faith. So far as the justification of believers is concerned, the governing theme of Paul's gospel is that Christ was put to death on account of their sins, and raised on account of their justification (*Rom.* 4:25). However, if justification refers to the believer's status in union with Christ, which is based upon the judicial verdict that God first declared in raising Christ from the dead, then imputation precisely corresponds to the nature of the justifying verdict itself. In justification, God declares the believer to be in the same judicial circumstance before him as Jesus Christ. This declaration presumes that all that Christ is and has done is equally the believer's by virtue of his or her faith-union with Christ.[19]

To deny that this transaction involves a legal component, equivalent to the declaration of a person's innocence in a court of law, would expunge the theme of justification from the gospel. The terminology of imputation functions as an expression of the believer's status before God on the basis of Christ's work on his behalf. To argue that the theme of incorporation into Christ offers an alternative explanation of how believers become righteous makes no sense, if justification essentially refers to the believer's standing in God's court. For the believer's justification on the basis of the imputation of Christ's righteousness is but a way of saying that the believer is justified by virtue of his or her judicial connection with the work of Christ. Imputation is a corollary of union with Christ, not an alternative to it.[20]

III. A 'LEGAL FICTION'?

The biblical doctrine of imputation is often charged with being a 'legal fiction'. God is said to regard sinners *as though they were righteous,* even though they still remain sinners. For the same reason that many object to the imputation of the guilt of Adam's sin to his posterity—the guilt is 'alien', not personal and real— imputation is often decried as a cold, legal transaction that leaves sinners in the same condition as before. This charge was not only a traditional component of Roman Catholic objections to the Reformation's teaching, but also plays an important role in recent criticisms of the doctrine of imputation.

There are two critical problems with this objection. The first, which is not so much our concern here, is that it ignores the way Christ, by his Spirit, sanctifies the believer whom he justifies. God, who declares the sinner righteous in justification, also makes the sinner righteous through the process of sanctification. The second problem, which is our concern, is that this objection ultimately charges God, who *declares the ungodly righteous on account of the work of Christ,* with declaring something to be real, which is in fact only a fiction. The same objection could be offered against God's declaration that all are subject to condemnation and death on account of the single trespass of the one man Adam. But the verdict of innocence, which God pronounces in freely justifying sinners for the sake of Christ's saving work, is no fiction. Rather, it is a divinely ordained and accomplished reality.[21] What could be more real than the perfect obedience and satisfaction of Jesus Christ, which are graciously granted and imputed to believers who place their trust in him alone? Perhaps the best answer to this objection, therefore, is to reply in the words of the apostle Paul:

> Who shall bring any charge against God's elect? It is God who justifies. Who is to condemn? Christ Jesus is the one who died — more than that, who was raised — who is at the right hand of God, who indeed is interceding for us (*Rom.* 8:33–34).

IV. THE ACTIVE AND PASSIVE OBEDIENCE OF CHRIST

At various points throughout our exposition of the Reformation view of justification we have referred to a traditional distinction between the 'active' and 'passive' obedience of Christ. According to this distinction, the righteousness of Christ, which is imputed to believers for their justification, consists both of Christ's active obedience to all the obligations of the law of God and his passive endurance of all the law's liabilities. The righteousness that under-girds the believer's acceptance with God consists of the obedience and satisfaction of Christ.[22] Though this distinction is a traditional one, it is often criticized as a theological conception that finds little or no scriptural support.[23] What biblical evidence is there to vindicate the doctrine of the imputation of the righteousness of Christ to believers, and that this righteousness includes both the obedience and satisfaction of Christ?

Several points need to be borne in mind, if this question is to be answered satisfactorily.

First, the distinction between the active and passive obedience of Christ aims primarily to clarify the twofold aspect of Christ's obedience. Whether or not the terminology of 'active' and 'passive' obedience is used, it is generally acknowledged that Christ's work involved not only his sinless obedience to his Father's will but also his suffering of the judicial consequence of sin on behalf of his people (*Rom.* 4:25). On the one hand, Christ was perfectly obed-ient to all that the Father called him to do. He willingly chose the course of obedience, an obedience that was ultimately manifested in his death upon the cross (*Rom.* 5:12–21; *Phil.* 2:6–11). Christ's 'active obedience' refers to this aspect of his life and ministry. On the other hand, Christ was 'made sin' for the sake of those on whose behalf he died (2 *Cor.* 5:19; cf. *Rom.* 8:3). Christ's 'passive obedience' emphasizes that his suffering and death were not on account of his own sin, but were endured for the sake of his people's redemption. Even among those who do not believe in the imputation of Christ's righteousness to believers, it is commonly acknowledged that Christ's sacrificial death was not on account of his own sins but on account of the sins of his people (*Rom.* 4:25; 8:3). Christ's so-called 'passive obedience' presupposes the kind of sinless obedience to God's will which theologians have described as his 'active obedience'. Though it is sometimes claimed that this terminology artificially separates the obedience of Christ into two disparate parts, the real interest of the distinction between the active and passive obedience is to underscore the richness of Christ's seamless life of obedience 'under the law' (*Gal.* 4:4).[24] In order to make atonement for his people, the sinless Christ endured the curse of the law resting upon those who have not continued to do all that the law demands (*Gal.* 3:13).[25] Therefore, even among those who would deny that the whole of Christ's obedience is imputed to believers for their justification, there is general agreement that the obedience of Christ includes both of these dimensions.

Second, the chief point in dispute regarding the active and passive obedience of Christ relates to the question whether through imputation believers share fully in both of these aspects of Christ's work. If it is granted that Paul teaches that believers are united to Christ by faith, and that God therefore regards or counts them to be *what Christ is*, the claim that believers have a full share in all the obedience, satisfaction, and righteousness of Christ seems undeniable. If there is a correlation between union with Christ and the imputation of his righteousness to believers, it hardly seems possible that believers would share in and benefit from only one aspect of the righteousness of Christ, namely, his death on account of their sins. The obedience, cross, and resurrection of Christ form one seamless act in which the righteousness of God is revealed (*Rom.* 5:12-21; *Phil.* 2:6-11).[26] When believers receive the free gift of God's righteousness in Christ, they are constituted righteous and are, accordingly, no longer subject to condemnation and death (*Rom.* 5:15–17).

Consequently, the claim that the whole of Christ's obedience and satisfaction are imputed to believers follows from several themes in Paul's writings: the unity of Christ's obedience, an obedience that took him to death upon the cross (*Phil.* 2:6–11); the union of believers with Christ such that Christ's life, death, and resurrection are as much theirs as his (*Rom.* 4:25; 6:1–11; *Gal.* 2:19–20); and the imputation to believers of the righteousness of God in Christ. The imputation of the whole of Christ's obedience is an implication of the great transaction that occurs in the redemption of believers. Christ was made to be sin in order that believers might become the righteousness of God in him (2 *Cor.* 5:19). Just as the believer's sin and guilt are imputed to Christ, so Christ's obedience and satisfaction are imputed to the believer. The traditional insistence upon the imputation of the whole obedience and satisfaction of Christ to believers is, accordingly, one that flows from the clear themes of Paul's teaching.

And third, the justification of believers involves a favourable verdict that goes beyond the mere forgiveness or non-imputation of the guilt of sin to believers. When God justifies the ungodly for the sake of Christ's saving work, he declares them to be in a positive state of innocence or righteousness. Justified believers are not simply declared to be without sin; they are declared to be positively righteous before God. In Christ the justified person enjoys a righteous standing before God that properly belongs to someone who has not only borne the curse of the law but also met all of its demands.[27] In the resurrection of Jesus Christ, which is the ground for the believer's justification, God vindicates his own righteousness and establishes the believer's right to be received into his favour as a righteous person. Not only is there now no condemnation for those who are in Christ Jesus, but there is no longer any basis for a charge to be brought against them (*Rom.* 8:33–34). As those who were crucified and raised with Christ, believers enjoy the privileged status of full acceptance with God. As John Murray observes:

. . . it is prejudicial to the grace and nature of justification to construe it merely in terms of remission. This is so to such an extent that the bare notion of remission does not express, nor does it of itself imply, the concept of justification. The latter means not simply that the person is free from guilt but is accepted as righteous; he is declared to be just. In the judicially constitutive and in the declarative sense he is righteous in God's sight. In other words, it is the positive judgment on God's part that gives to justification its specific character.[28]

Unless the righteousness of Christ in his obedience to the law as well as in his suffering of its curse is imputed to believers, they could not, strictly speaking, be justified in this full sense of being in the right before God.

The traditional distinction between the active and passive obedience of Christ, therefore, articulates the saving significance of the full scope of Christ's obedience under the law. The Saviour's death upon the cross by which he made atonement for sin was not an isolated act of obedience, but the epitome of an obedience that began with his readiness to 'take the form of a servant' for the sake of his people (*Phil.* 2:6–11). Believers who are united to Christ by faith receive the fullness of his righteousness, which includes his faithful obedience to the law and willing payment of its curse.

Only a complete share in the fullness of Christ's righteousness can explain the rich biblical teaching of free justification. God declares all who believe in Christ to be as acceptable to himself as Christ is: he is their righteousness from God (*1 Cor.* 1:30). The justification of believers, in this respect, is also the vindication of God's own righteousness, which is revealed in the law's demands as much as in its sanctions.

CONCLUSION

The story is told that J. Gresham Machen, shortly before his death, sent a telegram to his colleague John Murray with the words: 'I'm so thankful for active obedience of Christ. No hope without it.'[29] Machen's words perhaps express the truth of the imputation of Christ's righteousness in a more poignant and personal way.

Nevertheless, the doctrine of the imputation of Christ's right-eousness asserts that Christ's life, death, and resurrection are the sole basis upon which sinners are set right with God and become heirs of eternal life. Clothed in the perfect righteousness of Christ, believers may have confidence in the presence of God. They know that the punishment, which their sins merited, was fully paid by Christ. They know that their obligation to perfect obedience was perfectly fulfilled by Christ. They know that Christ continues to intercede for them as their Advocate before God. In short—being found in Christ, they know with the confidence of faith that 'There is therefore now no condemnation for those who are in Christ Jesus' (*Rom.* 8:1). And so they sing:

> Man's work faileth, Christ's availeth,
> He is all our righteousness;
> He, our Saviour, has for ever
> Set us free from dire distress.
> Through His merit we inherit
> Light and peace and happiness.

> *Venantius Fortunatus,* c. 530–609
> (translated by Augustus Nelson).

NOTES

[1] Though the traditional Roman Catholic view confuses justification and sanctification, the Council of Trent's definition of justification includes, as we noted in Chapter 2, an emphasis upon the sinner's 'reputation' and acceptance with God. Cf. *The Canons and Decrees of the Council of Trent,* Sixth Session, Chap. 7 (Schaff, *The Creeds of Christendom,* 2:95): '. . . we are not only reputed, but are truly called, and are just, receive justice within us, each one according to his own measure.' Cf. also the recent *Joint Declaration on the Doctrine of Justification,* by the Lutheran World Federation and the Roman Catholic Church, p. 13: 'Justification is the forgiveness of sins . . . liberation from the dominating power of sin and death (*Rom.* 5:12–21) and from the curse of the law (*Gal.* 3:10–14).'

[2] The *Heidelberg Catechism,* Q. & A. 60, provides an exemplary statement of the Reformation view that justification is based upon the imputed righteousness of Jesus Christ: 'How are you righteous before God? Only by a

true faith in Jesus Christ; that is, though my conscience accuse me that I have grievously sinned against all the commandments of God and kept none of them, and am still inclined to all evil, yet God, without any merit of mine, of mere grace, grants and imputes to me the perfect satisfaction, righteousness, and holiness of Christ, as if I had never had nor committed any sin, and myself had accomplished all the obedience which Christ has rendered for me; if only I accept such benefit with a believing heart.'

[3] See e.g. E. P. Sanders, *Paul and Palestinian Judaism*; pp. 492, 494; and James D. G. Dunn, *The Theology of Paul the Apostle*, pp. 341–2, 385–6. Neither Sanders nor Dunn make any significant use of the idea of imputation in their explanation of Paul's understanding of justification. Sanders dismisses the idea altogether (p. 492, footnote). When 'the righteousness of God' is viewed principally as God's covenant faithfulness in action, as is the case for writers of the new perspective, it can hardly be viewed as a gift that is freely granted or imputed to believers. The idea of imputation is a corollary of the idea of Christ's work as *substitutionary*. Since Dunn insists that Christ's work is 'representative' but not 'substitutionary' (that would leave us with a 'legal fiction'), it is not surprising that he does not affirm the imputation of Christ's righteousness to believers. Cf. Dunn, *The Theology of Paul the Apostle*, p. 386.

[4] *What Saint Paul Really Said*, p. 98. Not only does this comment present something of a caricature of the Protestant view, but it also misstates it. The Protestant view is not that the Judge (God) transfers his righteousness to us, but that he provides his Son as a substitute and surety whose righteousness becomes ours through imputation. Wright's statement suggests that he regards imputation to be a kind of 'infusion' of grace. The Protestant view, however, is that imputation is a judicial act in which God credits or accounts the righteousness of Christ to the person who believes in him.

[5] The diminishment of the importance of imputation is widespread and extends beyond the orbit of the new perspective. For example, in the recent documents, 'Evangelicals and Catholics Together' and 'The Gift of Salvation', which purport to give a consensus statement of the doctrine of justification by evangelical and Catholic authors, the doctrine of imputation receives short shrift. In the first of these statements, the subject of imputation is omitted, and in the second, it is mentioned as an item about which no consensus was reached. For recent examples of evangelical denials of imputation, see Don Garlington, 'Imputation or Union with Christ? A Response to John Piper', *Reformation & Revival Journal* 12/4 (Fall, 2003), pp. 45–113; Robert H. Gundry, 'The Nonimputation of Christ's Righteousness', in *Justification: What's At Stake in the Current Debates*, ed. Mark Husbands and Daniel J. Treier, pp. 17–45; and Michael F. Bird, 'Incorporated Righteousness: A Response to Recent Evangelical Discussion concerning the Imputation of Christ's Righteousness in Justification', *Journal of the Evangelical Theological Society* 47/2 (June, 2004), pp. 253–76. For recent defences of the doctrine of imputation against contemporary critics, see John Piper, *Counted Righteous in Christ: Should We Abandon the Imputation of Christ's Righteousness?* (Wheaton: Crossway Books, 2002); idem, 'A

Response to Don Garlington on Imputation', *Reformation & Revival Journal* 12/4 (Fall, 2003), pp. 121–8; and D. A. Carson, 'The Vindication of Imputation: On Fields of Discourse and Semantic Fields', in *Justification,* ed. Mark Husbands and Daniel J. Treier, pp. 46–78. For a cautious criticism of imputation by a critic of the new perspective, see Mark A. Seifrid, 'Luther, Melanchthon and Paul on the Question of Imputation', in *Justification,* ed. Mark Husbands and Daniel J. Treier, pp. 137–76.

[6] The Reformed confessions uniformly affirm that the justification of believers is upon the ground of the righteousness of Christ, which is granted and imputed to them from God and received by the hand of faith. See e.g. *Heidelberg Catechism,* Q.& A. 59; *Belgic Confession,* Art. 22-23; *Westminster Confession of Faith,* 11.1; *Westminster Larger Catechism,* Q. & A. 70–73, 77; *Westminster Shorter Catechism,* Q. & A. 33.

[7] For a treatment of the Old Testament background to the use of 'to count' or 'to reckon' in Genesis 15:6, see O. Palmer Robertson, 'Genesis 15:6: New Covenant Expositions of an Old Testament Text', 259–89; James R. White, *The God Who Justifies*, pp. 111–7; and Carson, 'The Vindication of Imputation', pp. 57–9.

[8] This language and distinction was expressed by the older Protestant writers on justification in the following dictum: *Fides iustificat non propter se, ut est in homine qualitas, sed propter Christum, quem apprehendit* ('Faith justifies not because of itself, insofar as it is a quality in man, but on account of Christ, of whom faith lays hold').

[9] For a more extensive argument against the view that the believer's righteousness 'consists of' his faith, see John Owen, *The Works of John Owen,* vol. 5, pp. 93–137; and John Murray, *The Epistle to the Romans,* vol. 1 (NICNT; Grand Rapids: Eerdmans, 1959), pp. 353–9. Though Murray holds the view that Genesis 15:6 takes Abraham's faith for his righteousness (incorrectly, in my judgment, as I shall shortly argue), he argues that this cannot mean that Paul regarded faith as the ground or basis for the believer's justification. That would contradict Paul's consistent emphasis upon justification on the basis of the righteousness of God in Christ. Cf. Gundry, 'The Non-imputation of Christ's Righteousness', who argues strongly that Paul does not view faith instrumentally, as the means to receive an imputed righteousness, but as that in which the believer's righteousness consists.

[10] 'Justification', *Evangelical Dictionary of Theology,* ed Walter A. Elwell (Grand Rapids: Baker, 1984), p. 596. Cf. Douglas Moo, *The Epistle to the Romans*, p. 262: 'The language ["counting Abraham's faith for righteousness"] could suggest that his faith is considered as the "equivalent" of righteousness — that God sees Abraham's faith as itself a "righteous" act, well pleasing to him. But if we compare other verses in which the same grammatical construction as is used in *Gen.* 15:6 occurs, we arrive at a different conclusion. These parallels suggest that the "reckoning" of Abraham's faith as righteousness means "to account to him a righteousness that does not inherently belong to him."'

[11] Cf. John Piper, *Counted Righteous in Christ*, p. 57: 'Would not the wording of verse 4 rather tell us that in Paul's mind "faith being credited for righteousness" is shorthand for faith being the way an external righteousness is received as credited to us by God—namely, not by *working* but by *trusting* him who justifies the ungodly?'

[12] Cf. Carson, 'The Vindication of Imputation', p. 60: 'In Paul's understanding, then, God's imputation of Abraham's faith to Abraham as righteousness *cannot* be grounded in the assumption that that faith is itself intrinsically righteous, so that God's "imputing" of it to Abraham is no more than a recognition of what it intrinsically is. If God is counting faith to Abraham *as* righteousness, *he is counting him righteous*—not because Abraham *is* righteous in some inherent way (How can he be? He is ἀσεβής), but simply because Abraham trusts God and his gracious promise. In that sense, then, we are dealing with what systematicians call an alien righteousness' (emphasis Carson's).

[13] For a more extensive treatment of Romans 5:12–21 and its implications for the imputation of Christ's righteousness, see Piper, *Counted Righteous in Christ*, pp. 90–114; and John Murray, *The Imputation of Adam's Sin* (Phillipsburg, NJ: Presbyterian & Reformed reprint, 1959). Reformation theology has traditionally read this passage to teach a parallel between the imputation of the guilt of Adam's sin to his posterity and the imputation of the righteousness of Christ to believers. Consistent with their denial of the imputation of Christ's righteousness to believers, new perspective authors are unclear on the subject of the relation between Adam's sin and the guilt of his posterity. Cf. Dunn, *Romans 1–8*, pp. 269–300; idem, *The Theology of Paul*, pp. 94-7; and Wright, *Romans*, pp. 522–32.

[14] *The Epistle to the Romans*, vol. 1, pp. 201-202. Cf. Piper, *Counted Righteous in Christ*, pp. 110-4. We will return to this distinction between Christ's active and passive obedience in the concluding section of this chapter.

[15] Charles Hodge, *A Commentary on 1 & 2 Corinthians* (London: Banner of Truth, 1958), pp. 526-7.

[16] Carson, 'Atonement in Romans 3:21–26', p. 134, note 53, makes an apt observation regarding the connection between substitution and imputation: 'Part of the contemporary (and frequently sterile) debate over whether or not Paul teaches "imputation", it seems to me, turns on a failure to recognize distinct domains of discourse. Strictly speaking, Paul never uses the verb λογίζομαι to say, explicitly, that Christ's righteousness is imputed to the sinner or that the sinner's righteousness is imputed to Christ. So if one remains in the domain of narrow exegesis, one can say that Paul does not explicitly teach "imputation", except to say slightly different things (e.g., that Abraham's faith was "imputed" to him for righteousness). But if one extends the discussion into the domain of constructive theology, and observes that *the Pauline texts themselves* (despite the critics' contentions) teach penal substitution, then "imputation" is merely another way of saying much the same thing.'

[17] 'Two Kinds of Righteousness', in *Martin Luther: Selections from His Writings*, ed. by John Dillenberger, pp. 86–7.

[18] Cf. Garlington, 'Imputation or Union with Christ?', p. 97: 'Hand in hand with the pre-eminence of the person of Christ is that union with him bespeaks a personal (covenant) relationship that is obscured when legal and transactional matters are given as much prominence as they are in traditional Reformed thought. "Imputation" is the transferral of a commodity from one person to another; but "union" means that we take up residence, as it were, within the sphere of the other's existence.'

[19] Cf. Richard B. Gaffin Jr., *Resurrection and Redemption: A Study in Paul's Soteriology* (2nd ed.; Phillipsburg, NJ: Presbyterian & Reformed, 1987), p. 123: 'Jesus' being delivered up (his death) on account of our transgressions identified him with us in the condemnation inevitably attendant on our transgressions; in fact his death is the pointed manifestation of this solidarity in condemnation. Consequently, his being raised on account of our justification identifies him with us in the justifying verdict inevitably attendant on the righteousness which he himself established for us (better, which he established for himself as he was one with us) by his obedience unto death; his resurrection is the pointed manifestation of this solidarity in justification.'

[20] Cf. John Murray, 'Justification', in *Collected Writings* (Edinburgh: Banner of Truth, 1977), vol. 2, p. 214: 'In reality the concept is richer than that of imputation; it is not simply reckoned as ours, but it is reckoned to us and we are identified with it. Christ is ours, and therefore all that is his is ours in union with him and we cannot think of him in his vicarious capacity or of anything that is his in this capacity except in union and communion with his people. . . . These are not legal fictions. They are the indispensable implicates of what union with Christ entails.'

[21] Cf. James Buchanan, *The Doctrine of Justification*, p. 337: 'When we are brought face to face with such realities as these, it is vain to talk of "legal fictions", whether under the Law or under the Gospel; for while condemnation, on the one hand, and justification, on the other, are strictly forensic or judicial acts, and must necessarily have some relation to the Law and Justice of God,— and while the representative character both of the first and second Adam, and the consequent imputation of their guilt and righteousness to those whom they respectively represented, can only be ascribed to the sovereign will and appointment of God,—yet the results are in their own nature real and true, and not, in any sense, fictitious or imaginary.'

[22] The imputation of Christ's active and passive obedience is implicitly or explicitly affirmed in the following Reformation confessions: *Heidelberg Catechism*, Q. & A.'s 15, 16–19, 21, 35–36, 37, 60, 62; *Belgic Confession*, Article 22; *Formula of Concord*, Article 3; *Canons of Dort*, I.8, 9; Rejection of Errors I.1, 3; *Westminster Confession of Faith*, Chapter 8.4, 5; Chapter 11.1, 3; *Westminster Larger Catechism*, Q. & A.'s 70–73; *Westminster Shorter Catechism*, Q. & A. 33; *London Confession (1689)*. Because some Lutheran

(Cargius) and Reformed theologians (Piscator) affirmed the imputation of Christ's passive obedience alone, these confessions reflect a history in which the affirmation of the imputation of Christ's active obedience became increasingly explicit. For historical and theological summaries of this subject, see Bill Berends, 'The Obedience of Christ: A Defence of the doctrine of Christ's Active Obedience', *Vox Reformata* 66 (2001), pp. 26–51; Nicolaas H. Gootjes, 'Christ's Obedience and Covenant Obedience', *Koivonia* 2 (Fall 2002), p. 2–22; and Turretin, *Institutes of Elenctic Theology*, 2, pp. 445–55.

[23] Cf., for example, Gundry, 'The Nonimputation of Christ's Righteousness', pp. 32–45.

[24] Cf. Carson, 'The Vindication of Imputation', p. 55, who speaks, incorrectly in my view, of the 'absolute bifurcation' this distinction introduces. Carson affirms, however, that the whole of Christ's obedience becomes ours when we are joined to Christ by faith and receive his righteousness as our own.

[25] John Murray, *Redemption, Accomplished and Applied* (London: Banner of Truth, 1961), pp. 20–1, offers a traditional explanation of this distinction: 'This obedience has frequently been designated the active and passive obedience. This formula when properly interpreted serves the good purpose of setting forth the two distinct aspects of Christ's work of obedience. But it is necessary at the outset to relieve the formula of some of the misapprehensions and misapplications to which it is subject. (a) The term "passive obedience" does not mean that in anything Christ did was he passive, the involuntary victim of obedience imposed upon him. . . . (b) Neither are we to suppose that we can allocate certain phases or acts of our Lord's life on earth to the active obedience and certain other phases and acts to the passive obedience. The distinction between the active and passive obedience is not a distinction of periods. It is our Lord's whole work of obedience in every phase and period that is described as active and passive, and we must avoid the mistake of thinking that the active obedience applies to the obedience of his life and the passive to the obedience of his final sufferings and death. The real use and purpose of the formula is to emphasize the two distinct aspects of our Lord's vicarious obedience. The truth expressed rests upon the recognition that the law of God has both penal sanctions and positive demands.'

[26] Cf. Turretin, *Institutes of Elenctic Theology*, 2, pp. 452: 'The whole paschal lamb was to be eaten. In like manner, a whole Christ is to be received by us, both as to what he did and what he suffered. This tends to the greater glory of Christ and to our richer consolation, which they obscure and lessen not a little who detract from the price of our salvation a part of his most perfect righteousness and obedience and thus rend his seamless tunic.'

[27] In this connection, defenders of the imputation of Christ's active obedience appeal to passages like Romans 10:5 and Galatians 3:12, which enunciate the principle that the law promises life only to those who do what it requires. Christ's active and passive obedience, accordingly, are understood to have met all the claims (perceptive and penal) of the law on behalf of his people. In this

way, the law is upheld in the gospel of Christ, and God is both just and the one who justifies those who believe in him (cf. *Rom.* 3:26). Cf. Turretin, *Institutes of Elenctic Theology*, pp. 445ff.

[28] *Collected Writings*, 2:218.

[29] As quoted by Ned B. Stonehouse, *J. Gresham Machen: A Biographical Memoir*, 3rd ed. (Edinburgh: Banner of Truth Trust, 1987 [1954]), p. 508.

10

JUSTIFICATION AND A FINAL JUDGMENT ACCORDING TO WORKS

In the course of our study of the new perspective on Paul, we have emphasized the important role played by E. P. Sanders' treatment of Second-Temple Judaism. According to Sanders, the Judaism of Paul's day practised a pattern of religion which he describes as 'covenantal nomism'. Covenantal nomism regards the covenant relationship between the Lord and his people Israel as being one based upon sovereign election and grace. Contrary to the assumptions of traditional Protestantism regarding the occasion for Paul's teaching on justification, the new perspective argues that Second-Temple Judaism did not teach a kind of Pelagian moralism or works righteousness. Not only did it teach that entrance into covenant with the Lord depends upon his gracious initiative and promise, but it also acknowledged the need for the Lord's continued gracious provision of forgiveness and atonement for sin. Works performed in obedience to the law were necessary to 'maintain' a covenant member's place within the covenant community. But they were never thought to 'merit' the Lord's favour or to serve as the basis for the covenant relationship itself.

One interesting issue raised by this understanding of covenantal nomism is that of the role of works in the present maintenance and the eschatological vindication of those who belong to the covenant community. Though Sanders, as we acknowledged previously, may have demonstrated that Second-Temple Judaism was not 'Pelagian' in its view of how one enters into the covenant, his assessment of Second-Temple Judaism still leaves unanswered the question whether it was not 'semi-Pelagian' in its understanding of how the covenant is maintained. If works play an indispensable role in the

maintenance of the covenant relationship and in the final vindication of those who belong to the covenant community, the
spectre of a doctrine of justification by works still remains. As we
have seen, according to writers of the new perspective, the doctrine
of justification is principally addressed to the issue of who belongs
to the covenant family of God. However, God's gracious initiative
in establishing the covenant does not secure or guarantee the future
inheritance of the covenant promises. The pattern of religion characteristic of Second-Temple Judaism is one of 'entrance' by grace
and 'maintenance' by works. Put in terms of the language of justification, this means that belonging to the covenant people of God
is partly by grace and partly by works.

Justification, which according to the new perspective means
belonging to the covenant community, remains 'unfinished business', since continued membership in the covenant community
requires its members to persevere in obedience to the law. Such
obedience, accordingly, would not only maintain but also finally
constitute the ground for future justification or acquittal.[1]

It is not surprising to find among proponents of the new perspective those who connect Paul's doctrine of justification with a
future or 'final' justification.[2] This future or final phase in the
justification of those who believe in Christ is related to the apostle's
understanding of the final judgment. Since this is clearly a judgment
'according to works', it seems that the justification of believers has
at least three distinct phases, past, present, and future.

N. T. Wright argues that justification in Paul's perspective occurs
in three tenses or stages. The present justification of the covenant
community is founded upon 'God's past accomplishment in Christ,
and anticipates the final verdict.'[3] In the past event of Christ's cross
and resurrection, God has accomplished in history something that
anticipates what he will do at the end of history, namely, vindicate
or justify his people for whom Christ acted as the 'representative
Messiah of Israel'. Through faith believers are united with Christ
and become participants and beneficiaries of this past event. Baptism, which is the event in the present that incorporates believers
into the covenant community, effects this present justification or
participation in Christ, and at the same time anticipates the

resurrection of believers in the future. According to Wright, the future justification of believers, which will occur in the context of the final judgment, represents the ultimate completion of the believer's justification. This future justification will be on the basis of the whole life of faith.[5]

These features of the new perspective's view of justification in relation to the final judgment and vindication of those who belong to the covenant community require our careful consideration. Since the final judgment is closely linked to works performed by those who are judged, it naturally raises the question of what this means for our understanding of justification. This is not a new question, of course, since it played an important role in the context of sixteenth-century debates regarding justification. One of the principal objections of the Roman Catholic Church to the Reformation's teaching of justification by faith alone was that it failed to do justice to the biblical theme of a works-based final acquittal before God.[6] Since justification and final judgment are judicial acts, which involve the pronouncement of a verdict by God as Judge, the place of works in the setting of the final judgment inescapably compels the question whether the doctrine of justification 'by faith alone' adequately summarizes the apostle Paul's teaching. Does the justification of believers require a final phase or 'completion', which will be determined by the works of those who are justified? And, does this mean that the justification of believers is, in the final analysis, based upon faith *plus works?*

THE REFORMATION'S ANSWER TO THE QUESTION

To address these questions we will summarize the Reformation's answer to them. During debates on the doctrine of justification, the Reformers, who insisted that the believer's justification is based wholly upon the righteousness of Christ received by faith alone, were compelled to consider how their position is compatible with a final judgment according to works. Since Roman Catholic objections often included an appeal to the scriptural teaching of a final judgment according to works, the subject of justification and the final judgment was an unavoidable feature of their teaching.

Looking at the treatment of justification and the final judgment in the Protestant confessions we can detect several important themes.

Fundamental to the Reformation view was the claim that justification was a judicial act of God that *irrevocably* and *definitively* declares believers to be right with God and heirs of eternal life. Justification is not like sanctification – a process that occurs over time as believers are renewed and conformed to Christ by the working of his Spirit. Instead justification is an act of God whereby he pronounces believers to be in a state of acceptance and favour with himself. This free acceptance with God is wholly based upon the work of Christ, whose righteousness is the sufficient and only basis for God's justifying verdict. When believers come to enjoy the benefit of Christ's saving work through faith, their justification declares, *here and now,* the favourable verdict that God will publicly confirm at the final judgment. Free justification declares all the believer's past, present, and future sins to be forgiven and covered by the perfect righteousness of Jesus Christ, whose life of obedience and sacrificial death constitute their righteousness before God. In this respect, justification *anticipates* the favourable verdict that will be declared openly at the final judgment. When believers are joined to Christ through faith they become beneficiaries of the verdict declared already by God in the resurrection of Christ from the dead (*Rom.* 4:25).

To state the matter conversely, if the final judgment were to undo or reverse the verdict already pronounced in the believer's justification, the believer's confidence that there 'is therefore now no condemnation for those who are in Christ Jesus' would be seriously compromised (*Rom.* 8:1). To speak of a 'future' or final justification that is partly based upon works jeopardizes the believer's assurance of full and irrevocable justification.

Nowhere in the confessions of the Reformation is this more emphatically stated than in the *Westminster Confession of Faith.*

> God doth continue to forgive the sins of those that are justified; and, *although they can never fall from the state of justification,* yet they may, by their sins, fall under God's fatherly displeasure,

and not have the light of his countenance restored unto them, until they humble themselves, confess their sins, beg pardon, and renew their faith and repentance (Chapter 7 'Of Justification', Section 5, emphasis added).

The Confession's language unmistakably declares that justification is a once-for-all judicial act, which secures the believer's right standing with God in an irrevocable manner. There is no room for the idea of a future justification that completes an otherwise unfinished reality. A similar point is made in the *Heidelberg Catechism*, although appearing in the express context of the Catechism's treatment of the final judgment. When the question is asked, 'What comfort is it to you that Christ *shall come to judge the living and the dead?*', the answer strongly insists that this judgment occurs within the framework of a solid confidence that Christ's obedience and sacrifice have *already secured*, permanently and irrevocably, the believer's freedom from the curse of the law:

That in all my sorrows and persecutions, with uplifted head I look for the very same Person who before has offered himself for my sake to the tribunal of God, and has removed all curse from me, to come as Judge from heaven (Q. & A. 52).

The final judgment does not represent a fearful prospect of loss for believers who place their trust in Christ, since Christ has secured once-for-all their freedom from the curse of the law and accomplished all that is necessary to secure their right standing with God (*Rom.* 8:31-39; *Phil.* 3:20; *Titus* 2:13).[6]

Since this definitive and irrevocable declaration of the believer's standing with God is based solely upon the righteousness of Christ, which is received by faith alone, the works that play a role in the context of the final judgment must not be regarded as the ultimate basis for the favourable verdict and acquittal which this judgment publicly declares. The confessions clearly and repeatedly assert that the only righteousness, which is the ground for the justifying verdict of God, is the righteousness revealed in the gospel of Jesus Christ (*Rom.* 3:21–24; 5:1, 2, 16; *Eph.* 2:8–9; *Phil.* 3:9; 2 *Cor.* 5:21).[7] Since believers are justified by faith 'apart from works', the final judgment's contemplation of the works of believers must not be construed as a justification *by works,* even though such works are the necessary and inevitable fruits of a true and living faith. Though it is acknowledged that the final judgment includes a public *confirmation* of the believer's present justification, this judgment is not described as a kind of future or final justification that completes an otherwise unfinished process. To regard the final judgment as a final justification would inevitably compel the view that justification, at least in its ultimate expression, is not a free gift of God's grace, granted for the sake of Christ's righteousness alone.

If the confessions of the Reformation clearly speak of justification as a once-for-all act of God, which does not comport with a final justification according to works, this still leaves open the question regarding the way they handle the final judgment and the obvious role that works play in this judgment. How do they treat the subject of the role of good works in the context of the final judgment?

To answer this question, it is significant to observe that the confessions of the Reformation clearly affirm the reality of a final judgment according to works. They also openly acknowledge that the good works of believers are genuine works that please God and are accordingly rewarded by him. However, they are careful to note that the good works God rewards in this context have at least three important characteristics.

First, they are not the kinds of works that could ever justly deserve the verdict of free justification. Such works could never be 'the whole or part of our righteousness before God', according to the *Heidelberg Catechism:*

> Because the righteousness which can stand before the tribunal of God must be absolutely perfect and wholly conformable to the divine law, while even our best works in this life are all imperfect and defiled with sin (Q. & A. 62; cf. *Rom.* 3:9, 20; 10:5; 7:23; *Gal.* 3:10; 5:3; *Deut.* 27:6; *Lev.* 18:5).

Second, the good works of believers are themselves the fruits of God's sanctifying grace at work in the hearts and lives of his people. They are those good works that God prepared beforehand for believers (*Eph.* 2:10).

And third, the works of believers are only 'good' in so far as they proceed from faith, the same faith that finds no other basis for acceptance with God than that provided by the righteousness of Jesus Christ. Good works are the inescapable fruits of a true and living faith; though faith alone – 'before we do good works' – is the exclusive instrument whereby believers receive the free gift of justification (*Matt.* 7:18; *John* 15:5; *James* 2:18, 22).[8]

Gratitude, borne out of the awareness of God's super-abounding grace in Christ, is the principal motive at work in the Christian life (*Rom.* 12:1). To suggest that the good works of a believer constitute the basis for final acceptance with God would be to transpose them into an unbiblical key. Were believers motivated to obey God by the prospect of the loss of their justification and inheritance in the covenant, their works would be performed in 'bad faith', that is, out of an ungrateful denial of the perfection of Christ's work on their behalf. When God rewards the works of faith, therefore, he is in fact rewarding works produced by his own Spirit in the lives of believers.

Since the genuine good works of believers, which play an important role in the final judgment, are not the kind of works that could justify anyone, the confessions also insist that their reward, though genuine, is not the gift of salvation itself or the title to eternal life (*1 Cor.* 3:14–15). Salvation is wholly a gift of God's grace in Christ (*Rom.* 6:13) and therefore cannot be a reward for good works. The reward that God grants to the good works of believers is a genuine and undeniable feature of the final judgment. However, the believer's acceptance with God and title to eternal life – whether in this life or in the setting of the final judgment – are always grounded upon the gracious work of Christ. Were these to depend upon who they are or what they have done, the assurance of free justification would be lost and works would become the way of salvation. This would also constitute a denial of justification by the instrumentality of *faith alone*.[9]

Among the more important features of the confessions' treatment of a final judgment according to works is their insistence that God's acceptance and reward of our good works is *by grace and not merit*. When God rewards the works of believers, he does not reward them in terms of their inherent value, as though, strictly speaking, there would be a sense in which they 'deserve' this reward. Since the works of believers are always imperfect and stained with sin, and since these works are themselves the fruits of Christ's Spirit at work within them, it is not possible to speak of their reward as properly merited. There is no sense in which the reward could be said to be 'due' to believers, as though it were like a wage that is due a worker who has satisfactorily fulfilled all his duties (cf. *Luke* 17:10; *Rom.* 4:4). Indeed, however genuine and praiseworthy the works performed by believers, their acceptance and reward from God *depends wholly upon a prior acceptance of their persons for the sake of the righteousness of Christ.*

In this connection, the confessions introduce a distinction, which is also found in the writings of John Calvin and other Reformed theologians of the sixteenth and seventeenth centuries, between the *justification of the believer's person* and the *justification of the believer's works.* Though present in several of the confessions, nowhere is this distinction more clearly stated than in the *Westminster Confession of Faith:*

> Notwithstanding, the persons of believers being accepted through Christ, their good works also are accepted in him; not as though they were in this life wholly unblameable and unreprovable in God's sight; but that he, looking upon them in his Son, is pleased to accept and reward that which is sincere, although accompanied with many weaknesses and imperfections (Chap. 16, Section 6).

The point of this distinction is to emphasize that whatever pleasure God takes in the otherwise imperfect works of his children, this pleasure wholly depends upon and is under girded by his prior pleasure in their persons, which is on account of the righteousness of Christ alone. By speaking of an acceptance or justification of the works of believers, the Confession clearly does not mean to speak of something that 'completes' or complements the believer's prior justification by faith alone. The acceptance of their works is altogether gracious and unmerited. It is not a second chapter in the ongoing process of the believer's justification; rather, it is a fruit and consequence that follows from a more basic act, namely, the free justification of believers themselves on account of work of Christ on their behalf.[10]

Within the context of these emphases, the confessions affirm that believers will not be acquitted in the final judgment, or receive the confirmation of their free justification and praise for their good works, unless their lives give evidence of the genuineness of their faith.[11] God will not declare the final acquittal of professed believers whose lives belie or deny their profession. In this respect, it is permissible to say that believers will only be vindicated in the final judgment within the context of *an acknowledgment of their good works, which prove the genuineness of their faith*. The good works that true faith produces are a necessary part of what belongs to the salvation of any believer (a genuine *conditio sine qua non*); however, they are not the cause or reason for the salvation of any believer.[12] In other words, believers will only be saved when they embrace the gospel with the kind of faith that necessarily produces good works. However, this certainly does not mean that we should view the final judgment as a kind of final chapter in the believer's justification that determines whether believers are worthy of eternal life on the basis of works.

Therefore, according to the confessions, the final judgment and acquittal of believers is 'according to' but not, strictly speaking, 'on account of' their good works. Because true faith is 'ever accompanied with all other saving graces' (*Westminster Confession of Faith,* Chapter 11, Section 2), including good works, the final judgment will openly confirm the salvation of those in whom the Spirit of Christ has worked. The final judgment will show that the faith that alone justifies is not alone in those who genuinely believe in Christ. None of those whom God justifies freely for the sake of Christ are left in the condition in which they were found. Rather, the Spirit of Christ, who is the Spirit of sanctification, always and simultaneously renews believers in new obedience to the law of God.

The purpose of the final judgment, accordingly, is to vindicate God's righteousness in declaring his justified and sanctified people to be the proper recipients of their open acquittal and praise. By contrast, the judgment of the unbelieving and impenitent will publicly declare that they remain in their sins and are deservedly recipients of condemnation and death.

SUMMARY

The Reformed confessions' treatment of the themes of justification and a final judgment according to works includes several inter-related themes. All believers, whose free justification is based upon the righteousness of Christ alone, received through faith alone, will be judged at Christ's coming. Because justification is a definitive and irrevocable declaration of the believer's acceptance with God and title to eternal life, this final judgment, though a judgment according to works, is not understood to be a final phase or step in an unfinished process of justification. Rather, this judgment will publicly declare and confirm what is already true, namely, that Christ has removed every accusation against his people and every reason for their remaining under the curse of God.

Furthermore, because the faith that receives the gift of Christ's righteousness for justification is also a faith that proves its genuineness by its fruits, the final judgment will declare the propriety of God's judgment in favour of believers by recognizing and rewarding the works of believers. The works of believers will not be the reason or basis for God's favourable verdict and acquittal of believers in the final judgment. Nor will the gift of eternal life be the reward of these works.

The role of good works in the final judgment will be to offer the occasion for God to reward graciously, and not according to merit, those good works of believers that are the fruits of his gracious working in them.

Believers will be judged 'according to' their works, but they will not be saved 'on the basis' or 'by reason' of such works. Though we may properly say that believers will only be acquitted in the final judgment when their profession is confirmed by their good works, we may not say that this acquittal is based upon their good works.

PAUL ON JUSTIFICATION AND THE FINAL JUDGMENT

The question now to be addressed is whether the Reformation understanding of the relation between justification and the final judgment accurately reflects Paul's teaching. One way to put the question would be to ask whether the Reformation view was born out of the desire merely to protect the Reformed doctrine of justification by grace alone through faith alone?

The Necessity of Sanctification

Before directly addressing Paul's understanding of the final judgment in relation to good works, we need to observe that his epistles clearly teach the sanctification of freely justified believers through union with Christ. Those who receive Christ for righteousness also receive him for sanctification (*1 Cor.* 1:30). However emphatic the apostle's declaration of free justification is, he nowhere countenances the conclusion that this is at the expense of the work of the Spirit of Christ in renewing them in obedience to the 'law of Christ' (*Gal.* 6:2). Expressed theologically, the apostle affirms that the gospel of God's grace in Christ includes both the benefits of justification and sanctification. Antinomianism, which teaches that the free grace of God permits the believer to live indifferently with respect to the requirements of the law, is expressly rejected as a false conclusion that fails to appreciate the fullness of the salvation given to the believer. Though justification is a principal benefit of the gospel, it must not be separated from sanctification. Salvation includes not only the grace of acceptance with God but also the grace of transformation into the image of his Son (*Rom.* 8:29).

We need only consider a few instances where Paul emphasizes the indispensable place of the obedience of faith in the Christian life.

One of the more remarkable instances of this is to be found in a section of the epistle to the Romans that follows immediately upon the heels of the apostle's treatment of the theme of free justification.

What shall we say then? Are we to continue in sin that grace may abound? By no means! How can we who died to sin still live in it? Do you know that all of us who have been baptized into Christ Jesus were baptized into his death? We were buried there-fore with him by baptism into death, in order that, just as Christ was raised from the dead by the glory of the Father, we too might walk in newness of life (*Rom.* 6:1–4).

In this transitional portion of the argument in Romans, Paul anticipates a possible response to his earlier exposition of God's 'super-abounding grace' in Jesus Christ. If salvation is a free gift, which is granted solely upon the basis of the obedience of Christ (*Rom.* 5:12–21), the conclusion may seem to follow that the more we sin, the more God's grace is magnified. What possible motive or reason for obedience remains, if we are justified by faith alone apart from works performed in obedience to the law?

Remarkably, without backtracking from his insistence upon the grace of free justification,[13] the apostle simply reminds his readers that those who are united to Christ by faith are thereby *participants in his death and resurrection*. By virtue of their incorporation into Christ, they have died to sin and are being raised in newness of life (verse 5). Through union with Christ, believers are 'set free from sin' and made alive to God (verses 7, 11). Therefore to conclude that believers may live as they please, since they have been saved by grace alone, represents a fundamental failure to comprehend what it means to be united with Christ. The believer's new life in union with Christ is not an optional 'extra', but an integral aspect of all that is entailed by being united to Christ by faith and indwelt by his Spirit. Consequently, the apostle sums up his response to any attempt to use the grace of God as a license for sin in the opening part of Romans 8:

You, however, are not in the flesh but in the Spirit, if in fact the Spirit of God dwells in you. Anyone who does not have the Spirit of Christ does not belong to him. But if Christ is in you, although the body is dead because of sin, the Spirit is life because of righteousness (verses 9–10).

This theme of 'life in the Spirit' is sounded at various important points in Paul's epistles. The believer has fellowship with Christ, the 'life-giving Spirit' (2 *Cor.* 3:17; cf. *1 Cor.* 15:45). This means that the believer no longer lives in the environment of the flesh, but in the environment of the Spirit. In his letter to the Galatians, which primarily argues that believers are justified by faith and not by the works of the law, Paul insists that those who are no longer 'under' the curse of the law may not use their new freedom as an opportunity for the flesh (*Gal.* 5:13). Believers have been crucified with Christ so that the life they now live is no longer their own because Christ lives in them (*Gal.* 2:19-20). Accordingly, they must 'walk by the Spirit' and bear the 'fruit of the Spirit [in] love, joy, peace, patience, kindness, goodness, faithfulness, gentleness, self-control' (*Gal.* 5:22-23). The same faith that receives the gracious promise of God and is opposed to justification by works, is also a faith that 'works through love' (*Gal.* 5:6). Just as in Romans 6, so in Colossians 3, the apostle appeals to the reality of the believer's union with Christ in his death and resurrection as the basis for calling believers to a distinctively Christian way of living:

> If then you have been raised with Christ, seek the things that are above, where Christ is, seated at the right hand of God. Set your minds on things that are above, not on things that are on the earth. For you have died, and your life is hidden with Christ in God. When Christ who is your life appears, then you also will appear with him in glory (verses 1–3).

Within the setting of this real incorporation into Christ crucified and risen from the dead, the apostle urges believers to 'put to death' the passions and ways of the flesh (verse 5), to 'put off the old self with its practices' (verse 9), and to 'put on the new self which is being renewed in knowledge after the image of its creator' (verse 10; cf. 2 *Cor.* 3:18).

Since justified believers are being progressively sanctified in union with Christ whose Spirit indwells them, the apostle Paul is also able to speak of their salvation as a still future reality. Indeed, only those who continue in faith and obedience will obtain the end of their salvation, eternal life (*Rom.* 6:22). The urgency of such persistence in the Christian life is the setting for Paul's use of the metaphor of a race when speaking of the Christian life. As he reminds the Corinthians, not all athletes who compete in the race obtain the prize. What is required is the kind of self-control and persistence that will enable the athlete to finish the race and not be disqualified (*1 Cor.* 9:24–27).[14] Believers are exhorted to work out their own salvation, because it is God who works in them both to will and to do for his good pleasure (*Phil.* 2:12). Full participation in Christ, not only in the likeness of his death but also in his resurrection, will only be obtained when perfection is reached in a yet future state of glory. For this reason, the apostle confesses that he has not already obtained this, nor is he perfect, but 'I press on to make it my own, because Jesus has made me his own' (*Phil.* 3:12).

Thus, the fullness of salvation includes more than God's act of free justification, which liberates the believer from condemnation and death. It also includes an incorporation into Christ after whose likeness the believer is being conformed. Since this has a future end or goal in view, Paul speaks of the believer's 'hope of salvation', which suggests that—from the vantage point of the future— salvation is yet to be obtained (*1 Thess.* 5:8, 9). The salvation of believers is, accordingly, nearer than when they first believed, though not yet their complete possession (*Rom.* 13:11). Since salvation, whether in its present, partial realization or its future, consummate perfection, involves a complete transformation after the likeness of Christ, it can be described as an ongoing, yet-unfinished process (cf. *1 Cor.* 1:18; *2 Cor.* 3:18).

A Final Judgment According to Works

Within the context of Paul's insistence upon the necessary trans-formation of the life of the believer by the Spirit of Christ, it is not surprising to find that he links the future experience of full salvation with a final judgment according to works. The believer's present enjoyment of salvation through union with the crucified and risen Christ ('already') does not represent the fullness of salvation which will be enjoyed when the end comes ('not yet'). According to the apostle, the present experience of salvation is an anticipation and beginning of a more glorious future of consummate blessing. To use the metaphor of harvest, the 'first fruits' of Christ's resurrection life, which are shared with believers through union with Christ by his indwelling Spirit (*Rom.* 8:1–11), are the beginnings of the complete harvest, when everything believers presently enjoy in the form of an earnest or down-payment will be received in full (2 *Cor.* 5:4–5). The obtaining of salvation in its fullest measure will only occur within the setting of Christ's coming and the final judgment.

The prospect of a final judgment is, therefore, a central and inescapable feature of the future. It is an unavoidable prospect for all believers and unbelievers, who will be judged according to their works and their respective responses to the gospel of Jesus Christ. Even believers, who enjoy the grace of acceptance with God on the basis of Christ's saving work, will be subject to a future judgment. Though they presently know that there 'is therefore now no condemnation for those who are in Christ Jesus' (*Rom.* 8:1), this fact does not exempt them from a future judgment that will include their public acquittal before others. Nor does it allow them to conclude that good works are not a necessary fruit of faith.

Some passages in Paul's epistles speak of the final judgment in the most comprehensive terms. All people, whether Jews or Gentiles, whether believers or non-believers, will be judged by God. In the opening chapters of Romans, which demonstrate that the divine condemnation hangs over the whole of fallen and sinful mankind, the apostle emphasizes that everyone will be judged by God in 'the day of wrath when God's righteous judgment will be revealed' (*Rom.* 2:5). At that time God 'will render to each one according to his works: to those who by patience in well-doing seek for glory and honour and immortality, he will give eternal life; but for those who are self-seeking and do not obey the truth, but obey unrighteousness, there will be wrath and fury' (verses 6–8). This judgment will fall upon all who have sinned, whether those who sinned 'under the law' or 'without the law'. No one will be spared the judgment of God 'on that day', says the apostle, 'when, according to my gospel, God judges the secrets of men by Christ Jesus' (verse 16). The point of Paul's insistence upon this universal judgment of

God is to maintain that all sinners, Jews as well as Gentiles, will not escape being examined by God and found guilty and worthy of condemnation. There is no escape available to anyone by means of the law. The advantage of having the law and the oracles of God, which distinguishes the Jews from the Gentiles, will not safeguard those who do not do what the law requires. The principle enunciated is that all will be judged according to what they have received, and no one will be found acceptable to God by that standard: 'For all who have sinned without the law will also perish without the law, and all who have sinned under the law will be judged by the law' (*Rom.* 2:12).

In other passages, the apostle speaks of the final judgment particularly with respect to those who obey or disobey the gospel. The final judgment will witness a separation between those who are saved and those who are not. In the case of non-believers who have disobeyed the gospel of Jesus Christ, the final judgment holds only a fearful certainty of divine wrath and displeasure. In a passage remarkable for its vivid imagery, the apostle portrays the second coming of Christ as a time when Christ will be 'revealed from heaven with his mighty angels in flaming fire, inflicting vengeance on those who do not know God and on those who do not obey the gospel of our Lord Jesus' (2 *Thess.* 1:7–8). The coming of Christ promises rest to his beleaguered people, but terrible distress for those who have rejected him. In the case of believers, the final judgment promises the fullness of salvation, provided they continue in their course of faith and obedience (2 *Cor.* 11:15).

Whether in those passages which speak of God's judgment in comprehensive terms or those which speak particularly of the judgment of believers, it is clear that this judgment will be 'according to' works. When defending his own apostolic ministry, Paul is not content to appeal to his own judgment concerning himself. Rather, he appeals to the judgment of the Lord who will either vindicate or condemn his ministry. In the face of opposition and division within the Corinthian church, he notes that it is the 'Lord who judges me' (and, by implication, all believers). There is a day coming in which we shall stand, not in a human court, but in the court of the Lord. 'Therefore', he warns, 'do not pronounce judgment before the time, before the Lord comes, who will bring to light the things now hidden in darkness and will disclose the purposes of the heart. Then each one will receive his commendation from God' (2 *Cor.* 4:5). The clearest statement of a final judgment of believers, however, is found in 2 Corinthians 5:10: 'For we must all appear before the judgment seat of Christ, so that each one may receive what is due for what he has done in the body, whether good or evil.'

If we consider all of these features of Paul's teaching, the general pattern seems fully consonant with the Reformation's confessional position. Since justification is always accompanied by sanctification in the lives of those who are in union with Christ by faith, the apostle insists that only those whose lives confirm the indwelling presence of the Spirit of Christ will be saved. Salvation includes the consummation of that saving work in the lives of believers, which begins in this life, but is only perfected in the life to come. Justification, which is a principal benefit of the gospel, does not encompass the whole of the believer's salvation. Those whom God justifies he also sanctifies.

Consequently, no one will be saved who does not exhibit the fruits of the Spirit's working in his life, and who does not persist in the way of new obedience. This is the context for Paul's clear teaching that all will be judged in the future and that this final judgment will be according to works. However, despite this clear emphasis upon a final judgment and vindication according to works, nowhere in the apostle's writings is this final judgment described as a completion or final chapter in the believer's justification. The grace of free justification remains the basis for the believer's acceptance with God.

There are, however, two passages in Paul's epistles that are of special importance to the question of justification and a final judgment according to works. The first of these, 1 Corinthians 3:10-15, is pertinent to the nature of the reward granted to believers for their works. The second of these, Romans 2:13, is the one passage in Paul's epistles that might appear to teach something like a future justification based upon good works. Before drawing our conclusion on Paul's teaching regarding justification and the final judgment, we need to examine these passages carefully.

1 CORINTHIANS 3:10–15

According to the grace of God given to me, like a skilled master builder I laid a foundation, and someone else is building upon it. Let each one take care how he builds upon it. For no one can lay a foundation other than that which is laid, which is Jesus Christ. Now if anyone builds on the foundation with gold, silver, precious stones, wood, hay, straw— each one's work will become manifest, for the Day will disclose it, because it will be revealed by fire, and the fire will test what sort of work each one has done. If the work that anyone has built on the foundation survives, he will receive a reward. If anyone's work is burned up, he will suffer loss, though he himself will be saved, but only as through fire.

The context for this passage is the apostle's sharp rebuke to the Corinthians for their unspiritual treatment of those who are ministers and teachers of the gospel. The chapter begins with Paul noting that he could not address them 'as spiritual people, but as people of the flesh, as infants in Christ' (verse 1). In the Corinthian church there was an unseemly factionalism that expressed itself in terms of some saying, 'I follow Paul' or 'I follow Apollos'. This party spirit was rife and led to many problems in the church. In his rebuke Paul argues that this factionalism betrays a fundamentally wrong view of Christ's servants. He reminds them that, though Christ's ministers may plant and water the seed of God's Word, they are nevertheless utterly dependent upon God. In the strongest possible language, he says that ministers are nothing by themselves: 'So neither he who plants nor he who waters is anything, but only God who gives the growth' (verse 7).

Having reminded them of the impropriety of boasting in those who are merely servants of Christ, the apostle raises the subject of rewards. Comparing the church to a building, ministers are described as God's workers, each of whom will receive his wages according to his labour (verse 8). Speaking of himself as a 'skilled master builder', Paul notes that his labour within God's building was based upon the one foundation, the Lord Jesus Christ. If anyone carries out his ministry on behalf of the Lord with the proper materials—gold, silver, and precious stones—his work will endure the fiery purification of the 'Day' when each one's work will become manifest. Christ's ministers, who build properly upon the true foundation of Jesus Christ, will receive a reward. However, those who build upon the foundation in an improper manner (using materials that are like wood, hay, or straw) will witness the fiery destruction of their work. Such inappropriate work will not receive a reward. Nevertheless, those whose work is unworthy of a reward will be saved, though only after having passed through the fiery judgment.

The significance of this passage for our consideration of the question of justification and a final judgment according to works is transparent. All servants of Christ are reminded to labour within God's building in a way that builds upon the one great foundation, Jesus Christ. The quality of the labour depends upon the means utilized in the church-building effort. Some means, which conform to the nature of the gospel, are like precious and abiding materials that, even when tested by fire, will endure in the day of judgment. Other means, which are not conformed to the gospel, are like worthless materials that, when tested by fire, will be utterly consumed. This passage is a clear affirmation of Paul's teaching that Christ's servants will undergo a judgment or testing according to their works.

What is particularly striking about this judgment-testing, however, is that it will not issue in the irrevocable loss of salvation for those who belong to Christ. The respective rewards granted to those who labour in God's building do not include the reward of salvation or eternal life, which is a gift of God's grace (cf. *Rom.* 6:13), but praise and honour, consistent with the quality of the work performed.[15] Though it does not expressly address the subject of justification, the teaching of this passage is certainly consistent with the idea that the reward associated with a final judgment according to works ought not to be understood as the gift of salvation itself. As it stands, there is nothing in the passage that contradicts the Reformation's teaching that free justification secures the believer's salvation and inheritance of eternal life, though it does not mitigate the reality of a future judgment according to works. Furthermore, although this passage focuses particularly upon a future judgment according to works as it affects ministers of Christ, it also carries an application to all believers.[16]

WHAT ABOUT ROMANS 2:13?

The most significant passage in Paul's writings regarding the subject of justification and a final judgment according to works may be Romans 2:13: 'For it is not the hearers of the law who are righteous before God, but the doers of the law who will be justified.' One possible reading of this passage could understand Paul to be affirming a positive connection between good works and a future justification presumably associated with the final judgment.[17] When it comes to the ultimate judgment of believers in the future, only those who have done what the law requires will be justified. Without further qualification, this could be interpreted to mean that the final phase of the believer's justification, which will occur in connection with a final judgment according to works, will be one in which works, and not faith alone, will be the basis for acquittal. Upon this reading, one might conclude that the believer's initial justification, which is by means of faith and apart from works, needs to be completed by a future justification, which is by means of the works of faith. If this is indeed the teaching of Romans 2:13, it would contradict Paul's teaching elsewhere that the believer's justification is by faith and not by the works of the law (cf. *Rom.* 3:28).

Many different and distinct interpretations of this verse have been offered in the history of the church.[18] For our purposes, we will only consider the three most prominent views, especially as they relate to whether Paul taught a doctrine of a future justification by works.

i. The first reading of this text, which was common among representatives of the Reformation view of justification in the sixteenth century, argues that the apostle Paul is refuting the empty boast of those who seek to be justified by obedience to the law. Within the context of his argument in the early chapters of

Romans, Paul is not stating that there are those who do what the law requires and thereby obtain justification; rather, he is simply stating a principle which is enunciated in the law of God: those who abide by the law's precepts will thereby possess a righteousness that would commend them to God (cf. *Lev.* 18:5). However, since it is not possible that anyone does what the law requires, the principle stated in this verse is *hypothetical: if* someone were to do what the law requires, *then* he would be righteous before God. But there are no such persons who do what the law requires and therefore no one can be justified by doing the law (cf. *Rom.* 3:10). Calvin summarizes this view in his commentary on the book of Romans:

> The sense of this verse, therefore, is that if righteousness is sought by the law, the law must be fulfilled, for the righteousness of the law consists in the perfection of works. . . . We do not deny that absolute righteousness is prescribed in the law, but since all men are convicted of offence, we assert the necessity of seeking for another righteousness. Indeed, we can prove from this passage that no one is justified by works. If only those who fulfil the law are justified by the law, it follows that no one is justified, for no one can be found who can boast of having fulfilled the law.[19]

Among the arguments for this understanding, two stand out as of special importance. The first is drawn from the immediate context of Romans 2:13. In the preceding verses, Paul is anxious to show that all people, Jews and Gentiles alike, are subject to God's righteous judgment. All will be judged by God who shows no partiality (verse 11). Whether someone sins 'without the law' as a Gentile or 'with the law' as a Jew, no one who sins will be able to escape the wrath and condemnation of God. To suggest, therefore, that those who have the law enjoy an advantage in distinction from those who do not have the law, is mistaken. For it is not enough to have the law or to be a 'hearer' of the law; only those who do what the law requires will be justified. In this setting of the epistle's argument, Paul seems to be saying to his opponents who are boasting in their possession of the law that this will be of no benefit to them since they are not doing what the law requires. Paul adduces the principle ('only doers of the law will be justified') for the express purpose of refuting the empty boast of those who seek to be justified by their obedience.

The second argument is drawn from the broader context of Romans chapters 2–4. Since the burden of Paul's argument in these chapters is to establish that 'all have sinned and fall short of God's glory'(*Rom.* 3:23), and that justification is a free gift of God's grace in Christ (3:24–26), it seems unlikely that the point of Romans 2:13 is to affirm a positive role for works in relation to justification. Throughout the epistle's opening chapters, Paul is making a case against any kind of self-justification, which appeals to works or works of the law as the basis for acceptance with God. Works of any kind are utterly excluded as a basis for justification (2:19–20) for two reasons: firstly, because there are no persons who are righteous by the standard of the law, and secondly, because God has now revealed a righteousness 'apart from the law', which is 'through faith in Jesus Christ for all who believe' (3:21–22). Thus, within both the immediate and broader context of Paul's argument in Romans, it does not seem likely that Romans 2:13 represents a positive statement regarding the role of good works in relation to justification.[20]

ii. A second reading of this text takes it as a positive description of believers whose faith is confirmed by their works of obedience. Though this reading does not claim that Paul is speaking of a final justification by works, it does view the passage as a character description of the believer who will be justified ultimately. Only those whose conduct confirms the genuineness of their faith will be justified. Since those who are truly joined to Christ are justified and sanctified by grace, there is a legitimate sense in which the works of faith are a necessary accompaniment of justification. Though the works of the believer are at no time the basis for their justification, this does not mean that the believer will be justified without having obeyed the law and thereby confirming the genuineness of their profession. The inseparable connection between justification and sanctification makes it possible for the apostle to insist that only those who do what the law requires (who are being sanctified) will enjoy the benefit of God's justifying verdict. The good works of justifying faith, though not, strictly speaking, the basis for the justification of believers or their acquittal in the final judgment, are nonetheless necessary evidences of the genuineness of that faith. Although believers are not justified *on account of* their doing the law, they will not be justified *without* doing what the law requires, however imperfect their obedience may be.

Thomas Schreiner is an able exponent of this second reading of Romans 2:13.[21] In his treatment of this text, several arguments are cited to show that Paul is enunciating a positive principle, namely, that only those who by the Spirit do what the law requires will be justified.

First, there is evidence in the context that Paul speaks positively about the actual obedience of Gentile believers, who are 'doers of the law' in contrast to those Jews who 'hear' the law but do not do what it requires. Of particular significance to Schreiner is the description offered at the close of Romans 2 regarding the obedience of such Gentile Christians.[22] In verses 26–27, Paul contrasts the conduct of uncircumcised Gentiles who 'keep the precepts of the law' with that of circumcised Jews who have the 'written code . . . but break the law'. Since Paul appeals to the actual (and not merely hypothetical) obedience of such Gentile Christians in the context of his sustained argument for the righteousness of God's judgment upon Jew and Gentile alike, the assertion that 'doers of the law will be justified' likely refers to the vindication of believers who obey the law.[23]

Second, in the verses preceding Romans 2:13, Paul has described the judgment of God as an event in which he 'will render to each one according to his works' (verse 6). This judgment will have a twofold outcome: some who 'by patience in well-doing seek for glory and honour and immortality' will receive 'eternal life', others who 'are self-seeking and do not obey the truth' will receive only 'wrath and fury' (verses 7-8). The distinct outcome of God's judgment for believers on the one hand and unbelievers on the other, suggests that Paul taught that only believers who do good will receive eternal life in the context of God's righteous judgment. And third, Schreiner appeals to the frequent emphasis in Paul's writings upon a final judgment which is according to works. This emphasis is fully compatible with a view of Romans 2:13 that understands it to be a positive affirmation of God's approval/vindication at the final judgment of those who do good.[24]

Though he defends the view that Paul is stating a positive principle in Romans 2:13, Schreiner insists that the apostle is not thereby contradicting his clear teaching that believers are justified by faith (alone) apart from works.[25] In the opening chapters of Romans, Paul emphatically rejects the idea that anyone, whether Jew or Gentile, can obtain justification on the basis of the works of the law (cf. *Rom.* 3:20, 28).[26] We should not take his statement that 'only the doers of the law will be justified', therefore, as a description of the basis or ground for the believer's justification. Like those who take the first view of this text, Schreiner rejects the idea that Paul is teaching a future justification based upon works, which completes a present or initial justification. Rather, Paul is reminding his readers that true faith produces good works by the Spirit of Christ, and that these works are a significant confirmation of the genuineness of faith. Indeed, such works, though imperfect, are such a necessary part of salvation that no one will be justified without them. Summarizing this view, Schreiner notes that

> we should understand the good works that do lead to an eschatological reward in different terms. They are *the result* of the Spirit's work in one's life, as the connection forged between verses 26-27 and 28-29 demonstrates. The Spirit's work on the heart logically precedes the observance of the law by the Gentiles. Autonomous works are rejected, but works that are the fruit of the Spirit's work are necessary to be saved. Paul is not speaking of perfect obedience, but of obedience that clarifies that one has been transformed. . . . The good works done are not an achieving of salvation, then, but the outflow of the Spirit's work in a person's life.[27]

iii. The third reading of this text claims that the apostle Paul is affirming that the final, eschatological justification of believers will be based upon their works. This understanding is the view of some contemporary theologians, including proponents of the new perspective on Paul.[28] In this interpretation of Romans 2:13, Paul is understood to teach that justification has a present and future phase. Though believers enjoy an initial justification by faith apart from works, there is a yet future justification that will be upon the basis of those works that belong to true faith. On this reading of the text, the apostle Paul is not speaking hypothetically; rather he is speaking about actual believers whose works not only prove the genuineness of their faith but also constitute the ground for their final vindication or justification. Justification, according to this view, has both an initial and a final stage.

There is no uniformity of understanding among the proponents of this third view. Some suggest that Paul is engaging in a polemic against some Jews who boasted that they, unlike the Gentiles, were given the Mosaic law. Refuting this boast, Paul reminds his readers that it is not enough to hear the law, since only those who do what the law requires will be justified. E. P. Sanders, for example, maintains that Paul affirms in this verse that the Gentiles who do the law will be justified upon that basis, which contradicts the apostle's teaching elsewhere that no one can be justified by the works of the law.[29] As we noted earlier, N. T. Wright also appeals to this text to support his claim that Paul taught a doctrine of final or eschatological justification based upon the believer's works.[30]

This view had proponents at the time of the Reformation, and has been suggested by interpreters of Romans at various times since.[31] At the end of the nineteenth century, F. Godet, in his commentary on the book of Romans, maintained that Paul speaks in this verse of a future justification that will be based upon works. Godet cited Paul's use of the future tense in Romans 2:13, when he says that only doers of the law 'will be justified'. Since the justification of which Paul speaks is a future event, it does not likely refer to a hypothetical circumstance, namely, that anyone who does what the law requires will be justified even though no such person exists. Godet also appealed to the words at the close of Romans 2, which speak of Gentiles who 'keep the law' (verse 27). This indicates that Paul is speaking, not hypothetically, but about specific instances of obedience to the law. Since Paul speaks here of a future justification, and since he appeals in the subsequent context to the specific obedience of Gentiles to the law, Godet concluded that we should distinguish between an 'initial' justification and a 'final' justification:

> It will certainly, therefore, be required of us that we *be* righteous in the day of judgment, if God is to *recognize* and *declare* us to be such; *imputed* righteousness is the beginning of the work of salvation, the means of entrance into the state of grace. But this initial justification, by restoring communion between God and man, should guide the latter to the *actual* possession of righteousness—that is to say, to the fulfilment of the law; otherwise, this first justification would not stand in the judgment. . . . And hence it is in keeping with Paul's views, whatever may be said by an antinomian and unsound tendency, to distinguish two justifications, the one initial, founded exclusively on faith, the other final, founded on faith *and its fruits.*[32]

This brief overview of the three most important readings of Romans 2:13 illustrates the difficulty of determining precisely what Paul means when he says 'only doers of the law will be justified'. While recognizing the difficulty of interpreting this verse in its context, I am persuaded that the first view remains the most likely reading of the text. There are several reasons that support this conclusion.

First, though the apostle Paul uses the future tense in this verse, it goes beyond the interest of Romans 2:13 to directly connect its language with his teaching in other places about a final judgment according to works, *as though these good works were a basis for a final justification.* We have noted that the subject of a final judgment according to works is a common one in Paul's epistles. However, neither in Romans 2:13 nor in any other text that refers explicitly to a final judgment does Paul speak of it as *another justification,* which is to be distinguished from a presumably initial justification that occurs by faith apart from works. To be sure, the final judgment, like justification, is a judicial act that occurs within a legal setting. But Paul never explicitly speaks of the final judgment as an act that completes or fulfils an earlier justification. If he did so in Romans 2:13, this text would be a noteworthy exception to his usual pattern.[33]

Second, the argument from the immediate and broader context of Romans seems to support the view that Paul is speaking hypothetically. The one point that Paul wishes to make by the statement, 'only the doers of the law will be justified', is a negative one, namely, that those who boast of their possession of the law make an idle boast since they do not do what the law requires. Paul states a principle in order to reject those who claim to be justified by their works. However, this claim is contradicted by their failure to do what the law demands. As John Murray remarks in his comments on this verse:

> It is quite unnecessary to find in this verse any doctrine of justification by works in conflict with the teaching of this epistle in later chapters. Whether any will be actually justified by works either in this life or at the final judgment is beside the apostle's interest and design at this juncture. The burden of this verse is that not the hearers or mere possessors of the law will be justified before God but that in terms of the law the criterion is *doing*, not hearing.[34]

The function of Paul's appeal in this text to the principle that 'only doers of the law will be justified' parallels his appeal elsewhere to the fact that justification by obedience to the law is precluded by the failure of anyone to do *all* that it requires (cf. *Rom.* 3:19–20; 10:5; *Gal.* 3:10; 5:1). Moreover, if the point made in this verse was that those who do what the law requires will be justified *on that basis,* the inconsistency of his overall argument in Romans 2-5 would be rather striking. The burden of the argument in the opening chapters of Romans is that the law, so far as justification before God is concerned, serves only to expose and aggravate the reality of human sin and guilt (*Rom.* 3:19-20, 28; *Rom.* 4:4). To maintain that Romans 2:13 states a positive connection between doing the law and justification is glaringly inconsistent with such an emphasis.

Third, the argument of Schreiner and others that Paul is enunciating a positive principle in this verse depends heavily upon the claim that Romans 2:27–29 describes Gentile Christians who 'keep the law' by the working of the Spirit of Christ. Though this is a possible interpretation, it does not seem finally to fit well with the argument of this section of Romans. Even if Paul alludes to the conduct of Christians in verse 29, when he speaks of those whose circumcision is a matter of the heart 'by the Spirit', his main point here reiterates what he argued earlier in verses 14-15. Paul's concern here and throughout Romans 2, is to teach that the mere possession of the law of God (the Mosaic law) does not suffice to save anyone. Only those who do what this law requires can find salvation by means of the law. Verses 27–28 repeat a theme that was developed already at an earlier point in verses 14–15 of Romans 2, namely, the contrast between the empty boast of those Jews who possess the law but do not do what it requires, and the keeping of the law by Gentiles, who do not possess the law but (sometimes) do what it requires.

This contrast, especially if it is a contrast between Jews and Gentile Christians, might suggest that Paul believes that the latter would be saved on the basis of their keeping the precepts of the law. However, the whole thread of Paul's argument in Romans 2 is tied together in chapter 3, where he insists that no one, whether Jew or Gentile, can be saved upon the basis of their own works (verses 9–10). It seems unlikely, therefore, that Paul means to speak positively of the keeping of the law by Gentile Christians, when declaring that 'only doers of the law will be justified'. This would not seem consistent with the great theme of this section of Romans that all Jews and Gentiles are shut off from finding acceptance with God by means of the works of the law.[35]

And fourth, Paul's doctrine of justification amounts to the claim that believers have a final, eschatological participation in Christ's death and resurrection, so far as this secures their acceptance and favour with God. Justification, in Paul's teaching, is a thoroughly eschatological blessing. It represents the *present, definitive* declaration of God's favourable verdict concerning those who are joined to his Son by faith. This verdict anticipates and secures the believer's acceptance with God (*Rom.* 5:1; 8:1). If Romans 2:13 taught a future, eschatological justification, which is based upon the works of faith and not upon the work of Christ alone, the believer's present justification would no longer secure a future reception of eternal life. Rather, the prospect of future justification (or condemnation) upon the basis of works would undermine the believer's present persuasion of God's favour, a persuasion that derives from the freeness of the gift of justification.

These considerations favour the first reading of Romans 2:13, though perhaps not in such a way as to rule out completely the second view. Because the second view does not claim that Paul is speaking in this verse of another, yet future justification, which is based upon works and not faith alone, it need not imperil Paul's teaching regarding justification as a free gift in Christ. Though I am not finally persuaded that it does justice to the place of this verse within the context of the apostle's teaching in the opening chapters of Romans, this second view rightly emphasizes the necessity of obedience as a confirmation and evidence of the genuineness of that faith which receives the grace of justification. It is true that Paul, at the close of Romans 2, speaks positively of those who 'keep the law'. This represents an argument that lends plausibility to the claim that he is positively affirming that only those who (imperfectly) obey the law by the work of the Spirit of Christ will be justified. It should also be noted that this second view, though at variance with the common reading of Romans 2:13 in the Reformation tradition, does not conflict with what we have represented as its consensus on the subject of justification and a final judgment according to works. However, what it does suggest is that, because justification and sanctification are inseparable benefits of the believer's union with Christ, no one will be justified who does not live by the Spirit.

CONCLUSION

Our review of Paul's teaching on the subject of justification and a final judgment according to works does not support the claim that Paul regarded the final judgment to be a kind of concluding chapter in the believer's justification.[36] Paul's teaching that works are absolutely excluded as a basis for the justification of believers is simply incompatible with the idea that (final) justification will ultimately be based upon the works of believers. Paul regards justification as a thoroughly eschatological blessing, which anticipates in the most definitive way the final verdict that God declares concerning those who are beneficiaries of the saving work of Christ. If the believer's present justification could be completed or undone in the context of a final justification, the gospel promise of free acceptance with God would be profoundly compromised. The notion of a final justification on the basis of works inevitably attenuates the assertion that there is now no condemnation for those who are in Christ Jesus (*Rom.* 8:1). A final justification on the basis of works also undermines Paul's bold declaration that no charge is able to be brought against those who belong to Christ (*Rom.* 8:33–34).

Rather than treating the final judgment as a kind of further justification, we can understand Paul's emphasis upon the role of works in this judgment in terms of his understanding of all that salvation in union with Christ means for believers. Since all believers, who are joined to Christ by faith and indwelt by his Spirit, are being renewed in obedience, their acquittal in the context of the final judgment will be a public confirmation of the genuineness of their faith and testimony. Since believers receive Christ for righteousness and sanctification (*1 Cor.* 1:30), they are not saved without good works. Though these good works are the fruits of faith and not the basis of their justification, they are an indispensable part of the work of salvation. Therefore, Paul's teaching of a final judgment according to works confirms his consistent teaching that, though no one is justified by works, no one is saved in the fullest sense without them.

NOTES

[1] We previously noted that the study of Simon J. Gathercole, *Where is Boasting?*, leaves open the question whether Paul may have taught, with Second-Temple Judaism, a final justification based upon works. According to Gathercole, though the present reality of justification may be by faith alone, Paul seems to teach that the eschatological vindication of believers in Christ will depend upon their good works (pp. 135, 265).

² In addition to the study of Simon J. Gathercole, see e.g., E. P. Sanders, *Paul and Palestinian Judaism*, pp. 293ff., 307–9, 515–18; Kent L. Yinger, *Paul, Judaism, and Judgment According to Deeds* (Cambridge: Cambridge University Press, 1999); Thomas R. Schreiner, *The Law and Its Fulfillment*, pp. 179ff.; James D. G. Dunn, *The Theology of Paul*, pp. 135–37, 490-2; James D. G. Dunn, *Romans 1–8*, pp. 97–8.

³ 'The Shape of Justification', p. 2.

⁴ 'The Shape of Justification', p. 2; and N. T. Wright, *What Did Saint Paul Really Say?*, p. 129. Cf. N. T. Wright, *Romans*, p. 440: 'Justification, at the last, will be on the basis of performance, not possession [of the law].'

⁵ The Council of Trent, for example, in its Sixth Session on the doctrine of justification, Chapter 16, states the following (Schaff, *The Creeds of Christendom*, 2:107): 'And, for this cause, life eternal is to be proposed to those working well *unto the* end, and hoping in God, both as a grace mercifully promised to the sons of God through Jesus Christ, and as a reward which is according to the promise of God himself, to be faithfully rendered to their good works and merits.'

⁶ The *Belgic Confession* makes the same point, but in its own striking manner, when it sets forth the doctrine of justification: 'And therefore we *always hold fast this foundation*, ascribing all glory to God, humbling ourselves before him, and acknowledging ourselves to be such as we really are, without presuming to trust in any thing in ourselves, or in any merit of ours, relying and resting upon the obedience of Christ crucified alone, which becomes ours when we believe in him. This is sufficient to cover *all our iniquities*, and to give us confidence in approaching God. . . . And, verily, *if we should appear before God,* relying on ourselves or on any other creature, though ever so little, we should, alas! Be consumed.'

⁷ The Reformation confessions consistently exclude believers' works as the ground or basis for their justification. See e.g., the *Heidelberg Catechism*, Q. & A. 59–62; *Belgic Confession*, Art. 22–24; *Westminster Confession of Faith*, chapter 11; *Westminster Larger Catechism*, Q. & A. 70–73; and *Westminster Shorter Catechism*, Q. & A. 33.

⁸ Cf. *Belgic Confession*, Art. 24: 'These works, as they proceed from the good root of faith, are good and acceptable in the sight of God, forasmuch as they are all sanctified by his grace. Nevertheless they are of no account towards justification, for it is by faith in Christ that we are justified, even before we do good works; otherwise they could not be good works, any more than the fruit of a tree can be good before the tree itself is good.' A similar emphasis upon the distinction between faith, which alone justifies, and the good works that are produced by faith, is found in the following confessional statements: *Heidelberg Catechism*, Q. & A. 64, 91; *Westminster Confession of Faith*, chapter 11, section 2; chapter 15, section 2; and *Westminster Larger Catechism*, Q. & A. 73.

⁹ Cf. *Westminster Confession of Faith*, chapter 16, section 5: 'We cannot by our best works merit pardon of sin, or eternal life at the hand of God, by reason of the great disproportion that is between them and the glory to come; and the infinite distance that is between us and God, whom, by them, we can neither profit, nor satisfy for the debt of our former sins, but when we have done all we can, we have done but our duty, and are unprofitable servants; and because, as they are good, they proceed from his Spirit; and as they are wrought by us, they are defiled, and mixed with so much weakness and imperfection, that they cannot endure the severity of God's judgment.'

¹⁰ Cf. Calvin, *Institutes*, III.xvii.5: 'For the Lord cannot fail to love and embrace the good things that he works in them [that is, believers] through his Spirit. But we must always remember that God "accepts" believers by reason of works only because he is their source and graciously, by way of adding to his liberality, deigns also to show "acceptance" toward the good works he himself has bestowed. . . . But because the godly, encompassed with mortal flesh, are still sinners, and their good works are as yet incomplete and redolent of the vices of the flesh, he can be propitious neither to the former nor to the latter unless he embrace them in Christ rather than in themselves.'

¹¹ In this connection, I am reminded of the remark made by Thomas Chalmers to James Buchanan: 'I would have every preacher insist strenuously on these two doctrines—a present Justification by grace, through faith alone—and a future Judgment according to works. All faithful ministers have made use of both, that they might guard equally against the peril of self-righteous legalism on the one hand and of practical Antinomianism on the other' (as quoted by James Buchanan, *The Doctrine of Justification*, pp. 238–9).

¹² The seventeenth-century theologian, Francis Turretin, expresses this point in more technical language than that used in the confessions (*Institutes of Elenctic Theology*, 3:63): 'However, although in this judgment to each one ought to be repaid "according to his works", as to quality, so that it may be well with the good and evil with the wicked; still there will not be the same relation of good and bad works to the reward and punishment. For evil works indeed will be properly the meritorious cause of the punishment which will be inflicted on the wicked; but there is not the same relation of good works . . . rather they will be brought forward not as the causes, but only as the consequence, testimonies and effects of faith and of grace which they obtained in Christ. . . . this pardoning sentence will not be so much a justification of them *a priori* (which is made only from faith and is intimated to them in this life in the court of conscience by the Holy Spirit), as the declaration of it *a posteriori* from their works, as the judgments and proofs of faith . . .' (p. 603). Turretin's point, to use the language of theology, is that we must not confuse the antecedent (faith alone justifies on account of the righteousness of Christ alone) with its consequent (which faith always and necessarily produces fruits by the working of Christ's Spirit), when it comes to the matter of acceptance with God and reception of salvation as a free gift. Another, more simple way of expressing it would be to say that, though justification and sanctification

are inseparable in the life of the believer, they must be distinguished, lest the latter be viewed as an antecedent condition or cause for the former.

[13] Cf. John Piper, *Counted Righteous in Christ*, p. 77: 'The doctrine of justification by faith apart from works (*Rom.* 3:28) raises the question, "Are we to continue in sin that grace may increase?" (*Rom.* 6:1). And: "Shall we sin because we are not under law but under grace?" (*Rom.* 6:15). The raising of these questions is a powerful indication that justification does *not* include liberation from the mastery of sin. For if it did, these questions would not plausibly arise.'

[14] For a good summary of Paul's use of this metaphor in connection with his teaching regarding sanctification, see Karl Paul Donfried, 'Justification and Last Judgment in Paul', *Interpretation* 30/2 (April, 1976), p. 143. Donfried summarizes Paul's view as follows: 'In short, the Christian life is a process which begins in justification, is actualized in sanctification, and is consummated with salvation. Critical for the final reception of salvation is man's continued obedience and continued reception of God's freely offered gift of the Spirit who is at work in the believer as a part of the body of Christ' (pp. 143-4).

[15] Since the passage does not specify the nature of these respective rewards, it is wise not to speculate too much as to what they might be. For a treatment of the general biblical teaching regarding rewards in the Christian life, see my *The Promise of the Future* (Edinburgh: Banner of Truth, 2000), pp. 405-19.

[16] Contra Donfried, 'Justification and Last Judgment in Paul', p. 149, who argues that this passage only applies to Christian ministers: 'The entire thrust of our argument has been that neither 1 Corinthians 3:15 or 4:5 have anything to do with the good works of the individual Christian nor with his personal salvation; both deal with a concrete situation in the life of the Corinthian congregation concerning the validity and effectiveness of apostolic ministry.' See Nigel M. Watson, 'Justified By Faith: Judged By Works—An Antinomy?' *New Testament Studies* 29 (1983), pp. 202-21. Watson applies this passage in a more general way and argues, correctly I believe, that Paul teaches the 'eschatological finality' of present justification while warning his listeners in concrete situations to avoid the 'false presumption' or illusion that it makes no difference how they live.

[17] I say, 'presumably associated with the final judgment', because the text itself does not expressly speak of a final judgment. However, the future tense of the verb suggests a final, eschatological judgment, and in the context Paul speaks of a final judgment according to works.

[18] For a survey and analysis of the various interpretations of this text in history, see Klyne R. Snodgrass, 'Justification by Grace—To the Doers: An Analysis of the Place of Romans 2 in the Theology of Paul', *New Testament Studies* 32 (1986), pp. 72-93; and Thomas Schreiner, *The Law and Its Fulfillment*, pp. 179-204.

[19] *Calvin's New Testament Commentaries*, 8:47. Cf. Francis Turretin,

Institutes of Elenctic Theology, 2:637: 'For as there are two covenants which God willed to make with men—the one legal and the other of grace—so also there is a twofold righteousness—legal and evangelical. The former consists in one's own obedience or a perfect conformity with the law, which is in him who is to be justified; the latter is another's obedience or a perfect observance of the law, which is rendered by a surety in the place of him who is to be justified—the former in us, the latter in Christ. Concerning the first, Paul says, "Not the hearers, but the doers of the law shall be justified" (*Rom.* 2:13).'

[20] I use this guarded language since, even if we take the language of Romans 2:13 to refer to those who actually do what the law requires, this does not require that justification is 'on account of' works. As we shall see, a contemporary exponent of this view, Thomas Schreiner, does not argue for a final justification on the basis of the believer's works.

[21] See *The Law and Its Fulfillment*, pp. 179–204. Cf. Snodgrass, 'Justification by Grace—To the Doers', pp. 72–93, who reaches a similar conclusion to that of Schreiner. Snodgrass argues that the 'hypothetical' view fails to see that the obedience required for vindication in the final judgment is not a perfect obedience or an obedience that is not itself the product of the working of the Spirit of Christ.

[22] Interestingly, Schreiner does not argue that Paul is referring to Gentile believers in verses 14–15. In these verses, Paul is simply describing Gentiles in general who have a natural acquaintance with the works of the law and even do by nature at times what the law requires. Cf. *The Law and Its Fulfillment*, pp. 193–6. See Moo, *Romans*, pp. 148–57, for a summary of the three views of the identity of the Gentiles in verses 14–16. Moo rightly maintains that Paul adduces the example of these Gentiles to explain further the phrase in verse 12a, 'without the law'. Because Paul says they sometimes do 'by nature' what the law requires, it is quite unlikely that he is speaking of Gentile Christians (who 'fulfill' the law 'by grace'; cf. *Rom.* 8:4).

[23] *The Law and Its Fulfillment*, pp. 184–5, 196–201.

[24] *The Law and Its Fulfillment*, p. 185: 'Even though justification is not by works of law, works are necessary for a person to obtain eternal life. Those who do not practice good works are threatened with judgment.'

[25] See e.g. E. P. Sanders, *Paul, the Law, and the Jewish People*, pp. 123–35; and Heikki Räisänen, *Paul and the Law*, pp. 98–101. Sanders and Räisänen offer different explanations for Paul's assumption in Romans 2:13-16 that even unbelieving Gentiles can fulfil the law and thereby be justified, an assumption that contradicts his teaching elsewhere and is one of the inconsistencies of Paul's theology of the law.

[26] *The Law and Its Fulfillment*, p. 181.

[27] *Romans* (Grand Rapids, MI: Baker Books, 1998), p. 145. Cf. also the general study of Kent L. Yinger, *Paul, Judaism, and Judgment According to Deeds*, esp. p.p. 283–91. Yinger's overall summary of Paul's view is similar to

Schreiner's reading of Romans 2:13: 'Those who had already been justified by grace through faith in Christ were expected (by God's grace and the Holy Spirit, of course) to live righteous lives as well. That is, their righteousness by faith would manifest itself in obedience, in works; though not necessarily in sinless perfection. . . . Thus, there is no tension in saying that the status of righteousness is conferred solely by means of faith in Christ, and that all (including the righteous) will be judged according to their deeds. This is not a second justification, nor does it somehow place one's present justification (by faith) in doubt' (Yinger, *Paul, Judaism, and Judgment*, p. 290). According to Yinger, more recent treatments of Paul's teaching on justification and the final judgment have fallen into two groups: some argue that Paul's teaching is contradictory, others argue that his teaching is harmonious. Among those who argue for the harmony of Paul's views, there are three approaches: first, some argue that justification secures salvation, while the final judgment apportions rewards (but not the gift of salvation); second, justification occurs in two phases, one present, the other future, and the final judgment represents the future phase; and three, the final judgment confirms the justification of believers. (pp. 6–16).

[28] In addition to the references listed earlier, see N. T. Wright, 'New Perspectives on Paul'.

[29] *Paul, the Law, and the Jewish People*, pp. 123–35.

[30] In his recent article, 'New Perspectives on Paul', Wright reiterates his earlier claim that Paul teaches a future justification upon the basis of works. In this article, Wright makes clear that these works 'show...that one is in Christ' and 'are produced ... as a result of the Spirit's indwelling and operation.' They are not perfect works, nor are they works that are self-produced. However, he insists that Romans 2:13 is speaking of a future judgment according to works that is the final phase of the believer's justification, and that this justification is 'on the basis of the entire life a person has led in the power of the Spirit.'

[31] That this view was also represented by Catholic theologians in the sixteenth century seems to be suggested by Calvin's comments on this verse: 'Those who misinterpret this passage for the purpose of building up justification by works deserve universal contempt' (*Calvin's New Testament Commentaries*, 8:47). Calvin does not mention to whom he refers, but it is certainly in keeping with the traditional Roman Catholic view to base justification, particularly in its final realization, upon the works of the believer whose faith is 'formed by love'.

[32] *Commentary on St Paul's Epistle to the Romans* (Edinburgh: T. & T. Clark, 1889), p. 204.

[33] Cf. Douglas J. Moo, *The Epistle to the Romans*, p. 147, fn. 21: 'Paul affirms that Christians must stand before God on the day of judgment (e.g., 2 Cor. 5:10). But he uses terms other than "justify" to denote this event; and the works that are taken into account in that judgment are the product of justifying faith and not the basis for justification itself.'

[34] *The Epistle to the Romans*, p. 71.

[35] Cf. Moo, *Romans*, p. 171, who appeals to this contextual argument against the view that Paul is speaking of Gentile Christians: "We therefore conclude that Paul is again here citing God's standard of judgment apart from the gospel as a means of erasing the distinction at this point between Jew and Gentile. Paul is not pointing the way to salvation but is showing Jews that their position, despite their covenant privileges, is essentially no different from that of the Gentiles: disobedience brings condemnation; obedience brings salvation. Paul's way of putting the matter in this context could, of course, suggest that there actually are people who meet this requirement for salvation; but his later argument quickly disabuses us of any such idea (cf. 3:9, 20)." Moo, *Romans*, p. 170, suggests a further argument against identifying the Gentiles in verses 27-28 as Christians: they are described as keeping the precepts of the Mosaic law, something which Paul teaches elsewhere is no longer required of Christians (cf. Rom. 6:14, 15; Gal. 6:2; 1 Cor. 9:20).

[36] Though the final judgment should not be connected with the believer's justification, as though it were something that completes it, it is certainly permissible to say that the final judgment will be a public manifestation of what is now reality, but known only to faith as it looks upon the things that are unseen (cf. 2 Cor. 4:18).

I I

CONCLUSION

At various points in this book I have acknowledged that my assessment of the new perspective on Paul addresses the subject in a manner different from that found in other studies. Such studies devote more attention to the historical debates regarding the nature of Second-Temple Judaism. Since E. P. Sanders' study of Second-Temple Judaism plays such a dominant role in the emergence of the new perspective, debate regarding the validity of his conclusions will constitute an important part of any on-going discussion of its claims. In contrast to these, my assessment does not seek to contribute directly to the contemporary study of Judaism.

In addition to the continued discussion of Sanders' conclusions, there are also a growing number of New Testament studies that address various aspects of the new perspective's reading of the apostle Paul. Many are highly technical and scholarly treatments of specific portions of the Pauline corpus. Though I have addressed many of the passages in Paul's writings that play an important role in the formulation of the new perspective, I have not treated them in the highly technical and more scholarly form of a New Testament specialist. My assessment is written from the standpoint of a systematic theologian who has an interest in Reformation studies and the new perspective's implications for any coherent understanding of the gospel in the present day.

While acknowledging the limitations of my assessment of the new perspective, I have written it out of the conviction that proponents as well as opponents of the new perspective have neglected to evaluate its claims within a broader theological framework. Regrettably, new-perspective authors frequently fail to demonstrate the kind of first-hand acquaintance with the older Reformation perspective that their far-reaching claims demand of them. For example, when advocates of the new perspective sweepingly assert that the western church has misunderstood the apostle Paul for fifteen centuries, they may succeed in gaining attention but they also assume an extraordinary burden of proof.

Minimally, even though their field of expertise is that of New Testament studies, they ought to interact far more directly with the history of Christian, and particularly Reformation theology, with regard to the issues that are in dispute. In the literature of the new perspective there is a notable absence of direct appeals to the history of Protestant theology in general and to the confessional summaries of the Reformation perspective on Paul in particular. Even though authors of the new perspective are quick to point out how theological disputes of the sixteenth century affected the reading of Paul's epistles by the Reformers, they are not always as ready to acknowledge the extra-scriptural factors that play a significant role in their own thinking.

The admission that my study does not fully engage all of the historical and exegetical considerations that inform the new perspective, therefore, is not to be construed as unduly concessive. My critical assessment of the new perspective deliberately focuses upon a broader set of theological concerns than is often the case in the literature. The study of Second-Temple Judaism and the new reading of the apostle Paul undergirding the new perspective need to be complemented by studies that place the debate in a larger historical and theological setting.

Fortunately, as we have seen throughout the course of this book, there are a growing number of historical and exegetical studies that are making a contribution to an evaluation of the claims of the new perspective. Unfortunately, there are few that have assessed the new perspective and its claims from the standpoint of historical and systematic theology. My assessment aims to answer particularly to this deficiency.

To conclude our study, we will begin by identifying several commendable features associated with the new perspective. Then we will summarize our assessment by taking note of its critical weaknesses.

COMMENDABLE FEATURES OF
THE NEW PERSPECTIVE

Though our assessment of the new perspective has criticized its claims at several crucial points, we do not want to leave the impression that the new perspective has no commendable features associated with it. We have argued against the new perspective's insistence that it provides a more historically and biblically satisfying understanding of the apostle Paul than that of the Reformation. However, our critical assessment of its principal claim should not be misunderstood. Writers of the new perspective have made some contributions to our understanding of the historical setting of Paul's writings.

Perhaps the foremost commendable feature of the new perspective is its insistence that we take a fresh look at Paul's writings in their historical context. Nothing we have argued throughout the course of this study should be interpreted as a rejection of this insistence.

N. T. Wright, for example, quite rightly maintains that a careful reading of the biblical writings is precisely what is demanded from those who would honour the intentions of the Reformers. The final test of any perspective on the teaching of the apostle Paul must surely be the New Testament epistles that bear his name. However respectful and deferential we should be to the consensus of opinion which is summarized in the Reformation confessions, the task of theology, and especially of biblical interpretation, requires a continual process of critical reflection upon the Scriptures. If, in the course of such critical reflection, the confessional summaries are shown to be inadequate or even mistaken, the Protestant principle of Scriptural authority requires that greater weight be given to the Scriptures' testimony than that of the confessions.

For this reason, we have not simply answered the claims of the new perspective by citing the confessional summaries of the Reformation. Rather, we have sought to appeal to the writings of the apostle Paul as the touchstone for determining whether the Reformation or new perspective on these writings is to be preferred. In so far as authors of the new perspective have sought to honour the authority of Scripture in their interpretation of the apostle Paul, they have rightly embraced a key methodological feature of historic Protestant theology.

Since the Reformation view of the apostle's teaching on justification assumes the presence of a form of legalism among his contemporaries, the new perspective also properly insists that we need to carefully examine the character of Second-Temple Judaism to see whether any such legalism was present in Paul's day. The character of Second-Temple Judaism at the time of the writing of the New Testament is clearly relevant to a determination of the kind of error Paul was opposing, when he insisted against the Judaizers that believers are justified by grace and not by works. Unless the apostle Paul was shadow boxing in his epistles when he opposed the teaching of justification by works, his opponents must be located within the spectrum of teaching that was present within Second-Temple Judaism. Writers of the new perspective, accordingly, have insisted that we need to read Paul's epistles in their first-century historical context, and beware of the temptation to read later theological disputes into the apostle's polemics.

The study of Second-Temple Judaism, which forms such an important component for the development of a new perspective on Paul, is undoubtedly a legitimate enterprise, and one that sheds light on the historical circumstances occasioning Paul's opposition to some of his contemporaries on the subject of justification. As we acknowledged in our consideration of Sanders' interpretation of Second-Temple Judaism, Paul was undoubtedly addressing a form of teaching that was present within the Judaism of the first century of the Christian era. If the Reformers wrongly interpreted the nature of Paul's opposition when he proclaimed that believers are not justified by the works of the law, as the new perspective argues on the basis of its interpretation of Second-Temple Judaism, this will have far-reaching implications for a proper understanding of his teaching.

Whether the new perspective's view of Second-Temple Judaism has the implications claimed for it needs to be disputed, as we have argued. What is not disputable, however, is that a proper understanding of Second-Temple Judaism may have some limited bearing upon our interpretation of Paul's teaching on the subject of justification.

One particularly commendable feature of the new perspective's approach to the interpretation of Paul's epistles is the attention it pays to the Old Testament background to Paul's preaching of the gospel. Writers of the new perspective insist that Paul's use of the terms 'righteousness', 'justification', and 'covenant', presuppose the traditional uses of such terms in the Old Testament and in the traditions of Second-Temple Judaism. 'The righteousness of God', for example, refers to God's covenant faithfulness in fulfilling his promises of salvation to Israel. Likewise, 'justification' has to be interpreted to refer to God's favourable judgment/vindication of those whom he counts as members of his covenant family and heirs to the promises made to Abraham and Old Testament believers. Paul's proclamation of the gospel of Jesus Christ declares that the covenant with Israel reaches its 'climax' (Wright) in the person and work of Jesus Christ, Israel's representative. Within the setting of God's previous dealings with his covenant people Israel, the work of Christ does not contradict but fulfils what was previously revealed through the law of Moses.

According to the new perspective, therefore, any failure to read Paul's account of the gospel within the framework of the Old Testament Scriptures and the expectations of Judaism is bound to produce misunderstanding and misinterpretation. The hermeneutical key to the apostle's writings is the biblical history of the covenant with Israel, especially the Old Testament expectation that all peoples will inherit the covenant blessing first promised to Abraham. The new perspective is undoubtedly correct, when it insists upon this kind of historical-redemptive and covenantal approach to the interpretation of the Pauline epistles. After all, it was the apostle himself who summarized his gospel by saying, 'I delivered to you as of first importance what I also received: that Christ died for our sins *in accordance with the Scriptures,* that he was buried, that he was raised on the third day *in accordance with the Scriptures*' (*I Cor.* 15:3–4, emphasis added).

Because the new perspective seeks to read Paul within the historical setting of Second-Temple Judaism and the history of the

covenant with Israel, it calls attention to the historical occasion for
Paul's articulation of the theme of justification. Authors of the new
perspective suggest that the Reformation perspective fails to
account adequately for the ecclesiological focus of the doctrine of
justification. Though I do not believe that this is true, it is correct
to say that the Reformation view of justification treats this theme
primarily from a soteriological perspective. Because the Reformation view focuses upon the way justification answers the question
of how believers, whether Jews or Gentiles, may find acceptance
with God, it tends to state the doctrine in the most general form
possible.

However, especially in the case of the epistle to the Galatians,
Paul articulates his understanding of justification in the face of
Judaizers who were refusing to admit Gentile believers into the
covenant community until they submitted to certain requirements
of the Mosaic law (circumcision, for example). One of the benefits
of the new perspective's re-consideration of the theme of justification in Paul's writings is the way the historical context and
texture of Paul's teaching comes into view. A careful reading of the
commentaries of the Reformers on Paul's writings will show that
they were also aware of the historical occasion for Paul's treatment
of justification. However, due to the force of historical circumstance, particularly their dispute with Roman Catholic teaching,
their treatments of Paul's writings tend to run rather quickly to the
broader theological implications of his teaching.

Another commendable feature of the new perspective emerges at
the point of its attention to the historical and covenant context for
Paul's teaching on justification. One of the new perspective's oft-
repeated criticisms of the Reformation perspective is that it tends to
reduce Paul's gospel to a question of individual salvation. It is
argued that the Protestant and evangelical doctrine of justification
focuses exclusively upon the question of how an individual sinner
can find favour with God. When the theme of justification is interpreted in this individual or existential form, it is usually assumed
that justification is the solution to the problem of an anxious conscience before God. In this view of justification, the gospel is no
longer primarily about the transforming lordship of Jesus Christ, as

it was for Paul, but about the deliverance of individual sinners from the guilt of their sin. Over against this narrowing of the theme of justification, authors of the new perspective maintain that it is a feature of the gospel that has broad social and ecclesiological implications. Justification is not primarily about individuals in their relationship with God; rather, it has immediate implications for the gracious inclusion of all kinds of people within the worldwide family of God.

The irony of the older perspective is that, despite its emphasis upon God's gracious acceptance of sinners into his favour, it often encouraged a kind of gracelessness toward those who did not affirm the Reformation view. According to Wright, this grace-lessness seems to lead to a position that maintains something like a doctrine of justification on the basis of believing the right doctrine of justification. Such individualism and exclusivism betrays the gospel of gracious justification, which teaches that God owns all who believe in Christ as members of his covenant family. While such criticisms are not entirely free from exaggeration and misrep-resentation, there is sufficient evidence of this kind of narrowing of the gospel's focus within evangelicalism to warrant some of the criticisms advanced by the new perspective.

A SUMMARY OF OUR CRITICAL ASSESSMENT OF THE NEW PERSPECTIVE

Despite these commendable features, this critical assessment of the new perspective argues that it does not offer a truly satisfying alternative to the older, Reformation perspective. Though the new perspective makes bold claims for its understanding of Paul's teach-ing on the subject of justification, we have not found these claims to be warranted. Indeed, we believe that the new perspective pro-foundly distorts the gospel of free acceptance with God on the basis of the work of Christ. Our critical assessment of the new per-spective can be summarized in several points.

First, the new perspective depends heavily upon E. P. Sanders' study of Second-Temple Judaism. A basic element in the argument for the new perspective is the thesis that the Reformers misunder-stood Paul's doctrine of justification because they misunderstood the nature of Second-Temple Judaism. When the Reformers opposed the medieval Roman Catholic teaching of justification by works, they read Paul's epistles as though they were addressed to a similar legalistic error among the Judaizers of the first century. According to the Reformation perspective on Paul, free justification was Paul's answer to the problem of moralism or legalism, which teaches that believers are saved by their works or obedience to the requirements of the law.

The new perspective rejects this view of Paul's doctrine of justification by arguing that no such legalism existed within the context of Second-Temple Judaism. Paul's teaching about justification by grace could hardly be his response to a form of teaching that had no attraction within Second-Temple Judaism. If Sanders' thesis is correct, namely, that Second-Temple Judaism was a form of 'covenantal nomism', then the Reformation reading of the apostle Paul appears to have been built upon sand.

Despite the apparent force of this fundamental element of the argument for a new perspective on Paul, we have found it to be, ironically, something of a confirmation of the Reformation's perspective. Though Sanders' study of Second-Temple Judaism remains a subject of on-going debate, nothing in his profile of its pattern of religion militates against the Reformation view. 'Covenantal nomism' corresponds rather closely to the kind of 'semi-Pelagian' teaching that the Reformers opposed in the sixteenth century. The Reformers never argued that the medieval Roman Catholic doctrine of justification was 'Pelagian' or, strictly speaking, grace-less. What they repudiated was the idea that works of any kind, even those prompted by grace, constitute part of the basis for the believer's acceptance with God.

Studies of Second-Temple Judaism, including those of Sanders, confirm that Paul was not only familiar with but could have opposed views that were comparable to the medieval Roman Catholic conception of justification by grace *and* works. Therefore, nothing in the contemporary study of Second-Temple Judaism requires the kind of radical revision of our understanding of Paul's doctrine of justification represented by the new perspective. If its advocates were more sensitive to the theological nuances of the

Reformation dispute regarding Paul's understanding of justification, they would not make the claims for the significance of Sanders' study of Second-Temple Judaism which often characterize their writings.

Second, the new perspective contends that Paul's view of the law was shaped, not by his opposition to a form of legalism, but by his opposition to Jewish exclusivism. Since Sanders' thesis regarding Second-Temple Judaism endeavours to debunk the assumption that Paul was opposing legalism, the new perspective offers a different view of the law and Paul's terminology of the 'works of the law' in its interpretation of his doctrine of justification.

Rather than opposing those who sought to justify themselves before God on the basis of their obedience to the law, Paul's doctrine of justification was formulated over against those who insisted upon obedience to the 'boundary-marker' requirements of the law in order to be included among the people of God. When Paul says that no one is justified by the works of the law, he is not exposing the boast of those who thought obedience to the law would obtain God's favour. Rather, Paul uses this terminology to reject the exclusionary policy of the Judaizers who were unwilling to admit Gentiles into the covenant people of God, unless they first submitted to those peculiar obligations of the law that distinguished Jews from Gentiles (circumcision, dietary laws, feast-day observances).

In our evaluation of this aspect of the new perspective, we noted that it fails to deal adequately with the radical contrast Paul draws between any acts of obedience to all that the law requires and the believing reception of the free gift of justification. When Paul appeals to the law to expose human sinfulness and inability to fulfil its requirements, he draws the kind of contrast between the law and the gospel that the Reformation perspective identified in its interpretation of Paul's doctrine of justification. Our analysis of Paul's understanding of the problem of human sin and guilt, which the law reveals and even aggravates, confirms the validity of the Reformation view. It is simply not possible to sustain the new perspective's claim that Paul's references to 'works' and 'works of the law' describe only those acts that conform to the boundary-marker requirements of the law. The problem to which Paul's doctrine of justification provides a solution is not merely one that concerns membership of the covenant people of God. His doctrine of free justification emphasizes the sheer graciousness of God's acceptance of Jews and Gentiles alike, all of whom are unable to obtain his favour on the basis of any works performed in obedience to the requirements of the law.

Third, the new perspective rejects the Reformation view that the term 'justification' refers to the way God receives otherwise undeserving and guilty sinners into his favour. According to its proponents, Paul's doctrine of justification primarily addresses the identity of those who belong to the covenant family of God. Justification is not so much a soteriological theme, which describes how sinners may be received into God's favour, as it is an ecclesiological theme, which describes those who belong to God's covenant family as heirs of the promise to Abraham.

In our evaluation of this aspect of the new perspective, we noted that it is unnecessarily reductionistic. Though Paul's doctrine of justification undoubtedly has ecclesiological implications, its principal meaning relates to the soteriological issue of how sinners, who have disobeyed the law of God and stand under its condemnation, can be acceptable to God.

When Paul presents the doctrine of justification, in the opening chapters of Romans, he begins with a lengthy indictment of Jews and Gentiles alike, who are all under the wrath and judgment of God because of their unrighteousness. The setting for the Pauline theme of justification indicates that it is a soteriological theme *before* it is an ecclesiological one. All who through faith are joined to Christ, whether Jews or Gentiles, are included in the number of God's people. But in order for believers to receive justification's favourable verdict, they must be made aware of their standing before God as sinners. Unless God intervenes graciously in Christ on behalf of those who are worthy of condemnation and death, there is no hope of favour with God. In contrast to the new perspective, the Reformation perspective on Paul captures far more powerfully and adequately the apostle's meaning when he speaks of the 'justification of the ungodly' on the basis of the atoning work of Christ. Nothing less than the favourable verdict of acceptance with God is at stake in the justification of any sinner.

Fourth, just as the new perspective reduces the weight and narrows the meaning of Paul's use of 'justification', so it offers an unsatisfying account of Paul's use of 'the righteousness of God'. Though we have no quarrel with the new perspective's observation that this terminology can refer to the faithfulness of God in fulfilling his covenant promises, we must insist that it also refers to the way in which the obedience and saving work of Christ benefits believers.

One of the most vexing features of the new perspective is its failure to explain the connection between the justification of believers and Christ's atoning work. In the Reformation perspective on Paul, there is a close and intimate connection between Christ's obedience, cross, and resurrection, and the benefit of free justification which believers derive from their union with him. Christ's objective work on behalf of sinners (his death for their sins and his resurrection for their justification) constitutes the basis of the verdict which justification declares. Since the sinless Christ bore the sins of his people upon the cross and was declared righteous before God in his resurrection, believers now enjoy through union with him a new status of acceptance and life in fellowship with God. The righteousness of God, which is revealed in the gospel and received through faith, is demonstrated in God's judgment upon sinners in the death of Christ and in God's vindication of sinners in Christ's resurrection.

In the Reformation perspective on justification, the revelation of God's righteousness in the work of Christ provides a sure basis for the acceptance of sinners joined to him by faith. Justification is the subjective benefit granted to believers on account of the objective work of Christ on their behalf. The righteousness of God requires that sinners be set right before God. In order for this to occur, their sins must be atoned for and their righteousness established.

However, in the new perspective, no comparable account is provided of the intimate conjunction between Christ's saving work and the believer's justification. Justification merely identifies those who belong to the covenant family of God, but no adequate explanation is provided as to why this identification required nothing less than the cross and resurrection of Christ on their behalf. The new perspective offers no satisfactory account of Paul's emphasis that believers are justified by the blood of Christ (*Rom.* 5:9) or through the redemption and propitiation he provided (*Rom.* 3:23). Nor does the new perspective's explanation of the righteousness of God explain why Paul insists that, were righteousness to come through the law, Christ would have died in vain (*Gal.* 2:21).

The point of these observations is not to suggest that advocates of the new perspective have no doctrine of atonement or explanation of Christ's representative death and resurrection. The point is that, unlike the Reformation perspective on Paul, the new perspective offers no coherent theological explanation of the inter-relation between Christ's work on behalf of his people on the one hand, and their enjoyment of the benefit of that work on the other. Since the problem addressed by justification in the new perspective is not primarily the problem of human sinfulness and guilt, Paul's account of Christ's atoning work for sinners does not seem as much to the purpose as in the Reformation perspective.

Fifth, unlike the Reformation perspective on justification, the new perspective does not view faith as an instrument whereby believers receive the benefit of free justification on the basis of the work of Christ. In the older Reformation view of justification, faith receives the free gift of God's righteousness in Christ. Justification involves a transaction in which Christ assumes the sin and guilt of his people in order that they might become the righteousness of God in him. Justification declares God's verdict that believers in Christ are acceptable to him. This verdict involves God's granting and imputing the righteousness of Christ to them. Believers are reckoned righteous by God when they receive the righteousness of Christ by faith.

In the new perspective, this emphasis upon faith as an instrument receiving the imputed righteousness of Christ is generally rejected. Faith in Christ is not a means to receive an imputed righteousness; rather it is merely the badge of identity that distinguishes those who belong to God's covenant family from those who do not. In the new perspective on Paul there is no need for the kind of transaction that imputation expresses since justification does not primarily address the soteriological question of how guilty sinners can become acceptable to God. Though authors of the new perspective acknowledge the legal or forensic nature of justification (that it is like the vindication of a defendant in a court of law), they offer no satisfactory explanation of the righteous character of God's verdict, when the believers he justifies are guilty sinners.

The language of imputation is necessary to express the gospel truth that God justifies the ungodly, not upon the basis of their own righteousness, but upon the basis of the righteousness of another. When God declares believers to be righteous, he reckons them to be innocent in Christ and on account of Christ's work. In the court of heaven, believers enjoy the reputation which properly belongs to Christ.

And *sixth*, one of the uncertain features of the new perspective is the question of justification and a final judgment according to works. Among some new-perspective authors, Paul's emphasis upon a final judgment according to works is viewed as a kind of final chapter in the believer's justification. Unlike the Reformation perspective, which distinguishes between justification by grace alone apart from works and a final judgment 'according to' but not 'on the basis of' works, this final justification concept suggests that the present membership of believers in the covenant family of God is suspended upon a future justification. Although believers enjoy a present justification in union with Christ, they face the prospect of a future justification whose verdict depends upon the quality of their whole life of faith.

Though it would not be correct to say that this idea of a future justification is a common or consensus opinion among new-perspective writers, it is suggested by a number of them. The presence of the idea of a final justification is a troubling, but not altogether unexpected, feature of the new perspective. As we noted in our discussion of Sanders' treatment of Second-Temple Judaism, one of the unresolved questions of his studies is whether Judaism taught that, in the eschatological justification/vindication of the covenant people, the basis for their acceptance by God would be their continuance in and conformity to the requirements of his law. If this were the case, the initial reception of believers into the covenant community would be by God's grace, but the ultimate justification of believers would be by their works.

In our review of Paul's teaching on justification and a final judgment according to works, we argued that the final judgment may not be construed as a kind of completion of the justification of believers.

An unqualified affirmation of a future, yet-to-be-determined justification based upon works would radically undermine or destroy Paul's teaching that there is now no condemnation for those who are in Christ Jesus. The Reformation's handling of this question, we maintained, does justice both to Paul's teaching of justification by grace alone and a final judgment according to works.

In the Reformation view, free justification and the sanctification of believers in union with Christ are inseparable, though distinct, benefits of the gospel. The carelessness with which writers of the new perspective speak of a final justification on the basis of works threatens the heart of Paul's gospel, which teaches that the acceptance and standing of believers before God rests on the work of Christ alone. An unqualified doctrine of a final justification, which is suspended upon the works of believers, is tantamount to 'another gospel' and merits the Paul's apostolic 'anathema' of Galatians 1:8–9.

In each of these respects, the older Reformation perspective on the apostle Paul captures the heart of the gospel in a way that the new perspective does not. Our assessment of the new perspective demonstrates that it is neither as new as its proponents aver, nor as capable of providing a more satisfying interpretation of Paul as they promise. The older perspective of the Reformation still remains a faithful presentation of what the apostle Paul boldly terms 'my gospel' (*Rom.* 2:16). In one of the well-known summaries of that gospel, Paul speaks in language that the Reformation perspective reflects:

> For while we were still weak, at the right time Christ died for the ungodly. For one will scarcely die for a righteous person—though

perhaps for a good person one would dare even to die—but God shows his love for us in that while we were still sinners, Christ died for us.

Such a gospel speaks compellingly in every age – in the twenty-first as much as the sixteenth century. It is also the kind of gospel in which all believers, Jew and Gentile alike, are invited to sit in fraternal fellowship at the same table and to glory in the same Lord Jesus Christ, in whom alone salvation is found.

SELECTED BIBLIOGRAPHY

AKERS, J. N., *et al.*, eds. *This We Believe: The Good News of Jesus Christ for the World*. Grand Rapids: Zondervan, 2000.

ALTHAUS, PAUL. *The Theology of Martin Luther*. Philadelphia: Fortress Press, 1966.

ANDERSON, CHARLES C. *Critical Quests of Jesus*. Grand Rapids: Eerdmans, 1969.

ANDERSON, H. GEORGE, *et al.*, eds. *Justification by Faith. Lutherans and Catholics in Dialogue VII*. Minneapolis: Augsburg, 1985.

BARAUCH, MANFRED T. 'Perspectives on "God's righteousness" in recent German Discussion.' In *Paul and Palestinian Judaism: A Comparison of Patterns of Religion,* by E. P. Sanders. London: SCM, 1977, pp. 523–42.

BARCLAY, JOHN M. G. 'Paul and the Law: Observations on Some Recent Debates', *Themelios* 12/1 (1986), pp. 5–15.

BARNETT, PAUL. 'Tom Wright and the New Perspective.' www. anglicanmedia sydney.asn.au/ pwb/ntwright_perspective. htm.

BARRETT, C. K. *The Epistle to the Romans*. Rev. ed. London: A. & C. Black, 1991 (1957).

BARTH, KARL. *Church Dogmatics*. Vol. 4/1: *The Doctrine of Reconciliation*. Edinburgh: T. & T. Clark, 1956.

BARTH, MARKUS. *Justification. Pauline Texts Interpreted in the Light of the Old and New Testaments*. Grand Rapids: Eerdmans, 1971.

BAVINCK, HERMAN. *Our Reasonable Faith: A Survey of Christian Doctrine*. Grand Rapids: Baker reprint, 1977 (1956).

BEKER, CHRISTIAAN J. *Paul the Apostle: The Triumph of God in Life and Thought*. Philadelphia: Fortress Press, 1984.

BERENDS, BILL. 'The Obedience of Christ: A Defence of the Doctrine of Christ's Active Obedience', *Vox Reformata* 66 (2001), pp. 26–51.

BERKHOF, LOUIS. *Systematic Theology*. London: Banner of Truth, 1958.

BERKOUWER, G. C. *Faith and Justification*. Grand Rapids: Eerdmans, 1954.

BIRD, MICHAEL F. 'Incorporated Righteousness: A Response to Recent Evangelical Discussion concerning the Imputation of Christ's Righteousness in Justification', *Journal of the Evangelical Theological Society* 47/2 (June 2004), pp. 253–76.

BROWN, COLIN, ed. *The New International Dictionary of New Testament Theology*. 3 vols. Grand Rapids: Zondervan, 1975–78.

BRUCE, F. F. *The Epistle of Paul to the Romans*. 2nd ed. Grand Rapids: Eerdmans, 1985.

BUCHANAN, JAMES. *The Doctrine of Justification*. Edinburgh: Banner of Truth, 1997 (1867).

BULTMANN, RUDOLF. *Theology of the New Testament*. Vol. 1. New York: Charles Scribner's Sons, 1951.

CALVIN, JOHN. *Calvin's New Testament Commentaries*. 12 vols. Ed. by D. W. Torrance and T. F. Torrance. Grand Rapids: Eerdmans, 1965.

_____. *Commentary on the Book of Psalms*. Vol. 2. Reprint. Grand Rapids: Baker Book House, 1979 (1843).

_____. *Institutes of the Christian Religion*. Ed. by John T. McNeill. Philadelphia: The Westminster Press, 1960.

_____. *Selected Works of John Calvin: Tracts and Letters*. 7 vols. Ed. Henry Beveridge. Reprint. Grand Rapids: Baker Book House, 1983 (1851).

CARSON, D. A., ed. *Justification and Variegated Nomism*. Vol. 1, *The Complexities of Second Temple Judaism*. Grand Rapids: Baker, 2001.

_____, ed. *Justification and Variegated Nomism*. Vol. 2, *The Paradoxes of Paul*. Grand Rapids: Baker, 2004.

_____. 'Atonement in Romans 3:21-26.' In *The Glory of the Atonement: Biblical, Historical & Practical Perspectives (Essays in Honor of Roger Nicole)*, ed. Charles E. Hill and Frank A. James III. Downers Grove, IL: InterVarsity, 2004, pp. 119–39.

_____. 'The Vindication of Imputation: On Fields of Discourse and Semantic Fields.' In *Justification: What's At Stake in the Current Debates*, ed. Mark Husbands and Daniel J. Treier. Downers Grove, IL: InterVarsity Press, 2004, pp. 46–78.

CHAMBLIN, KNOX. 'The Law of Moses and the Law of Christ', in John Feinberg, ed., *Continuity and Discontinuity: Perspectives on the Relationship Between the Old and New Testaments* (Westchester: Crossway Books, 1988), pp. 181–202.

COLSON, CHARLES, AND NEUHAUS, RICHARD JOHN, eds. *Evangelicals and Catholics Together: Toward a Common Mission*. London: Hodder & Stoughton, 1996.

CRANFIELD, CHARLES E. B. '"The Works of the Law" in the Epistle to the Romans', *Journal for the Study of the New Testament*, 43 (1991), pp. 89–101.

_____. *On Romans and Other New Testament Essays*. Edinburgh: T. & T. Clark, 1998.

_____. *A Critical and Exegetical Commentary on the Epistle to the Romans*. 2 vols. Edinburgh: T. & T. Clark, 1975, 1979.

DAS, A. ANDREW. *Paul, the Law, and the Covenant*. Peabody, MS: Hendrickson, 2001.

DAVIDS, PETER. *Commentary on James*. NIGTC. Grand Rapids: Eerdmans, 1982.

DAVIES, W. D. *Jewish and Pauline Studies*. Philadelphia: Fortress Press, 1984.

_____. *Paul and Rabbinic Judaism: Some Rabbinic Elements in Pauline Theology*. 4th ed. Philadelphia: Fortress Press, 1980.

DIBELIUS, MARTIN. *James*. Hermeneia. Philadelphia: Fortress Press, 1975.

DILLENBERGER, JOHN, ed. *Martin Luther: Selections from His Writings*. Garden City, NY: Anchor Books, 1961.

DONFRIED, KARL PAUL. 'Justification and Last Judgment in Paul', *Interpretation* 30/2 (April, 1976), pp. 140–52.

DUNN, JAMES D. G. *Jesus, Paul, and the Law: Studies in Mark and Galatians.* Louisville: Westminster, 1990.

_____. *The Parting of the Ways Between Christianity and Judaism and their Significance for the Character of Christianity.* Philadelphia: Trinity Press International, 1991.

_____. *The Theology of Paul the Apostle.* Grand Rapids: Eerdmans, 1998.

_____. *Romans.* 2 vols. Dallas: Word, 1988.

_____. 'Works of the Law and the Curse of the Law (Galatians 3.10-14).' *New Testament Studies* 31 (1985), pp. 523-42.

_____. 'Yet Once More—"The Works of the Law": A Response.' *Journal for the Study of the New Testament* 46 (1992), pp. 99-117.

_____ ed. *Paul and the Mosaic Law.* Grand Rapids: Eerdmans, 1996.

DUNN, JAMES D. G., AND SUGGATE, ALAN M. *The Justice of God: A Fresh Look at the Old Doctrine of Justification by Faith.* Carlisle, UK: The Paternoster Press, 1993.

DYER, SIDNEY. 'N. T. Wright's View of Justification: An Ecumenical Interpretation of Paul', *Greenville Seminary: katekômen* (Summer, 2002), pp. 17-21.

ECUMENICAL AND REFORMED CREEDS AND CONFESSIONS. Classroom edition. Dyer, IN: Mid-America Reformed Seminary, 1991.

'EVANGELICALS AND CATHOLICS TOGETHER: The Christian Mission in the Third Millennium', *First Things* 43 (May, 1994), pp. 15-22.

EVESON, PHILIP. *The Great Exchange: Justification by Faith Alone in the Light of Recent Discussion.* Bromley, Kent: Day One Publications, 1996.

FESKO, J. V. 'N. T. Wright and the Sign of the Covenant', *Scottish Bulletin of Evangelical Theology* 23/1 (Spring, 2005), pp. 30-9.

FORDE, GERHARD O. *Justification by Faith—A Matter of Death and Life.* Philadelphia: Fortress, 1982.

FULLER, DANIEL. 'Another Reply to *Counted Righteous in Christ*', *Reformation & Revival Journal* 12/4 (Fall, 2003), pp. 115–20.

_____ *Gospel and Law: Contrast or Continuum?* Grand Rapids: Eerdmans, 1980.

FUNG, RONALD Y. K. '"Justification" in the Epistle of James', in *Right With God: Justification in the Bible and the World*, ed. by D. A. Carson (Grand Rapids: Baker, 1992), pp. 146–62.

GABLER, JOHANN PHILIPP. 'Von der richtigen Unterscheidung der biblischen und der dogmatischen Theologie und der rechten Bestimmung ihrer beider Zeile.' In *Biblische Theologie des Neuen Testaments in ihrer Anfangszeit*. Marburg: N. G. Elwert, 1972, pp. 272–84.

GAFFIN, RICHARD B., Jr. 'Paul the Theologian', *Westminster Theological Journal*, 62/1 (Spring, 2000), pp. 121–41.

_____ 'Atonement in the Pauline Corpus'. In *The Glory of the Atonement: Biblical, Theological & Practical Perspectives*, ed. Charles E. Hill and Frank A. James III. Downers Grove, IL: Intervarsity Press, 2004, pp. 140–162.

_____ *Resurrection and Redemption: A Study in Paul's Soteriology*. 2nd ed. Phillipsburg, NJ: Presbyterian & Reformed, 1987.

GARLINGTON, DON. 'Imputation or Union with Christ? A Response to John Piper', *Reformation & Revival Journal* 12/4 (Fall, 2003), pp. 45113.

_____ 'The Obedience of Faith in the Letter to the Romans; Part I: The Meaning of ὑπακοὴν πίστεως (*Rom.* 1:5; 16:26)', *Westminster Theological Journal* 52 (1990), pp. 201–24.

_____ 'The Obedience of Faith in the Letter to the Romans; Part II: The Obedience of Faith and Judgment by Works', *Westminster Theological Journal* 53 (1991), pp. 47-72.

GATHERCOLE, SIMON J. *Where is Boasting? Early Jewish Soteriology and Paul's Response in Romans 1–5*. Grand Rapids: Eerdmans, 2002.

GEISLER, NORMAN, AND MACKENZIE, R. E. *Roman Catholics and Evangelicals: Agreements and Differences*. Grand Rapids: Baker, 1995.

GEORGE, TIMOTHY. 'Evangelicals and Catholics Together: A New Initiative', *Christianity Today* (December 8, 1997), pp. 34–8.

_____ '"A Right Strawy Epistle": Reformation Perspectives on James'. *Review & Expositor* 83 (1986), pp. 369–82.

'THE GIFT OF SALVATION', *First Things* 79 (Jan. 1998), pp. 20–3.

GODET, F. *Commentary on St Paul's Epistle to the Romans.* Vol. 1. Edinburgh: T. & T. Clark, 1889.

GODFREY, W. ROBERT. 'The Lutheran-Roman Catholic Joint Declaration', *The Banner of Truth*, Issue 432 (January 2000), pp. 17–20.

GOOTJES, NICOLAAS H. 'Christ's Obedience and Covenant Obedience', Koinwnia 19/2 (Fall, 2002), pp. 2–22.

GORDON, T. DAVID. 'Why Israel Did Not Obtain Torah Righteousness: A Translation Note on Rom. 9:32', *WTJ* 54/1 (1992), pp. 163–6.

GUNDRY, ROBERT H. 'The Nonimputation of Christ's Righteousness'. In *Justification: What's At Stake in the Current Debates,* ed. Mark Husbands and Daniel J. Treier. Downers Grove, IL: InterVarsity Press, 2004), pp. 17–45.

HAMILTON, JAMES M., Jr. 'N. T. Wright and Saul's Moral Bootstraps: Newer Light on "The New Perspective"'. *Trinity Journal* 25/2 (Fall 2004), pp. 139–55.

HARTIN, PATRICK J. *James.* Collegeville, MN: Liturgical Press, 2003.

HILL, CHARLES. 'N. T. Wright on Justification.' *IIIM Magazine Online* 3/22 (May 28 to June 3, 2001), pp. 1–8.

HINLICKY, P. R., *et al.,* eds. 'An Ecumenical Symposium on "A Call to Evangelical Unity"', *Pro Ecclesia* 9 (2000), pp. 133–49.

HODGE, CHARLES. *A Commentary on 1 and 2 Corinthians.* London: Banner of Truth, 1958–9.

_____. *A Commentary on Romans.* [1835]; Edinburgh: Banner of Truth, 1986.

HODGES, ZANE. *Dead Faith: What Is It?* Dallas, TX: Redención Viva, 1987.

_____. *The Gospel Under Siege*. Dallas: Redención Viva, 1981.

HOLMES, C. RAYMOND. "Recent Developments in Luther Research: Implications for the Adventist Understanding of Christ our Righteousness," *Journal of the Adventist Theological Society* 12/2 (Autumn, 2001), pp. 76–86.

HORTON, MICHAEL. *Putting Amazing Back into Grace: Who Does What in Salvation?* Grand Rapids: Baker, 1991.

_____, ed. *Christ the Lord: The Reformation and Lordship Salvation*. Grand Rapids: Baker, 1992.

HUGHES, R. KENT. *James: Faith That Works*. Wheaton, IL: Crossways, 1991.

HUSBANDS, MARK, AND TREIER, DANIEL J., eds. *Justification: What's at Stake in the Current Debates?* Downers Grove, IL: Intervarsity Press, 2004.

JOHNSON, LUKE TIMOTHY. *The Letter of James*. Garden City, NY: Doubleday, 1995.

JOINT DECLARATION ON THE DOCTRINE OF JUSTIFICATION. Lutheran World Federation and The Pontifical Council for Promoting Christian Unity. Grand Rapids: Eerdmans, 2000.

JÜNGEL, EBERHARD. *Justification: The Heart of the Christian Faith*. New York: T. & T. Clark, 2001.

KÄSEMANN, ERNST. *Commentary on Romans*. Grand Rapids: Eerdmans, 1980.

_____. 'The Righteousness of God in Paul.' In *New Testament Questions of Today*. London: SCM, 1969. Pp. 168-82.

KARLBERG, MARK. 'The Search for an Evangelical Consensus on Paul and the Law', *JETS* 40/4 (December, 1997), pp. 563–79.

KIM, SEYOON. *Paul and the New Perspective. Second Thoughts on the Origin of Paul's Gospel*. Grand Rapids: Eerdmans, 2000.

KISTEMAKER, SIMON J. *James and I-III John*. NTC. Grand Rapids: Baker, 1986.

KLINE, MEREDITH G. 'Gospel Until the Law', *JETS* 34/4 (1991), pp. 433–46.

KOPERSKI, VERONICA. *What Are They Saying about Paul and the Law?* Mahwah, NJ: Paulist Press, 2001.

KRUSE, COLIN G. *Paul, the Law, and Justification.* Peabody, MS: Henrickson, 1997.

KÜNG, HANS. *Justification. The Doctrine of Karl Barth and a Catholic Reflection.* Rev. ed. Philadelphia: The Westminster Press, 1981.

LAATO, TIMO. 'Justification According to James: A Comparison With Paul', *Trinity Journal* 18/1 (Spring, 1997), pp. 43–84.

LANE, ANTHONY N. S. *Justification by Faith in Catholic-Protestant Dialogue: An Evangelical Assessment.* London: T. & T. Clark Ltd., 2002.

LEHMANN, K. AND PANNENBERG, WOLFHART, eds. *The Condemnations of the Reformation Era: Do They Still Divide?* Minneapolis: Fortress Press, 1990.

LETHAM, ROBERT. *The Work of Christ.* Downers Grove, IL: InterVarsity, 1993.

LORENZEN, THORWALD. 'Faith without works does not count before God! James 2:14-26', *ExpT* 89 (1978), pp. 231–5.

LUTHER, MARTIN. *A Commentary on St Paul's Epistle to the Galatians.* Ed. P. S. Watson. Cambridge: James Clarke & Co. reprint, 1972.

_____. *Luther's Works.* Ed. Jaroslav Pelikan and Helmut T. Lehmann. American ed. 55 vols. St. Louis: Concordia Publishing House, and Philadelphia: Fortress Press, 1957-1986.

MACARTHUR, JOHN F., Jr., *et al. Justification by Faith Alone.* Morgan, PA: Soli Deo Gloria, 1995.

MCCARTNEY, DAN G. 'No Grace Without Weakness', *WTJ* 61/1 (Spring, 1999), pp. 1–13.

MCGRATH, ALISTAIR E. *Iustitia Dei: A History of the Christian Doctrine of Justification.* 2nd ed. New York: Cambridge University Press, 1998 (1986).

MONTEFIORE, CLAUDE G. *Judaism and St Paul.* London: Max Goschen, 1914.

MOO, DOUGLAS. *The Epistle to the Romans*. Grand Rapids: Eerdmans, 1996.

_____. '"Law", "Works of the Law", and Legalism in Paul.' *Westminster Theological Journal* 45 (1983), pp. 73–100.

_____. 'Paul and the Law in the Last Ten Years', *Scottish Journal of Theology* 40 (1986), pp. 287–307.

_____. 'The Law of Moses or the Law of Christ', in Feinberg, ed., *Continuity and Discontinuity*, 203–20.

_____. *The Letter of James*. Grand Rapids: Eerdmans, 1985.

MOORE, GEORGE FOOT. 'Christian Writers on Judaism', *Harvard Theological Review* 14 (1921), pp. 197–254.

MORRIS, LEON. *New Testament Theology*. Grand Rapids: Zondervan, 1986.

_____. *The Apostolic Preaching of the Cross*. 3rd ed. Grand Rapids: Eerdmans, 1965.

_____. *The Cross in the New Testament*. Grand Rapids: Eerdmans, 1965.

MURRAY, JOHN. *The Epistle to the Romans*. Vol. 1–2. Grand Rapids: Eerdmans, 1959.

_____. *The Imputation of Adam's Sin*. Reprint. Phillipsburg, NJ: Presbyterian & Reformed, 1959.

_____. *Collected Writings*. Vol. 1–4. Edinburgh: Banner of Truth, 1976, 1977, 1982.

_____. *Redemption, Accomplished and Applied*. London: Banner of Truth, 1961.

NEITZEL, HEINZ. 'Eine alte crux interpretum im Jakobusbrief 2:18.' *Zeitschrift für die neutestamentliche Wissenschaft* 73 (1982), pp. 286–93.

NEUSNER, JACOB. *Rabbinic Judaism: Structure and System*. Minneapolis: Fortress Press, 1995.

_____. *The Rabbinic Traditions About the Pharisees Before 70*. 3 vols. Reprint. Atlanta: Scholars Press, 1999 (1971).

NOLL, MARK A., AND NYSTROM, CAROLYN. *Is the Reformation Over? An Evangelical Assessment of Contemporary Roman Catholicism.* Grand Rapids: Baker Academic, 2005.

ODEN, THOMAS C. *The Justification Reader.* Grand Rapids: Eerdmans, 2002.

OWEN, JOHN. *The Works of John Owen.* Vol. 5: *Faith and Its Evidences.* [1850-53]; London: Banner of Truth, 1965.

PACKER, J. I. 'Justification.' In *Evangelical Dictionary of Theology,* ed. Walter A. Elwell. Grand Rapids: Baker Book House, 1984.

PATE, C. MARVIN. *The Reverse of the Curse: Paul, Wisdom, and the Law.* Tübingen: Mohr/Siebeck, 2000.

PIPER, JOHN. *Counted Righteous in Christ: Should We Abandon the Imputation of Christ's Righteousness?* (Wheaton, IL: Crossway Books, 2002).

_____. 'A Response to Don Garlington on Imputation', *Reformation & Revival Journal* 12/4 (Fall, 2003), pp. 121-8.

PREUS, ROBERT D. *Justification and Rome: An Evaluation of Recent Dialogues.* Saint Louis: Concordia Publishing House, 1997.

RAHNER, KARL, ed. *Sacramentum Mundi: An Encyclopedia of Theology.* Vol. 4: *Matter to Phenomenology.* London: Search Press Limited, 1969.

RÄISÄNEN, HEIKKI. *Paul and the Law.* Philadelphia: Fortress Press, 1983.

_____. *The Torah and Christ: Essays in German and English on the Problem of the Law in Early Christianity.* Helsinki: Finnish Exegetical Society, 1986.

RAUSCH, T. P., ed. *Catholics and Evangelicals: Do They Share a Common Future?* Downers Grove: Intervarsity Press, 2000.

REISINGER, ERNEST C. *Lord & Christ: The Implications of Lordship for Faith and Life.* Phillipsburg, NJ: Presbyterian & Reformed, 1994.

REUMANN, JOHN. *'Righteousness' in the New Testament.* Philadelphia: Fortress Press, 1982.

RIDDERBOS, HERMAN. *Paul: An Outline of His Theology*. Grand Rapids: Eerdmans, 1975.

ROBERTSON, O. PALMER. 'Genesis 15:6: New Covenant Expositions of an Old Covenant Text.' *Westminster Theological Journal* 42 (1980), pp. 259–89.

ROPES, JAMES HARDY. *A Critical and Exegetical Commentary on the Epistle of St. James*. Edinburgh: T. & T. Clark, 1916.

_____. '"Righteousness" and "The Righteousness of God" in the Old Testament and in St. Paul', *Journal of Biblical Literature* 22 (1903), pp. 211–27.

ROSS, ALEXANDER. *The Epistles of James and John*. Grand Rapids: Eerdmans, 1967.

RUSCH, WILLIAM G., ed. *Justification and the Future of the Ecumenical Movement: The Joint Declaration on the Doctrine of Justification*. Collegeville, MN: Liturgical Press, 2003.

SANDERS, E. P. *Paul and Palestinian Judaism: A Comparison of Patterns of Religion*. London: SCM, 1977.

_____. *Paul, the Law, and the Jewish People*. Minneapolis: Fortress Press, 1983.

SCHAFF, PHILIP. *The Creeds of Christendom*. 3 vols. Grand Rapids: Baker reprint, 1985 (1931).

SCHREINER, THOMAS R. *The Law and Its Fulfillment: A Pauline Theology of Law*. Grand Rapids: Baker, 1993.

_____, 'Paul and Perfect Obedience to the Law: An Evaluation of the View of E. P. Sanders', *WTJ* 47 (1985), pp. 245-78.

_____. 'Is Perfect Obedience to the Law Possible? A Re-examination of Galatians 3:10', *Journal of the Evangelical Theological Society* 27 (1984), pp. 151-60.

SCHWEITZER, ALBERT. *The Mysticism of Paul the Apostle*. London: A. and C. Black, 1931.

_____. *The Quest of the Historical Jesus: A Critical Study of Its Progess from Reimarus to Wrede*. New York: MacMillan, 1968 (1961).

SEIFRID, MARK A. *Christ, Our Righteousness. Paul's Theology of Justification.* Downers Grove, IL: InterVarsity, 2000.

_____. '"The Gift of Salvation": Its Failure to Address the Crux of Justification', *Journal of the Evangelical Theological Society* 42 (1999), pp. 679–88.

_____. 'Luther, Melanchthon and Paul on the Question of Imputation.' In *Justification: What's at Stake in the Current Debates?*, ed. Mark Husbands and Daniel J. Treier. Downers Grove, IL: InterVarsity Press, 2004, pp. 137–76.

SILVA, MOISÉS. 'The Law and Christianity: Dunn's New Synthesis', *Westminster Theological Journal* 53 (1991), pp. 339–53.

_____. 'Abraham, Faith, and Works: Paul's Use of Scripture in Galatians 3:6-14', *Westminster Theological Journal* 63 (2001), pp. 251–67.

_____. 'Is the Law Against the Promises? The Significance of Galatians 3:21 for Covenant Continuity.' In *Theonomy: A Reformed Critique,* ed. William S. Baker and W. R. Godfrey. Grand Rapids: Zondervan, 1990, pp. 153–67.

_____. 'The Place of Historical Reconstruction in New Testament Criticism', in *Hermeneutics, Authority, and Canon,* ed. D. A. Carson and John D. Woodbridge (Grand Rapids: Zondervan, 1986), pp. 109–33.

SNODGRASS, KLYNE R. 'Justification by Grace — To the Doers: An Analysis of the Place of Romans 2 in the Theology of Paul', *New Testament Studies* 32 (1986), pp. 72–93.

SPROUL, R. C. *Faith Alone: The Evangelical Doctrine of Justification.* Grand Rapids: Baker, 1995.

_____. *Getting the Gospel Right: The Tie that Binds Evangelicals Together.* Grand Rapids: Baker, 1999.

STAFFORD, TIM. 'N. T. Wright.' *Christianity Today* (Feb. 8, 1999), pp. 42–6.

STEIN, ROBERT H. 'N. T. Wright's *Jesus and the Victory of God*: A Review Article', *JETS* 44/2 (June 2001), pp. 207–18.

STENDAHL, KRISTER. *Paul Among Jews and Gentiles and Other Essays.* London: SCM, 1977.

STONEHOUSE, NED B. *J. Gresham Machen: A Biographical Memoir.* 3rd ed. Edinburgh: Banner of Truth, 1987 (1954).

STOTT, JOHN R. W. *The Cross of Christ.* Downers Grove, IL: Intervarsity, 1986.

_____. *Romans: God's Good News for the World.* Downers Grove, IL: Intervarsity, 1994.

STRIMPLE, ROBERT B. *The Modern Search for the Real Jesus.* Phillipsburg, NJ: Presbyterian & Reformed, 1995.

STUHLMACHER, PETER. *Revisiting Paul's Doctrine of Justification. With an essay by Donald A. Hagner.* Downers Grove, IL: InterVarsity, 2001.

TAPPERT, THEODORE G., ed. *The Book of Concord: The Confessions of the Evangelical Lutheran Church.* Philadelphia: Fortress Press, 1959.

TASKER, R. V. G. *The General Epistle of James.* Grand Rapids: Eerdmans, 1956.

THAYER, Joseph Henry, ed. *A Greek-English Lexicon of the New Testament.* New York: American Book Co. ed., 1889.

THIELMAN, FRANK. *Paul and the Law: A Contextual Approach.* Downers Grove, IL: InterVarsity, 1994.

_____. *From Plight to Solution: A Jewish Framework for Understanding Paul's View of the Law in Galatians and Romans.* Leiden: E. J. Brill, 1989.

_____. 'Law', in Gerald Hawthorne & Ralph Martin, eds., *The Dictionary of Paul and His Letters* (Downers Grove: Intervarsity, 1993), 529-43.

TRAILL, ROBERT. *Justification Vindicated,* [1692]; Edinburgh: Banner of Truth, 2002.

TRAVIS, A. E. 'James and Paul. A Comparative Study', *Southwestern Journal of Theology* 12 (1969), pp. 57–70.

TURRETIN, FRANCIS. *Institutes of Elenctic Theology*. 3 vols. Phillipsburg, NJ: Presbyterian & Reformed, 1994.

VENEMA, CORNELIS P. *The Twofold Nature of the Gospel in Calvin's Theology*. Ph.D. dissertation. Ann Arbor, MI: University Microfilms International, 1985.

_____. *The Promise of the Future*. Edinburgh: Banner of Truth, 2000.

_____. 'N. T. Wright on Romans 5:12–21 and Justification: A Case Study in Exegesis, Theological Method, and the "New Perspective on Paul"', *Mid-America Journal of Theology* 16 (2005).

_____. 'Justification and the Imputation of Christ's Righteousness', *The Banner of Truth*, Issue 479–80 (August-September 2003), pp. 8–20.

_____. 'Justification by Faith: The Ecumenical, Biblical and Theological Dimensions of Current Debates', in *Always Reforming*, ed. A. T. B. McGowan (Leicester: Inter-Varsity Press, 2006), pp. 289–327.

VISSCHER, GERHARD H. 'New Views Regarding Legalism and Exclusivism in Judaism: Is there a need to reinterpret Paul?', *Koinonia* 18/2 (1999), pp. 15–42.

WALLACE, DANIEL B. *Greek Grammar Beyond the Basics— Exegetical Syntax of the New Testament*. Grand Rapids: Zondervan, 1999.

_____. 'Galatians 3:19–20: A *Crux Interpretum* for Paul's View of the Law', *Westminster Theological Journal* 52 (1990), pp. 225–45.

WATERS, GUY PRENTISS. *Justification and the New Perspectives on Paul. A Review and Response*. Phillipsburg, NJ: Presbyterian and Reformed Publishing Co., 2004, chap. 1.

WATSON, NIGEL M. 'Justified By Faith: Judged By Works—An Antinomy?', *New Testament Studies* 29 (1983), pp. 209–21.

WENDEL, FRANCOIS. *Calvin*. London: Collins, 1963.

WESTERHOLM, STEPHEN. *Israel's Law and the Church's Faith: Paul and His Recent Interpreters*. Grand Rapids: Eerdmans, 1998.

_____. 'Torah, *nomos*, and Law: A Question of "Meaning".' *Studies in Religion* 15 (1986), pp. 327-36.

_____. *Perspectives Old and New on Paul: The 'Lutheran' Paul and His Critics*. Grand Rapids: Eerdmans, 2004.

WHITE, JAMES. *The God Who Justifies*. Minneapolis: Bethany House, 2001.

WILLIAMS, SAM K. 'The "Righteousness of God" in Romans.' *Journal of Biblical Literature* 99 (1980), pp. 241-90.

WITHERINGTON, BEN, III. *The Jesus Quest: The Third Search for the Jew of Nazareth*. Downers Grove, IL: InterVarsity, 1997.

WRIGHT, N. T. *The Climax of the Covenant: Christ and the Law in Pauline Theology*. Minneapolis: Fortress, 1991.

_____. *What Saint Paul Really Said. Was Paul of Tarsus the Real Founder of Christianity?* Grand Rapids: Eerdmans, 1997.

_____. *The New Testament and the People of God*. Minneapolis: Fortress Press, 1992.

_____. *Christian Origins and the Question of God*. 3 vols. Minneapolis: Fortress Press, 1992, 1996, 2003.

_____. 'A *Reformation & Revival Journal* Interview with N. T. Wright: Part One.' *Reformation & Revival Journal* 11/1 (Winter, 2002), pp. 117–39.

_____. 'New Perspectives on Paul.' http://www.ntwrightpage.com/Wright_New_Perspectives.htm.

_____. 'The Paul of History and the Apostle of Faith.' *Tyndale Bulletin* 29 (1978), pp. 61–88.

_____. *Who Was Jesus?* Grand Rapids: Eerdmans, 1992.

_____. 'The Law in Romans 2.' In *Paul and the Mosaic Law*, ed. James D. G. Dunn. Grand Rapids: Eerdmans, 1996, pp. 131–50.

_____. 'The Shape of Justification.' http://www.thepaulpage.com/Shape.html.

_____. *The Letter to the Romans*. Vol. 10 of *The New Interpreter's Bible*. Nashville, TN: Abingdon Press, 2002.

_____. 'On Becoming the Righteousness of God: 2 Corinthians 5:21', in *Pauline Theology*, vol. 2, ed. David M. Hay (Minneapolis, MN: Augsburg Fortress, 1993), pp. 200–8, (chap. 5)

_____. *Paul in Fresh Perspective*. Minneapolis: Fortress Press, 2005.

YINGER, KENT L. *Paul, Judaism, and Judgment Acoording to Deeds*. Cambridge: Cambridge University Press, 1999.

ZIESLER, J. A. *The Meaning of Righteousness in Paul: A Linguistic and Theological Enquiry*. Cambridge: University Press, 1972.

ZODHIATES, SPIROS. *The Epistle of James and the Life of Faith*. Grand Rapids: Eerdmans, 1966.

INDEX OF PERSONS

⸺⟨☙⟩⸺

INDEX OF SELECTED SUBJECTS

―⟨ை⟩―

INDEX OF SCRIPTURE
REFERENCES